Ruling Myanmar

The **Institute of Southeast Asian Studies (ISEAS)** was established as an autonomous organization in 1968. It is a regional centre dedicated to the study of socio-political, security and economic trends and developments in Southeast Asia and its wider geostrategic and economic environment.

The Institute's research programmes are the Regional Economic Studies (RES, including ASEAN and APEC), Regional Strategic and Political Studies (RSPS), and Regional Social and Cultural Studies (RSCS).

ISEAS Publishing, an established academic press, has issued more than 2,000 books and journals. It is the largest scholarly publisher of research about Southeast Asia from within the region. ISEAS Publications works with many other academic and trade publishers and distributors to disseminate important research and analyses from and about Southeast Asia to the rest of the world.

Ruling Myanmar

From Cyclone Nargis to National Elections

Edited by
Nick Cheesman, Monique Skidmore
and Trevor Wilson

INSTITUTE OF SOUTHEAST ASIAN STUDIES
SINGAPORE

First published in Singapore in 2010 by
ISEAS Publishing
Institute of Southeast Asian Studies
30 Heng Mui Keng Terrace
Pasir Panjang
Singapore 119614

E-mail: publish@iseas.edu.sg
Website: http://bookshop.iseas.edu.sg

ISEAS Library Cataloguing-in-Publication Data

Ruling Myanmar : from cyclone nargis to national elections / edited by Nick Cheesman, Monique Skidmore and Trevor Wilson.
Based on 2009 Myanmar/Burma Update Conference organized by the Dept. of Political & Social Change, The Australian National University Research School of Pacific and Asian Studies, Canberra, held 17–18 August.
1. Burma—Politics and government—1988—Congresses.
2. Burma—Economic conditions—1948—Congresses.
3. Cyclone Nargis, 2008—Congresses.
4. Humanitarian assistance—Burma—International cooperation—Congresses.
I. Cheesman, Nick.
II. Skidmore, Monique.
III. Wilson, Trevor.
IV. Australian National University. Dept. of Political and Social Change.
V. Myanmar/Burma Update Conference (2009 : Canberra, Australia)
DS530.4 B972 2009 2010

ISBN 978-981-4311-46-5 (soft cover)
ISBN 978-981-4311-47-2 (hard cover)
ISBN 978-981-4311-48-9 (e-book PDF)

Cover photo: People walk away from a polling station for the constitutional referendum, May 2008. The slogan on the roof reads: "National Discipline begins at school"
Photographer/Artist: Khin Maung Win
Courtesy of Getty Images

Typeset by Superskill Graphics Pte Ltd
Printed in Singapore by Utopia Press Pte Ltd

CONTENTS

LIST OF TABLES

LIST OF FIGURES

BACKGROUND ON ANU 2009 MYANMAR/BURMA UPDATE CONFERENCE

Preparations are under way for the first elections in Myanmar/Burma since 1990, to be held in 2010 as part of the military regime's "Road Map for Democracy". The conditions under which the elections will be held are far from favourable, although the laws and procedures under which they will be conducted have not yet been announced. Political controls remain repressive, freedom of expression and assembly does not exist, and international access is restricted by government controls as well as sanctions. Nevertheless, is this a turning point for Myanmar/Burma? Presenters at the Australian National University 2009 Myanmar/Burma Update conference examined these questions and more. Speakers were leading experts from the United States, Japan, France, and Australia, as well as from Myanmar/Burma.

ACKNOWLEDGEMENTS

We greatly appreciate the ongoing and generous support of the Australian Agency for International Development (AusAID), without whose financial support the 2009 Australian National University Myanmar/Burma Update Conference would not have been possible. AusAID's encouragement has gone much further that just providing financial support, and helped organizers improve the focus and structure on the conference. We are also grateful for the steadfast backing we have always received from the Department of Political and Social Change, in the ANU College of Asia and the Pacific, especially from the current and former Heads of Department, Paul Hutchcroft and Ed Aspinall, respectively. Finally, we thank the Institute of Southeast Asian Studies (ISEAS) in Singapore, which was once again prepared to publish the conference papers, and copy-editor John Owen for his prompt and fine copy-editing. Last but not least, this publication would not have amounted to anything without the willingness of the contributors to devote time and thought to their chapters, which makes this project worthwhile.

CONTRIBUTORS AND EDITORS

David Allan: Independent Consultant based in Yangon, working mostly with local non-government organizations.

David Camroux: Senior Researcher at the Centre d'Etudes et des Recherches Internationales, at Sciences Po, Paris.

Nick Cheesman: Doctoral candidate, Department of Political & Social Change at the Australian National University, Canberra.

Priscilla Clapp: Retired Minister-Counsellor in the US Foreign Service, and former Chief of Mission, US Embassy, Yangon. Currently involved in various community and policy institutions in Washington DC.

Renaud Egreteau: Research Assistant Professor, Hong Kong Institute for the Humanities and Social Sciences, University of Hong Kong. Formerly, researcher at Institut d'Etudes Politiques de Paris (Sciences Po), Paris.

Jane Ferguson: Lecturer, Mainland Southeast Asian Studies, Faculty of Asian Studies, Australian National University.

Nancy Hudson-Rodd: Honorary Research Fellow in human geography at Edith Cowan University and previously Foundation Director, Centre for Development Studies, Edith Cowan University, Perth.

Khin Maung Nyo: Editor in Chief of the *World Economic Journal*, in Yangon. Graduated in economics from the Institute of Economics in Yangon.

Khin Zaw Win: Director of Tampadipa Institute, a think-tank and civil society capacity building organization. Previously worked on providing care, treatment and support for people with HIV/AIDS.

Ikuko Okamoto: Resident Visiting Fellow at the Resources Management in the Asia-Pacific program at the ANU. Senior Research Fellow, Institute of Developing Economies, Tokyo.

William Sabandar: Special Envoy of ASEAN Secretary-General for Post-Nargis Recovery, Myanmar, from May 2009. During 2005–April 2009, served as head of the Indonesian post-tsunami recovery programme for Nias.

Sein Htay: Independent researcher, formerly with the Burma Fund and the Federation of Trade Unions-Burma.

Monique Skidmore: Dean of the Faculty of Arts and Design at the University of Canberra, and Adjunct Professor at the School of Humanities, Australian National University. Co-convener of the ANU's Myanmar/Burma Update Conference since 2006.

Ashley South: Independent writer and consultant, specializing in political and humanitarian issues in Burma/Myanmar and Southeast Asia.

Sean Turnell: Associate Professor in the Department of Economics and Finance, Macquarie University, Sydney. Co-founder of Burma Economic Watch, an online website at Macquarie University.

Alison Vicary: Lecturer in the Department of Economics and Finance, Macquarie University, Sydney. Economic analyst at the Burma Economic Watch website at Macquarie University.

Trevor Wilson: Visiting Fellow in the Department of Political & Social Change at the Australian National University. Co-convener of the Myanmar/Burma Update Conference since 2004, and former Australian Ambassador to Myanmar (2000–03).

NOTE ON TERMINOLOGY AND GEOGRAPHICAL NAMES

In 1989, the military regime changed the official romanized name of Burma to Myanmar and changed the names of most cities and towns from the spelling used prior to that date. Inside the country today, the revised names and spellings are used. Opponents of the regime objected to these changes and so different authors have their preferred different usages (Myanmar/Burma, Myanmar, Burma, Rangoon/Yangon, Rangoon, Yangon, etc.). In this publication, the editors have not adjusted contributors' preferences to a single consistent usage.

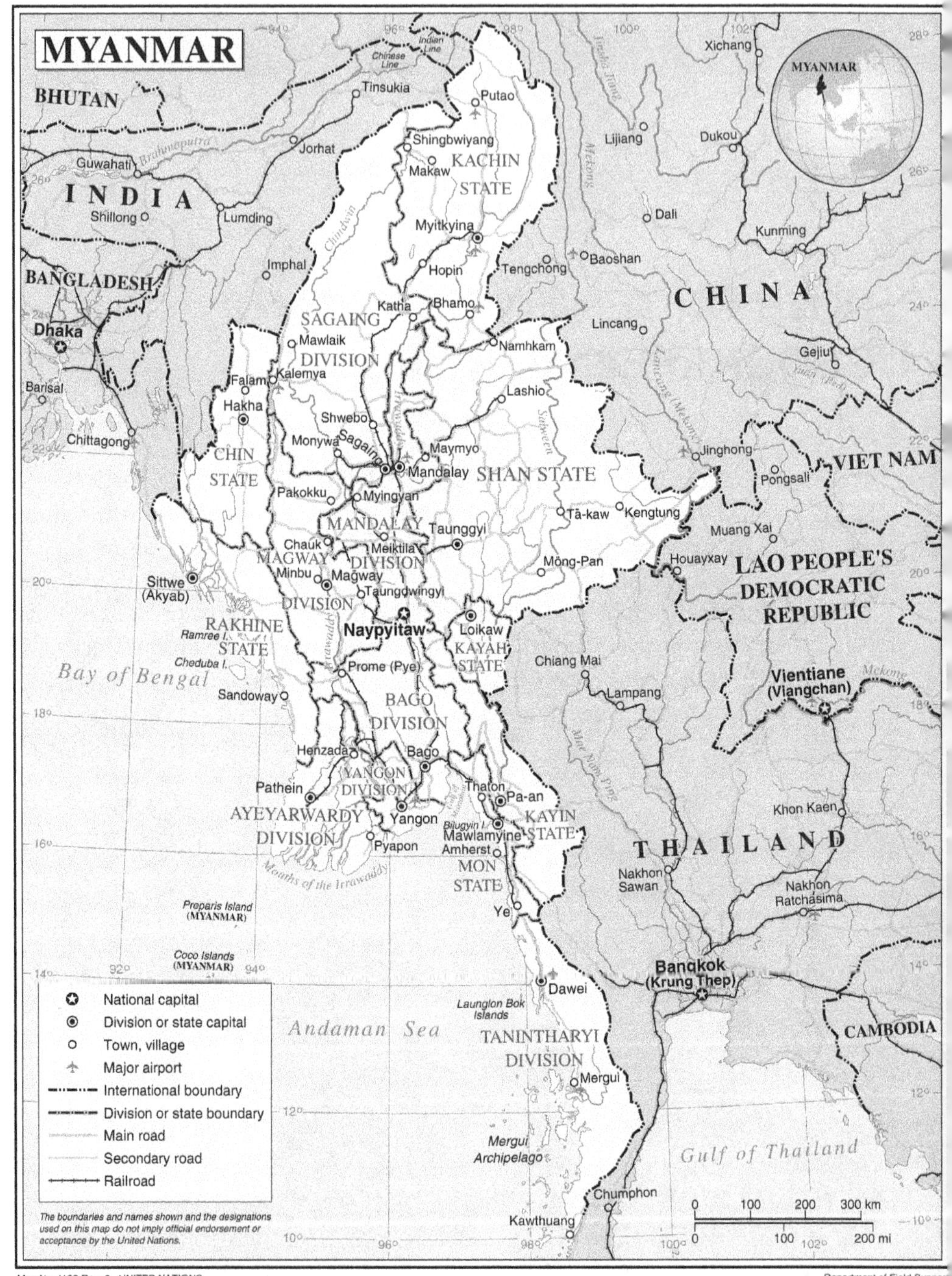

Source: Map of Myanmar, no. 4168 Rev. 2 May 2008, reproduced with permission of the UN Cartographic Section.

I

Overview

1

PERSPECTIVES ON A TRANSITIONAL SITUATION

Monique Skidmore and Trevor Wilson

BACKGROUND: POLITICAL AND ECONOMIC CHALLENGES TO AUTHORITY

Significant changes in Myanmar/Burma since the popular demonstrations of 2007 mask a situation that seems superficially to be "more of the same". The adoption of a new constitution, through a referendum conducted under questionable arrangements in May 2008, on paper restores a form of legal governance for the first time since 1988. However, few observers, in Myanmar or outside, have any illusions that this will mean a real transfer of power to a popularly elected government. Yet increasingly commentators and interested parties are taking the view that the elections, scheduled to take place in 2010 for the first time since 1990, at both the nationwide and regional level, will mark a new or accelerated phase in the agonizingly slow transitions purported to be occurring to bring about an end to military rule, even if they do not purport to restore participative government. This situation represents a major challenge for the citizens of Myanmar/Burma, whose ability to influence state decision-making is extraordinarily constrained, as well as for the international community.

Myanmar's military regime, the State Peace and Development Council (SPDC), not only maintains its tight grip on power, but since 2007 has moved to reduce further the space in which its authority can be contested and challenged. During 2008/09, the regime intensified its military campaigns against its opponents along its eastern border with Thailand. A new crackdown against political opponents during 2008, apparently aimed at weakening opposition groups before the 2010 elections, resulted in more than 2,100 political prisoners, more than at any other time in the modern period. Throughout 2009, the military leadership orchestrated a concerted (but poorly executed) campaign to convert armed minority groups into border security forces but, as tensions rose in August 2009, fighting between the army and the Kokang militia resulted in the first serious breakdown among the various ceasefire groups. The military regime has, however, still not been significantly challenged politically, despite the new array of sanctions (imposed outside the United Nations) since the 2007 crackdown against civil protests. Those UN Security Council members supporting Myanmar maintain their support, even though during 2008 they occasionally urged the military regime to cooperate more fully with the United Nations, as the UN's apparent impotence in dealing with the problem of Myanmar/Burma continued.

A striking feature of the SPDC's ongoing authoritarian socio-political controls remains the extraordinary secrecy with which the military leadership continues to conceal its own political intentions. The public does not know what kind of accommodation, if any, is to be forged between the military leadership and non-military elements. There is still no process of political negotiation, which means that any outcome is unlikely to command credible legitimacy or wider support. There is no sign of any political compromise that might acknowledge some legitimate interests of the military while allowing greater participation by non-military representatives. The long delay in introducing the election law and the rules governing the formation and membership of political parties suggests the considerable difficulties the military leadership must be experiencing in deciding how to move forward. Yet, at the same time, anecdotal evidence is growing about the military leadership's confidential plans to organize officially sponsored candidates, either for national and regional assemblies, involving current senior military administrators "resigning" from the army to do so.[1] The delays in finalizing arrangements for the election exacerbate widespread concerns inside and outside the country about the extent of tight control the authorities expect to retain over the election process and the outcome.

Nevertheless, as Myanmar/Burma approaches its 2010 elections in the course of its largely discredited "Road Map for National Reconciliation", observers inside and outside the country are detecting a slight breeze of political change and are becoming more interested than before in the potential for some longer-term beneficial changes to emerge. In particular, sections of the international community, including some aid donors, are starting to contemplate strategies to reinforce the trend towards change and underpin marginally improved conditions in the country. Against this backdrop, some discussion is beginning about ways to achieve better governance in Myanmar/Burma over time. Nobody has any illusions about how difficult this might be, how long it might take, and how far Myanmar/Burma is from any modicum of "good governance". Thus these topics formed the backdrop also of the 2009 Myanmar/Burma update conference at the Australian National University.

As with all publications of the Myanmar/Burma Update, the coverage of issues and parts of the country is wide-ranging but not necessarily exhaustive. Some leading scholars and policymakers may not contribute to a particular volume because their current work is not related to the topical theme of the Update. More often, however, Myanmar/Burma Update volumes reflect a depth of specific expertise rather than aspiring to overall consistency of analysis and comprehensive coverage, but continue to be constrained by the difficulties in gaining recent in-country data. This volume is no exception. Data about recent changes to the SPDC as elements become "civilian politicians", as well as details about the constitution drafting and election process, is scanty. Similarly, information about the processes occurring amongst armed minority groups as they negotiate with the SPDC about transforming themselves into "Border Guard Forces" is incomplete at the time of publication. The current volume contains both current in-country research results as well as high-quality analysis from policymakers whose work in and on Burma often spans several decades.

Although political circumstances in Myanmar/Burma remain stalemated, without noticeable improvement in the authoritarian way politics is conducted, both participants and observers are starting to contemplate the prospect of some form of change ahead. As a concerned Burmese, **Khin Zaw Win** in his chapter describes 2010 as "a time of reckoning" for nation-building in Myanmar/Burma, and argues that the time has come for a "bottom-up" approach because of the "sorry record" of the top-down style of leadership. He maintains that ethnic and religious minority interests can only flourish in Myanmar/Burma under principles of liberal democracy.

How the military authorities envisage managing the transition to a new arrangement for political and legal governance is also not clear. Myanmar/Burma has almost no prior experience of a peaceful transfer of power, and the trust that might provide a foundation for a smooth transfer of power does not exist in any sense. Will any "new" government in Myanmar ever be able to mobilize public support behind its policies and programmes, when almost none of the mechanisms that would facilitate this process yet exist in any recognizable or robust form? Drawing from decades of in-country experience and high-level policy work, **Priscilla Clapp** draws attention to the importance of the process of political transition and she suggests that after the departure of the current SPDC leader, Senior General Than Shwe, a new landscape is likely to throw up new issues, and challenge existing power structures and orthodoxies. She argues that new centres of power will inevitably emerge under the new constitution, which could have loosening and liberalizing effects, making it easier for further, more targeted and more powerful international engagement by the United States and, therefore, others.

Elsewhere in the world, a shift in thinking about political authority has long placed greater weight on devolution of authority, decentralization of controls, and local "ownership" of institutions and processes. This is no less the case in Myanmar/Burma, although this is not likely to have been the primary reason for the new constitution restoring state assemblies, after the country under the SPDC witnessed an unprecedented degree of centralized authority and control. The cessation of armed hostilities across most of the country and a measure of local control over resources has, however, nourished desires for greater local autonomy, though these have mostly yet to be realized. In areas under ceasefire agreement, political structures are not static and alliances continue to rise and fall. **Ashley South** presents the results of recent immersive fieldwork in Karen State where, he explains, new regional structures have been functioning, albeit they are changing rapidly and are perhaps excessively dependent on personal authority.

Very different but equally serious choices are faced by the ethnic groups such as the Kachin, Mon and the various groups in Shan State which already have ceasefire agreements with the State Peace and Development

Council. Under pressure, but reluctant, to agree to convert their armed forces into "border security guards", they are keen to find better expression of their political aspirations by participating in the 2010 elections as well as to secure long-promised increased delegation of economic and other authority. From the military regime's perspective, its protracted negotiations with these groups remain to be consummated, have already descended into armed clashes in the Kokang Special Region, and threaten the very unity and integrity of the state that the SPDC prizes above all. At a time when greater certainty about these important matters should have been assured, there is perhaps less certainty than there has been since the military took over direct rule in 1988. **Jane Ferguson** reflects upon the changes that have occurred between the Myanmar regime and the two Wa organizations that exercise de facto authority in the Wa Special Regions. She raises doubts about the underlying legitimacy of some of these groups.

Meanwhile, Myanmar/Burma continues to stagnate economically and socially, worsening the quality of life for ordinary Burmese. In the three-year period 2007–09, economic growth was, according to the Economist Intelligence Unit, 2.5, 0.2 and 1.1 per cent respectively,[2] a performance well behind its neighbours. No improvement in economic governance is in sight as the regime's appetite for economic reform becomes even more questionable. Centres of political and economic power continue to shift between Naypyitaw and Yangon (Rangoon). Internal security remains somewhat fragile, but while no real threats to state unity and stability are in evidence, security and unity remain the dominant concerns of the regime. Improved rules and predictability for the so-called private sector have yet to materialize. Patronage of cronies, lack of effective financial and regulatory systems, arbitrary intervention by the authorities, and the extreme short-term approach to the building of critical infrastructure and other "enabling" policies continue to hold back sound economic opportunities. Evidence of this lies in the clear failure of recent projects and programmes to deliver meaningful improvement in the availability of electric power, create more employment opportunities or attact more foreign firms bringing investment funds, technological advances, and access to markets. In other words, the continued absence of most of the fundamentals of economic governance (transparency, contestable procedures, and market-driven decision-making) underlines how far Myanmar/Burma is from achieving sustainable development.

Analysing economic data officially endorsed by the SPDC leadership, **Khin Maung Nyo** demonstrates the "other worldly" quality of official economic policy. This argued that Myanmar/Burma would be relatively unaffected by the global financial crisis, when the reality was revealed in chaotic movements in domestic commodity markets and trade. In-country economic research has been particularly productive over the past year, and in his analysis of agricultural credit arrangements, **Sean Turnell** notes that any reform — including in micro-credit — will face stiff barriers of regulation, corruption and entrenched community distrust of the country's financial institutions. Recent economic policies generally show the very mixed results that can be found under such constrained political and economic policy parameters. **Ikuko Okamoto** similarly presents new research findings as she meticulously documents the difficulties faced by labourers in the fishing industry seeking to take up jobs wherever they could find them. She draws some important conclusions about pressures to gain a much higher income than could be achieved at the present rate; the emergence of regional economic disparity in Myanmar; and the undeveloped state of the labour market. All of this points to the fundamental absence of opportunities for ordinary people to lead productive lives, to improve their prospects with any certainty, and to base critical decisions on expectations of sound arrangements and systems to protect property and allow for capital accumulation in rural livelihoods.

In Myanmar/Burma, dysfunctional courts and legal processes contribute significantly to stultification of many forms of human endeavour and business. **Nick Cheesman** interrogates the new constitution and practices of the courts in Myanmar through the reintroduction of habeas corpus. He presents a substantive analysis of the current circumstances of the judiciary as compared with those of earlier periods, as well as with those in parts of South Asia. He distinguishes the type of judiciary in Myanmar, which is fully integrated into administrative arrangements and executive goals, from that found in many other contemporary authoritarian settings, and considers the possibilities for exercise of legal rights under heavy constraints. Nor are property rights adequately defined and defended in current circumstances. **Nancy Hudson-Rodd** and **Sein-Htay** observes problems posed by the phenomenon of land confiscation, and explains how this cripples agricultural production and planning in communities. They include in their analysis the lack of compensation, property rights-driven incentives, certainty, poor production decisions and the use of unskilled imported labour that characterize the agricultural sector in

Myanmar today. The whole area of finding a pathway to improve property rights for individuals and corporate entities, to allow for reasonable livelihoods as well as to form the foundations of sound economic development has yet to be mapped in any future governance scenario.

BEYOND CYCLONE NARGIS: THE ROLE OF THE STATE AND THE INTERNATIONAL COMMUNITY

Leaving 140,000 people dead or missing and destroying 800,000 homes in south-eastern Myanmar in May 2008, Cyclone Nargis was a major humanitarian disaster which prompted greater international focus on the question of appropriate assistance to Myanmar and provided an opportunity for both the regime and the international community to review their positions. UN Secretary General Ban Ki-Moon visited Myanmar in July 2008 for the first time ever, to provide UN leadership for the international community's response to the post-Nargis humanitarian crisis and ensure a larger flow of assistance than might have otherwise occurred. The Myanmar regime's insistence on controlling humanitarian assistance jarred strongly with the United Nations and international donors, whose generosity was significantly dampened by evidence of the military leadership's disregard for the plight of the populace. This situation was only partially alleviated by the unprecedented facilitating role played by the Association of Southeast Asian Nations (ASEAN) via the Tripartite Core Group (of the SPDC, the United Nations and ASEAN). The Special ASEAN Envoy in charge of the ASEAN role, **William Sabandar**, outlines some of the TCG's successes in a chapter in this book.[3]

The cyclone coincided with a debate in the United Nations about the "responsibility to protect", and some leaders, such as French Foreign Minister Bernard Kouchner, used the Myanmar/Burma case to justify forcible intervention, but this was not taken up as a viable or generally desirable option by the members of the Security Council. In one sense this debate was also overtaken by ASEAN's unprecedented intervention to oversee disaster relief for the international community. For the first time since ASEAN's inception as a regional cooperation body, Myanmar's fellow members of ASEAN stepped forward to provide significant political leadership in managing the recovery efforts, inducing the regime to pursue a somewhat more cooperative approach through 2008 and 2009. Ultimately, the regime was its own worst enemy on international assistance, as on many other matters. While negative perceptions of its performance persist among different observers, the overall record of this period is more positive and encouraging than for some time as it ultimately resulted in the highest level of in-country aid, international political oversight, and international development assistance and personnel since the regime took office as the State Law and Restoration Council (SLORC) in 1988.

At the ANU conference, international perspectives on conditions in Myanmar/Burma drew some encouragement from the prospect of elections ahead, and from recent experiences. Dr William Sabandar observed that, from the ASEAN perspective, more opportunities for a direct ASEAN contribution to development and governance could lie ahead, based on the success of the Tripartite Core Group model. He notes specifically in reference to the ASEAN Charter, that "Among the fourteen principles in the Charter were adherence to the rule of law, good governance, the principles of democracy and constitutional government, upholding the Charter and upholding international law". **David Camroux and Renaud Egreteau** make a powerful case for more-effective engagement with Myanmar/Burma right now, given the failure of international approaches to date. They are not advocating isolation of the military regime or increased sanctions against it, but seek more realistic, rational and strategically sensible policies. They see the 2010 elections as an opportunity for a different emphasis in international approaches which should have some normative underpinnings.

Severely questioned after Cyclone Nargis, state capacity in Myanmar/Burma for smooth administration, let alone good governance, remains a long-term aspirational goal rather than an immediate objective.[4] Official accounts of the problems faced by communities, not only in cyclone-hit areas but elsewhere, stressed the wide range of needs that had to be met by massive injection of funds from the government or from international assistance.[5] Reports from non-government groups that worked in relief operations drew attention to the dimension of the human tragedies that occurred on many levels, with or without appropriate government interventions, and sometimes found hope in the increased openness that eventually emerged following the authorities' initial highly restrictive response.[6] It was as much the organization, management and matching of responses to needs that demonstrated gaps in systemic capacity. This is hardly surprising. While Myanmar/Burma possesses government structures and procedures similar to most comparable developing countries, its operating systems and machinery of government have not undergone serious reform or change to make it more responsive, more effective, or more accountable.

In reality, Myanmar/Burma has almost no experience of participatory responsible government; little acquaintance with the consultative processes that might help achieve more open forms of governance; and equally little practice in implementing accountability systems to assist in introducing more dispersed forms of governance. Apart from a few technocratic areas such as medicine, civil engineering, and agricultural science, government and national capacities in Myanmar/Burma have not really been expected to achieve at a high level and to do so honestly and accurately. However, remarkably few detailed assessments have been done on governance issues in Myanmar/Burma, and this volume only partially adds to the stock of knowledge and analysis. What is intuitively clear is that there is a great gulf between present practice in Myanmar/Burma and what would be regarded as satisfactory in most countries in this situation. Workable habits of political and economic governance simply do not exist, even in embryonic form. Relative isolation from relevant developments in the Southeast Asian region or elsewhere in the world has compounded the problem.

The first steps in political change may occur during and after the elections, but transparency and accountability, genuine consultative rule, and policies that are consciously responsive and tailored to popular needs are still a long way off. Moreover, as yet there are few signs of how such good governance might emerge, either through indigenous development or borrowing from elsewhere. According to *Webster's Revised Complete Dictionary* (1913), "governance" may be defined as the "exercise of authority; control; government; arrangement". This encompasses all the systemic and institutional arrangements that influence the sound operation of the state and society and form the foundations of its legitimacy. It includes politics and political systems, the law and related legal arrangements, social and economic practices and procedures that provide social equality and opportunity, predictability and fairness for economic activities, and, above all, avenues for popular recourse in the event of system failure. It may seem unrealistic to discuss such comprehensive mechanisms in Myanmar/Burma when the very state itself is struggling to function and survives only by the threat of political violence. However, the rudiments of most of these systems are present or aspired to by a reasonably well-educated population that repeatedly calls for a return to sound and fair governance.

So the overall state of governance in Myanmar/Burma remains bad. The former UN Humanitarian Coordinator, Charles Petrie, commented that "There is no transparency and accountability within the government system, and even less towards the people or vis-à-vis the outside world."[7] The impact of inadequate governance arrangements affect even Myanmar's closest collaborator, China. According to the International Crisis Group: "Political instability and uncertainty have resulted in a lack of confidence in Myanmar's investment environment, and weak governance and widespread corruption have made it difficult for even strong Chinese companies to operate there."[8] In any listing of indicators of governance, Myanmar's performance is very poor[9] but, in some situations, assessments-based independent analyses of actual performance can be more useful, and since 2007 there have been several attempts at producing such assessments for Myanmar.[10]

What should be the role of international assistance in the case of Myanmar/Burma? How far should it go in seeking to underpin the fundamental livelihood of the people, enhance their basic food security, and help them withstand and recover from future natural disasters? To what extent should it seek to influence broader socio-economic conditions outside the purely humanitarian area? In what ways and through which organizations can assistance be most effectively delivered without providing unintended support for the military regime? Can international assistance be the vehicle or catalyst for transition to a form of state authority and non-state behaviour that is not necessarily the subject of specific popular mandate?

What conditions should be met when humanitarian crises occur but effective governance cannot be assured? Cyclone Nargis starkly highlighted once again the lack of transparency, lack of legitimacy, and lack of integrity of the regime in Myanmar and again raised profound questions about broader governance in Myanmar/Burma as well as about the role of international assistance. Anecdotally, corruption associated with the Burmese Army and with the activities of military-owned business corporations (Union of Myanmar Economic Holdings and Myanmar Economic Corporation) has worsened. No end is in sight of the army's harmful and distorting domination of the economy without any rules to govern effectively its role.

To what extent, if any, do the return to constitutional government and the anticipated 2010 election followed by the partial transfer of power to civilian representatives raise prospects for improved governance in Myanmar? Are they steps, albeit small, towards some genuine change or merely towards more of the same? What sort of interventions at this time could realistically effect more far-reaching and durable improvements? Can a highly introverted regime, which has insisted on total state control for most of the past five decades, learn to tolerate differences and other groups or parties contesting its world view? Does it have any intention of doing so?

Alison Vicary's chapter illustrates the cumulative negative impact of poor economic policy on the part of the Myanmar government and grossly inconsiderate responses to the specific disaster of Cyclone Nargis. Her analysis is weighed against the military regime and those that work directly under it, but cannot answer the question of how non-government organizations (local as well as international) ever manage to work effectively and achieve the sort of positive outcomes in Myanmar for which other accounts, based on in-country evidence, provide testimony. The answer may be that while the operating environment is oppressive, local ingenuity can sometimes overcome many, but not all, difficulties.

Inside Myanmar/Burma many organizations and groups are anticipating the transition and readying themselves for it, to the extent that they can. As political groups and individuals decide whether to register political parties for the purpose of participating in the elections, others seem to be regrouping for a post-election situation. Many civil-society groups have been emboldened by their experiences and achievements after Cyclone Nargis and have restructured themselves for a more active role after the elections. Indigenous businesses are reconfiguring their operations in the event that their operating environment changes and perhaps improves. At the state and division level, nationality groups are consolidating their organizations for the greater authority they hope will come. Only government agencies seem unable to react and prepare, yet their functions are among those that need greatest reform.[11] Do these moves create opportunities or risks for the international community?

LOOKING AHEAD TO WHAT?

With so little known of what lies ahead, and with the strong possibility of something unexpected occurring, it is not surprising that it is difficult to foresee what might lie ahead. Moreover, the bulk of capacity-building international assistance to date has been humanitarian or simply responding to emergencies and urgent gaps. There is little effort directed strategically towards preparing for a changed political situation in which the socio-economic determinants can still be shaped.

What steps can be taken gradually to establish the rule of law and the proper functioning of the judiciary? When so little regard is paid to laws generally, how can a legal environment be created in which reliance can be placed on regular observance of laws, proper respect for others' rights, and mutual acceptance of negotiation or compromise as a reasonable outcome in disputes? How can improved socio-economic opportunities be made available ahead of wider political and social reforms, in the interests of better protecting the people's rights in the short term? In current circumstances, it is hard to devise a grand strategy to help achieve these reforms when political leadership is still in doubt. But this need not be an excuse for doing nothing. An alternative might be to press for a range of smaller reforms whose cumulative effect, if sustained, might be significant and place Myanmar/Burma on the right road, even if there is still a long way to go.

Case studies of limited successes already being achieved through normative approaches are provided in the final chapters here. In his consideration of what might be possible to work towards, rather than what might be difficult to achieve, **David Allan** notes the policy progress which has been made already on some important issues such as human trafficking, narcotics control, and agricultural education. He suggests that donors should not be blinkered by the challenges involved in new policy opportunities such as disability policy/strategy, extractive industries regulation, and mainstreaming sustainable-development principles. His own experience underlines the importance of working closely with the Myanmar/Burma authorities on a wide variety of policy issues that may not capture the headlines in the same way as the truly "big issues" around political reform in Myanmar, but which in their own way can achieve real and positive results. Cumulatively, working with the military regime on many small and mid-level policy issues may build trust and capacity, and involve knowledge transfer in addition to incorporating international norms and best practices into governance. It is perhaps an overly optimistic view of the ability of international organizations and consultants to effect lasting or significant change, but his message is central to the modus operandi of international organizations working in-country.

Finally, **Trevor Wilson** offers a case study of ways in which normative pressures have been used to bring about substantive changes, although these changes are not nearly enough to satisfy most observers. He identifies external factors (such as universally accepted international authority) and internal circumstances (such as regime readiness to change as well as the positive impact of advocacy by engagement), but also points out that expectations about what is achievable need to be realistic. He acknowledges the difficulty of knowing whether any movement toward apparent compliance with norms is accompanied by real behavioural change.[12]

These issues are among many that will play out in the wake of the country's first elections in more than twenty years. This edited collection, on the eve of the national elections and in the shadow of the great destruction and loss of life brought by Cyclone Nargis, presents a series of snapshots of a nation poised to begin a new stage in its political life. However, the country still faces serious gulfs between capacity and ambitions, between entrenched blockages to socio-economic development and under-nourished civil-society aspirations, and is without guarantees for improvement in socio-economic conditions or the ability to advance or protect basic freedoms in the future. Standards of transparency, accountability and responsiveness that underpin effective governance anywhere generally remain elusive in Myanmar/Burma.

Notes

1. According to Win Min, quoted by Marwaan Macan-Markar 2009.
2. *Myanmar economy: Country outlook*. Economist Intelligence Unit, 2010.
3. ASEAN's role in the Tripartite Core Group has been criticized for being politically naive (by Dr Zarni of the Free Burma Coalition) and economically unsound (by Burma Economic Watch 2009 Macquarie University). Such commentary may have some validity, but does not detract from observations made by Dr Sabandar in this volume and leading ASEAN officials in various public statements.
4. See Englehart (2005).
5. For example, the two major reports from the Tripartite Core Group of the SPDC/UN/ASEAN, were The Post-Nargis Joint Assessment (PONJA) of July 2008, and The Post-Nargis Recovery and Preparedness Plan (PONREPP) of December 2008.
6. For example, *After the Storm: Voices from the Delta*, by the Emergency Assistance Team of Johns Hopkins University in March 2009; the Joint INGO Response to "After the Storm: Voices from the Delta" (April 2009); *Burma/Myanmar: Views*

from the Ground and the International Community, National Bureau of Asian Research, Washington, May 2009; *Listening to Voices from Inside: Myanmar Civil Society's Response to Cyclone Nargis*, Centre for Peace and Conflict Studies, Phnom Penh, 2009.

7. Charles Petrie, "End of Mission Report", 2008.
8. International Crisis Group, "China's Myanmar Dilemma", September 2009.
9. The World Bank Indicators of governance cover (i) Voice & Accountability, (ii) Political Stability and Lack of Violence/Terrorism, (iii) Government Effectiveness, (iv) Regulatory Quality, (v) Rule of Law, and (vi) Control of Corruption. In all categories, Myanmar's score is at the lowest end of the scale.
10. For example, UNDP *Integrated Household Living Conditions Survey* (summary available at <http://www.mm.undp.org/HDI> Project Activities); and FAO 2008.
11. *The Irrawaddy* in January 2010 reported new privatization initiatives by the military regime to protect some of their military economic interests after the elections. See Wai Moe 2010.
12. In his comments at the Update Conference, Morten Pedersen warned that symbolic policies could be useful and had their place, but would lose credibility quite seriously if they were seen as being empty.

References

Burma Economic Watch. "Statement on PONREPP" February 2009. Available at <http://www.econ.mq.edu.au/Econ_docs/bew/BEWStatementPONREPP.pdf>.

Englehart, Neil A. "Is Regime Change Enough for Burma? The Problem of State Capacity". *Asian Survey* 45, no. 4, (July/August 2005): 622–44.

Food and Agricultural Organization (FAO). *Needs Assessment for the Cyclone Nargis Affected Areas*. Rome: FAO Emergency & Rehabilitation Programme, 2008.

Htet Aung. "Civil Society's Role Beyond the Election". *The Irrawaddy*, 28 December 2009.

IDEA International Institute for United Nations Development Programme (UNDP). *Integrated Household Living Conditions Survey*.Yangon, 2007.

International Crisis Group. *Myanmar Towards the Elections*, Report No. 174, 20 August 2009.

Jayasuriya, Kanishka. "Regulatory Regionalism in the Asia Pacific". *Australian Journal of International Affairs* 63, no. 3 (September 2009).

Wai Moe. "Regime Privatizing to Retain Control of Resources". *The Irrawaddy*, 7 January 2010.

Macan-Markar, Marwaan. "Burma: Junta under Scrutiny for Concrete Pre-election Signs", International Press Service, 29 November 2009, at <http://www.ipsnews.net/news.asp?idnews=49463>. Accessed 14 January 2010.

II

Political Legitimacy, Governance and Justice

2

2010 AND THE UNFINISHED TASK OF NATION-BUILDING

Khin Zaw Win

INTRODUCTION

The term "nation-building" is enjoying a revival in scholarly circles as well as becoming common in international politics. It has come to prominence in the debate on failing states, conflict management and development theory. In the post-colonial nation-states of South and Southeast Asia particularly, it has been on the political agenda since the 1950s (Derichs and Heberer 2006). This earlier usage needs to be distinguished from the term now widely being used, especially in the United States, to mean creating a "nation" in a country undergoing conflict. The latter usage denotes the employment of armed force and civil authority in putting together a workable government in a country recovering from war or still embroiled in it. There is a growing literature on this, but the meaning differs greatly from that intended in this paper.

Anthony Smith defines the nation as "a named human population which shares myths and memories, a mass public culture, a designated homeland, economic unity, and equal rights and duties for all members"

(1995, pp. 56–57). It does not take much effort to realize that by this definition Myanmar still has a long way to go before attaining nationhood. At the present time, there is little sharing of myths among its peoples, and there would be marked differences particularly in the memories of the post-independence period, which has been witness to what is perhaps the longest-running civil conflict in the world.

According to Jochen Hippler (1998), nation-building consists of three major elements:

1. An integrative ideology, that might be nationalist, but could also be religious, racist, developmentalist, or shaped along other lines, as long as it provides for integrating the sub-groups of the inhabitants of a country into one society.
2. An integrated society, with its several elements communicating more often with each other than with outsiders. This implies a "nationwide" integration of geographic regions, economic sectors, and politics. It also presupposes a functioning infrastructure and intellectual discourse of "national" scale.
3. An existing state apparatus, which actually fulfils its functions on all of the national territory.

The concept of the nation-state would imply that nation-building and state-building are twin processes, but they do not necessarily go together. There are nations without a state, like the Palestinians and the Kurds, and states without a nation, as evidenced vividly by the intractable cases of Iraq and Afghanistan. Myanmar comes across as a country where both nation- and state-building have met with little success.

Nation-building in Hippler's sense has not been seriously attempted in Myanmar before. There is a pressing need now to look at it anew, in light of the civil conflict, military rule, setbacks to democratization, and economic decline that have marked the past seventy-odd years. The question arises: have the half-hearted and ineffectual efforts to build a nation ultimately contributed to its ills? And what implications are there for the less-than-rosy-looking future?

HISTORICAL SETTING

At different times in history and up to now, the political and administrative entity referred to as Burma/Myanmar was assumed to be a single state.

Most people involved in politics and governance in Myanmar would also accept that Myanmar is a nation-state. However, a measure of circumspection is called for in using those terms in a meaningful sense. Myanmar still falls short of becoming a nation, and the purported state is a weak one. The troubles that beset the country — including those related to democracy — can be said to stem from this.

Pre-modern states have existed in the central riverine plains of Myanmar since at least the eighth century AD. Burman kings established "empires" centred at Bagan (eleventh–thirteenth centuries), Toungoo (fourteenth–sixteenth–centuries) and Ava (eighteenth–nineteenth centuries), ruling over a diverse array of ethno-linguistic groups. The two dominant cultures were Bamar and Mon and, at the British incursions of the nineteenth century, the Bamar kingdom, centred at Amarapura and later Mandalay, had recently conquered the other states as well as Arakan (Rakhine) on the western coast. True to *mandala* form, the smaller principalities in the Shan regions owed allegiance to the dominant Bamar court, as did some of the lesser ethno-political entities in the mountainous arc at the rim of the riverine plains.

Mary Callahan has written that in 1885, when the British annexed the last Bamar kingdom:

> They drew boundaries around territory that hosted one of the world's widest diversities of indigenous populations, in one of the most fractured geographical settings...For purposes of bureaucratic simplification and fiscal cheese-paring, they partitioned the country into two zones: "Ministerial Burma" or "Burma Proper" and the "Frontier" of "Excluded" areas...[N]o other Asian colony suffered such a radical bifurcation in its population's fate. (2009, p. 32)

The writing of this history has not been of help in nation-building in Myanmar. When national historians took up the story of national origins as an anti-colonial and, later, post-independence enterprise, they concentrated on the chronicles and narratives of the Bamar majority.[1] This version of history has been reinforced–more recently by the symbolic trappings of the present regime.

ETHNIC DIVERSITY AND CONFLICT

Most states in East and Southeast Asia are multi-ethnic, marked by ethnic conflict, and internal colonialism. States have attempted to enforce ethnic assimilation, unity through a common language, internal migration and military solutions to movements for autonomy. All these elements are found in Myanmar. Nationalism in this wide region is seen less as an aggressive, externally oriented ideology but, rather, as entertaining domestic functions. These include an integrative nationalism aiming at further state- and nation-building, and a modernizing nationalism designed to mobilize the people in the interest of the shared, "solidarity" goal of modernization (Derichs and Heberer 2006). Myanmar's present acute situation is a reflection of the failure of both functions.

Again, in common with a number of other countries, the nation is defined in distinct cultural terms (Bamar Buddhism in Myanmar's case). Brown (1996, pp. 260–61) asserts that this "hinders the effective management of ethnic-state relations" and thus efficacious nation-building. The dominant ethnic group and its political elite pass off their values and their concept of development as those of the entire nation, arguing that these are in the interest of political cohesion, integration and societal loyalty. Political elites have taken an unbelievably shallow perspective on ethnic and cultural diversity, and this is not limited to those from the Bamar majority. The cleavages are not merely those between the Bamar majority and the other nationalities. Differences and tensions exist between the other groups and within sub-groups as well.

The Panglong conference and agreement in 1947 can be seen as a first attempt at nation-building; sadly, its promise did not come to fruition. Now, sixty years later, one of the present regime's many slogans is national reconsolidation, which is a very poor choice of terms. The opposition has mooted a "Second Panglong", but it has not progressed beyond words. Matthew Walton has asked whether there could be a collective reappraisal of Panglong, constructing, in Prasenjit Duara's words, an "alternative history which emphasizes the dynamic, multiple, and contested nature of historical identities" (2008, p. 910). He adds that,

> As a national myth, Panglong is crucial to deciphering the persistent ethnic conflict that has plagued Burma since independence, but it is also necessary to reinterpret this "common history" in a way that recognizes ethnic diversity and even ethnic conflict, particularly if the "spirit of Panglong" is to have any resonance in fostering national unity. (2008, p. 910)

MISSED OPPORTUNITIES SINCE 1988

The 1988 uprising, which had been sparked off by students and later drew in people from all walks of life, was centred in Yangon and major towns, including those in the ethnic-nationality states. It was a nationwide groundswell of protest against the authoritarian one-party system and the economic and conflict-related hardships that it entailed. We know what the uprising was against, but we are less clear what it was for. "Democracy" was the rallying cry and leaders such as Aung San Suu Kyi rode to prominence on this wave. Huge amounts of hope and expectation were riding on it too, including the naïve assumption that democracy would solve all the accumulated shortcomings and grievances.

Following the coup of 1988, partly to continue with the promises made earlier by Burma Socialist Programme Party leaders and partly to placate smouldering bitterness over the crushed democracy uprising, the military council announced that multi-party democracy elections would be held and parties allowed to register. Two developments are worthy of note — the formation of the National League for Democracy as a largely Bamar party and the emergence of dozens of ethnic-based parties. There was no grand alliance of these parties in the subsequent elections in 1990, nor was there a genuinely multi-ethnic political party. Much later, with the backlash against democratic parties and the de-registration of hundreds of them, a loose, informal grouping known as the United Nationalities Alliance came into being. It is composed of a handful of ethnic parties and is linked to the former National League for Democracy (NLD).

A word needs to be added on where the NLD figures in all this, and on its (missing) input into this game-changing process. It has become virtually a single-issue party. In a public, official statement earlier in 2009, economic development was treated in a cursory, cavalier fashion. It would now seem that the matter of a political solution to the ceasefires and to the larger ethnic-nationalities question is being accorded the same treatment. This shirking of national responsibility will no doubt add to the long list of developments that will happen without the NLD.

In parallel with the democratic debacle, the institution that came to be called "the ceasefires" came into existence. The first ceasefires celebrated their twentieth anniversary early in 2009. These two decades have been "lost" decades in a number of ways. The peace dividend was not forthcoming and there was no progress beyond the cessation of hostilities. At the final session of the National Convention on 18 July 2007, the Kachin Independence Organization (KIO) delegates put up nineteen points that were endorsed by the other nationalities to be included in the constitution. However, all of them were rejected.

In April 2009, the government proposed that ceasefire groups surrender their arms and transform into border-guard forces (BGF) and political parties for the electoral process. Three deadlines (June, October and December 2009) for transformation into BGF have passed and although two ceasefire groups — the New Democratic Army–Kachin and the ethnic-Kokang group, Myanmar National Democratic Alliance Army — have taken up the offer, a final and comprehensive settlement has not yet been reached. Everything militates against it under the present circumstances.

Whereas Senior General Than Shwe is going for a maximum-advantage, high-risk solution, most, if not all, the generals at regional and division levels — closer to reality than Than Shwe is — would gladly opt for a maximum-advantage, low-risk arrangement. This would translate into having many of the present benefits continue to accrue to them (which wouldn't happen if fighting resumes), while being on good terms with the ethnic forces. They should be able to understand — at least more than Than Shwe does — that the limits have been reached for military options and that the possibility of a political solution lies with the parliament-to-come.

It needs to be underscored here that the defence forces' leadership has placed that institution in a position where it stands to lose either way. If it sticks to having its way, employing the force of arms to achieve this, it would undermine one of its few accomplishments: the post-1988 ceasefires. Moreover, a complete military victory is by no means assured, taking into account the decline in combat capabilities.

When it comes to the alternative of a more-or-less favourable settlement, the longer-term portents for the defence forces aren't that good either. When they were initiated two decades ago, the ceasefires were meant to be the first step to a long-overdue political solution. However, the junta, the main opposition and the international community failed to give them the recognition that they deserved, and in consequence they languished. The advent of a broadly acceptable outcome now could relegate a military solution to an inferior status (despite advice to the contrary from irrelevant personages like the Sri Lankan President). It could also open the door to truer pluralism, and autonomy and decentralization. (It has to be borne in mind, though, that there are positive and negative sides to each of these.) The likelihood is lessened of everything revolving around the pivot of a centralized, military-dominated state.

The major concern through much of 2009 was the wholesale collapse of the ceasefires and the resumption of hostilities. Would it be hazardous to state that the likelihood of this has lessened now? If so, the closeness of the elections, the possibility of re-engagement with the United States, and subtle interventions by China might all have lent a hand. The realization may have seeped in that nothing is going to be served by hostilities. The new post-election state structure and the accompanying change in outlook might contribute to a peaceful and more conclusive settlement, but it will still require political will on all sides.

COMPARISONS

Desperately short of new ideas, the lingering adherents to authoritarianism have slapped together a constitution that they presume will perpetuate their hold over the country. One of their keystones is a mass organization and legislative assembly modelled after what Indonesia had before the fall of Suharto. Taking the failed models of yesteryear as a template may seem self-defeating but this regime appears to be serious. Indonesia's swift and successful turnaround after 1998 may be unsettling to some people in Naypyitaw. What really should be emulated are the developments in Indonesia since 2004.

It has been shown that in multi-ethnic societies, periods of actual or expected change constitute "critical junctures" where ethnic groups tend to worry about a deterioration of their position or to struggle for its improvement. The last years of Suharto's rule and the first years after the demise of the New Order were critical junctures for Indonesia, when communal conflict sharply increased (Meuleman 2006).

Furthermore, Schulte Nordholt has shown that the processes of decentralization, democratization and development of civil society, although often brought about in relation to each other, are non-parallel. Nation-building may be included as a fourth element in this set of partially related but different and non-parallel socio-political processes. He also points out the risks involved in decentralization. After comparing developments in South Asia and West Africa, Crook and Manor (1998) conclude that instead of bringing fundamental changes, decentralization tends to reinforce existing political patterns at the regional level. Regional elites in Myanmar would consist of military commanders, ceasefire forces and the "complexes" they form with local and foreign business interests.[2]

Quite a number of people in these elites are bound to get elected. In a country where so many things tend to go wrong and have gone wrong, the coming decentralization will have to be handled with care.

Besides the shared legacy of having been part of Britain's Indian Empire and having extended periods of post-independence military rule, there are other similarities between Myanmar's and Pakistan's failed attempts at nation-building. Hippler (1997) writes of Pakistan that:

> While some of the arguments the Army put forward to justify its taking power (like incompetence and corruption of many civilian politicians) are not without merit, military rule has not strengthened, but weakened the social fabric of the country. A very important point has been that all political parties are organized as internal dictatorships. Office holders are not elected, but appointed by the chairperson, or the governing bodies. Parties are hardly the instruments of people to express their will, but oligarchies and political machines. Internal democracy is completely absent, and political programs do not matter.

One could perhaps be grateful that no part of Myanmar has broken away, as did East Pakistan in 1971, and that there is no country bordering it that is undergoing a greater degree of conflict and instability. Outright secession of any ethnic homeland can be ruled out in Myanmar's case; what is more likely is that the Wa region, for instance, becomes entrenched as the equivalent of Pakistan's tribal areas on the borders of Afghanistan. The country may be spared the ignominy of secession of one of its regions, but the end-result is a sub-state with a high degree of de facto autonomy, practically governing itself and defying the central government.

Despite the symbolic edifices being constructed at Naypyitaw, the period since 1988 has seen a decline in state capacity. This accentuates the risk in venturing upon an innovative state structure following the elections; that is, provincial legislatures and governments. Whether all this will help or hinder state- and nation-cohesiveness is one of the major questions hanging over the country. One important factor that could prevent fissures from widening is China's political and economic hegemony. With Myanmar's geo-strategic importance to her, it would not serve China well if Myanmar were to follow in the footsteps of Pakistan.

THE ROADMAP AND 2010

As far as the military is concerned, the Myanmar nation already exists, heir to the illustrious (Bamar) empires that flourished in history. Their nation is not only Bamar-centred but military-centred as well. The configuration following 2010 will not be a departure from this set pattern, despite the formal measure of autonomy given to the provincial legislatures and governments. The Union Solidarity and Development Association (USDA) is one of the primary tools to ensure this. On 1 June 2010 it was turned into a political party. It is by far the biggest of the current political parties and will contest all 1,000 plus seats in the three tiers of parliament. This is an integral part of the seven-stage Roadmap.

Most perspectives and opinions on the Roadmap — from the opposition and the international community and even the Myanmar public — are on how much it does or does not facilitate democracy in Myanmar. The implications for nation-building are only mentioned in passing, if at all. It is eerily familiar with the situations in 1947–48 and 1988–89. It has to be underscored that despite the Myanmar public's longing for the resumption of a democratic system, the current arrangements again point to a majoritarian democracy that will not be a cure-all for what afflicts them; a genuinely plural system that presages a plural nation has to be the goal from the outset. Contrary to most popular assumptions, a nation will not ensue with the re-advent of democracy.

For whatever it is worth, following the 2010 elections, there will be a bicameral Union legislature, as well as fourteen provincial (state and region) legislatures and governments, elected along parliamentary lines. Sectors that fall under the jurisdiction of the state and region governments include the budget, economy, agriculture, industry and transport. When provincial institutions come into being following the elections, the staffing of those departments will invariably draw from the ethnic groups of those provinces.[3] The end-result will be that more non-Bamar government employees are recruited and appointed. These will have to join with Union-appointed employees in running a government. Some attention and effort, cutting across ethnic lines, will then come to be devoted to nation-building, whether there is an overarching national direction or not.

For those of us beyond the army's constricted circle, a favourable outcome of the ceasefires could lead the way to a widely acceptable and therefore lasting solution to the age-old conundrum of centre–periphery, majority–minority relations.

It is perhaps a measure of the Myanmar polity that, with elections due to be held in late 2010, a multi-ethnic political organization is still not on the cards. It is true that circumstances do not yet permit such preparations on the opposition side. As such, voting is expected to be along ethnic rather than multi-ethnic lines. But this hiatus is nonetheless worrying, knowing that a multi-ethnic alliance contesting the election is in the realm of the possible. And expectations should not stop at the elections; a caucus of elected representatives at both national and provincial levels could and should continue with the work. This is one structure and vehicle that can be looked forward to. The present constitution for all its flaws presents a tool that may be harnessed and utilized for this purpose. The first term of semi-democratic legislatures could be used as the period to work on this.

Ironically, the priority given to democracy is a low-key issue of contention amongst the opposition; notably between the major political parties and the ethnic-based organizations. Put simply, for the major parties, democracy comes first and is above all else, whereas for almost all ethnic-based organizations, ethnic rights take precedence over democracy. The NLD still thinks bilateral dialogue must come before inclusion of ethnic nationalities. The reliance upon dialogue at the top is getting wearisome, and the relegation of the minorities issue to secondary status is as persistent as it is self-defeating.

For the rest of the opposition, a symbiotic arrangement is an urgent necessity. It could be called a multi-ethnic democracy or a democratic devolution. Something like integrative nationalism would be too much to hope for even in the near future. It has to be understood that for aspirations on all sides to be fulfilled, people have to work and build together. This sounds like a party or government slogan but it is quite amazing that those who have aspired to national leadership have given lip-service to but actually neglected this rather basic fact.

Well, times have changed. In the semi-democracy that will most likely emerge, is it going to be the same story of demanding more democracy? It will still make good copy in the media abroad, but how much will it serve political goals domestically? At the same time, members of the new parliaments will have to push for greater devolution to make it happen. Will these be ethnic voices alone? Non-democratic bastions would dearly love this cleavage and would avidly continue the *divide et impera*. Manoeuvring and coalition-building to pre-empt this could provide fresh impetus for nation-building.

On the other side, there has been intense interest in federalism among the ethnic nationalities. There was even the very controversial "eight states" proposal, which would have the Bamars grouped or mapped into the eighth state. Voices calling for this have died down in the past decade, to the relief of many. It goes without saying that federalism is anathema to the successive authoritarian regimes.

So where and to what extent does federalism figure in nation-building, and vice versa? One does get the impression that the vision that is espoused for a federal system stops rather short of the nation-that-is-to-be-desired. It appears to be, first and last, a means of distancing from the unworkable Bamar centralism. The question that the ethnic nationalities have to face now is what lies beyond the federalism that they hanker for.

CONCLUSION

There is an ongoing crisis with the ceasefires. Needless to say, nation-building — which has lagged behind, from the beginning — is facing yet another possible setback. If hostilities are to be averted, all sides will have to concede ground, and a face-saving formula has to be found and put into effect. It will have to be a workable formula that is not about just give-and-take.

The year 2010 will be a time of reckoning for nation-building in Myanmar. The performances of the Bamar polity and its poor leadership have held centre stage since, and even before, independence. No Bamar leader then and now has had the capability to shape and forge a nation. This assessment does not see attitudes and policies changing in time for 2010. It is now time that the issues central to Myanmar are reframed. With the sorry record of top-down nation-building, more attention should be paid to the possibilities for a bottom-up approach. As in the field of development, civil society has been at the fore in bringing different ethnic nationalities to work together on common objectives. Civil society is one element that has been missing in the past, but its efforts are still very much in the initial stage. And there is considerable variation in its presence and activity among different ethnic groups.

Taking into account the multiple demands that 2010 will bring to an exhausted people, Callahan points to the need to:

> overcome the deep divisions fostered by the British, the continuation of which under the *thakins* and their military successors constitutes Myanmar's great failure. It would need to rally both the minorities and the deeply impoverished centre, as well as sectors of the armed forces, behind an

> economic programme that would heal the country's gaping inequalities, and in support of a constitutional settlement at once federal and democratic. (2009, p. 63)

The issue should not be about "what should come first", although hard lessons worldwide incline towards the nation. A good part of the problem in Myanmar lies in the way ethnic aspirations and federalism have been labelled and boxed in. Both the military and the left have regarded these warily, if not suspiciously. When former military officers and the old left constitute the leadership of a democratic party, one can perhaps gauge what that party's stand would be. The present exponents of democracy in Myanmar have difficulty with minority views. Instead of wrangling over which to put first, it has to be realized that, leaving aside the civil conflict, a democracy is not going to be complete nor will it be sound and stable if significant ethnic and religious views are not incorporated. In the same vein, ethnic rights are not going to make headway if the present authoritarianism is not cut back and attenuated by liberal-democratic inroads.

Notes

1. There is a discussion of this in South 2005.
2. To give one instance, the Pa-O National Organization, a ceasefire group, controls practically everything in Pa-O ethnic areas. This is a widespread pattern in the ethnic areas. There will be a Pa-O self-governing region under the new constitution.
3. There is no published ethnic composition of government employees but the non-Bamar strength is generally low. Nowhere is this more apparent than in the military.

References

Brown, David. *The State and Ethnic Politics in Southeast Asia*. London: Routledge, 1996.

Callahan, Mary. "Myanmar's Perpetual Junta: Solving the Riddle of the Tatmadaw's Long Reign". *New Left Review* 60 (2009): 27–63.

Crook, Richard C. and James Manor. *Democracy and decentralization in South Asia and West Africa; Participation, accountability and performance*. Cambridge: Cambridge University Press, 1998.

Derichs, Claudia and Thomas Heberer. "Introduction: Diversity of Nation-Building in East and Southeast Asia". *European Journal of East Asian Studies* 5, no. 1 (2006): 1–13.

Holliday, Ian. "Voting and Violence in Myanmar: Nation-building for a Transition to Democracy". *Asian Survey* 48, no. 6 (2008): 1038–58.

Hippler, Jochen. "Problems of Democracy and Nation-Building in Pakistan". <http://www.jochen-hippler.de/Aufsatze/Nation-Building_in_Pakistan/nation-building_in_pakistan.html>. Accessed 1 December 2009.

Meuleman, Johan. "Between Unity and Diversity: The Construction of the Indonesian Nation". *European Journal of East Asian Studies* 5, no. 1 (2006): 45–69.

Nordholt, Henk Schulte. "Renegotiating boundaries". *Bijdragen tot de Taal, Land en Volkenkunde* 159, no. 4 (2003): 550–89.

Postill, John. *Media and Nation Building: How the Iban Became Malaysian*. Oxford and New York: Berghahn Books, 2006.

Smith, Anthony D. *Nations and Nationalism in a Global Era*. Cambridge: Polity Press, 1995.

South, Ashley. *Mon Nationalism and Civil War in Burma: The Golden Sheldrake.* London and New York: Routledge, 2005.

Walton, Matthew J. "Ethnicity, Conflict, and History in Burma: The Myths of Panglong". *Asian Survey* 48, no. 6 (2008): 889–910.

3

BURMA'S POLITICAL TRANSITION
Implications for U.S. Policy

Priscilla Clapp

INTRODUCTION

Burma will be undergoing a political transition over the coming decade. The new constitution promulgated to guide this transition provides for a highly "disciplined", military-dominated, quasi-parliamentary system with wide-ranging constraints on the participants in election politics and elected bodies. Some believe that this transition, despite the authoritarian constitution, may ultimately prove to be the long-awaited opportunity to develop alternatives to military rule in Burma. Others see the constitution and the coming elections simply as a codification of permanent authoritarian rule in the guise of democracy. Even a careful reading of the constitution does not answer this dilemma; the answer will only become apparent in its implementation, both near-term and long-term. In the near term, outside actors are likely to have very little impact on the 2010 elections and the formation of the newly elected government. Over the longer term, however, Burma's political transition could lead the country to greater international interaction, both politically and economically, depending upon the nature of the new leadership that emerges and the policies that Asian neighbours, Western governments, and international institutions adopt toward the new government. This paper will examine the possible outcomes of Burma's political transition and speculate on how different outcomes might affect U.S. policy.

LEGISLATING "DISCIPLINED DEMOCRACY"

The 2008 Burmese constitution has been carefully crafted by Burma's military rulers to guide the country into a new era of multi-party quasi-parliamentary government in which the military itself plays a central role in assuring political "discipline."[1] Although the 2008 constitution has been dismissed by most observers as a thoroughly undemocratic document, the State Peace and Development Council (SPDC) has been clearly unwilling to entertain any suggestion of modification and appears determined to follow through with its plans for elections and transition to quasi-parliamentary government in 2010. We must therefore view the constitution as the blueprint for the transition process and the new government it will produce.

According to the constitution, the structure of the new government will be based on:

1. Seven states, seven regions, one Union territory (Naypyitaw), and six self-administered areas for ceasefire groups;
2. A bicameral national parliament, with the lower house elected by township and the upper house consisting of 12 elected representatives for each state and region; a unicameral parliament in each state and region; and a legislative/executive Leading Body in each self-administered area;
3. 25 per cent appointed military representation in each parliament and Leading Body;
4. A separate executive branch, headed by a President elected by the parliament;
5. A military Commander-in-Chief, appointed by the President and approved by the parliament;
6. A National Defence and Security Council that rules on all matters of security and foreign affairs;
7. A separate judicial branch with a Supreme Court at the apex;
8. A Constitutional Tribunal, whose membership is reconstituted with

each parliamentary election, to rule on matters of constitutional interpretation; and,

9. Courts Martial for military justice, under the authority of the Commander-in-Chief.

The constitution provides for the following sequence of events to put the new government in place:

1. After elections in November 2010, the sitting of the new parliament brings the constitution into effect;
2. The SPDC itself ceases to exist, but its structures of government remain valid and authoritative until various institutions of the new government are formed;
3. The parliament elects speakers and a President;
4. The President appoints a Commander-in-Chief, forms ministries, and appoints ministers;
5. The President forms a National Defence and Security Council, a Financial Commission, and an Election Commission;
6. Simultaneously, the state and region parliaments sit;
7. The President appoints Chief Ministers for the states and regions from among elected members of their parliaments;
8. As state and region governments are being duly constituted, Leading Bodies are formed in self-administered areas (The Leading Body chairperson becomes a minister in the state or region government);
9. The President appoints a Chief Justice and members of the Supreme Court; and,
10. High Courts for states and regions and a system of civilian courts are formed.

Much of the constitution is devoted to detail about how the new system of government must operate to achieve "disciplined democracy". For example:

1. The military is embedded firmly in the political system under the authority of the Commander-in-Chief, who serves on the powerful National Defence and Security Council and commands all the military representatives in parliament, constituting the single-most disciplined bloc of parliamentary votes. The Commander-

in-Chief names the ministers of defence, home affairs, and border affairs and their equivalents in states, regions, and self-administered areas.

2. Strict rules determine who can run for office or be appointed to senior executive and judicial positions. The election laws published in March 2010 added further draconian restrictions, notably one forbidding political parties from including members currently serving prison terms.
3. Executive power is heavily concentrated in the President, whose election is carefully choreographed to give the military a key role in his choice, and the qualifications for President required by the constitution make it virtually certain that he must be a retired military officer. The President makes all major appointments, and authority for major legislative and executive decisions extends upward to the President and Commander-in-Chief.
4. In constitutional or security emergencies, the constitution may be suspended partially or nearly in full. In the worst case, the President may suspend the parliament, declare martial law, and hand power over to the Commander-in-Chief for as much as two years.
5. Despite purported guarantees of individual rights, they are all subject to concerns for security, public order, and morality. The tone of the constitution makes it clear that current norms will continue to dictate public morality.

RECIPE FOR CONTINUED MILITARY CONTROL

The constitution leaves wide latitude for authoritarian manipulation and control and it exempts the military from all of the provisions that govern the country's civilian population. For example, military forces will be appointed to one-quarter of all the parliamentary seats at both the national and state/division levels, the military will maintain strict control of its own budget and finances, military companies will remain a major component of the formal economy, military personnel will be judged by their own tribunals, and military leaders will occupy key ministerial and political positions.[2] Furthermore, many of the senior officials of the SPDC will take off their uniforms, compete in the elections, and be appointed to senior legislative and executive positions in the new government. Thus, despite the pretence of democratic process through elections and the formation of parliamentary structures, the government will continue to be heavily militarized.

A number of serious questions about the elections remain unresolved. The election laws setting the rules for formation of political parties and for competing in the elections have imposed heavy burdens on parties and candidates that seem designed to limit the number of parties and guarantee the predominance of the party favoured by the government, the newly formed Union Solidarity and Development Party (USDP).[3] The harsh restrictions placed on the formation of parties and the conduct of elections have led the National League for Democracy (NLD) to decide against competing in the elections. The Election Commission's implementation of the election laws displays a clear bias in favour of the USDP. For example, the USDP members have resigned from the military, but not from their ministerial positions, despite regulations against civil servants running for office. Also, the USDP candidates are openly employing government resources in their campaigns, despite elections rules against this. Although a substantial number of minority-nationality parties and independent democracy parties have applied to register, the Election Commission has been slow to approve many of these applications, effectively denying the parties the right to organize and campaign. And finally, the Election Commission was late setting a date for the elections, even though they are supposed to occur before the end of 2010.

The regime also faces a serious unresolved point of contention with several of the major ceasefire groups,[4] who are challenging the government's demand that they agree to place their armed militias under the command of the Burmese Army as part of a new border guard. Having initially made this a condition for participating in the elections and the new government, the SPDC now seems to be backing off in the face of adamant resistance by the largest of these groups and pressure from China. The SPDC's attack on the leadership of the Kokang ceasefire group in August 2009, which sent more than 30,000 refugees into China, drew an angry reaction from Beijing and hardened the resistance of the larger Wa ceasefire group, which has a well-armed and well-trained force of an estimated 20,000–30,000 troops. Chinese Premier Wen Jiabao's visit to Napyitaw in June 2010 appears to have elicited a promise from Senior General Than Shwe that the SPDC will not let its differences with the ceasefire groups lead to further violence.[5]

After the 2010 elections finally take place, there will be critical questions about how the new government is to be formed. The constitution does not specify the sequencing for the establishment of the new government and the phase-out of the SPDC. It states that the constitution will come into operation on the day that the new parliament is called into session by the SPDC after the elections. At this point, the SPDC cedes the exercise of sovereignty to the new government and the parliament proceeds with the business of electing speakers, deputy-speakers, vice-presidents and a President. The appointment of ministers and the reconstitution of the executive branch, including the military itself, will take time, and the structures and remaining officials of the SPDC are likely to remain in place for quite a while, running the risk that the new government could wind up adopting the governance patterns of the SPDC. This risk is reinforced by the constitutional provision that all structures and personnel of the current government and judicial system will remain in place until the new government replaces them. The constitution further decrees that all laws, regulations, policies, and so on, of the SPDC will devolve to the new government and remain in effect until repealed or amended by the government.

Even before the elections, however, the SPDC has already begun to change its face significantly, because many of its senior officials have resigned from the military to run for parliamentary seats and position themselves for senior office in the new government. Those who have replaced them in the military command structure are from a much younger generation than the current membership of the SPDC, because, according to knowledgeable Burmese sources, the mandatory retirement age of 60 for military service will be strictly observed after the elections. A military officer designated for a senior military position such as the commander-in-chief will probably be under 55, so that he will not be forced into retirement before the end of the first parliamentary term. Therefore, as the SPDC withers away, its members will slide into senior government positions one way or another. Senior General Than Shwe and Vice Senior General Maung Aye will probably retire into advisory positions and continue to exercise considerable authority over the new government.

Many in Burma see the new constitution and the transition that will take place after the 2010 elections as a carefully crafted exit strategy for the country's strongman, Senior General Than Shwe, which he has designed personally to ensure his legacy, as well as the welfare of his family, once he is no longer the head of the military. They expect that in order to guarantee the security and reliability of this plan Than Shwe will remain a strongman either as president or from behind the scenes, as General Ne Win did after he stepped down in 1988. In any case, there is no question that Than Shwe has absolute control over the SPDC today, that he makes all the critical decisions — more often than not on his own counsel — and that he will remain in close control of the transition process as long as his health allows. At the same time, because he has built his own strength by keeping those around him guessing, he has not developed an obvious line of leadership succession and, once he steps back, he is not likely to be replaced soon by another unassailable strongman.

If Than Shwe and the leadership of the new government determine that they must recreate some of the mechanisms and procedures currently used by the SPDC to allow an inner circle to control all the functions of government, despite the provisions of the 2008 constitution for new executive institutions, the country will clearly remain stuck in the authoritarian quagmire that has held it back for the last few decades. This situation would probably persist for at least the first five years of the new government, until a post-Than Shwe generation of leaders, somewhat removed from the "cult" of the SPDC, begins to emerge. Ultimately, how the leadership elected in 2010 decides to resolve all of these questions the first time around will have a strong effect in determining whether the new government is capable of addressing the country's major issues; namely, creating adequate space for political opposition and minority nationalities in the system of governance, laying the foundation for economic development, and establishing the rule of law.

CONTEMPLATING THE LONGER TERM

At this stage, there is no reliable means of measuring how this transition to a quasi-parliamentary system will affect the prospects for building democracy in Burma over the longer term. Even discounting the debilitating impact of repressive military control, the country is so bereft of the fundamental institutions and political culture required to support democratic governance, that it will take decades to establish stable democracy in Burma under the best of circumstances. While the constitution appears on the surface to be a blueprint for legalizing indefinite military control of the country's political system and is likely to be so as long as Than Shwe remains a major force, the post-Than Shwe era could be more promising. As things have been arranged during the past decades of military rule, first under Ne Win's one-party government and centralized economy, then under the iron grip of the SLORC/SPDC regimes, lines of control over decision-making led back to a single strongman.[6] Once Than Shwe steps back, it is not clear that this pattern of control can be perpetuated for very long under the system contemplated by the new constitution, despite its military complexion, for a number of reasons.

First, sooner or later — if not during the first five-year parliament, then perhaps after subsequent elections — the authority that currently resides in the SPDC will be dispersed to legislative bodies, civilian ministries, and other executive committees, introducing the possibility of more broadly informed management and decision-making, especially with regard to economic matters, but also in health, education, and social welfare. The brunt of continued military control over the political system will be concentrated on national security and foreign policy, and other areas of national decision-making will no longer be conditioned strictly by a military-command psychology. Government officials will also have to answer increasingly to elected representatives in parliament who, in turn, must respond to constituents' concerns. Although the widespread placement of former military officers in civilian ministries ensures that the military mentality will linger throughout the government for a long time, if elected government survives long enough, better civilian governance practices may eventually have a chance to incubate.

Second, the reintroduction of at least quasi-parliamentary procedure, particularly the multi-party, multi-level, multi-national make-up prescribed by the 2008 constitution, offers the promise of bringing a more diverse group of people into the government than has been the practice under the predominantly Burman male-chauvinistic military regime. Over the longer term, no amount of military discipline is likely to prevent a more ethnically and politically representative legislature — despite its twenty-five per cent military composition — from developing its own ideas about how the country should be governed. The key to political reform will be whether a new majority can eventually force the possibility of amending the 2008 constitution.

Third, the racial diversity of the new system of governance will present additional challenges to military control. During the SLORC/SPDC decades, minority nationalities have been largely excluded from national government and their responsibility for local governance has been subject to the whims of regional military commanders in most areas. The constitution opens space for them to participate in legislative affairs at the state/division level, albeit without giving them much, if any, authority over education or natural resources, both of which are important components of self-determination. Although the constitution is clearly designed to standardize central-government access, influence, and control in all the ethnic minority areas of the country, the Wa, Kachin, and others — who have managed to develop considerable autonomy in governing the areas they were granted by ceasefire agreements — are clearly dissatisfied with the new constitution and are resisting the regime's efforts to force their militias under Burmese Army control before the elections. Having used force to bring the Kokang into line, the SPDC has been attempting to negotiate compromise solutions with the others, under considerable pressure from China. Even if a peaceful resolution can be found, these groups are likely to remain determined to limit the central government's control over their territory after the elections. China will play a significant role, both before and after the elections, in facilitating a *modus vivendi* between the government and the ethnic-Chinese groups on the border to prevent these tensions from developing into hostile resistance.[7]

In the areas along the Thai border where small-scale armed insurgency remains active, implementation of the constitution is not likely to ease tension in the near term. On the contrary, those involved in the insurgencies believe the new constitution totally ignores their interests and they fear that the elections and transition could draw their compatriots into wider cooperation with the ruling powers and diminish their insurgency's support base. This trend is already evident in rising tensions among various Burmese groups on the Thai side of the border and could easily translate into sporadic intra- and inter-ethnic tension in the Shan, Karen, Karenni, and Mon areas inside Burma. Therefore, it is not unrealistic to anticipate a greater degree of instability and tension in various non-Burman areas during the transition period.

Fourth, because the new constitution does not offer any immediate relief from military domination of political life in Burma, the most significant near-term gain from transition to the new government could be an improvement in the prospects for the country's economic development. When the generals finally stop meddling in economic management, neighbouring countries — which have been frustrated to see their investments in Burma mismanaged and squandered by the military — are likely to intensify pressure to correct the serious macro-economic distortions that have been inhibiting economic development for decades. China, Japan, and key Association of Southeast Asian Nations (ASEAN) countries will undoubtedly see this as an opportunity to encourage economic reforms. International financial institutions will come into play and donor governments will have to reassess the rationale for continuing their restrictions on IMF, World Bank, and ADB advice and assistance to Burma. Under these circumstances, the international community could make a valuable contribution to improved governance, particularly in the areas of economic management, health, and social welfare, by training civil servants to strengthen the competence of civilian government structures that may no longer be burdened by strict military control.[8]

Fifth, the transition to multi-party parliamentary government is likely in the longer term — that is, after the 2015 elections — to produce new, competing centres of power in Burma, diminishing the military's totalitarian grip on the country. Ironically, the powers the constitution confers on the President amount to a recipe for competition with the Commander-in-Chief, regardless of the fact that the President will most probably be a former general himself. Whether or not he occupies a formal position in the new government, Than Shwe is likely to remain behind the scenes, in substantial control of the government for as long as his health allows. Once Than Shwe is no longer the strongman pulling the strings of government, competition for power and authority will begin in earnest. The post-Than Shwe President, for example, is likely to find it in his interest to avoid any situation that would require him to hand the reins of government over to the Commander-in-Chief. The Commander-in-Chief is likely to try to keep security concerns at the top of the government agenda to enhance the military's grip on political power, but he will no longer enjoy the overwhelming authority that Than Shwe has built up through years of bullying and terrorizing his perceived challengers. Initially, the Union Solidarity and Development Party (USDP) will be a source of support for the President and, by virtue of its control over parliamentary seats and a number of senior executive positions, will have a strong interest in keeping the civilian government in place. In other words, despite the "killer clause" that gives the military constitutional authority to return to martial law, the elected officials who must initiate and approve the suspension of parliament — namely, the President and the parliament — could be unwilling to put themselves out of business.

Under these circumstances, it probably won't take long for significant splits to occur in the leadership itself, because the USDP is not an intrinsically well-disciplined organization, it does not share uniformly common interests with the military, and its branches at the national and state levels are likely to develop different and potentially competing interests, as they move increasingly into the business of governance. The downside of expanding political diversity in the parliaments, however, could be the advantage it gives the uniformed military bloc in the parliaments, which will remain loyal to the Commander-in-Chief.

There is also the possibility that the minority nationalities could eventually become a more potent political force at the state and regional level, particularly if they are able over time to develop discipline to act in concert at the national level in pursuit of their common interests. The development of an effective political culture among these groups, however, will take considerable time and education. It is nonetheless something to watch and perhaps even an opportunity to encourage democratic development at the local level.

Sixth, when genuine economic development gets under way, a more potent free-market business class is likely to develop. As people begin to grasp the potential of parliamentary governance, it would be natural for this business class to begin developing its own set of political interests. This, along with a continuing effort to promote community development, could serve to strengthen the skills and independence of elected officials. It could also force the development of a sense of downward responsibility to communities and constituencies on the part of elected officials.

Seventh and finally, the constitution makes amendment of its provisions so difficult that the government is likely to be the first victim of this ruse. It is not difficult to imagine that amendments will be required almost immediately to correct some of the contradictions, blanks, and inconsistencies in this highly detailed constitution, when the government is confronted with them during the implementation phase. Changes in essentially procedural matters can be managed by assuring a 75 per cent vote in the parliament without a referendum, but changes touching on structural matters will require an onerous political process. Perhaps, in the end, the difficulty of amendment is not so important as how practical necessity will define the way the new system works.

THE UNITED STATES REVISITS ITS SANCTIONS POLICY

For the past two decades, U.S. policy toward Burma has tended to focus more on efforts to sanction and exclude the Burmese government —

especially its military leaders — from the international community, rather than to promote engagement. This trend has been inspired and reinforced by Burmese exile groups and their advocates, in the name of the National League for Democracy (NLD) and its leader Aung San Suu Kyi. The greatest impetus for U.S. sanctions policy, however, has been the military regime itself, whose brutal assaults on its domestic opposition have only invited further international outrage. It could even be argued that the military leadership has so demonized the idea of Western influence on Burmese society as to suggest that it may, perversely, welcome Western sanctions and isolation, so long as its Asian neighbours remain engaged.

Beginning with a ban on providing aid and the withdrawal of USAID from Burma after the events of 1988, U.S. sanctions were extended in the 1990s to private investment, military exchanges and military assistance, travel visas, high-level official meetings, and educational exchanges, and during the next decade to trade with the United States, gems, and financial services. As a result, formal economic and political relations between the two countries today are negligible. Nonetheless, a large volume of U.S. dollars finds its way into Burma through tourism, humanitarian assistance programmes, and remittances from overseas Burmese, notwithstanding U.S. financial sanctions on the Burmese banking system, the government, and the generals and their business cronies.

Even as sanctions were being tightened over the past two decades, the U.S. foreign-assistance budget continued to carry a line item earmarked for Burma. During the 1990s this assistance was directed almost exclusively to the support of Burmese exile groups, in order to promote the return of democratic governance in Burma and to address the severe needs of displaced minority nationalities. With the gradual expansion of UN agencies and international humanitarian organizations in Burma and their outreach to the impoverished Burmese population, the U.S. government began to channel assistance increasingly through UN agencies and international NGOs to humanitarian programmes inside Burma, with the proviso that none of this aid was to go to the Burmese government itself. With the development of reliable mechanisms for delivering assistance inside the country and under increasing pressure from U.S. advocates of humanitarian assistance, the budget earmarked for Burma has more than doubled in recent years, to more than US$17 million in 2009. An additional US$18 million was added to this in two 2009 budget supplementals, for a total of US$35 million. In response to Cyclone Nargis, the United States pumped another US$75 million into the emergency and recovery effort in the Irrawaddy Delta and, in October 2009, announced an additional US$10 million contribution to post-Nargis assistance. Furthermore, the emergence of a more robust civil-society movement in Burma during the last two years has presented a variety of new channels for engaging at the grassroots level, making it possible to disburse more than half of the designated amount and the lion's share of the Nargis money inside Burma.

When the Obama Administration came to office in February 2009, U.S. Burma policy became an early candidate for review. This first became explicit during Secretary of State Hillary Clinton's February 2009 trip to Asia when she foreshadowed this policy review, remarking that neither sanctions nor engagement seemed to have influenced the stubborn military regime. She also signalled that the United States would be open to more constructive discussion with ASEAN and other Asian governments on the question of what to do about Burma. With Clinton's return to Washington, a wide-ranging review of Burma policy was initiated which slowly gained momentum during the next six months, engaging policymakers at all levels and including all major elements of the U.S. government involved with enforcing the sanctions. It was perhaps the most thorough and far-reaching policy review of U.S. relations with Burma that has been undertaken by the U.S. government in recent memory.

While the policy review was under way, the SPDC decided to prosecute NLD leader Aung San Suu Kyi for allowing an American intruder to remain in her compound overnight when his health prevented him from swimming back across the lake from whence he had come. Baffled by the absurdity of this trial — which was launched just as the United States was considering easing its sanctions policy — U.S. policymakers decided to hold the review in abeyance pending the outcome of the trial. In the meantime, Senator Jim Webb had approached Burmese authorities about visiting the country as part of a tour of ASEAN countries during the Congressional recess in August. Perhaps sensing an opportunity to correct its message to the new administration in Washington, the SPDC (probably Senior General Than Shwe himself) decided to bring the trial to a grand finale on the eve of Webb's visit, handing down a commuted sentence of 18 months under house arrest for Aung San Suu Kyi[9] and a prison term of seven years for the American intruder, John Yettaw. When Webb arrived in Rangoon, he found that he had become the first senior U.S. official to be granted a meeting with

Senior General Than Shwe and that he would also be allowed to meet with Aung San Suu Kyi. The SPDC also handed Yettaw over to Webb for repatriation to the United States. Although Webb's meetings in Burma have not caused the regime to relax its repressive policies, his unusually cordial reception by the SPDC created the impression that U.S. relations with Burma had suddenly reached a turning point — a classic manoeuvre by the military leadership to trump substance with form.

With the trial concluded, Washington was finally able to bring its policy review to a conclusion. Senior administration officials announced the initial results in September, when Secretary of State Clinton met with the "Friends of Burma" group at the United Nations during the General Assembly. Assistant Secretary of State for Pacific and East Asian Affairs Kurt Campbell then gave a more detailed exposition of the policy decisions in his testimony before the Senate Foreign Relations Committee Subcommittee on the Pacific and East Asian Affairs hearings, chaired by Senator Jim Webb on 30 September 2009. Explaining that the United States had decided to balance its sanctions policy with an effort to engage Burma's senior leadership in dialogue, Campbell said:

> While our goals in Burma remain the same as before, the policy review confirmed that we need additional tools to augment those that we have been using in pursuit of our objectives. A policy of pragmatic engagement with the Burmese authorities holds the best hope for advancing our goals. A central element of this approach is a direct, senior-level dialogue with representatives of the Burmese leadership. As the Secretary previewed in her remarks to the Friends of Burma last week, we hope a dialogue with the Burmese regime will lay out a path forward towards change in Burma and a better, more productive bilateral relationship. (2009, p. 2)

Campbell told the subcommittee that the administration expected the policy of "pragmatic engagement" to be a "long, slow, and step-by-step process" and that progress would be measured by the willingness of the Burmese regime to address fundamental U.S. concerns with democracy and human rights. In particular, the United States intended to use engagement to press the regime for the unconditional release of Aung San Suu Kyi and other political prisoners, for an end to conflict with ethnic-minority groups, and for genuine dialogue among the Burmese government, the democratic opposition, and the non-Burman nationalities to develop a shared vision of the country's future. The administration also intended to address U.S. non-proliferation concerns over Burma's growing relationship with North Korea.

With regard to economic sanctions, Campbell explained that existing sanctions would not be lifted in the absence of meaningful progress and that the United States would reserve the option of tightening the sanctions in response to events in Burma. He argued against those who advocate lifting sanctions for the benefit of the Burmese people, saying that the state of the Burmese economy was not a result of sanctions, but rather of gross mismanagement by decades of military leadership and that it would take fundamental economic reform to turn the economy around. As for the 2010 elections, he said, the administration expected that, judging by the constitutional referendum of 2008, they would not be free and fair, but the United States would continue to stress the basic requirements of a credible electoral process and ask that others do the same. The United States would also stress the need to begin genuine dialogue immediately before the elections. "We must be prepared to sustain our efforts beyond the planned 2010 elections," Campbell concluded. "Some day a new generation of leaders in Burma will come to power. If the country is more open to the outside world we can hope to influence that transition and encourage Burma's leader to take a more positive, constructive, and inclusive path."

In early November 2009, Assistant Secretary Campbell led an "exploratory mission" to Burma to meet with senior government officials, including Prime Minister General Thein Sein, and with political opposition, including Aung San Suu Kyi. Despite a second visit to Burma in May 2010, Campbell's meetings with government officials appear to have produced no visible progress on fundamental U.S. concerns, leading some prominent voices in the United States to question the viability of the engagement policy.

The new U.S. engagement policy, however, was not limited to U.S. relations with Burma, but applied also to relations with other concerned Asian countries, including ASEAN, Japan, and China. This aspect of the policy began to emerge even before the policy review was complete, during Secretary of State Clinton's visit to Thailand in July 2009 to attend the ASEAN Regional Forum. Her objective in this meeting, aside from the important consultations that took place on North Korea and Burma, appears to have been to reinvigorate U.S. support for, and relations with, ASEAN. For example, she committed the United States to the ASEAN Treaty of

Amity and Cooperation and pledged the United States to an active role in the Mekong River initiative. Many consider that her participation in this and subsequent ASEAN ministerial meetings has effectively brought an end to more than a decade of strain between the United States and ASEAN, owing to ASEAN's decision to bring Burma into the group and its subsequent failure to translate this membership into improvements in Burma's political and human-rights performance. President Obama's decision to participate in the first U.S.–ASEAN leaders' summit in November 2009 in Singapore consolidated the new U.S. relationship with ASEAN.

FUTURE DIRECTIONS IN U.S. BURMA POLICY

The administration's decision to modify its sanctions policy with "pragmatic engagement" with Burmese leadership and to work in coordination with Burma's Asian neighbours has not materially changed U.S. relations with Burma in the absence of positive responses from the SPDC itself. Unfortunately, the regime is not likely to respond positively to the most fundamental U.S. concerns about democracy and human rights before the 2010 elections.

The development of U.S. policy after the elections will be critically affected by how the elections are handled. If they are manipulated and unfair, as seems the case, U.S. relations with the new government will remain in the deep freeze. In fact, it is possible that, as Campbell foreshadowed in his testimony before Congress, financial sanctions could be tightened against specific individuals and institutions, similar to measures the U.S. Treasury is currently pursuing against Iran.

Furthermore, Washington has expressed support for those advocating the establishment of an international commission of Inquiry to determine whether there is evidence of international crimes on the part of Burma's military leaders. Even if this effort bears no fruit, the U.S. move has undoubtedly signalled to Naypyitaw that engagement is not high on the U.S. agenda for now.

On the other hand, U.S. engagement with Burmese civil society through humanitarian and community-development assistance and engagement with Burma's Asian neighbours, however, will continue to expand. Like other governments, the United States sees assistance to community development as an investment in the country's democratic base.

If the elections, despite being unfair, result in a government that is more inclusive and reform-minded than currently expected, the U.S. policy of pragmatic engagement could still leave the United States well positioned to work on a wider range of democracy-building programmes than is currently possible. The issues of human rights, the promotion of democracy, the fate of political prisoners, and the well-being of Burma's minority nationalities will remain serious concerns for U.S. policy. Should the new government move in positive directions on these issues, U.S. policy toward Burma could ease considerably. The decision by the NLD to forgo participation in the 2010 elections and to disband as a political party, however, has already conditioned a negative U.S. response to the elections, which is not likely to be reversed soon under any circumstances.

In fact, it is likely to be years before substantial changes in U.S. policy, aside from humanitarian assistance, will emerge. Such changes would include, for example, symbolically significant adjustments like official U.S. acceptance of the name "Myanmar" or upgrading diplomatic representation to ambassador level in both capitals. Substantial movement on political prisoners and human rights would be required before the U.S. Congress would consider easing U.S. economic, trade, and financial sanctions. At the same time, the U.S. government will probably continue to seek wider channels of communication with the new Burmese government, including the new military leadership after the elections.

Over the longer term — that is, beyond 2015 — another level of improvement in bilateral relations might come if Burma's leadership transition brings real change in the central government's interaction with its own people and the international community. Specifically, this would involve the conclusion of a bilateral assistance agreement with the Burmese government, as USAID normally does with its individual country programmes, paving the way for U.S. assistance to be administered in coordination with the Burmese government. At this stage, U.S. assistance might focus also on government programmes and capacity-building, as took place in South Africa after the 1994 elections. U.S. scholarship and visitor programmes could be expanded to include Burmese government officials. Positive developments in human rights and a clear intention to professionalize Burmese military forces could lead to an expansion of bilateral military-to-military relations and the restoration of military assistance, particularly military-training assistance with a human-rights component. Under these circumstances, the United States would also have a strong interest in expanding counter-narcotics cooperation and other programmes related to international criminal activity.

The continuation of U.S. efforts to promote advances in Burma's civil society and community development does not depend on the elections, as is already evident in the expansion of U.S. humanitarian assistance at the community level. This is a long-term policy aimed at strengthening the capacity of Burmese society to cope with decades of inadequate support from the government. It is also designed to build a stronger civil society as the foundation of sustainable democracy. If the transition brings simply a rerun of the current military leadership and no improvements in governance, U.S. assistance will continue to be limited to humanitarian efforts at the community level.

U.S. policy will also continue, despite the election process in Burma, to focus on how Asian ties can be employed more effectively to build economic and political foundations in Burma. Regardless of developments inside Burma over the coming few years, we are likely to see more-positive U.S. engagement with key ASEAN countries on Burma and an easing of U.S. restrictions on high-level contacts with Burma in the ASEAN context. This, in turn, will lead to more-serious dialogue with Japan and China, as key ASEAN partners. If the political transition in Burma produces a markedly different leadership group and greater receptivity to internal reform and external engagement, U.S. coordination with Asian partners might blossom rather rapidly into cooperative efforts to stimulate economic development in Burma and to provide governance capacity-building. Among other things, this could bring ADB, IMF, and World Bank technical assistance into play.

In the final analysis, while President Obama has some leeway to adjust the tenor and conduct of U.S. relations in response to developments in Burma, in the case of economic sanctions, the Congress will remain an immovable object unless Burma's political transition brings definitive results on human rights. Clearly this is a bridge that cannot be crossed in a single stride. One can only hope that the President's new policy of pragmatic engagement will eventually help to open channels of interaction and communication with Burma after the elections, which — along with a positive political transition in Burma — can serve ultimately to accelerate improvements in bilateral U.S.-Burmese relations and build confidence in the new Burmese government to embrace an inclusive political culture.

Notes

1. This discussion of the 2008 constitution is based on original research and analysis by the author. Readers may also wish to consult similar studies by Ghai (2009) and the International Crisis Group (2009).
2. David C. Williams, Executive Director, Center for Constitutional Democracy, Indiana University Maurer School of Law, in testimony before the U.S. Senate Committee on Foreign Relations Subcommittee on East Asia and Pacific Affairs on 30 September 2009, described in detail how the constitution ensures continuing military control over both military and national affairs.
3. For a detailed analysis of the implications of the 2010 election laws, see International Crisis Group (2010).
4. The "ceasefire" groups are former minority-nationality insurgent groups who concluded agreements with the SPDC, ending their insurgencies in return for special rights. In some cases, these rights included autonomy over territory, economic concessions, and the right to maintain armed militias.
5. "China Signs Agreement with Myanmar on Border Stability", Reuters, 3 June 2010.
6. For a detailed analysis of this phenomenon, see Callahan (2009).
7. For an excellent analysis of the current power structures in ethnic-minority areas, see Callahan (2007).
8. The Asia Society Task Force Report of March 2010 offers more detail on the possibilities for economic reform that could emerge during transition.
9. The judge actually sentenced Aung San Suu Kyi to three years' hard labour, but the Home Affairs minister dramatically announced that out of humanitarian concern Senior General Than Shwe had commuted the sentence to eighteen months of house arrest, with the option of early release for good behaviour.

References

Callahan, Mary. "Political Authority in Burma's Ethnic Minority States: Devolution, Occupation, and Coexistence". *Policy Studies* 31 (2007). Washington, D.C.: East-West Center.

———. "Myanmar's Perpetual Junta". *New Left Review* 60 (November–December, 2009).

Campbell, Kurt. "U.S. Policy Toward Burma". Testimony before the U.S. Senate Committee on Foreign Relations, Subcommittee on East Asia and Pacific Affairs, 30 September 2009.

Ghai, Yash. *The 2008 Myanmar Constitution: Analysis and Assessment*. UNDP Constitution Advisory Support Unit, 2009.

International Crisis Group. "Myanmar: Towards the Elections". *Asia Report* No. 174, Yangon/Brussels: 20 August 2009.

———. "The Myanmar Elections". *Asia Briefing* No. 105. Jakarta/Brussels: 2010.

The Asia Society. *Current Realities and Future Possibilities in Burma/Myanmar,* Task Force Report. Washington, D.C.: The Asia Society, 2010.

Williams, David C. Testimony before the U.S. Senate Committee on Foreign Relations, Subcommittee on East Asia and Pacific Affairs, 30 September 2009.

4

SOVEREIGNTY IN THE SHAN STATE
A Case Study of the United Wa State Army

Jane M. Ferguson

More than twenty years have now passed since the beginning of the organization of large-scale ceasefire agreements in Burma, with Khin Nyunt having taken the historical credit for spearheading this spate of accords. The United Wa State Army, or UWSA, is one such ceasefire group (in Burmese, a *nyein chan yay apwe*) and claims territories in the Northern and Eastern Shan State. Particularly in the past decade, the UWSA has repeatedly engaged in combat with the Shan State Army South, at the behest — and to the potential benefit — of the Burmese Tatmadaw. While ten years ago, the UWSA's tenth-anniversary celebrations were marked with fanfare, and attended and sanctioned by Khin Nyunt himself, the ceasefire group's twentieth-anniversary celebrations in April 2009 were markedly different in tone. Although the celebrations in the Wa capital of Panghsang were attended by roughly twenty thousand people and 2,400 UWSA troops, only a handful of lower-ranking SPDC military men were in attendance in 2009. Arguably, this diminished enthusiasm on the part of the SPDC foreshadows a lesser role ascribed to the ceasefire groups in the upcoming elections, and whether this will be a viable option for these organized groups in the context of the Shan State political economies remains to be seen.

These tense relations, with some observers waiting to see which side fires first[1] will certainly have a significant effect on the political future of the Shan State. Of particular interest for the context of this conference on governance in the region is the Wa organizations' overt refusal to accept and participate in the SPDC's recent ultimatum that they become a proxy force, or a Border Guard Force (BGF) ultimately supervised by the Tatmadaw (*The Irrawaddy*, 20 April 2010). All of the major ceasefire groups were urged to join the fold of the Burmese Tatmadaw, and out of the seventeen ceasefire groups given this ultimatum, the largest of these groups, including the UWSA as well as the Kachin Independence Organization (KIO), have rejected these proposals, claiming that they would only negotiate with a democratically elected government in the future (*The Irrawaddy*, 18 May 2010).

This chapter details the ways in which the UWSA, in its particular status as a ceasefire group, has operated. First, it gives an overview of the UWSA's beginnings as a ceasefire group, and its relations within a context of other political and military stakeholders in the Shan State in the 1990s. It then discusses how demographic changes and the increased material wealth of UWSA leadership have affected their political relations in the region. Finally, it describes how the current tense situation is potentially creating a political deadlock for the future of this area of the Shan State, and causing an obstacle for the SPDC's plans for securing more complete territorial sovereignty in the region. It calls into question the role of the Wa military and political apparatus as a bona fide sovereign power over the Wa special region in relation to state and national sovereignty and its implications for future prospects of governance, or even equitable political participation amongst citizens in the region. Given the number and variety of ceasefire groups in Burma at present, by focusing exclusively on the Wa organizations I am not suggesting that this group is a representative one, but the common economic, strategic and political implications of the SPDC–UWSA relationship have relevance for other geographically peripheral stakeholders in Burma. By offering a specific case study of arguably the most powerful of the ceasefire organizations, the discussion on governance in Burma/Myanmar is moved away from centralist approaches, which would likely focus on those with visible presence in the country's capital. These geographically peripheral powers, such as the UWSA (as well as Kokang, Karen, Kachin, Pa-O and Shan ceasefire organizations, to name but a few) have played a decisive role in Burma's political economy for decades, but have been overlooked by the popular media and mainstream debate on Burmese politics.

COMPETING FOR SOVEREIGNTY IN THE SHAN STATE

From independence onwards, scores of armed militias have operated in the Shan States. Indeed, the sheer number of groups during the height of the Cold War makes it difficult to summarize, but for purposes of clarity, these can be condensed into five major categories:

1. soldiers of the Burmese military, the Tatmadaw, ostensibly bankrolled by the Burmese state[2]
2. the Kuomintang, or the soldiers of the insurrection against the Maoist regime in China, supported by the Taiwanese government and the CIA, as well as the profits from their trade networks[3]
3. the soldiers of the Communist Party of Burma (CPB)[4]
4. state separatists or ethnic militias seeking autonomy from the Burmese state, such as many of the Shan armies, which were supported by taxes, trafficking, or alliances with other groups[5]
5. the *Ka Kwe Yay*, or home-guard militias, which were organized privately but allowed concessions (and sometimes even given arms) by the Burmese government provided that they acted as a counter-insurgent force against the other groups considered hostile to the Burmese government.

The last of these proves an interesting case study regarding state power in the region, and the model has relevance for studying the ceasefire groups following 1989, as ruling by proxy is by no means new to the region nor to the Burmese government since independence. In acknowledging their inability to control these vast insurgent territories, particularly those of the Kuomintang, during the 1950s, the Burmese military instituted the *Ka Kwe Yay*, the home-guard militias. These groups served as counter-insurgents for the Burmese government, and in exchange for their services, were allowed trafficking concessions, which included one of the most lucrative commodities: opium/heroin. Because these groups were not bankrolled by the Burmese state (though sometimes supplied with arms), this strategy proved very cost-effective from the government accountant's point of view. The profits reaped by the militias, however, started to tell another story. On average, a Ka Kway Yay militia would make two annual trips to trade depots. The percentage of commercial value that the Ka Kway Yay could exact ranged from 10 to 50 per cent (Chao Tzang 1987, p. 128).

A crucial new distinction between the twentieth-century Home Guard militias and the proxy forces of vassal states in the pre-colonial era was that the drug-trafficking networks of the proxy forces put them into contact with the lucrative trade of the international mafias, the Chinese triads, and massive profits. In other words, the proxy forces had the ability to accumulate massive amounts of capital. In the Shan plateau, the power dynamics which linked these trade economies to political actors partially represents a survival of the pre-colonial system of economic and political organization, but it is one that is intensified by the nationalization of the economy by the Burmese Socialist Programme Party, and further bolstered by the transnational economic networks and allegiances of Cold War processes. Because these mercenary soldiers were able to tap into the transnational capitalistic shadow economies, their power posed a significantly greater threat than could had been anticipated previously. At the time, few could have predicted the extent to which Cold War agendas would interlock with transnational crime networks and collude to make heroin #4 one of the most lucrative trades on the planet.

THE UNITED WA STATE ARMY (1989–2000)

The United Wa State Army was born out of the coinciding collapse of the Burmese Communist Party and the spate of ceasefire agreements instigated by the changing Yangon government in 1989. In some ways, we could consider these ceasefire accords to have significant parallels with the former strategy of the Burmese government in its establishment of the Home Guard militia. In this particular context in the late 1980s, these agreements were negotiated between the Kokang and Wa insurgent leadership and the then-Military Intelligence Chief, Khin Nyunt. With the 1989 ceasefire agreement, the Burmese central government had given the Wa not only the right to maintain their territory and their army, but also promises of development assistance (Callahan 2007, p. 28). The Wa leadership's sovereignty covered its area in Panghsang in the Northern Shan State, the former Communist stronghold on the border with China, and the rest of the areas in Wa Special Region 2. While groups self-identifying as Wa have long inhabited areas in the Northeast Shan State and across the border into China, their rank-and-file membership in the Communist insurgency allowed a relatively seamless re-configuration as troops of the UWSA. Observers have noted that the UWSA leadership is almost-exclusively ethnic Han, while the soldiers are Wa, and the leadership of some of the Wa battalions in the Southern Shan State has even been identified as Shan or Shan-Chinese.[6]

At the time of the initial ceasefire agreement between the Kokang, Wa and the SPDC, it was the Mong Tai Army (MTA), the umbrella organization representing the merger of the armies of Kon Jerng and Khun Sa, which was the most powerful force in the Shan State. The MTA marketed itself as the army of the Shan (Hkun Loi Laeng 1991, p. 166) and commanded approximately 15,000 troops over vast insurgent territories from the Salween River east to the Thai border. The Salween river gorge had for many years formed an impassible boundary for the soldiers of the Tatmadaw. As a ceasefire group in collusion with the SPDC, the UWSA made use of former Communist Party of Burma artillery to fight the Mong Tai Army. For example, in their ongoing battle over Loi Larng, a strategic access point to the Thai border, an estimated 1,000 lives were lost (Smith 1999, p. 440). The presence of the Wa proxy armies was undoubtedly instrumental in pressuring Khun Sa to surrender; and when he did in 1996, the UWSA (as well as the SPDC) successfully encroached on much of the territory formerly controlled by the MTA. These territorial gains by the UWSA were seen as the spoils of victory for their role in expediting the surrender of Khun Sa (Callahan 2007, p. 29).

In 2001, David Steinberg predicted that by the time a new constitution would be formed, the autonomous area of the Wa would have expanded greatly, at the expense of those of the Shan (Steinberg 2001, p. 59). It was during the early part of that decade that the UWSA, at the behest of the SPDC, moved approximately 126,000 Wa people from the Chinese-border area down to the Thai-border area, to settle in the areas of Mongton, Mong Hsat and Tachileik (SHAN 2009), former (and current) strategic areas of the Shan insurgency. Prior to the recent tensions there was the possibility that the presence of such large numbers of Wa in these areas would present a potential electoral challenge for the SPDC: should the political branch of the USWA, the UWSP, choose to run candidates, and the Wa electorate vote along ethnic lines, there would be the possibility that a Wa political presence would dominate.[7] But again, this political strength in numbers is predicated on an investment in electoral politics which has yet to manifest itself in Burma. In this context, it is crucial to consider the military strength of the Wa, and how this might affect their position in this changing political climate.

THE UNITED WA STATE ARMY IN THE TWENTY-FIRST CENTURY

The UWSA, boasting an army of over 20,000 troops, is the largest and most powerful of the armed ethnic groups in Burma. Part of its strength has to do with the profits reaped through its methamphetamine[8] production and trafficking. Among the more sensational products available on the black market are bootlegged Hollywood DVDs lining the stalls of the Thai-Shan State border town marketplaces of Mae Sai–Tachileik. Many of these goods are imported via the trade networks of the UWSA. With their control of these particularly lucrative trades, the UWSA is able to sustain itself quite well without assistance from the SPDC, but its leadership crucially depends on amicable relations with China, particularly for the maintenance of its supply of firearms. Furthermore, one analyst, Kheun Sai Jaiyen of the Shan Herald Agency for News, has predicted that China would aid the UWSA if fighting were to erupt between the UWSA and the SPDC, though another analyst, Bertil Lintner, believes this is "highly unlikely" (Wade 2010). In any case, with the shared border with China's Yunnan Province, the Chinese authorities will almost inevitably be an important consideration for the future of UWSA–SPDC relations.

In spite of the vast wealth accumulated by the UWSA leadership as a result of its commercial endeavours, progress toward the development goals of the Wa areas has failed to meet expectations. The development of roads and other infrastructure was one of the hopes of the initial agreements signed twenty years ago. One UWSA official has admitted that though the Wa armed forces have been considerably strengthened over the past two decades, the infrastructural development of the Wa autonomous region has lagged far behind (Solomon 2009).

This is not the only concern regarding the future strength of the Wa military apparatus. Although the UWSA has been able to secure relative economic and military superiority in the region because of its status as a ceasefire group, there have been noted tactical disadvantages arising from a comparatively mismanaged, and ideologically haphazard military apparatus. For example, throughout a month-long attack against the Shan State Army South in 2005, the Wa lost more than 700 troops, compared with fewer than 50 SSA losses (Wechsler 2009). Furthermore, a rift amongst Wa leadership has further hampered a united political front. The fracture occurred between those who support Bao Youxiang and those who support Wei Xuegang; these respective factions have their roots in the times of their support of the red-flag CPB (Bao) and the white-flag Kuomintang (Wei). Compounding the rift between the factions is the SPDC's non-identical ultimatums issued to both Bao and Wei.

With former Prime Minister and head of Military Intelligence Khin Nyunt out of the picture since 2004, to many observers it would seem that the SPDC's stance toward ceasefire groups has gone from amicable to tolerant. But subsequent developments with the UWSA suggest these relations have become antagonistic, even though at the end of last year the UWSP had indicated its support for the 2010 elections. The year of 2009 was especially tense. The overturning of a Tatmadaw truck carrying a number of heavy weapons en route to the Wa capital of Panghsang in January 2009 marks the beginning of these souring relations (Hseng Khio Fa 2009). Although the UWSA is not dependent economically on the SPDC, there is concern that should fighting break out between the UWSA and the Tatmadaw, the aggressor would have to deal with the consequences of being blamed by Chinese authorities (Sai Wansai 2009). Losing trade with Chinese markets and investors would effectively cripple either side. Perhaps some SPDC officials sense this as well, and this may explain the lack of enthusiasm for the UWSA at its twentieth-anniversary celebrations. It was at these celebrations that the commander of the UWSA, Bao Youxiang, voiced his hope for a prosperous and united Wa State, and a peaceful settlement of the disagreement with the SPDC (Solomon 2009).

This leaves analysts to speculate as to why the SPDC would show less enthusiasm for the cooperation of the ceasefire groups. A possible answer may lie in the fact that these negotiations were largely spearheaded by Khin Nyunt. Alternatively, it may be the case that the SPDC is pressuring the UWSA to run candidates for the 2010 elections in order to incorporate the former autonomous regions into the fold of the central government; the recent ultimatum surely made the relations worse. The former push for candidature could be viewed as an SPDC strategy to neutralize the military wings of the various groups, thus replacing the UWSA with the UWSP (United Wa State Party) and the Kachin Independence Army with the Kachin Independence Organization. It could be argued, though, that the UWSP and the KIO are more accurately described as political "front" organizations for a more militant movement with goals for more complete autonomy and, ultimately, independence. As such, spokespeople from the Wa continue to iterate that they strive only for autonomy and self-governance in their areas (Solomon 2009).

Following the UWSA's twentieth-anniversary celebrations in April 2009, the SPDC added potential injury to insult: in overtures made to the ceasefire groups in May, the SPDC command detailed a plan by which the groups would be allowed to manage their daily affairs. However, the broader command structure would share command with, and ultimately be submissive to, the regional commanders of the Tatmadaw (*The Irrawaddy* 2009). This new organizational scheme would involve an estimated 326 military battalions, commanded by their respective ceasefire group leadership, but supervised by, and ultimately subordinate to, the officers of the Burmese Tatmadaw. As one ceasefire commander has said, "Before this they (the SPDC) only wanted us to surrender our arms. Now they want us to surrender ourselves and our men also" (Sai Wansai 2009). This agreement does, however, contain the provision that the UWSA would have the right to fix the maximum number of Tatmadaw soldiers and the kinds of weapons they would carry into Wa domains. The UWSA was given a deadline of 31 May to comply with this ultimatum, but the Wa leadership voted overwhelmingly to reject the junta's proposal.

The most pressing development in 2009 was the SPDC push to make the UWSA a proxy security force, or a Border Guard Force (BGF), for the Tatmadaw in the Wa areas. Wa commanders must increasingly report to SPDC authorities when they travel, or when they procure troops or supplies. Conversely, within some of the Wa ceasefire territories, people who are "Burman" (according to the ethnicity shown on their government ID cards) have purportedly not been allowed to enter, although this has only been an official proclamation on the part of the Wa leadership (Hseng Khio Fah 2009).

CONCLUSION

Ceasefire agreements have served a limited purpose for the tactical needs of the SPDC, and have allowed the upper echelons of these groups to become extremely wealthy. As has been the tendency in this ongoing internal conflict, those who pay the price have been the local villagers and the rank-and-file subordinates. Tremendous wealth has been concentrated in the hands of Wa elites such as Bao Youxiang and Wei Xuegang, as evidenced by Wei's recently built $60 million mansion near Panghsang. Whether Wei will continue to act as a tactical commander, or will strike a political deal with the SPDC in a similar fashion to that struck by Khun Sa more than ten years ago, remains to be seen. Undoubtedly, the relationship between the political and military leadership of these Wa parties and those of the SPDC will be a crucial question in the next few years.

Notes

1. See, for example, *Hkawn Kaw* (2009).
2. There are numerous useful sources detailing the history of the Tatmadaw, including Callahan (2003); Aung Myoe (2009); and Selth (1996).
3. For more on the role of the Kuomintang in Burma, see Taylor (1973); Kaufman (2001); and Chang (1999).
4. For a history of the Burmese Communist Party, see Lintner (1990).
5. See Smith (1999); Lintner (1994); and Pedersen (2008).
6. Lacking direct experience amongst members of the UWSA myself, I can only comment on the ways in which the UWSA functions as a political and military apparatus, rather than the ways in which ethno-nationalism plays out at the local level amongst Wa recruits. Certainly the ethnic composition is worthy of further investigation; Shan informants have told me of local Shan leadership of UWSA detachments.
7. It is worth noting that these three areas voted for the National League for Democracy and the Shan Nationalities League for Democracy in the 1990 elections.
8. Referred to in Shan as *Ya Haeng* ("strength medicine") and in Thai as *Ya Ba* ("crazy medicine").

References

Aung Myoe, Maung. *Building the Tatmadaw: Myanmar armed forces since 1948*. Singapore: Institute of Southeast Asian Studies, 2009.

Callahan, Mary P. *Making Enemies: War and State Building in Burma*. Ithaca: Cornell University Press, 2003.

———. *Political Authority in Burma's Ethnic Minority States: Devolution, Occupation, and Coexistence*. Singapore: Institute of Southeast Asian Studies, 2007.

Chang, Wen-Chin. "Beyond the Military: The complex migration and resettlement of the KMT Yunnanese Chinese in Northern Thailand". Ph.D Dissertation, Katholieke Universiteit te Leuven, 1999.

Chao Tzang Yawnghwe. *The Shan of Burma: Memoirs of a Shan Exile*. Singapore: Institute of Southeast Asian Studies, 1987.

Hseng Khio Fah. "Wa commander's trucks destroyed, men injured in fire in Panghsang" *Shan Herald Agency for News* 11, no. 4 (20 April 2009).

Kawn Hkaw 26, no. 256 (2009): 10. "*Suek Wa Main Kaeng Kan Saeng Kawng Te Lan Wan Laü* ["The Wa and Burmese armies are tense. On which day will firing start?"].

Hkun Loi Laeng. "Apwe Loi Maw Am Mi Yao". *Söng Laew* 8 (1991): 163–67.

Hseng Khio Fah. "Junta steps up formation of militia battalions" Shan Herald Agency for News. 26 November 2009.

Kaufman, Victor. "Trouble in the Golden Triangle: The United States, Taiwan and the 93rd Nationalist Division" *The China Quarterly*, no. 166 (2001), pp. 440–456.

Kramer, Tom. *The United Wa State Party: Narco-Army or Ethnic Nationalist Party?* Policy Studies Series, Washington, D.C.: East-West Center/Institute of Southeast Asian Studies, 2007.

Lintner, Bertil. *The rise and fall of the Communist Party of Burma (CPB)*. Ithaca: Cornell Southeast Asia Program, 1990.

———. *Burma in revolt: Opium and insurgency since 1948*. Boulder: Westview Press, 1994.

Pedersen, Morten. "Burma's Ethnic Minorites". *Critical Asian Studies* 40, no. 1 (2008): 45–66.

Sai Wansai. "Aung San Suu Kyi, ceasefire armies and the Junta". *Shan Herald Agency for News*, 16 May 2009.

Selth, Andrew. *Transforming the Tatmadaw: The Burmese armed forces since 1988*. Canberra: Strategic and Defence Studies Centre, Australian National University, 1996.

Shan Herald Agency for News. "Ceasefire group defies junta over land grab", 22 January 2008.

———. "Wa votes count in 2010", 22 July 2009.

Smith, Martin. *Burma: Insurgency and the Politics of Ethnicity*. Bangkok: White Lotus, 1999.

Solomon. "UWSA goals remain elusive after 20 years". *Mizzima News*, 20 April 2009.

Steinberg, David I. *Burma: The State of Myanmar*. Washington: Georgetown University Press, 2001.

Taylor, Robert. *Foreign and domestic consequences of the KMT intervention in Burma*. Ithaca: Cornell University Press, 1973.

The Irrawaddy. "Generals call the ceasefire groups' hands". 8 May 2009.

Wade, Francis. "China's fears over Wa fighting grow". *Democratic Voice of Burma*, 4 May 2010.

Wai Moe. "Wa Still Say 'No' to Border Guard Force". *The Irrawaddy*, 20 April 2010.

Wechsler, Maxmillian. "The News from Shan State". *Bangkok Post*, 24 May 2009.

Weng, Lawi. "Militias to Become Border Guard Forces". *The Irrawaddy*, 18 May 2010.

5

GOVERNANCE AND LEGITIMACY IN KAREN STATE

Ashley South

INTRODUCTION[1]

Karen-populated areas of Burma/Myanmar have been affected by armed conflict since 1949, the year after independence. For much of this period, the Karen National Union (KNU) operated as a *de facto* government, controlling large swathes of territory across Karen State, and adjacent areas of Mon State, and Pegu and Tenasserim Divisions. Although not recognized internationally, the KNU administration aspired to reproduce in areas under its control the (Weberian) "modern/rational-bureaucratic" state, fielding departments for health, education, and civil administration, and making claims to a legitimate monopolization of violence, and rights to extract taxes from the population.[2]

By the 1990s the KNU had lost control of most of its once-extensive "liberated zones" — although the organization still exerted varying degrees of influence over areas contested with government forces and proxy militias. This process was accompanied by a dramatic fall in revenues which the organization derived from taxing the black-market cross-border trade, and from logging deals. The decline of the KNU was exacerbated by the defection in late 1994 of several hundred battle-hardened soldiers, who established the government-allied Democratic Karen Buddhist Army (DKBA), in protest against the Christian domination of the KNU, and the failure of its long-term leader, the charismatic General Bo Mya (who died in 2006), to discipline adequately field commanders operating under his authority.[3]

Ten years later, the DKBA had displaced the KNU's armed wing — the Karen National Liberation Army (KNLA) — as the militarily and economically most powerful Karen non-state actor in Burma. Other ex-KNU/KNLA armed factions included the Karen Peace Force (KPF, established 1997) in southern Karen State, the "P'doh Aung San Group" (1998) and KNU-KNLA Peace Council (PC, 2007) in central Karen State, and two small ceasefire groups in northern Karen State (which split from the KNU in 1997), as well as various local militias. Whereas in previous years the KNU had been strong enough to demand at least symbolic loyalty from locally based field commanders — many of whom operated under the umbrella of the Karen national movement — the collapse of the organization's fortunes in the 1990s led to the splintering of the old insurgent paradigm, and the reorientation of specialists in violence towards the military government and its networks of control.

In late April 2009 the military government proposed that those armed groups with which it had negotiated ceasefires (see below) transform themselves into Border Guard Forces (BGF), under the direct control of the Burmese Army (*Tatmadaw*). In exchange for its compliance, the Burma Army encouraged the DKBA (specifically 999 Special Battalion, led by Maung Chit Thu) to increase its troop strength from 6,000 to 9,000 men, and to displace the KNLA from the remaining areas of insurgent control and influence in central Karen state. Thus in June 2009 the DKBA — with significant military and logistical support from its sponsor, the Burmese Army — overran a series of strategically important KNLA bases situated on the west (Burmese) bank of the Moei River (which constitutes the Thailand–Burma border). As a result, some 3,500 Karen civilians fled to Thailand, where they joined approximately 150,000 ethnic Karen (and also Karenni and other nationality groups) living as refugees in the kingdom.[4] Villagers fled to Thailand, not primarily as a direct result of armed conflict but mostly to avoid landmines (used widely by all sides in the conflict) and forcible conscription of young men and boys into the DKBA forces, either as porters or poorly trained soldiers (and/or the levying of huge fines in lieu of such service).

This latest round of fighting was initially perceived as another offensive in the interminable civil war. However, the loss of the remaining KNLA bases in Seventh Brigade (the "mother brigade", operating in central Karen State) represented a particularly significant symbolic reversal for the beleaguered KNU, denying Burma's longest-established insurgent organization access to the central Karen heartland and the population (and natural resources) therein. Although these military setbacks did not represent the very end of the KNU insurgency, they signalled that insurgency along the Thailand–Burma border was entering its final phase.

The decline of the KNU, and the ascendancy of the other Karen armed groups (and, above all, of the government forces) make it timely to assess the state of governance and legitimacy in Karen-populated areas of the south-eastern borderlands.[5] This chapter will focus on areas controlled or influenced by armed non-state actors. Particularly with the collapse of the KNU since the 1990s, the majority of people in Karen State and adjacent areas live under the direct control and administration of the military government, or in areas where control is contested, and/or comes under the authority of more than one armed group (for example, Burmese Army and DKBA, and/or KPF). For civilians in such "mixed administration" areas, the situation is particularly difficult, as they generally have to pay taxes (and other forms of tribute) to "multiple masters".

DEMOGRAPHICS AND ADMINISTRATION

An estimated (maximum of) 20 per cent of the Karen population are Christian (Gravers 2007, p. 228). There are some twelve Karen language dialects, of which the majority speak S'ghaw (particularly in hill areas, and among the Christian community) and Pwo (especially in the lowlands, and among the Buddhist community). The size of the Karen population is unknown, no reliable census having been undertaken since the colonial period. As Martin Smith (2003, pp. 10–11) notes: "Karen population statistics are disputed; rebel leaders' estimates are over 7 million Karens in modern-day Burma, but government figures are less than half that number." Only a minority of the Karen population live within the borders of Karen State (established in 1952). The majority live in Tenasserim (KNU Mergui-Tavoy District), eastern Pegu Division, Mon State, and Yangon and Irrawaddy Divisions.

The government divides Kayin (Karen) State into seven townships: Pa'an, Kawkareik, Kya-In Seik-Gyi, Myawaddy, Papun, Thandaung, and Hlaingbwe. The KNU meanwhile has organized the Karen free state of Kaw Thoo Lei into seven districts, each of which corresponds to a KNLA brigade area: First Brigade (Thaton District), Second Brigade (Toungoo District), Third Brigade (Nyaunglebin District), Fourth Brigade (Mergui-Tavoy District, in Tenasserim Division), Fifth Brigade (Papun District), Sixth Brigade (Duplaya District) and Seventh Brigade (Pa'an District). Each KNU district is divided into townships (twenty-eight in total), and thence into village tracts — groups of villages which are administered as a unit by the KNU (that is, in areas where the KNU still exercises some skeleton administration — which often overlaps with elements of central government administration: for example, a Karen village may have both a "KNU headman" and a "government headman"). This civilian structure is paralleled by an often more-extensive KNLA military administration. In addition, the KNLA deploys a number of Special Battalions, based in economically important border areas, which tend to be personally loyal to local commanders.

THE DEMOCRATIC KAREN BUDDHIST ARMY

The DKBA, which emerged in 1994, lacks a coherent command-and-control structure, and often acts as a proxy militia for the *Tatmadaw*, deflecting some (domestic and international) criticism for the state's harsh policies. Like the Burmese Army, the DKBA uses forced displacement as a means of controlling populations and resources, and to undermine the KNU, its main rival for leadership of the Karen community in Burma. Like some of their counterparts in the KNLA, many DKBA commanders and soldiers are "conflict entrepreneurs", for whom military and political status is a means to personal power and enrichment. However, DKBA leaders often also employ strong ethno-nationalist rhetoric, and in some areas have implemented local infrastructure-development projects. Furthermore, research indicates that conditions for Internally Displaced Persons (IDPs) in DKBA-controlled ceasefire areas are better than those in zones of ongoing armed conflict or government-controlled relocation sites (see South 2007). Despite its name, there are a number of Christians within the ranks of the

DKBA, including some commanders, many of whom enjoy considerable autonomy, answering to local Burmese Army commanders, in addition to the leadership at Myaing Gyi Ngu (DKBA Headquarters).

In August 2009 senior DKBA commanders agreed to transform their militia into a Border Guard Force (BGF). However, this decision remains controversial. In October 2009 the DKBA's founder and chief patron, the monk U Thuzana, met with KNU/KNLA leaders to discuss the possibility of an armistice between the two groups. Although these talks did not progress, they demonstrate that some in the DKBA leadership were unwilling to transform the organization into a militia directly controlled by the *Tatmadaw*. At the time of writing, it seems that (several deadlines having passed) the military government is willing to allow those ceasefire groups which have not already transformed into BGF formations to retain their current status — at least until after the elections scheduled for later in 2010 (see below). If pressure is exerted on the DKBA to transform itself, it seems likely that some commanders will resist (perhaps disbanding their units, and in some cases re-allying with the KNU), while others (for example, 999 Special Battalion) will grudgingly accept the proposal. The latter will be motivated by a desire not to expose Karen villagers to further conflict, combined with the powerful incentive of protecting extensive economic interests.

In the meantime, it remains unclear how much support the DKBA enjoys within the wider Karen population — many of whom are disappointed by the organization's inability to promote a Karen nationalist agenda. For example, although there are schools in DKBA-controlled areas, these — with a few exceptions — do not teach Karen language but, rather, follow the government (Burmese-language) curriculum.

DKBA commanders acknowledge that some within the organization are sometimes involved in human-rights violations, but argue that it is necessary for a people to accept certain privations and suffering in order to build a nation. Such arguments involve appeals to ends, over means. One DKBA commander relates such concerns to social, economic and cultural development. According to this argument, the DKBA has brought political-military security to the areas under its control — or at least to the 999 Special Battalion headquarters area at Shwe Ko Ko, just north of Myawaddy (opposite Mae Sot). He argues that the "Shwe Ko Ko" model can be reproduced in other areas, *once* the KNU has been eliminated.[6] Therefore, in order to safeguard the longer-term interests of the Karen population, he has argued that it is sometimes necessary to engage in some unpleasant short-term practices. This argument ignores the particular economic opportunities available at Shwe Ko Ko — a strategic and economically important border pass — which are unlikely to be reproduced in other Karen-populated areas. It also fails to address criticisms that the DKBA model of development is similar to that of the military government: a top-down understanding of "development as infrastructure", with little genuine participation by local populations.

PETTY MANDALAS AND PARA-STATES

The "traditional" pattern of governance (and state-formation) in the south-eastern borderlands of Burma has been similar to that in other peripheral areas of Southeast Asia. Emergent leaders (some imbued with Weberian "charismatic authority") constructed fiefdoms, mobilizing populations through a combination of violence and other forms of coercion, by controlling access to political-economic goods (often in the form of licit or illicit natural resources, or trading opportunities), and via claims to legitimate authority, based on locally relevant criteria (including ethno-linguistic and religious identities).

When such local chiefs were able to consolidate power, their emergent *mandalas* (zones of personalized power, the authority of which declines towards the geographic and symbolic periphery) expanded in scope and cultural-symbolic significance, attracting increasing numbers of followers (and potential levies). The degree of (often loose) control exercised by such princelings tended to be dispersed, with distance from the symbolic centre of power (Anderson 1991,[7] drawing on Wolters). Various principalities often enjoyed overlapping claims of sovereignty in a particular geographic area, or over certain populations and/or types of resources. While their chieftains were often in conflict, loose alliances often also emerged between different mandalas (which traditionally would be cemented by marriage).

The key to the fulfilment of patron–client obligations was power, and the various strata of society were loosely integrated in a series of fluctuating patrimonial relations. Thus, the princeling-warlord stood in a patron–client relationship to his followers (or subjects). Especially if he was the leader of a peasant rebellion, the strongman may have claimed legitimacy as a charismatic *min laung* pretender to Buddhist kinghood (South 2005, ch.4; and Gravers 1999). Petty chieftains sought to expand their authority and prestige through accepting vassal status vis-à-vis a greater power, either in the form of the chief of a larger mandala, or through paying tribute to (and thus seeking the endorsement of) the ruler of a more firmly established kingdom. This pattern of governance characterized mainland Southeast Asia in the pre-colonial period.[8] In the case of Burma, Mikael Gravers (1999) has described how such patterns persisted in the Southeast (particularly Karen areas) into the colonial era, under the British system of "indirect rule".

With the outbreak of widespread insurgency following independence in 1948, such localized, "neo-patrimonial" forms of governance re-emerged, as a myriad of insurgent organizations — motivated by a combination of socio-economic and political grievances (articulated through appeals to communism or ethnic nationalist agendas), and political-economic interests (economic agenda for conflict) — vied for control over vast areas of the country and, in particular, the remote and underdeveloped, often mountainous and forested, border areas (Smith 1999; South 2008). Just as during the pre-colonial period, local strongmen sought to mobilize populations through a combination of charisma, violence, economic incentive and appeals to various forms of legitimacy. In particular, insurgent commanders tended to fuse their personal and "professional" roles and finances, leading to the re-emergence of neo-patrimonial forms of governance.

The "unbounded"[9] characteristics of the insurgent para-state which emerged in the 1950s, and its extensions among refugees and exile communities, were first described by Ananda Rajah (1996; 2002). He analyzed the manner in which, unlike the modern nation-state with its clear territorial boundaries, the insurgent para-state has a "frontier" area or zone (characteristic of the mandala), rather than a border, which may overlap with the frontier zones of other para-states, or with more firmly established governance structures of the internationally recognized state.

During the 1950s, government forces regained control over most of the (predominantly Burman-populated) lowlands, and by the late 1970s had driven the diverse insurgent armies up into the hills bordering China and Thailand. Over the following two decades, the Burmese Army succeeded in neutralizing most of its remaining battlefield enemies, particularly through negotiation of a series of ceasefires with most of the armed ethnic groups — including four ethnic nationality-based militias, which emerged following the collapse of the Communist Party Burma (CPB) in 1989 (South 2008, Ch. 5).

Under the ceasefire agreements, the insurgents' "liberated zones" were transformed into government-recognized "Special Regions". In many cases, the ceasefire areas continued to be ruled as personal fiefdoms, with ill-defined borders which overlapped with those of the state and other non-state actors.[10] These ceasefire zones included those under the control of several previously KNU-allied local commanders. As the KNU and other insurgent organizations lost ground, so too they lost their ability to enforce a minimum degree of at least symbolic compliance upon neo-patrimonial strongmen operating on the peripheries of their shrinking fields of influence. The authority of the old insurgent mandalas had at one time permeated most border networks; by the1990s, however, the Burmese Army and government constituted the dominant centre of power in these contested areas.

Following the fall of Khin Nyunt in October 2004, the government moved to incorporate some of these networks of compliance into more-formal relationships, under a new constitutional arrangement. A number of ceasefire groups supported the governance structures emerging through the National Convention process — either because they had no choice, because they considered acquiescence politically expedient, or because they perceived advantages in doing so for their communities (and/or their leaders' vested interests). A further example of the reorientation of Karen armed groups is provided by the defection of elements of the KNLA's Seventh Brigade in January 2007, when the elderly commander, Brigadier-General Htein Maung, split from the KNU to make a separate peace with the government. Following the death of his old KNU ally and patron, General Bo Mya, Htein Maung and his advisers negotiated a separate truce, in the name of the KNU-KNLA Peace Council (PC). Although the PC's relationship with the government remained fraught, with the organization refusing to become a BGF, it continued to maintain control over a dozen or so villages in central Karen State, where civilians received some respite from the ongoing armed conflict.

However, this scenario could hardly be described as "peace". Along most of the Thailand border, the *Tatmadaw* still operated as a marauding army, terrorizing the local population. In areas of "mixed administration", overlapping centres of power exerted authority (and extracted resources) from the civilian population. Even in areas of greater stability, day-to-day life for most people was a struggle for survival, in the face of deteriorating local economies, and systematic injustices and structural violence, perpetrated by a range of predatory power-holders. In addition to the militarized forms of governance outlined above, at the local (micro-) level, mandalas existed also in the form of zones of influence (and, indeed, of safety), exercised by non-military patrons and, in particular, charismatic religious leaders.

CIVIL MANDALAS

For centuries, monasteries in Burma have functioned as havens of peace and refuge (Gravers 2007), and Karen monks have long provided assistance to vulnerable members of the laity. In recent years in Karen State, this has especially been the case at the DKBA's Myaing Gyi Ngu headquarters, and most famously at the Thamanya monastery near Pa'an. The late *sayadaw* of this large monastic complex (an ethnic PaO) oversaw a programme feeding more than 10,000 people a day, supported mainly by the donations of pilgrims. These displaced villagers were protected from forced portering and other abuses on the part of the Burmese Army and DKBA. Although the venerable 93-year-old monk passed away in December 2003, his successors continued his work — albeit on a somewhat reduced scale. The Thamanya monastery is a prime example of localized relative autonomy, dependent upon the charismatic power of an ascendant civilian patron.

One of the most prominent of a younger generation of Karen monks is the abbot of a monastery just north of Pa'an. A highly perceptive and charismatic individual, this *sayadaw* has been able to mobilize the community around agricultural and other local development projects; he also played a leading role in inter-faith dialogue with Karen Christian leaders. His influence extended throughout central Karen State, where he was regarded as a "democracy monk", and something of a competitor to U Thuzana, patron of the DKBA. Again, this religious leader's personal patronage and authority are central to the creation of a zone of relative local autonomy.

In addition to "indigenous" actors (the KNU and pretenders, civil society leaders, the military government etc.), external and transnational organizations and networks may demonstrate mandala-like qualities. The shifting mosaic of donors and international NGOs which constitute the "humanitarian industry"[11] on the Thailand–Burma border, and the activist and lobbying networks beyond, may be considered as a collection of (often collaborating, but sometimes competing) centres of power, the authority of which expands and/or declines, according to various criteria. Like other patrons, the influence of "humanitarian princes" is diminished, as their clients (for example, the KNU and affiliates), decline in power.

Among Burma's many and diverse armed ethnic groups, the KNU has received by far the most support from international sympathisers. Unlike most other insurgent groups in Burma, the KNU has not agreed to a ceasefire with the military government. It may be that, during the 1990s, foreign support — particularly for the refugee camps in Thailand — insulated the organization from the reality of its declining authority in southeast Burma, allowing its leaders to remain at war, during a period when most of their counterparts (for example, in the Kachin armed nationalist movement) agreed to ceasefires with the Burma Army.

THE QUEST FOR LEGITIMACY

The KNU articulates its programme through appeals to supposedly universal values, such as ethnic self-determination, human rights, and international law. During the 1960s and '70s it adopted a left-wing "national democratic" ideology (see Smith 1999; KNU 1992). By the 1970s, the KNU had abandoned ideas of an independent *Kaw Thoo Lei*, in favour of a federalist platform, epitomized by the organization's status as a founding member of the pan-ethnic insurgent National Democratic Front (established 1976). By the 1980s, the KNU was articulating a position that "the Karen revolution is a fight for self-determination and true democracy" (KNU 1986, pp. 3–4). Today, the KNU continues to appeal to values, such as "private ownership ... democratic rights — politically, economically, socially and culturally. Freedom and equality of all religions is guaranteed." Furthermore, it says, "we strongly believe in the Charter of the United Nations, its Declaration on Human Rights, the principle of Determination and the Democratic Rights of Peoples" (KNU 1992, pp. 13–14).

According to Gravers (2007, p. 250), the KNU struggle involves the construction of a "pan-Karen global and cosmopolitan identity". In this, the organization has been supported by a network of Thailand-and-overseas-based (transnational) activists and lobbyists, with linkages to the Burmese opposition-in-exile (which emerged following the suppression of the 1988 "democracy uprising" and the SLORC junta's refusal to recognize the results of the 1990 elections).[12]

Between the 1960s and late 1980s, the KNU had derived support (and thus some legitimacy among Western policymakers) through its role as a "buffer" between communist insurgents in Thailand and Burma. The organization consolidated a strong anti-communist identity, which made it a useful minor ally of the United States during the Cold War (Smith 1999). However, with the collapse of communism in Southeast Asia, the KNU's geo-strategic importance — and value as a client — declined. In addition to Thai (and, by proxy, American) business — and above all security — interests, foreign influences on the KNU came to include Western aid agencies and donors, many of which have been mobilized through transnational networks. Material support has generally been provided in the form of refugee and IDP relief, which since the 1980s has become a major "humanitarian industry" operating along the Thailand border. Such activities have helped to secure the KNU's control and influence over a substantial civilian support base, with KNU families (and soldiers on "R & R") living in refugee camps. Western support has served to feed portions of the KNLA, and legitimize the KNU.[13]

The KNU — an organization dominated by Christian men — presents itself as unproblematically representative of a linguistically and religiously diverse Karen community (many members of which do not identify with the insurgency). Since the 1960s, the KNU leadership has reproduced a stylized form of S'ghaw Christian culture as the culture-language of the nationalist movement, and thus (at least by implication) as the authentic expression of Karen identity. This "S'ghaw-ization" of Karen society in the borderlands and refugee camps resembled aspects of the central state's Burmanization of national culture, for which the military government has been criticized by ethno-nationalist opposition groups. This phenomenon helps to explain the frustration felt by many non-Christian Karen, and thus the emergence of the DKBA.

Although little discussed in the literature, these various armed factions, as well as non-armed civil-society groups and "above ground" political parties, compete with the KNU for leadership of the diverse Karen community living in various parts of Burma (South 2008). Many of these non-KNU stakeholders are less closely linked to international networks (in part due to lack of English-language skills, and their non-Christian faiths), or less likely to reproduce the liberal-democratic, rights-oriented discourse favoured by international donors. (Interestingly, the ex-KNU Peace Council employs some of the same rhetoric as the KNU, but towards arguing for a negotiated settlement with the military government.) Therefore, although they enjoy considerable influence at the community level, and in relation to the government (of Myanmar), such stakeholders tend to be marginalized in international discourse and practice.[14]

These include the "Union Karen" perspective, which incorporates ideas of Karen nationalism quite different from the KNU's militarized nation-building programme. Associated with elites in Yangon and the Irrawaddy Delta, this less aggressive nationalist stance has sought an accommodation with the state of Burma/Myanmar, rather than challenging its foundations. Since the imposition of military rule in 1962, and especially following the events of 1988–90, the Union Karen voice has been marginalized, in comparison with the uncompromising rhetoric produced by opposition groups along the Thailand border.

In part, this exclusion is explained by government restrictions on international access to Karen groups working inside the country — and thus to the lack of a Union Karen voice in reporting on the country. However, relatively few outside agencies have actually made efforts to engage with this sector of Karen political and civil society. Members of the Burma activist community often assume that any socio-political actors working "inside" the country must be stooges of the military government. Furthermore, due to the restrictions and frustrations of working in military-ruled Burma, the Union Karen have had to adopt strategies of subterfuge, working behind the scenes, in ways which do not attract attention, and producing writings which have to be read between the lines.

Karen community and nationalist/"small-p" political leaders have been active in government-controlled areas of Burma throughout the period of military rule (Maung Thawnghmung 2008). In most cases, these Union Karen networks operate under the patronage (and "umbrella of protection") of a handful of mostly elderly politicians, many of whom are retired state officials, or politicians who "returned to the legal fold" in the 1950s and '60s (often due to frustration with the KNU's hard-line nationalist position). They do not perceive a fundamental contradiction between citizenship of a centrally governed state and the pursuit of greater economic, social, cultural and linguistic autonomy for their community.

Karen actors inside Burma operate in a very constricted and shifting political space. In general, this diverse community has sought to engage with the government, to win limited concessions, and create the social and political space within which civil society actors may operate. The wide range of activities carried out by community-based organizations (CBOs) and local NGOs within this loose network demonstrate that it is possible to forge space for autonomous community organization, at least at the local level, in Burma.

The danger of exposing vulnerable groups and individuals precludes a detailed description of Karen networks operating inside Burma. However, at least thirty-five Karen groups are legally registered with the authorities.[15] In addition, three new Karen political parties have emerged to contest forthcoming elections (see below). Alan Saw U, a key Karen civil-society actor in Burma, has described how many Karen inside Burma have become weary of the internal struggle (in Ganesan and Kyaw Yin Hlaing 2007, p. 221).

With the fragmentation of the once-dominant KNU mandala, newly ascendant DKBA and other faction leaders have sought to establish their power and legitimacy. Claims to legitimacy (that is, legitimate authority, and thus uncontested sovereignty) beyond the KNU's decreasing circle of influence have tended to rely on a combination of coercion and other forms of violence, the purchase of loyalty, and appeal to traditional values. As Gravers notes (1999), the Karen princelings of Southeast Burma in the nineteenth century sought to mobilize support (against British and/or Burman overlords) through appeals to religious symbolism and, in particular, a Karen version of the *min laung* myths. Likewise, for many Karen mandalas, legitimacy is derived from (or claimed through appeals to) a variety of sources, both modern and "traditional". For the DKBA and other groups, legitimacy derives from their roles as local strongmen (whose exercise of power is proof of legitimacy), and as guardians and protectors of non-Christian (particularly Buddhist) Karen religion, and non-S'ghaw (particularly Pwo-speaking) Karen dialects.[16]

Such agendas are not peculiarly new in the Karen context: earlier claims to the status of custodian and legitimate political vanguard of "traditional" Karen ethno-culture were made by the Telecon and other groups (including "God's Army", in Tenasserim Division in the late 1990s: South 2008). However, observers have generally regarded such traditionally oriented movements as historical or cultural oddities. The Telecon and others have not been deemed serious political actors — largely because such groups have expressed their concerns and aspirations, and organized their activities, according to traditional conceptions of power.

Like these supposedly atavistic elements within the highly diverse Karen political-cultural community, the DKBA has been dismissed by

The Democratic Karen Buddhist Army (DKBA)

The DKBA, which emerged in 1994, lacks a coherent command-and-control structure, and often acts as a proxy militia for the *Tatmadaw*, deflecting some (domestic and international) criticism for the state's harsh policies. Like the Burmese Army, the DKBA uses forced displacement as a means of controlling populations and resources and to undermine the KNU, its main rival for leadership of the Karen community in Burma. Like some of their counterparts in the KNLA, many DKBA commanders and soldiers are "conflict entrepreneurs", for whom military and political status is a means to personal power and enrichment. However, DKBA leaders often also employ strong ethno-nationalist rhetoric, and have implemented several well-regarded local infrastructure-development projects. Furthermore, research indicates that conditions for internally displaced persons (IDPs) in DKBA-controlled ceasefire areas are better than those in zones of on-going armed conflict or government-controlled relocation sites (see South 2007). Despite its name, there are a number of Christians within the ranks of the DKBA, including some ranking commanders, many of whom enjoy considerable autonomy, answering to local Burmese Army commanders, in addition to the leadership at Myaing Gyi Ngu.

As the DKBA transforms itself into a Border Guard Force, it is likely to enjoy decreasing levels of autonomy — which may cause significant dissatisfaction, at least in the lower ranks. It remains unclear how much support the DKBA enjoys within the wider Karen population — many of whom are disappointed by the organization's inability to promote a Karen nationalist agenda. For example, although there are schools in DKBA-controlled areas, these — with a few exceptions — do not teach Karen language, but follow the government (Burmese-language) curriculum.

DKBA commanders acknowledge that some within the organization are sometimes involved in human rights violations, but argue that it is necessary for a people to accept certain privations and suffering, in order to build a nation. Such arguments involve appeals to ends, over means. One DKBA commander relates such concerns to social, economic and cultural development. According to this argument, the DKBA has brought political-military security to the areas under its control — or at least to the 999 Special Battalion headquarters area at Shwe Ko Ko, just north of Myawaddy (opposite Mae Sot). He argues that the 'Shwe Ko Ko model' can be reproduced in other areas, once the KNU has been eliminated. Therefore, in order to safeguard the longer-term interests of the Karen population, he argued that it is sometimes necessary to engage in some unpleasant short-term practices. This argument ignores the particular economic opportunities available at Shwe Ko Ko — a strategic, and economically important border pass — which are unlikely to be reproduced in other Karen-populated areas. It also fails to address criticisms that the DKBA model of development is similar to that of the military government: a top-down understanding of 'development as infrastructure', with little genuine participation by local populations.

many observers and activists as an illegitimate phenomenon, entirely directed by the military government. However, as Ingrid Jordt observes regarding legitimization in Burma, understandings of "political authority ... must be situated from the point of view of the governed" (2007, p. 171). Although it is certainly true that the DKBA is a fragmentary organization, and does act as a proxy for the Burma Army, forwarding the military government's strategic objectives, its leaders nevertheless make (often implicit) claims to legitimacy which seem to resonate with sections of the Karen community.[17] To a degree, such agendas may be characterized as "modernist", inasmuch as individual DKBA commanders (particularly Maung Chit Thu) are promoting a model of economic development and patronage of their organization (the "Shwe Ko Ko" model).

Other appeals to legitimization are not couched in the rational-bureaucratic, rights-based language and rationale familiar to — and sponsored by — the international humanitarian and human-rights community, as represented by humanitarian groups on the Thailand–Burma border. Rather, the DKBA's agenda resonates within non-Westernized elements of the Karen community. According to Gravers (2007, p. 249), the "zone of peace and Buddhist merit [as devised by U Thuzana and U Thamanya] is probably still a model, that can attract Karen across denominations and intra-ethnic boundaries".

However, under the traditional forms of governance described above the king has had a well-founded interest in ensuring that tributary powers do not gather too much strength to themselves, thus challenging the authority of the centre. It is for this reason that the military government in Burma has regularly rotated powerful regional commanders, in order to ensure that they do not consolidate too much local control. However, the DKBA cannot be so easily "rotated".

NEW DISPENSATIONS

It seems clear that the KNU's attempt to reconfigure *Kaw Thoo Lei* as a "modern" state has failed.[18] This issue relates to another important point. In the context of its loss of territory and increasing confinement to the border areas, the KNU has lost touch with the majority of the Karen population in Burma. Although it retains a following among those populations in the hills to which it still has access, the majority of Karen people are alienated, or feel marginalized and distant from the KNU (especially non-Christians). This is the single greatest challenge facing any pan-Karen political organization: to connect with both S'ghaw- and Pwo-speaking, Christian and non-Christian (particularly Buddhist) communities. Large numbers of Pwo-speaking Buddhists regard themselves as Karen, and could probably be persuaded to support a specifically Karen political organization; they generally despise the government (and respect Aung San Suu Kyi), but do not feel represented by the KNU. Many Buddhists have supported the DKBA — but most feel disappointed by the outcome of its political-military enterprise.

Nevertheless, the Karen population in Burma remains available for socio-political mobilization. Large numbers of Karen people living beyond the hills (for example, in central Karen State, Rangoon and the Irrawaddy Delta) have had little contact with the KNU for many years, and regard the organization as having become irrelevant to their concerns. Many of these communities retain a strong Karen identity, but consider the KNU's continued insurgency as unhelpful. Indeed, for such people, the ongoing armed conflict provides the government with a pretext for militarization and repression, and represents a constraint on their ability to undertake development activities and mobilize politically, particularly in government-controlled areas (where the great majority of Karen people live.[19]

At the October 2008 Congress, a group of progressive leaders failed to persuade their colleagues of the need to reform the KNU systematically, to adopt more accountable procedures, and to review key policy positions. Instead — in a reflection of the infighting which has undermined the organization's coherence — hardliners within the KNU prevailed (backed by exile-Burmese political formations, which have a strong interest in prolonging the armed conflict in Burma). For critical observers, this was perhaps the organization's last chance to embrace reform. Instead, the KNU re-committed itself to armed conflict, and all-or-nothing victory in its battle against the military government. Despite its declining military and political capacities, however, the KNU retains a symbolic significance arising from the historic role it has played in Burma's ethnic politics.

For many Karen nationalists (and particularly Christians), the KNU enjoys a special status as the vanguard party of "the revolution". The organization's long struggle also gives it a symbolic weight in Burmese politics, beyond the KNU's actual military and political capacities. Nevertheless, the KNU's authority is in steep decline. Although its supporters may attempt to present the organization as the sole legitimate representative of the Karen people, such presumptions are not necessarily shared by the wider Karen community.

This is not necessarily to state that non-KNU armed groups enjoy uncontested support and legitimacy from the communities they seek to represent. The DKBA's widespread use of coercion and arbitrary taxation and conscription tactics, employed in its 2009 campaign against the KNU, is widely resented by people living in the border areas. Indeed, it seems unlikely that the DKBA can continue with this strategy into 2010 and beyond, as to do so would risk depopulating the area newly under its control, as civilians flee, being unable to bear increased demands for taxation and/or to provide recruits. It remains to be seen whether the DKBA can (or is interested in trying to) reinvent itself as an organization which enjoys positive support from at least some elements of the community (rather than being obeyed through coercion and fear). The DKBA (or individual commanders) make appeals to locally relevant aspects of legitimacy, based on "traditional Karen values", rather than on Western-originated norms of democracy and human rights. For example, DKBA Brigade 999 Commander Pah Nwe has in the past been ordained as a monk, and is well known for building pagodas in areas under his control.

2010 AND ALL THAT

Units of the DKBA (especially the 999 Special Battalion, under Maung Chit Thoo) will probably, sooner or later, accept the government's proposal that they transform into Burma Army-controlled Border Guard Force battalions. In exchange, DKBA commanders are likely to expand their economic interests in Karen State, including various logging, mining (and possibly also *ya ba* drug production and trafficking) activities. The military government is also planning a series of economic zones in the newly occupied border zones stretching from Myawaddy, north to the confluence of the Salween and Moeie Rivers. It is expected that Thai business and security interests will invest in these projects — perhaps eventually providing a justification for repatriating refugees to a "pacified" Karen State.

In contrast, the KNU/KNLA Peace Council (under the control of the KNLA's previous Seventh Brigade commander) has repeatedly (most recently, in April 2010) rejected the government's BGF proposal. Peace

Council (PC) leaders fear that this refusal may earn the wrath of the military government. In the meantime, the PC retains control over about a dozen villages along the Moei River, as well as its headquarters areas at Taw Ko Ko, where schooling is available for local children, together with some protection for their families from the depredations of the DKBA and Burmese Army — at least for those villagers aligned with the PC.

Meanwhile, the situation for many people in government-controlled areas, and those under the influence of various (and multiple) local militias, remains dire. Livelihoods continue to be undermined, not least by economic mismanagement and corruption.

The emergence of the DKBA (and, to a lesser extent, other non-KNU armed groups, such as the PC and KPF) has fundamentally altered the balance of power in Karen State. Despite its decline, however, the KNU is likely to hang on for some years in a few patches of jungle in southern and (particularly) northern Karen State. In fact, the persistence of low-level insurgency in the Karen hills is probably welcomed by Burmese Army commanders, providing a pretext for the continued militarization of the borderlands. Ironically, therefore, both Burmese Army and KNU leaders may have some interest in maintaining the insurgency. (Indeed, it might be argued that a co-dependency exists between several of the key stakeholders: the Burmese Army and KNU need each other to justify their existence and strategies; the aid agencies need the KNU and displaced populations — refugees and IDPs — in order to continue their work; the victims of armed conflict in Burma look to the KNU for some protection, and to the humanitarian agencies for limited relief supplies.)

If the future of the historic KNU's state/nation-building project is no longer viable, what are the alternatives? It may be that the DKBA and its like will assume positions of dominance within the diverse Karen community, similar structurally to that previously occupied by the KNU. This scenario would see the emergence of new "princes" (the DKBA leaders), to replace the old KNU *mandala* — with the important difference that the DKBA para-state shores up its limited sovereignty through paying (actual and symbolic) tribute to the Burmese military government, while the KNU looked to the "international community" — and its supposedly universal values — as a primary source of legitimacy.

Such an outcome to the current chaos in Karen State might approximate the "Give War a Chance" position, outlined most famously by Edward Luttwak (1999). According to this view, "an unpleasant truth often overlooked is that although war is a great evil, it does have a great virtue ... War brings peace only after passing a culminating phase of violence" (p. 36). Luttwak warns against "premature peacemaking", saying: "[I]mposed armistices ... artificially freeze conflict and perpetuate a state of war indefinitely by shielding the weaker side from the consequences of refusing to make concessions for peace" (p. 37). While he overlooks the humanitarian arguments for ceasefires, and employs a very simplistic, binary opposition between the notions of "peace" and "war", Luttwak's basic argument is relevant to the Karen case. *If* it can be shown that the centuries-long European experience of "war as state-making" can be compressed into a few short years, in the very different historical, cultural and political-economic context of early twenty-first-century Southeast Burma, then perhaps the ascendancy of the DKBA is to be welcomed, and will prepare the way for a new phase of state/nation-building in the Karen borderlands.

Stabilization of this kind might constitute what Keen (in Berdal and Malone 2000) refers to as "the creation of a new type of political economy, not simply the destruction of the old one". This would involve the — at least partial — transformation of primarily greed-oriented conflict actors, and the investment of their profits into the licit economy. This could be achieved through the incentives of achieving the transition from "warlord to statesman". In this case, international agencies (and donors) should be asking *if* — and *how* — they should engage with the DKBA, and other non-KNU armed groups. At a minimum, the iconoclasm of Luttwak and others should warn against the manner in which the existence of refugee camps can — perhaps inadvertently — sabotage the opportunities for peace, sustaining warrior "nations intact and [preserving] their resentments forever ... [as well as] inserting material aid into ongoing conflict ... By [intervening] to help, NGOs systematically impede the progress of their enemies towards a decisive victory that could [bring the] end of the war" (p. 43).

However, an alternative future scenario is one of continued fragmentation. The military government is unlikely to regard the emergence of a strong and stable DKBA-controlled Karen zone as beneficial. It will be interesting to observe over the next few years whether the DKBA attempts to enhance its legitimacy and systematize governance in the areas under its control — and whether the Burmese Army will let it. As Mark Duffield (2007) has noted, Burmese military strategists are experts at crisis management (rule by emergency decree, and the politics of punitive brinkmanship). Therefore they will probably seek to maintain a high level of instability and chaos in the Karen-populated border areas.

Under current circumstances, it seems unlikely that the DKBA (or the PC or KPF) can muster the political will, or organizational and human capacities, necessary to develop substantial civilian administrations. The short-to-middle-term scenario for civilians living in Karen areas therefore remains bleak. Further humanitarian crises can be expected, at least until a political settlement is reached — which at present is a remote prospect.

An alternative framework of power relates to the military government's goal of consolidating control within Myanmar, by means of implementing the 2008 constitution, which would come into effect following elections scheduled for 2010. A range of ethnic nationality parties will compete for seats in the two nationwide assemblies (the *Amyotha Hluttaw* and *Pyithu Hluttaw* — the upper and lower houses, respectively). Most, however, will focus on winning seats in the fourteen assemblies representing States and Divisions (the latter being renamed "Regions" under the new constitution). Ethnic-nationality parties are hoping that, with significant blocks of seats in these provincial assemblies, they will be able to leverage some control over the allocation of government revenues (including from natural-resource extraction), and over language policy; for example, in schools, public administration, and the court system.

For some parties associated with communities that have long-standing histories of insurgency (the Karen, for instance), the formation of non-armed political groups represents something of a "declaration of independence" from the politics of border-based insurgency. Many parties are currently in the process of registration, following which they hope to begin organizing on the ground.

Several parties seem likely to compete for support within the Karen community. Of the main contenders, one — the Karen People's Party — is primarily based in Yangon and the Delta, and led by relatively well-educated, urban (predominately Christian) elites; another — the Ploung-Sqaw Democracy Party (PSDP) — is based in Karen State (although it will also campaign in Mon State, and perhaps the Delta), and is well-grounded in local (Pwo and S'ghaw, Christian and Buddhist) communities. However, the PSDP is conscious of lacking "human capital" and, especially, plausible candidates. It will be interesting to observe whether inexperienced political leaders from the two parties — who do not always enjoy smooth relationships — will be able to agree among themselves how best to corporate.

Union Karen politicians seem confident that their parties can do well, *if* votes are counted fairly. However, many of the most able individuals are unwilling to stand for election themselves, seeking rather to mobilize others to participate. For many, the forthcoming elections are a necessary evil — prior to the next round of polls (if there is one), when electoral politics can start in earnest.

In the meantime, government agents are reportedly busy in Karen-populated areas, gauging local sentiment, and making various promises to communities regarding benefits to be delivered after the election, if they vote as instructed (for example, for the regime's Union Solidarity Development Party, which has co-opted a number of Karen community leaders to stand in the government interest).

Groups such as DKBA are most likely to position themselves to be in as strong a position as possible, to engage with whatever power structures emerge following the elections. Therefore, the planned election is likely to have limited impacts on patterns of governance in Karen State — although it may create the "space" within which new civil society and political actors might gradually emerge. Although civil-society actors themselves can also become patrons in the game of neo-mediaeval power politics, local associations and leaders can nevertheless play important roles in establishing the beginnings of a system of accountability, at least in certain pockets and localities. At a minimum, such local (non-militarized) pockets of authority provide some protection to hard-pressed civilian populations.

Post-2010 politics may see the "civilizing role" of civil society become more important. It is therefore important to strengthen the positions and voices of civil-society actors — in the border areas, and particularly "inside Burma".[20] Given its weakness, and the near impossibility of reinserting itself into the current political-military scene, it is quite rational for the rump KNU to hold out for the (albeit increasingly unlikely) prospect of "decapitation" of the SPDC, and the radical transformation of national politics. Although the strategy of refusing to engage with the military government has not served the KNU well in the past, this is probably now the organization's only option. In the meantime, it is interesting to speculate whether "unifying princes" (or princesses) might emerge in the Karen context, and the different scenarios. These may include prominent political and civil-society leaders from within the community ("inside" the country, and in exile), including those living beyond Karen State.

Consolidation of power by local leaders can be facilitated by external (financial and legitimization) support. Various local and international NGOs, and donors (including governments), have interests at stake in the future governance of Karen State — which may or may not be grounded in a comprehensive understanding of the situation. Ultimately, however, in the age of globalization, more influential than the civil society and aid sectors will be the role of capital, and business more generally.

CONCLUSIONS

The great majority of studies regarding armed conflict and its humanitarian consequences in southeast Burma derive from the perspective of anti-government armed ethnic groups and their civilian support bases, and, in particular, the KNU, and that subgroup of internally displaced people who make themselves available to insurgent and affiliated organizations (South 2007). The existing literature is therefore distorted by a significant "selection (or access) bias". This distortion is of more than "academic" relevance, as the policies of key external stakeholders (for example, humanitarian donors and Western governments) are structured by the limitations of their access and knowledge, and ultimately reflect the presumed legitimacy of particular conflict and aid actors.

If politico-economic, social and humanitarian analysis and action are to be grounded in well-informed understanding of the situation, then researchers and policymakers must do more to ensure that their work covers the full range of stakeholders, and is not limited to the "usual suspects" along the Thailand–Burma border. This would require greater conflict-sensitivity in needs-analysis and other planning activities on the part of aid agencies, taking at least some account of the positions of "non-system" actors. Donors and aid agencies should do more to examine the socio-political impact of their assistance, and ensure that at a minimum they "Do No Harm".[21] Such analysis should include reflections on the relationship between foreign aid and the protracted nature of armed conflict along the Thailand–Burma border.

This observation relates to an aspect of the conflict, and the interventions of various actors, which most stakeholders would prefer not to explore: the agendas outlined above are not value-free, but serve particular interests. For many aid workers along the border, and those in the wider activist community, their identities (and much emotional capital) are invested in understanding the conflict according to the insurgent/border-based paradigm. This perspective embodies a set of assumptions which run through most Western discourse and practice regarding conflict-affected countries. For some conflict actors (and their affiliates in the welfare wings of armed groups) the stakes are higher, as foreign aid — and the legitimacy this brings — supports their ongoing political and military struggles, both directly and indirectly, while also serving to reinforce the positions of individuals within insurgent and affiliated hierarchies.

Although in some respects the ascendancy of these values is fairly recent — and indeed, inconsistent and contested — they derive ultimately from the European Enlightenment. This Western-oriented approach focuses in particular on individual rights, the promotion of democratization, and efforts to create systems of liberal governance, at the expense of more indigenous notions of governance and legitimacy (including those associated with authoritarian "Asian values").

However, the first decade of the twenty-first century has witnessed the end of post-Cold War Western triumphalism: the global financial crisis — and associated shifts in geopolitical power — have accelerated the declining influence of the liberal-democratic model. This is not to deny the importance of rights-based approaches, but rather to recognize their historical contingency, and declining political capital.

The epochal decline of international humanitarian and political interventions based on notions of human rights will have profound consequences for conflict-affected countries, such as Burma. In the case of Karen State, this finding cuts both ways: given the precipitous decline of the KNU, Western actors seeking to re-model Karen society may have to seek new clients among the diverse Karen community (focusing perhaps on the indigenous civil-society sector "inside" Burma, rather than the old border-based paradigm of regime-change driven by externally funded exile groups); for conflict/political actors (such as the KNU), it will be necessary to decrease their reliance on the Western-based human-rights and humanitarian industry and, instead, look for support to more local sources of legitimacy and patronage.[22]

Notes

This chapter was drafted before the DKBA units were transformed into government-controlled Border Guard Forces in August 2010.

1. This chapter is based on a series of interviews, focus-group discussions and workshops conducted in Thailand and Burma (Yangon and Karen State) between 2008–10, with displaced (Karen and other) villagers; members of armed (insurgent and ceasefire) groups and political organizations; Burmese (primarily Karen) CBOs; and international organizations (diplomats, INGOs, the UN, etc). Many thanks for comments on drafts of this paper to Tom Sheaham, Ruth Bradley-Jones, Nils Carstensen, Martin Smith, Alan Smith, David Eubank, Hazel Lang, Mandy Sadan, Trevor Wilson, and several Karen friends who would rather not been named.
2. On the politics of Karen ethnic-national identity, and the history and dynamics of the KNU, see South 2008; see also Gravers 1999 and Smith 1999.
3. The KNU's problems were exacerbated by the assassination (on Valentine's Day 2008) of its General Secretary, P'doh Mahn Sha, who had played a key role in shoring-up the organization.
4. In May 2010 the Thai authorities repatriated many of these civilians to Burma.
5. For discussions of legitimacy in Burma/Myanmar, see Steinberg (2007) and Maung Thawnghmung's (2004) important study of the relationship between state agencies and rural populations.
6. "The KNU had 60 years to build the Karen State, but has failed. Now it's our turn."
7. As Benedict Anderson (1991, p. 19) notes, "states were defined by centres, borders were porous and indistinct, and sovereignties faded imperceptibly into one another."
8. Since the 1980s, the mandala model has become a standard trope of Southeast Asian studies. As such, it is ripe for critical re-evaluation. However, this is not the purpose of the present chapter.
9. Thongchai Winichakul (in Tonnesson and Antlov 1996, pp. 73–74) describes pre-colonial boundaries as "not necessarily connected or joined ... It was the limit within which the authorities of a country could exercise their power... the areas left over became a huge corridor between the two countries... The two sovereignties did not interface."
10. For a typography of the ceasefire administrations, see Callaghan 2008.
11. This phrase is coined by Duffield (2001).
12. The opposition-in-exile has influenced the KNU's positions on a range of issues (South 2008, Ch. 4).
13. With the KNU's future looking increasingly precarious, there is a warning from history. For so long as there were Hmong refugee camps in Thailand, the Hmong ethnic insurgency in Laos could continue, using the camps as fall-back bases. However, in the 1990s, with the closure of the last Laos-origin refugee camps along the northern border, the Hmong insurgency was reduced to a few rag-tag guerrilla bands that pose no threat to the Lao government — but did

serve as a pretext for the continued militarization of remote, ethnic minority-populated areas.

14. Fiona Terry (2002) notes that in the process of negotiating access to needy populations, humanitarian actors often serve to legitimize non-state groups, whose cause they perceive as just. Likewise, in his classic study of "Global Governance and the New Wars", Mark Duffield (2001, p. 253) analyzes the ways in which relief and development aid can "change and reinforce the dominant relations and forms of discourse that it encounters and through which it flows… Such effects are not confined to the material or organizational sphere; they can also include social matters of legitimacy, political recognition or moral authority."
15. Documents shown to the author in confidence.
16. For accounts of the DKBA, and its appeals to religion for purposes of legitimization, see the following reports by the Karen Human Rights Group: <http://khrg.org/khrg2009/khrg09b8.html>; <http://www.khrg.org/khrg2009/khrg09f4.html>; <http://www.khrg.org/khrg2007/khrg07f5.html>.
17. This approach is illustrated by Col. Chit Thu, who has stated his "solemn vow" that he will promote and protect the Karen peoples' "existence, foundation, culture and tradition, our heredity, religion, way of life and convention … though the labyrinth will be violent" (no date). Further details of DKBA ideology and instructions to troops are to be found in its soldiers' Handbook (no date).
18. The KNU's failure was prefigured in the manner in which its field commanders have, for many years, acted as neo-patrimonial warlords in the areas under their control, rather than rational-bureaucratic governors.
19. In addition to populations in the southeast of Burma, and the vicinity of Rangoon, large numbers of (particularly S'ghaw and Pwo) Karen people live in the Irrawaddy Delta (including areas devastated by Cyclone Nargis in May 2008). Although many of these communities are proud to identify themselves as Karen, for most people the tough reality of day-to-day survival is the main priority, with issues of political affiliation being very much secondary considerations (as, of course, is also the case for many civilians in the armed conflict-affected southeast).
20. Duffield (2007) has advised against strengthening an abusive state, but rather to support those (primarily civil-society and non-state) actors working to hold the military/government accountable.
21. According to the influential "Do No Harm" doctrine (Anderson 1996), humanitarian agencies should seek to minimize the negative impacts that can arise from the provision of assistance — for example, the empowerment of conflict actors or distortion of local markets.
22. On the "marketing of rebellion", and the manner in which insurgent

organizations model their rhetoric and position representations of their struggle, in order to attract international patrons and support, see Bob (2005).

References

Anderson, Benedict. *Imagined communities: Reflections on the origin and spread of nationalism*. London and New York: Verso, revised edition, 1991.

Anderson, Mary. *Do No Harm: supporting local capacities for peace through aid.* Local Capacities for Peace Project, Cambridge, Massachusetts: The Collaborative for Development Action, 1996.

Berdal, Mats, and David Malone, eds. *Greed and Grievance: economic agendas in civil wars.* Boulder, Colorado: Lynne Rienner, 2000.

Bob, Clifford. *The marketing of rebellion: Insurgents, media, and international activism* Cambridge: Cambridge University Press, 2005.

Callahan, Mary. *Political authority in Burma's ethnic minority states: devolution, occupation and coexistence.* Washington, D.C.: East-West Centre, Policy Studies 21, 2007.

Chit Thu, Maung. *My solemn vow* (Burmese and English language mss). No Date.

Democratic Karen Buddhist Army, *Handbook* (Burmese language mss). No Date.

Duffield, Mark. *Global governance and the new wars: the merging of development and security.* London: Zed Books, 2001.

———. "On the edge of 'No Man's Land': Chronic emergency in Myanmar". Independent report commissioned by the Office of the UN RC/HC, Yangon and UNOCHA, New York: published by Centre for Governance and International Affairs, University of Bristol, *Working Paper* 01, 2008.

Ganesan, N. and Kyaw Yin Hlaing, eds. *Myanmar: state, society and ethnicity.* Singapore: Institute of Southeast Asia Studies, 2007.

Gravers, Mikael. *Nationalism as Political Paranoia in Burma: an essay on the historical practice of power.* London: Curzon, 1999.

———, ed. *Exploring ethnic diversity in Burma.* Copenhagen: Nordic Institute for Asian Studies Press, 2007.

Jordt, Ingrid. *Burma's mass lay meditation movement: Buddhism and the cultural construction of power.* Athens, Ohio: Ohio University Press, 2007.

Karen National Union. "The struggle of KNU for justice". *KNU Bulletin* 7 (1986).

———. *The Karens and their struggle for freedom*. Mannerplaw, 1992.

Luttwak, Edward. "Give war a chance". *Foreign Affairs* 78, no. 4 (1999).

Maung Thawnghmung, Ardeth. *Behind the Teak Curtain: Authoritarianism, agricultural policies and political legitimacy in rural Burma/Myanmar.* London, New York, Bahrain: Kegan Paul, 2004.

———. *The Karen Revolution in Burma: diverse voices, uncertain ends*. Washington: East-West Center, Policy Studies 45, 2008.

Rajah, Ananda. "Nationalism and the nation-state: the Karen in Burma and Thailand". In *Ethnic groups across boundaries in mainland Southeast Asia,* edited by G. Wijeyewardene. Singapore: Institute of Southeast Asian Studies, 1996.

———. "A 'Nation of Intent' in Burma: Karen ethno-nationalism, nationalism and narrations of nation". *The Pacific Review* 15, no. 4 (2002).

Smith, Martin. "Burma: the Karen conflict". In *Encyclopaedia of modern ethnic conflicts,* edited by Joseph Rudolph Jr. London and Connecticut: Greenwood Press, 2003.

———. *Burma: Insurgency and the politics of ethnicity.* 2nd ed. London: Zed Books, 1999.

South, Ashley. *Mon nationalism and civil war in Burma: The golden sheldrake.* Reprint ed. London: Routledge Curzon, 2005.

———. "Burma: The changing nature of displacement crises". Refugee Studies Centre, Oxford University, *Working Paper No.3,* 2007.

———. *Ethnic Politics in Burma: States of conflict.* London: Routledge, 2008.

Steinberg, David. *Turmoil in Burma: Contested legitimacies in Myanmar.* Connecticut: EastBridge, 2007.

Terry, Fiona. *Condemned to repeat? The paradox of humanitarian action.* Ithaca: Cornell University Press, 2002.

Tonnesson, Stein, and Hans Antlov, eds. *Asian forms of the nation.* London: Curzon, 1997.

6

THE INCONGRUOUS RETURN OF HABEAS CORPUS TO MYANMAR

Nick Cheesman

INTRODUCTION

A cartoon published in the state-run periodical *Shwenaingan* during May 2009 neatly captured the contradictory features of the 2008 Constitution of Myanmar. While the charter purports to guarantee its citizens equality, in cartoon form it stands with arms and legs outstretched, guarding the entrance to a new peaceful, modern, developed and discipline-flourishing democratic nation. Outside the entrance is the reason for its posture: darkly clad troublemakers are trying to get in. But the constitution has foiled them. It is not treating them as equals at all. They belong to some category of persons for whom the rights it proclaims do not belong even in principle, let alone in practice.

The new charter is not so much a supreme law as it is a supreme statement of how law in Myanmar has been subordinated to ruling group interests, evoking certain ideas of the Nazi jurist Carl Schmitt. Its obsessive concern with dangers to national sovereignty of the type visualized in the cartoon speak to his dictum that, "The specific political distinction to which political motives and actions can be reduced is that between friend

FIGURE 6.1
***Shwenainggan* Cartoon "The Constitution Guarding the Nation"**

and enemy" (Schmitt 2007, p. 26). Its section 20(f) situates the armed forces in the place of his executive president as guardian of the constitution. How they are to play that role is not explained, but by Schmitt's criterion — that the sovereign is he who decides the exception (Schmitt 1985, p. 5) — Myanmar's top military officer, not its president, remains the ultimate authority. And a full chapter of the constitution is devoted to undefined states of emergency during which the commander has unrestrained authority, again as Schmitt would have it. Its subtext is that anyhow he has the prerogative to ignore its terms where expedient.[1]

At the same time, the charter restores features of the 1947 Constitution that were written out of its 1974 counterpart. Among these, the constitution has reassigned the Supreme Court authority to hear writ petitions, including for habeas corpus.[2] This writ holds a special place not only in the emergence of civil rights globally but also in the earlier constitutional history of Myanmar or, as it was known then, Burma. By studying its return we can obtain a better understanding of the current troubled status of civil rights in Myanmar and can also interrogate the contents of the 2008 Constitution as a whole, and situate those contents with reference to the institutional arrangements of the contemporary state. With these objectives, I have organized the body of this chapter in four parts, as follows.

First, I locate the return of habeas corpus to Myanmar against a global backdrop. The writ's long pedigree is attractive for judiciaries and governments seeking to enhance their standing in the international community through safeguards of citizens' rights on paper. In reality, it has often done much less to protect liberties than applicants and advocates have hoped, especially at times when it is needed most. Therefore, any prospects for its use in Myanmar must be tempered by acknowledgement of its inherent practical limits.

Second, I examine habeas corpus as an important element in the legal and political dynamics of Burma in the years after independence and before military rule. Its rise and fall in earlier decades paralleled those of the independent judiciary. To understand why its return is incongruous, we need to be aware of how the country's criminal justice institutions lost stature in the past, and with what consequences for the present.

Third, I sketch some broad categories of possible applicants for habeas corpus in Myanmar under the new constitution, consider the reasons that they might apply, and identify some barriers that they are likely to encounter, drawing on the experiences of people in other authoritarian settings, particularly in parts of South Asia with a shared colonial legal heritage. But citizens of Myanmar face peculiar difficulties when seeking to obtain redress for wrongs, which are distinctive from those of their neighbours and that again go to the constitution's incongruity.

Fourth, I consider how some applicants might succeed in an environment profoundly hostile to the defence of individual rights against the interests of the state. I argue that these hypothetical cases speak not to judicial capacity to monitor and constrain government personnel — the capacity upon which habeas corpus is premised — but to how the country's judiciary is a surrogate of the executive, its authority extending only so far as non-judicial officials allow. The new constitution itself firmly establishes this fact, by declaring powers formally separated only "to the extent possible".[3] Thus the constitution negates normative commitments even as it pretends to declare them, at once dividing yet combining the apparatus of state, guaranteeing yet denying the equality of its subjects, and entertaining complaints yet confining them to the parameters set by its guardian.

HABEAS CORPUS

The new constitution empowers the Supreme Court of Myanmar to issue a number of prerogative writs — written orders on matters given priority over others on the court's docket — yet globally habeas corpus stands apart from the others as "the great writ of liberty" (Duker 1980, p. 3). It has obtained this title by virtue of its original and ancient principle: that upon request a court is entitled to call for a detainee to be brought before it, literally to "have the body". It is an extraordinary remedy, in that if within the law there are other possibilities for a detainee to be called before a court within a lawful time period then those ordinary avenues may be used in lieu of habeas corpus.[4] Robert Sharpe sketches it as follows:

> The writ is directed to the gaoler or person having custody or control of the applicant. It requires that person to return to the court, on the day specified, the body of the applicant and the cause of his detention. The process focuses upon the cause returned. If the return discloses lawful cause, the prisoner is remanded; if the cause returned is insufficient or unlawful, the prisoner is released. The matter directly at issue is simply the excuse or reason given by the party who is exercising restraint over the applicant (Sharpe 1989, p. 23).

Habeas corpus was from early on an important defence against arbitrary and illegal custody and over time increasingly also against custodial abuses like torture, cruel and inhuman treatment and extrajudicial killing. In his landmark work on the law of the English constitution, Albert Dicey went so far as to say that the right to issue directives in the manner of habeas corpus is at the crux of the relationship between the judiciary and executive (Dicey 1982, p. 135). Its force in common law was such that Lord Justice Farwell warned that its use in British-controlled territories could undermine colonial rule, observing that: "The truth is that in countries inhabited by natives who outnumber the whites, such laws [as the Habeas Corpus Act], although bulwarks of freedom in the United Kingdom, might very probably become the death sentence of the whites if they were applied there" (in Neumann 1957, p. 35).

In some places the importance of habeas corpus has been reaffirmed through extensive use and jurisprudence. Courts in India have interpreted their authority to issue habeas corpus writs widely, so as to afford a range of remedies that go far beyond those available via the writ in other common-law countries.[5] In Brazil, the courts historically extended the ambit of the writ considerably beyond its original scope (Nadorff 1982, p. 299). The Inter-American Court of Human Rights in 1987 unanimously opined that under the American Convention on Human Rights state parties are prohibited from suspending habeas corpus, including during times of emergency. The United Nations Working Group on Arbitrary Detention has described habeas corpus as "the best remedy" against abuse of powers to arrest and detain (1994, p. 17). Contemporary jurist and philosopher Larry May has argued that habeas corpus should under international law be a right from which no government is permitted to derogate.[6] And proposals for a system of world habeas corpus have been on the table for several decades.[7]

Others have been less enthusiastic, pointing out that the image of habeas corpus as a bulwark of liberty is exaggerated.[8] Rights experts have acknowledged that while habeas corpus is in principle the most powerful tool to address certain types of abuses, in practice it disappoints.[9] At times of emergency the writ is invariably suspended, as the new constitution of Myanmar permits.[10] Where it is not suspended, under authoritarian regimes it has not proven effective at securing the release of illegally detained persons. And as its efficacy depends upon the extent to which other laws authorize and delimit arrest and custody, where those laws allow for custodial orders that ordinary citizens might consider repugnant, if the law has been properly applied then the writ is still liable to fail applicants. This was often the case in Burma, before the demise of habeas corpus along with the independent judiciary, to which this chapter now turns.

THE RISE AND FALL OF HABEAS CORPUS IN BURMA

At independence in 1948, there were two ways to apply for habeas corpus in Burma. One was via the writ jurisdiction of the Supreme Court, established under the new constitution, which guaranteed all persons the right to approach the court directly for relief. The other way was via the appellate criminal jurisdiction of the High Court, under section 491 of the Criminal Procedure Code, which permitted applications "in the nature of habeas corpus".[11]

In the two years immediately after independence, when government authorities used emergency powers to combat myriad insurgencies and related violence, habeas corpus was according to Maung Maung— later chief justice and architect of the so-called people's justice system — "the most popularly invoked remedy" (Maung Maung 1961, p. 99). The courts interpreted their role liberally. Justice E Maung in the definitive 1948 G.N. Banerji ruling described the authority of the Supreme Court in issuing habeas corpus writs to be "whole and unimpaired in extent but shorn of antiquated technicalities in procedure" (pp. 203–204). In 1950, as chief justice, he stressed in the Tinsa Maw Naing case that, "The personal liberty of a citizen, guaranteed to him by the Constitution, is not lightly to be interfered with and the conditions and circumstances under which the legislature allows such interference must be clearly satisfied and present" (p. 37). He and other senior judges ruled to release many detainees on various grounds, including that orders for arrest had been improperly prepared or implemented, that indefinitely detaining someone was illegal, and that police or prison officers were without grounds to justify arrest, be it of an alleged insurgent sympathizer or notorious criminal. On the other hand, they did not order to release detainees in cases where procedure had been followed and the person's confinement justified, even when the law under which they had been detained had been written so as to reduce judicial oversight of custodial powers, as in the U Ba Yi case.

After the 1958 constitutional coup, things began to change. Applicants continued to file for habeas corpus in cases of alleged wrongful arrest and custody.[12] However, the courts were given fewer opportunities to exercise their authority than under civilian government. The military and police promptly rounded up hundreds of political opponents and other perceived threats and sent them, without warning, to a prison camp on a remote island. They were held in barbaric conditions and without any means for effective judicial inquiries.[13]

With the military takeover of 1962, although writs were not formally abolished and the statutory allowance for habeas corpus as a form of criminal appeal remained, there was no longer an independent superior court to receive petitions. None of the hundreds or perhaps thousands of persons detained without charge or placed under protective custody successfully challenged the orders against them.[14] A new parallel system of army-controlled special courts heard cases that would have been most likely to give rise to complaints of unlawful confinement. Illegal arrest and imprisonment ceased to be an issue with which the judicial system was practically concerned. The last reported petition for habeas corpus that the apex court entertained was that of U Aung Nyunt in 1965, and it was not a complaint against custody at all but one against an order prohibiting movement into a special frontier area.

There was no reference to writs in the 1974 constitution, and since then the only explicit writ-equivalent petition entertained has been for review of lower courts' proceedings on the ground of errors in law (U Min Lwin Oo 2004, p. 58). The 1975 Law Safeguarding Citizens' Rights was supposed to offer an alternative avenue for complaints of unlawful custody and other abuses, but as it was unaccompanied by any procedural guarantees, complaints were either delayed or ignored.[15] In 1976 the *Working People's Daily* carried a front-page article on a request for release from the central jail of a father and son whom military intelligence had arrested without charge in 1964. The apex court finally ordered that they be freed some seventeen months after it received the request, and then after the public prosecutor had repeatedly caused the case to be postponed, only to report that he had nothing special to say. In another case of this sort, an army battalion held an alleged insurgent without charge for around three years before a new commander discovered him and sent him up for trial. The judge found him guilty and sentenced him to imprisonment. Although his illegal confinement was acknowledged in court, the judge did not deduct it from the sentence, as it was not officially time served.[16] And during the 1988 protests when families of detained students applied to the chief justice for their release, he in turn just handed the documents over to the attorney general's office, where they were put on file.[17]

The sabotage of Burma's criminal justice system in the 1960s and 1970s is revisited daily in the denial of rudimentary rights to detainees in Myanmar today. At no time in recent years was the absence of judicial remedies for persons in custody more blatant than in the aftermath of the September 2007 protests, when state media acknowledged that thousands of people were being detained and released after questioning — often after signing promissory documents with no basis in law — entirely outside of the system. That the government did not declare either a state of emergency or martial law to allow for this wholesale departure from ordinary legal procedure was immaterial; the families and friends of detainees had no ways to approach the courts. Judges did nothing when lawyers for persons accused of being protest organizers brought to their notice that their clients had been illegally detained. The investigating officer in one case admitted on record that two accused had been held in the central prison for over three months without charge. He denied that the imprisonment was unlawful because, he said, remand had been obtained for the pair in other related cases, but when defence counsel asked him to provide details he was unable to do so. The court did not take up the matter.

Lacking judicial avenues to have their grievances heard, citizens instead make complaints direct to the agencies responsible for wrongdoing. Some people complain because conflicts with local authorities have forced them to go higher up, others for want of alternatives. The family of a man who disappeared from army custody in April 2007 lodged a formal complaint about his disappearance with senior commanders and government ministries. According to them, an army unit had come to the victim's fishery in Kyauk Kyi during early 2006 and demanded money. The disappeared person had not been able to give it at the time but apparently had persuaded the soldiers that he would do so after he sold his fish; however, the unit came again shortly thereafter and took him with them. The family searched various facilities and located him at the regional strategic command headquarters, where they were told that if they paid the money immediately then he would be released. But before they could collect the amount required, they learned that another unit had taken him to carry supplies in a remote area. Over a year later, they lodged their complaint with the help of a human-rights defender, who submitted a copy to the International Labour Office in Yangon. There is only one matching complaint for the period concerned in the office's anonymous public register of cases. It is recorded as closed, with comments that, "Government denied portering and alleged victim to be an insurgent who was captured but subsequently escaped."[18]

Could the return of habeas corpus make any difference for this family or other persons in similar situations? The remainder of this chapter is taken up with that question. What are some of the obstacles that applicants are likely to face? How do they compare with those in other places where writs have been sought before authoritarian governments? And what do these indicate about the incongruities of Myanmar's new constitution?

THE RETURN OF HABEAS CORPUS TO MYANMAR?

Who could now apply for habeas corpus and why would they bother? The cartoon constitution barring the entrance to the new developed nation suggests the existence of at least two general categories of plausible applicants: those on the outside of the gateway, aiming to demonstrate that its return is a fraud; and those on the inside, hoping that it is not.

The first category includes those detained for political reasons, or other reasons of special concern to the state or senior state officials, over whose cases the courts have no real authority. Applicants from this category and their legal counsel might apply for habeas corpus to demonstrate that it is a sham rather than in hope of obtaining relief. They could include the chairman and general secretary of the Shan Nationalities League for Democracy, Hkun Htun Oo and Sai Nyunt Lwin, jailed since 2005 and convicted of — among other things — high treason and sedition, but whose trial and imprisonment the UN Working Group on Arbitrary Detention in 2008 opined is arbitrary. They could also include the family members of 35 political detainees who in October 2008 lodged a complaint with the chief justice over the authorities' refusal to grant them access to the trials of their relatives going on inside the central prison. Given that the order to conduct the trials in this manner itself came from the Supreme Court, the complaint was evidently framed to make a point rather than in a belief that he would reverse the order.[19] And they could include persons detained because of conflict with senior officials or persons close to senior officials, such as businesspeople and other government personnel embroiled in financial or personal disputes.

One advantage of lodging petitions for these applicants would be that their complaints could at least be formally recorded, or they could say that they tried and failed to set down the details of alleged abuses. A writ petition is a formal accusal that obliges an official response. An applicant's affidavit carries weight that other paperwork does not. The evidence needed to lodge a request also makes for a more detailed and accurate narrative than might otherwise be the case. In this way the judiciary can be used as a record-keeper: if not a bulwark against the denial of human rights then at least one against the denial of historical fact. In Chile under the Pinochet regime, the vigorous filing of requests for writs had the effect of ensuring that something of the personal details of each illegally abducted and detained person is known to this day, even though in the period of dictatorship the Supreme Court only accepted thirty out of almost 9,000 petitions filed (Hilbink 2007, p. 115). The body of cases also served to make the forced disappearance of some persons more difficult (Fruhling 1983, p. 524).

But in Myanmar the value of habeas corpus for public advocacy is reduced by the lack of scope for publicity around court cases. Local news journals and civic groups do their best to create some space for coverage, but it remains painfully small in comparison even to most other countries across the region. The work of the courts goes virtually unreported in state media: during the 2009 trial of democracy-party leader Aung San Suu Kyi, which was a notable exception to this pattern, writers for the state newspaper demonstrated unfamiliarity with legal terms, using them awkwardly and inconsistently. There are no domestic or international rights groups operating in the country with the capacity or mandate to document and report on most of the types of cases that could be taken up in requests for habeas corpus in this first category. There are as yet no independent professional bodies to train members and lobby on issues of special concern. In the absence of these, the efficacy of the writ for advocacy is greatly diminished. This is already a problem for lawyers and others who are fighting cases behind closed doors and without means to communicate directly with large parts of the populace, other than via short-wave radio broadcasts from abroad. Whereas ultimately the writ is about bringing into the open that which is ordinarily shut away, without the means to communicate about the rights of detainees and abuses of these rights, habeas corpus is ineffectual. It remains to be seen whether or not after 2010 anticipated changes in government allow for more space to communicate than exists at present — as some analysts predict — but for the time being the domestic media for the most part must persist with writing between the lines rather than on them.

The second category of persons who might apply for habeas corpus includes a wide variety of subtypes, among them applicants who feel they have nothing to lose and applicants who for one reason or another cannot or do not choose to negotiate through the usual channels. The former subtype includes the family of the Kyauk Kyi fisherman, who having exhausted all prior available avenues may be prepared to try any new ones, knowing that his life is probably already lost. The latter subtype includes a group of residents in New Dagon who, during March 2007, made a complaint against ward officials and police and fire brigade personnel for allegedly illegally arresting and detaining nine persons whom the officers claimed were residing in the area without having been registered, although the complainants maintained that the detainees had already been put onto the household lists after some earlier delays caused by tardy ward officials. In this case, like others of its type involving complaints to higher levels, a dispute between the residents and the local authorities that led to the arrests also forced the unsatisfied inhabitants to seek the involvement of people further up the administrative hierarchy.

One common experience in countries where citizens have sought habeas corpus during times of repressive government is that authorities accused of having — or having had — people in their custody simply deny it. A few admit that they had the person, but that they let him go afterwards and do not know what happened to him next. In areas affected by civil war or occupied by various armed groups, the alleged perpetrators may acknowledge that they had the person but say — as in the Kyauk Kyi disappearance case — that he was an insurgent or sympathizer; that he escaped or was killed in an encounter. Outright disavowal of responsibility is easy, and often difficult to prove false. Because of the requirement that the applicant show grounds for the court to consider issuing a writ, if no evidence can be produced then the court will usually reject the request outright.[20] The courts in Burma during earlier decades sided with government officials where the matter rested on the mere say-so of the applicant against that of the respondent.[21] And in present-day Myanmar where lawyers accuse police in court of keeping detainees in illegal custody, the officers also simply deny knowledge of wrongdoing.[22]

In times of authoritarianism, requests for habeas corpus may have the perverse effect of encouraging judges and prosecutors to collude with police and soldiers. The methods used to frustrate applicants can be subtle or crude. Courts and their personnel can erect all sorts of barriers to cause delays without appearing to deviate from normal practice. In Sri Lanka, where people lodged at least 2,755 separate writ petitions for victims of forced disappearances in three provinces from 1989 to 1997, it took around seven years for the courts to hand down their orders (Presidential Commission 1997, ch. 10). This was in part because the system was overburdened and delays were the norm, but also because officers would fail to appear in court on appointed dates and judges would accommodatingly set new dates for them to fail to turn up again. Nor did lawyers feel obliged to serve their clients properly or keep them informed of proceedings. Not only did people disappear, but so too did files on them. Families never learned of the outcomes of their cases. Staff at the attorney general's office appeared for police and soldiers responding to habeas corpus petitions — as they did in Burma when the writ was in effect during earlier decades, and as they will in cases arising under the new constitution. Some coached the respondents on how to contribute to delays and submit false or misleading evidence. In this way they developed conspiratorial relationships with police officers and later on when they needed favours of the police the latter would help them in return.[23] When judges finally handed down their orders, many rejected petitioners' requests on spurious grounds of questionable legality.

Where advocacy and record-keeping through habeas corpus is aimed at incremental change but does not lead to any tangible benefits for the victims and families of detained or disappeared persons, it can even have a corrosive effect. In Sri Lanka, the presidential commissions of inquiry into disappearances paid special heed to the filing of the thousands of petitions for habeas corpus writs and the reasons for their failure in protecting the rights of citizens; however, they did not result in criminal cases against alleged perpetrators, and the families of disappeared persons at best received no more than paltry compensation. Most accused continued serving in official posts, many in higher posts, despite attempts to bring them to justice. The cumulative effect of all the work on these cases, while putting down the basic facts for posterity, has been to demoralize and exhaust people whom it was supposed to benefit.[24] People become frustrated and lose hope after years of trying to obtain justice, further diminishing the standing of the judiciary as a whole. Habeas corpus in Myanmar ultimately could have the same sort of detrimental rather than beneficial effects on a society that is already profoundly demoralized.

Even if judges and government lawyers try to perform their tasks conscientiously, the perpetrators of abuses in authoritarian settings have many opportunities to thwart the system, with or without inside help. They can botch or manipulate inquiries to ensure that when instructed to locate and bring a person to a hearing, or explain what has happened to them, they conceal more facts than they reveal. In places where the work of the police is militarized and a variety of other groups have quasi-policing duties — as is the case in Myanmar — a number of agencies may be involved in holding a detainee. Sorting out whether they were last in the hands of the army, police or a vigilante group may be all but impossible. Police or other officers may re-arrest people whom the courts order to be released, as happened frequently in Nepal from about 1999 to 2004, where sometimes the same police who brought a person to court effected her re-arrest as soon as she emerged from the premises. In Sri Lanka, security forces resorted to abducting people from their houses at night rather than bothering to re-arrest them. Some lawyers, witnesses and family members who insisted on lodging requests for writs suffered the same fate. Judges too can be put in harm's way and, even where not in fear of their lives, they may risk their jobs or chances of being promoted and, at very least, their reputations if they are repeatedly humiliated when their orders for release of detainees are ignored or ridiculed through these sorts of practices.

Among the material and technical obstacles to the return of habeas corpus to Myanmar, some are common to other countries and others are not. Under the new constitution, only the Supreme Court can issue writs, which means that applicants or their counsel must use time and money simply to lodge a petition, let alone to get it heard. In a country where most detained people do not have access to attorneys there is no prospect of more than a tiny percentage of the total number of plausible applicants approaching the court.[25] On top of this, there is no longer any practice of filing for writs. Lawyers don't know what habeas corpus is. There is no continuity with the habits of earlier periods as in parts of South Asia where legal traditions were kept alive even in the worst times, and where courts retained formal authority over other parts of state, even if they couldn't exercise it. The technicalities of reintroducing the use of writs to Myanmar at present remain a mystery, and will have to be sorted out, through issuance of directives and administrative rearrangements, before applicants are able to approach the court at all.

Attempts to use the writ could backfire on individual applicants, their lawyers and supporters, as well as society as a whole. Persons who accuse state officers of wrongdoing in Myanmar — and people helping them — are targeted through counter-complaints, not only in high-profile cases but in ordinary ones too.[26] Lawyers assisting applicants are easy prey for vindictive officials, as their licences can be suspended or revoked on any number of spurious grounds.[27] And there is the risk that the Supreme Court could respond to habeas corpus requests with regressive orders that formally endorse the arrogating of policing powers by the army or otherwise authorize state officers to do as they please.[28] The constitution has itself opened the way for rulings of this nature through its deliberate ambiguity on the statutory limit of twenty-four hours before a detainee is brought to court, which it reaffirms but qualifies, excluding "matters on precautionary measures taken for the security of the Union or prevalence of law and order [rule of law], peace and tranquility in accord with the law in the interest of the public".[29]

But if certain types of applicants might fail for these and other reasons, how might others succeed? The somewhat counterintuitive answer to that question goes to the incongruity of Myanmar's legal and political arrangements, an incongruity which has in turn been written into its new constitution.

WHY SOME CASES MIGHT SUCCEED

To understand how some applicants for habeas corpus under the new constitution might succeed in their plaints, we need to distinguish more clearly between the type of authoritarian legality in Myanmar as against that in recent periods in Sri Lanka or Nepal. To do this we must draw a line, with Otto Kirchheimer (1961, pp. 18–19), between a judiciary seeking its own adjustments and answers to the pressures of the times and one that has been integrated with the goals and objectives of the political authorities. During periods of dictatorship, judiciaries in South Asia have been coerced into making compromises with executive authorities, but have retained a degree of autonomy. After the overthrow of Nepal's absolute monarchy, the Supreme Court brought forward hundreds of habeas corpus requests that it had kept pending indefinitely. It issued the wide-ranging and unprecedented Rabindra Prasad Dhakal ruling on a batch of eighty-three cases in which it roundly condemned the government for the incidence of enforced disappearances and the failure to investigate, and directed it to pass a law to criminalize the offence in accordance with international standards and establish a special inquiry body with a view to prosecuting perpetrators, as well as compensating families of victims. By contrast, the Supreme Court of Myanmar today is altogether subordinate to and integrated with other parts of the state. To imagine that it can adopt proceedings devoted to resolving a dispute between the individual and the state of the likes of habeas corpus is, to paraphrase Mirjan Damaška, to smuggle ideological assumptions into a hostile environment. "The state interest" in this type of setting, he writes, "is lexically superior, indeed supreme, rather than placed on the same plane with individual interests wherein the two could be 'balanced' " (1986, p. 86).

In this setting, where the courts have an administrative rather than a judicial function, certain types of cases could be successful because of the need to comply with policy dictates rather than enforce law. For instance, Myanmar has joined international instruments concerning children's and women's rights and has sought to demonstrate commitment to these categories of rights. There is a lot written on them in professional journals and texts, and some attorneys are specializing in cases where women and children are the victims of abuse. Official groups and international agencies are helping to make space for debate and reportage on abuses of women and children that does not exist for lots of other issues. And in many cases of illegal confinement involving women and children, especially teenage girls brought to the towns and cities for employment, the perpetrators are private citizens rather than state officers, or the latter acting in a private capacity. These types of cases, if coming within the ambit of habeas corpus as an extraordinary remedy could succeed for administrative rather than judicial reasons.

The success of a few habeas corpus petitions, resulting in the release of detainees, could mislead well-intended outside agencies and serve as propaganda to raise money for in-country projects, as is already being done on issues like human trafficking and child soldiers. The government of Myanmar could seize on cautiously optimistic reports from international bodies keen to identify any change as a sign of some progress so as to impress faraway experts that it is sincerely promoting the rule of law and upholding judicial independence, just as the government of Argentina did during the 1970s even as its military was abducting, torturing and killing tens of thousands (Osiel 1995, p. 485). For some years officials from Myanmar's courts and its attorney general's office have sought to convince counterparts at meetings in other parts of Asia and further abroad that their country too shares in the common-law heritage and its values.

Reintroducing the writ may be one useful way for them to boost these claims in attempts to enhance not only their own credibility but also that of the new constitution, without much risk of actually achieving anything.

Finally, any habeas corpus petition without special policy interest to the state or senior officialdom could also succeed through the simple expedient of money given to judges, prosecutors and police. Anecdotally, the criminal-justice system in Myanmar is extremely corrupt. At present, virtually every stage in the criminal process, including arrest, filing of charges, granting of bail and hearing of an ordinary criminal case — both in the court of first instance and upon appeal — can be accompanied with payment of money to secure a desired result or at least mitigate the consequences of an undesirable one. Perhaps the prospect of further profit through brokerage and manipulating of the system, rather than any sense of justice or professional responsibility, will be the greatest motivator for lawyers interested to learn how to revive the ancient practice of writ petitions in Myanmar through the terms of the new constitution, however incongruous they may be.

CONCLUSION

Where the role of the courts is to assist in a state programme, rather than check executive power, policy directives can be implemented through the judiciary in the same way as through the administrative bureaucracy. By contrast, systems like those in Sri Lanka or Nepal may be defective and compromised but judges in them do still adjudicate more according to the terms of law than according to the dictates of executive officers. Ironically, a corrupted policy-implementing judicial system like that in Myanmar can be mistaken for an efficient system in contrast to its functionally separate counterparts, because its efficiency derives from the carrying out of orders and urgency to make money through the exercise of authority, not from integrity or professionalism of the sort that courts in other countries struggle to achieve, however imperfectly and half-heartedly.

This is the real incongruity of habeas corpus as an element in the 2008 Constitution of Myanmar. Habeas corpus is premised on the idea that courts have the power to compel soldiers, police and other officials to follow their orders. In Myanmar, where the judiciary is a proxy for the executive, judges have this power only where they have the approval and backing of higher executive authorities. Whereas in certain authoritarian settings the courts have retained nominal legal power over other parts of government but have been unable or unwilling to exercise it at certain times because of extenuating circumstances, in Myanmar the problem is much more basic. Myanmar's courts don't have effective authority over other parts of government at all. Their capacity to review the activities of state agencies and agents is limited to what the executive permits them. Under these circumstances, not only is the reintroducing of habeas corpus a figment but so too is any constitutional commitment to protect the individual, because all such legal commitments are delimited by higher administrative imperatives. Only where legal and administrative objectives coincide can the former prevail.

The incongruity of habeas corpus in the new constitution percolates throughout the charter's contents, and through the extant state institutions that will be responsible for establishing new institutions in accordance with its terms following general elections. Where the armed forces rather than the judiciary have responsibility to safeguard the constitution and uphold the rule of law, statements of citizens' rights are perverse. Where the state has subordinated legality to policy and detached policy from any coherent ideology, no amount of technical or procedural rearranging can effect significant change. Because the new constitution is a vague expression that is not binding on its guardian, ultimately it contains no guarantees, whether for a political detainee, an ordinary under-trial accused or anyone else.

Notes

1. Richard Horsey (2008, p. 4) correctly points out that analysis of the charter that assumes either the commander or his institution will faithfully adhere to its terms "overstates both the legal competence and procedural rigidity of the military".
2. Constitution 2008, sections 296(a)(i) and 378(a)(i). The apex court had this authority under section 25(2) of the 1947 Constitution, but not under the one of 1974.
3. Constitution 2008, section 11(a). In any event, the placing of guardianship over the charter in the hands of the armed forces itself negates the concept of judicial independence. Speeches of senior officers, too, routinely reinforce the message that the judiciary, police and administrative bureaucracy are functionally united. On 13 May 2009, for instance, the New Light of Myanmar (p. 9) reported Prime Minister General Thein Sein as reminding judges that,

"The administrative and judicial systems cannot operate separately but need to be in harmony to be able to protect public interests."

4. The writ is not discretionary, meaning that it should be issued by right, and unlike other writs cannot be denied simply on the basis that an alternative remedy exists. However, the law on the extent to which the writ can be entertained by right varies markedly according to jurisdiction.
5. In Mohd. Ikram Hussain the Supreme Court of India held that in matters of habeas corpus every procedure is open to a court to make inquiries unless they are expressly prohibited. In T.V. Eachara Varier the Kerala High Court held against the police and state government and demanded that they produce evidence of what happened to a young disappeared detainee even though the authorities denied ever having held him in custody. Justice Subramonian Poti stated that "so long as it is the duty of this court to protect the freedom of a citizen and his immunity from illegal detention we cannot decline to exercise our jurisdiction merely because a dispute has arisen on the issue of detention" (para. 14).
6. May 2008. Thanks to Larry May for reading and commenting upon a draft of this paper that I presented to the 2009 Myanmar/Burma Update conference.
7. See, for instance, Kutner 1962.
8. See, for instance, Clark and McCoy 2000, ch. 2.
9. See, for instance, United Nations Commission on Human Rights 1992, para. 202.
10. Constitution, 2008, sections 296(b), 379. The 1947 Constitution in its section 25(3) made the same provision, which the government applied in certain times and places prior to 1962, but not nationwide.
11. The section remains on the code to the present day but has not been used since the mid-1960s and is a narrower provision than that provided under the former constitution; hence, in this paper I refer to the formal "return" of habeas corpus through the new constitution.
12. Director of Information 1960, p. 60. For a reported case from the same year, see Lim Lyam Hwat.
13. For a detailed recount of a former detainee, see Ko Ko Lay 1960, who records that some detainees were taken to the island in error, among them juveniles, small traders and at least one unfortunate who had the same name as a notorious criminal. Meaningful legal and political challenges to the camp were not launched until late 1959; the authorities closed it the following year. The island was again used to hold prisoners from 1968–70.
14. Myint Zan 2000, p. 19. For a short account of a meeting with a detained former minister, see Singh 2001, pp. 140–41.
15. Under the law, a citizen whose rights had been infringed could report to the "concerned authorities" or their superiors, who were then duty-bound to

investigate promptly and take further action where the grievance was found to be genuine or take other steps as necessary to redress the grievance and inform the complainant of the outcome. I have not been able to find any cases deliberated under this law in the law reports.

16. Information provided by a professional intimate with the case, March 2009. In other cases cited in this paper where no specific reference is given, the details have been drawn from relevant documents.
17. Maung Maung 1999, pp. 47, 61. According to Maung Maung, when Ne Win asked the attorney general if arrested students had been brought before the courts within twenty-four hours as required by law, the latter "could only mumble that he couldn't say" (p. 48).
18. International Labour Organization 2009, p. 29. The ILO appears to have waited around two years for this reply; in a March 2009 report the case was still recorded as "open", with "further government information awaited".
19. In court daily diaries for these cases where defence attorneys applied to have the hearings held in the open, the trial judges invoked Supreme Court orders No. 16/2008 as the basis for holding the trials inside the central prison.
20. In the Kodippilage Seetha case the Court of Appeal, Sri Lanka, went so far as to say that not only did the burden to prove an enforced disappearance lie with the petitioner for a writ of habeas corpus, but that the standard required was proof beyond reasonable doubt (p. 234). The jurisprudence on the standard of proof in Sri Lanka has been inconsistent. At other times the courts have issued writs on prima facie evidence.
21. See, for example, the Mrs. G. Latt case.
22. In cases where persons have allegedly been illegally detained and these facts have come to the notice of the courts in which they have been tried, police have replied that as they have been assigned only to investigate they know nothing about arrangements for keeping the accused in custody.
23. Thanks to Basil Fernando for these observations and for his comments on an early draft of this chapter.
24. See the stories in Asian Legal Resource Centre 2004.
25. During visits to two prisons in 2008 a United Nations expert who spoke at random with detainees did not meet anyone who had been represented in court, and according to him many prisoners did not even know the meaning of the word "lawyer". Quintana 2009, pp. 6–7.
26. In the disappearance case from Kyauk Kyi, the ILO register further records: "Any connection between the facilitator['s] subsequent imprisonment and this case was denied." International Labour Organization 2009, p. 29.
27. In May 2009 two prominent rights lawyers had their licences revoked following four months' imprisonment for contempt of court because they had presented documents withdrawing their powers of attorney citing the reason given by

their clients for no longer requiring counsel as that they "no longer trust the judiciary".

28. This happened in the U Ye Naung case, in which the court found that there was no reason why a confession to a military intelligence officer should not also be admissible as evidence, although the finding contradicts all prior law and precedent.
29. Constitution, 2008, section 376. The English version of the constitution uses "prevalence of law and order" where in the original text the expression is "rule of law". On the ambiguities of rule-of-law language in Myanmar, see Cheesman 2009. The statutory requirement of 24-hour detention in section 61 of the Criminal Procedure Code is that, "No police officer shall detain in custody a person arrested without a warrant for a longer period than... twenty four hours" excluding time taken for transporting the detainee to the police station and court, unless the police officer obtains an order from a judge under section 167.

Reported Cases

G.N. Banerji v. Superintendent, Insein Jail Annexe, Insein. BLR (1948) SC 203–04.
Kodippilage Seetha v. Saravanathan. [1986] 2 Sri LR 228.
Lim Lyam Hwat v. Secretary, Home Ministry. BLR (1960) SC 128.
Mohd. Ikram Hussain v. State of U.P. & Others. [1964] 5 SCR 86.
Mrs. G. Latt v. The Commissioner of Police & One. BLR (1949) SC 102.
Tinsa Maw Naing v. Commissioner of Police, Rangoon & Another. BLR (1950) SC 37.
T.V. Eachara Varier v. Secretary to the Minister of Home Affairs & Others. [1977] KLT 335.
U Aung Nyunt v. Union of Burma (Sub-Divisional Magistrate, Tachilek). BLR (1965) CC 578.
U Ba Yi & Eight Others v. The Officer-in-Charge of Jail, Yamèthin. BLR (1950) SC 130.
Union of Myanmar v. U Ye Naung & Another. MLR (1991) SC 63.

References

Asian Legal Resource Centre. *An Exceptional Collapse of the Rule of Law: Told through Stories by the Families of the Disappeared in Sri Lanka*. Hong Kong: Asian Legal Resource Centre, 2004.

Burma Director of Information. *Is Trust Vindicated?* Rangoon: Director of Information, Government of the Union of Burma, 1960.

Cheesman, Nick. "Thin Rule of Law or Un-Rule of Law in Myanmar?" *Pacific Affairs* 82, no. 4 (2009): 597–613.

Clark, David and Gerard McCoy. *The Most Fundamental Legal Right: Habeas Corpus in the Commonwealth*. Oxford: Clarendon Press, 2000.

Constitution of the Republic of the Union of Myanmar (2008). Printing and Publishing Enterprise, Ministry of Information, 2008.

Damaška, Mirjan R. *The Faces of Justice and State Authority: A Comparative Approach to the Legal Process*. New Haven & London: Yale University Press, 1986.

Dicey, A.V. *Introduction to the Study of the Law of the Constitution*. 8th ed. Indianapolis: Liberty Fund, 1982.

Duker, William F. *A Constitutional History of Habeas Corpus*. Contributions in Legal Studies, edited by Paul L. Murphy, Westport, Connecticut and London: Greenwood Press, 1980.

Final Report of the Commission of Inquiry into Involuntary Removal or Disappearance of Persons in the Western, Southern and Sabaragamuwa Provinces, Presidential Commission on Disappearances (Western, Southern and Sabaragamuwa Provinces). Sri Lanka, 1997.

Fruhling, Hugo. "Stages of Repression and Legal Strategy for the Defence of Human Rights in Chile: 1973–1980". *Human Rights Quarterly* 5, no. 4 (1983): 510–33.

Habeas Corpus in Emergency Situations [Arts. 27(2) and 7(6) of the American Convention on Human Rights]. Advisory Opinion OC-8/87 (Ser. A) No. 8 (1987), Inter-American Court of Human Rights 1987.

Hilbink, Lisa. *Judges Beyond Politics in Democracy and Dictatorship: Lessons from Chile*. Cambridge Studies in Law and Society, eds. Chris Arup, Martin Chanock, Pat O'Malley, Sally Engle Merry and Susan Silbey, Cambridge and New York: Cambridge University Press, 2007.

Horsey, Richard. "A Preliminary Analysis of Myanmar's 2008 Constitution". Conflict Prevention and Peace Forum, 2008.

Kirchheimer, Otto. *Political Justice: The Use of Legal Procedure for Political Ends*. Princeton, NJ: Princeton University Press, 1961.

Ko Ko Lay. *Balehe-Kokokyun* [What is Coco Island]. Rangoon: Khin Maung Yi and Sons Press, 1960.

Kutner, Luis. *World Habeas Corpus*. New York: Oceana Publications, Inc., 1962.

Maung Maung. *Burma's Constitution*. 2nd ed., The Hague: Martinus Nijhoff, 1961.

———. *The 1988 Uprising in Burma*. Yale Southeast Asia Studies, ed. Marvel Kay Mansfield, New Haven: Yale University Southeast Asia Studies, 1999.

May, Larry. "Why Habeas Corpus Should Be a *Jus Cogens* Norm in International Law". Talk given at the Centre for International and Public Law, Australian National University, 13 November 2008.

Myint Zan. "Judicial Independence in Burma: No March Backwards Towards the Past". *Asian-Pacific Law & Policy Journal* 1, no. 1 (2000): 1–38.

Nadorff, Norman J. "Habeas corpus and the protection of political and civil rights in Brazil: 1964–1978". *Lawyer of the Americas* 14, no. 2 (1982): 297–336.

Neumann, Franz. *The Democratic and the Authoritarian State*. Glencoe, Il: The Free Press, 1957.

New Light of Myanmar. "Judgements passed by court must be free from corruption and should be a salutary lesson". *New Light of Myanmar*, 13 May 2009, pp. 8, 9, 16.

Opinion No. 26/2008, Working Group on Arbitrary Detention, 16 August 2008.

Osiel, Mark J. "Dialogue with Dictators: Judicial Resistance in Argentina and Brazil". *Law and Social Inquiry* 20, no. 2 (1995): 481–560.

Quintana, Tomas Ojea. Report of the Special Rapporteur on the Situation of Human Rights in Myanmar. United Nations Human Rights Council, 2009.

Report of the Working Group on Arbitrary Detention. United Nations Commission on Human Rights, 1994.

Report on the Visit to Sri Lanka by Three Members of the Working Group on Enforced or Involuntary Disappearances (7–18 October 1991). United Nations Commission on Human Rights, 1992.

Schmitt, Carl. *Political Theology: Four Chapters on the Concept of Sovereignty*. Trans. George Schwab, Chicago & London: University of Chicago Press, 1985.

———. *The Concept of the Political*. Trans. George Schwab, Chicago & London: University of Chicago Press, 2007.

Sharpe, R.J. *The Law of Habeas Corpus*. 2nd ed., Oxford: Clarendon Press, 1989.

Shwenaingnan, 1 May 2009.

Singh, Balwant. *Burma's Democratic Decade, 1952–1962: Prelude to Dictatorship*. Tempe, Az: Arizona State University, 2001.

Special Sitting to Examine Developments Concerning the Question of the Observance by the Government of Myanmar of the Forced Labour Convention, 1930 (No. 29). International Labour Organization, 2009.

U Min Lwin Oo. "Shedawthwin-sachundawmya-agyaung-thigaungsayar" [What to Know about Habeas Corpus Writs]. *Constitutional Affairs Journal* 19 (2004): 48–60.

Working People's Daily. "Father and son released after ten years' detention". 8 November 1976, p. 1.

III

Economic Development, the Rural Economy and Labour Rights

7

MYANMAR'S RESPONSE TO THE 2008 GLOBAL FINANCIAL CRISIS

Khin Maung Nyo

INTRODUCTION

Some studies[1] suggest that the Myanmar government spending will remain heavily focused on military expenditure, with few (if any) initiatives in the pipeline to support households and businesses or to stimulate the economy in the face of the global economic downturn. The Myanmar government announced that the current global economic slowdown has had only a marginal impact on Myanmar.[2] It seems doubtful, however, that it would be capable of taking effective action to limit damage, as indicated by the speeches of military leaders and articles in the daily papers.

In an article entitled "Resilient Country, Resilient People", which appeared in the *New Light of Myanmar* on 18 December 2008, Kyaw Ye Min (the pseudonym of an official) claimed that Myanmar had suffered no spill-over effects from the crisis of neighbouring Southeast Asian countries during the Asian financial crisis in 1997. Myanmar, he said, was capable of managing the economy to stabilize it and of isolating itself from economic crises in other countries. A country without any external aid and help could survive easily in the face of difficulties, it was assumed.

In 2003, Myanmar experienced a banking crisis.[3] Problems in sub-prime financial services infected banks, creating a liquidity crisis. To make things worse, rumours spread which influenced people to withdraw their deposits. Some private banks had a poor record of financial discipline and depositors had a low level of trust and confidence in Myanmar's banks. The government provided 59.90 billion kyat of credit to banks as emergency liquidity during this period. In addition, as a lender of last resort, the central bank extended a credit line of a further 50.68 billion kyat. With a total of 110.58 billion s given to thirteen private banks, the banks recovered by January 2004, which was an indication, the article said, that the Myanmar government was willing and capable of helping people in times of need and emergency.

To help victims of Cyclone Nargis, which left Irrawaddy Division and Yangon Division helpless in May 2008, subsidies of 88.44 billion kyat were provided by the government, with 42.32 billion kyat more coming from private donors. Even if Myanmar is a poor country, the help from government should be recognized, the columnist added.

Myanmar is a developing country with a very low level of financial and trade relations with the United States and Western industrialized countries, which means there will be almost no direct impact from the global financial crisis. As Myanmar's major trading partners are India, China and ASEAN countries, any impact would come indirectly through any recession in those countries. However, remittances from Myanmar workers working abroad would also be significantly reduced and some of these workers were likely to become unemployed. As these workers returned to Myanmar, measures for their re-employment in the domestic economy would need to be considered, the article continued.

The tourism and hospitality sectors were likely to suffer most, which would be followed by a decline in trade. The export of garments and fishery products would decline and the import of luxury goods would be reduced, the article predicted.

However, some blessings and positive impact could be expected, the columnist asserted. The price of fuel would decline and reduce the cost of Myanmar's oil imports. India and China, Myanmar's major trading partners, were less vulnerable to the effects of the global financial crisis. As an agricultural economy which meets its own basic food requirements and necessities, Myanmar relied less on imports, reducing the demand for hard currency and thus making Myanmar less vulnerable to the crisis.

This article reflects the optimistic and less realistic outlook of Myanmar's government. But it would pay us to examine what is really happening in Myanmar's domestic market and Myanmar's response to the impact of the global financial crisis.

WHAT HAPPENED IN MYANMAR'S MARKETS?

The first signs of the global financial crisis hitting Burma could be traced in the plummeting prices of goods such as rice, beans and palm oil in the Rangoon marketplace. The price of a 50 kg (108 lb) sack of rice at Bayintnaung Market fell from 16,200 kyat (US$12.85) to about 14,200 kyat (US$11.25) within a month, even though demand for rice traditionally increases in November. The price of beans dropped 50 per cent, from 740,000 kyat (US$580) per ton to about 500,000 kyat (US$394) per ton, according to businesspeople in Rangoon as demand dropped. Indian companies suspended imports from Burma when the crisis began (see *Irrawaddy News*, 19 November 2008). This problem resulted in the non-payment by bean traders of the moneys they owed to bean sellers.

The Burmese military government's income from selling natural gas abroad is likely to suffer from falling prices triggered by the global financial crisis. Income from gas sales — mostly to Thailand — had already slumped in the first nine months of the 2009 financial year, the Burmese Ministry of National Planning and Economic Development disclosed in its "Quarterly Economic Indicators".[4]

The ministry said gas exports, which account for about 40 per cent of all export income, fell 28.5 per cent in value between April and December — a loss of US$670 million compared with the same period a year earlier. At the same time the cost of imports rose, resulting in a 39 per cent drop in trade surplus.

Against the backdrop of plummeting prices of pulses and beans in the Indian market as a result of the global recession, some Myanmar wholesale traders were put on trial for non-payment to sellers. The wholesale traders joined futures trading in green beans and other beans in the export market and owed billions of kyat to the sellers and their sub-contractors, who in turn bought these commodities from the producers. These big buyers bought hundreds of tons of beans for anything between 500 and 1,000 tons. Trading in beans had become sluggish as prices were falling. The small traders suffered and big traders lost a lot of money. Their profit fell by about 33 per cent over the previous year. The futures traders paid high prices when they bought the commodity and then could not pay their dues when they had to settle their accounts because of the falling prices. The big wholesale traders from Rangoon usually appoint their agents to buy commodities on their behalf from the producers by paying 1 per cent commission as fees on the trade value. They were having difficulty when their principals did not pay on time. Most of these agents could not pay their dues on behalf of the wholesale traders.[5]

This problem in the agricultural commodity market spread to other areas and caused a liquidity crisis in the private sector. The root causes of the problem might be poor understanding of international markets and a low level of education among traders. In his chapter, Sean Turnell explains the problems in regard to rural credit.

Gold dealers said that prices were heading downward, with a strong kyat and weak demand to blame. As of 3 March 2009, on the London market the price of gold was US$912.50 per ounce. The price of an ounce of gold in Myanmar was about K831,666, or about US$832 and it was expected to fall further because of the reduced demand for gold. Some dealers reported that they had lost a lot of customers, particularly farmers from the countryside. The dollar/kyat exchange rate is indirectly linked to the gold price. If gold rises, the value of the kyat usually goes down. Even if the world gold price increased to US$1,000 an ounce, if the dollar is worth less than K1,000, the domestic price cannot reflect the international price.[6]

Hit by a 46 per cent shortfall in its target for fisheries exports in 2008, the government lowered the target for 2009 to US$700 million. Export income for this key sector in the financial year 2008/09 was only US$480 million, falling far short of the targeted US$850 million. Officials blame Cyclone Nargis, which hit the country in early May 2008, and the world financial crisis for falling fisheries income. The falling prices of fisheries products around the world were still hitting Myanmar products in mid-2009, and exporters said that although orders are nearly back to normal, prices are still low. Prices were still 30 per cent down compared to before the crisis.[7]

Education service firms in Myanmar, which organize students from Myanmar to study at universities abroad, introduced innovative ways to attract students. As the universities could not reduce tuition fees, they offered full scholarships, partial scholarships or study grants. Singapore universities use these promotional techniques to attract students (*Kumudra*

Journal, 24 July 2009) in recognition of the reality that family incomes had been affected by the crisis and that some Myanmar parents would no longer be able to afford foreign tuition fees.

According to *The Economist* magazine, more than a million people from Myanmar have opted to work in Thailand. However, the global downturn has conspired to make their prospects even bleaker, with garment workers typically taking home about 70 baht ($2) a day, less than half the legal minimum wage in Thailand. The downturn was quick to hit Mae Sot's export-focused garment factories, where many Burmese workers are employed. Workers reported that production had dwindled and the value of their remittances was further eroded by the appreciation of the kyat, which had risen by a quarter against the baht over the previous year. Because of low levels of border trade, Myanmar traders bought less Thai currency, which later caused the price of the baht to decline.

The plight of migrant workers in Thailand is worsened by many of them being unregistered: the illegal status makes at least half of them vulnerable to exploitation by employers, frequent extortion by the police and periodic clampdowns. Migrant workers have been quietly encouraged, but no new registrations have been accepted by the Myanmar authorities since 2006. The impact of the slump on migrant labour may not be straightforward. Garment workers will doubtless continue to feel the pinch and suffer redundancy and lost income. But those working in dirty and dangerous jobs may still be in demand, even as prices and incomes fall, as cheap labour is rarely scorned in a downturn.[8]

Sometimes falling commodity prices were not attributable solely to the global financial crisis: government policy and actions have also had an impact. The price of leaf tea declined by about 40 per cent after a number of pickled-tea brands were banned from sale locally by the Myanmar government. In April 2009, the US Food and Drug Administration (FDA) banned forty-three brands of pickled tealeaves after discovering the chemical dye O Auramine — considered dangerous for human consumption — in packets of tea. The U.S. government ban reduced tea consumption, which led to a fall in the Myanmar price. The result of the decreased sales revenues from the sales of tea products has been severely felt by workers at tea plantations, where wages declined by 30 per cent.[9]

According to news reports,[10] Myanmar youth no longer hope to get employment abroad, but they try to find local employment. As a result, enrolment at training schools which could provide the necessary skills increased. Up until 2008, young people had tended to opt for courses, such as in tourism and the hospitality industry, which would be useful for working abroad. After 2009, however, their interests shifted back to employment in the local market.

In October 2008, the strong flow of computers and accessories through stock-clearing sales caused a remarkable decline in prices. However, in mid-June 2009 prices increased again in line with the change in the exchange rate and the price of imported goods — personal computers, laptop computers, mother boards and graphic cards. Generally, prices increased by between 5–7 per cent. Industry experts complained that producers controlled production and inventory, thus causing prices to jump. However, they estimated that there would be no change in demand for computers. Wholesalers are no longer practising cut-throat competition to attract customers. Rather, they are using post-purchase services to promote sales in the domestic market.[11]

Each year, on 29 July thousands of people gather at a site near Mandalay for one of Burma's most popular festivals, the week-long Taung Pyone Pwe, a celebration of the ancient belief in *nats*, inhabitants of the spirit world, which many believe have the power to grant them good luck, health and wealth. Many make the pilgrimage to Taung Pyone to give thanks for good fortune. A typical three-day excursion from Rangoon costs 35,000 kyat (US$35). In 2009, tour companies reported a drop in interest by half, which they attributed to Burma's economic difficulties and the slowing economy.[12]

MYANMAR'S RESPONSE TO THE IMPACT OF THE GLOBAL FINANCIAL CRISIS

Myanmar's military leaders pride themselves on their ability to keep outside influences at bay. Thus, in December 2008 Prime Minister General Thein Sein was widely reported as saying that Myanmar would not be affected by the global financial crisis and that workers returning from neighbouring countries could be employed in the cyclone-devastated rice fields of the Irrawaddy Delta and in the rubber plantations in other areas.[13] However, on the ground, no returnees have joined the rice fields and rubber plantations.[14]

The Ministry of Commerce announced a series of measures to mitigate the potential impact of the crisis.[15] Firstly, it encouraged expansion of market share through finding new and potential markets and attempts are being made to access end-user markets directly, without going through a third country. Quality improvements, standardization, and waste control, better packaging, storage facilities and the development of post-harvest technologies were among other measures mentioned as means of improving value and gaining market share.

When applying for export licenses, current prices need to be specified. Adjustments, which used to be made fortnightly, are now made on a weekly basis to be consistent with changing international markets and to facilitate trade.

Inputs for the agriculture sector, such as fertilizer and insecticide, could be imported easily to encourage and support farmers. Red tape was to be reduced to ease the import of raw materials for small and medium-sized domestic industry and to encourage employment. The smooth flow of capital and commodities would be maintained, the ministry announced.

During the crisis, expenditure on unnecessary and luxury items would be controlled.

Trade — sea-borne and cross-border — was to be promoted; research teams and information networks were to be established. Trading associations, commodity exchanges and traders were advised to join hands with the public sector in the broader interest of people.

Such measures seemed designed to solve long-term structural issues and cannot expect immediate results.

The government seemed to be trying to utilize resources from the private sector in economic and social-sector development. It has instructed twenty-five companies to disburse agricultural loans to farmers. Businessmen dealing in rice have been asked to provide agricultural loans of 50,000 to 100,000 kyat (approximately US$50) per acre to farmers in the Irrawaddy and Pegu Divisions at two per cent interest rates per month. The loans are to cover production costs and provide technology and farm implements to rice producers. Htoo Trading Company will invest three billion kyat in the business. Local businessmen from Bogale invested two billion kyat. Gold Delta Company invested ten billion kyat and will provide loans of 100,000 kyat per acre to the farmers in about 500 villages.[16] Even private-sector funding of certain high-profile sporting activities seemed to be timed and designed to underpin economic activity. Thus, Yangon United FC spent over 500 million kyat (approximately US$450,000) on the club for the recently established Myanmar National League (MNL) soccer tournament.

In an effort to legalize citizens working illegally in Thailand, the Burmese government has opened "citizen identification centres" at three immigration checkpoints along the Thai border, at Ranong, Chiang Rai's Mae Sai District, and Mae Sot District in Tak province.[17]

Thai employers had until 30 July 2009 to register their intent to hire Burmese workers at local employment offices. Those whose citizenship is confirmed by Burma will then be issued with a "worker's passport" which enables them enter the country legally after getting a 2,000-baht "work visa" stamped at the Thai border. These visas would allow them to work for up to two years. Citizenship verification has long been a stumbling block in getting workers properly registered. Unofficial estimates of the number of Burmese working in Thailand surpassed the one million mark in the year 2000 and have now reached 1.2 million. The Thai Deputy Minister for Foreign Affairs hoped that by this arrangement all parties — both governments, the workers and their employers — stand to benefit.[18]

At another level, the authorities sought to encourage confidence in the currency and underwrote credit for some public services. The Central Bank of Myanmar announced that it was making arrangements to replace some old and worn banknotes that are no longer suitable to be kept in circulation. The central bank also provided small change to the All Bus Lines Supervisory Committee and Market Departments of the municipal authorities of Naypyitaw, Yangon and Mandalay on a weekly basis.

Official measures for improving electricity supplies, another key indicator, had mixed results. The supply of electricity for daily household consumption in Yangon Division increased to some extent in mid-July 2009. All households had power from 11pm to 5am, with electricity shared among three households for other periods. Meanwhile, industrial zones receive nine hours' supply daily during the day, but could not operate around the clock. Hospitals, police forces, and gas stations usually have constant supply of energy. Improvements in electricity supply were achieved by buying energy from China-Myanmar Joint Venture Shweli River electricity production, as generators using natural gas are still under repair.[19]

CONCLUSION

Usually academics in Myanmar refer to the country indirectly when they make comments which could displease authorities. For example,

Dr U Myint has referred to Myanmar as one of the Bottom Billion least-developed countries.[20] Bottom Billion countries like us think that, because we have few dealings with the United States and the outside world, have no stock market, rudimentary banking, no multinationals and a low-level economy, we are immune to the global financial crisis. Indeed, official statistics give no indication of there being any economic problems in the country. But, globalization affects all such countries. The unofficial, underground economy plays a dominant part in these countries.[21] In any event, the credibility of official statistics is always being called into question.[22]

We believed that, as underdeveloped countries, financial disease could be kept out by taking "administrative measures" — closing border trade, cancelling import and export licenses, arresting foreign-exchange dealers. However, we are not in an isolation ward. No border can be totally closed. Official statistics deal with the formal or official economy, but the majority of people live in the informal economy which, since it is linked with the outside world, can be devastated by a global financial crisis.

Moreover, the large human costs borne by young people and poor families can never be quantified and reflected in official statistics. With an undiversified economic structure, poor infrastructure, insufficient foreign reserves, and limited administrative capability, we do not have any shock absorbers, or resilience or the capacity to cope with any type of economic disturbance. And when the crunch comes, the burden falls heaviest on the poor and the masses on the lowest rung of society.

As Professor Suiwah Leung warned at the 2009 Myanmar/Burma Update Conference in Canberra, Australia, when the world economy emerges from this recession, Myanmar will be further behind in the competitiveness stakes than it was before the crisis.[23]

Notes

1. See, for example, Economist Intelligent Unit (2009).
2. However, in his September 2009 General Assembly address, Prime Minister Thein Sein stated: "The global financial and economic crisis and the climate change crisis have compounded the problems we face in the last few years".
3. See Sean Turnell's article "Myanmar's banking crisis" in *ASEAN Economic Bulletin*, December 2003.
4. See *The Irrawaddy News*, 8 January 2009.
5. See *Mizzima News*, 18 November 2008; *Modern News*, 26 December 2008.

6. See *Myanmar Times*, 19 March 2009.
7. *Myanmar Times*, 4 March 2009.
8. *The Economist*, 19 March 2009.
9. *Myanmar Times*, 4 March 2009.
10. This was reported in journals such as *Weekly Eleven News* at that time in 2009.
11. *Myanmar Times*, 3 June 2009.
12. See *The Irrawaddy News*, 29 July 2009; *Mizzima News*, 29 July 2009.
13. See Myanmar News Agency 2008. However, when the Prime Minster spoke at the 64th United National General Assembly on 28 September 2009, he said: "The global and financial crisis and the climate change crisis have compounded the problems we face in the last few years."
14. *The Irrawaddy News*, 7 December 2008.
15. See Myanmar Ministry of Commerce 2008.
16. *Mizzima News*, 22 July 2009.
17. *Phuket Gazette*, 14 July 2009.
18. Ibid.
19. *Mizzima News*, 28 July 2009.
20. Myint (2009).
21. For an explanation of the role of the informal economy, see Mya Than and Myat Thein (2007).
22. See Steinberg (2001), p. xxxiii, for example.
23. Remarks by Professor Suiwah Leung, Crawford School of Economics and Government, Australian National University, at the Myanmar/Burma Update Conference, Canberra, 17 August 2009.

References

Economist Intelligence Unit. *Country Report Burma*, 19 March 2009.

Kyaw Ye Min. "We are not perturbed". *New Light of Myanmar,* 17–18 December 2008.

Mya Than and Myat Thein. "Transitional Economy of Myanmar: Present Status, Developmental Divide, and Future Prospects". *ASEAN Economic Bulletin* 24, no. 1 (2007): 98–118. Retrieved 21 December 2009 from ABI/INFORM Global. (Document ID:1382667751).

Myanmar Central Statistics Organization. *Selected Monthly Indicators*. <http://www.csostat.gov.mm/csomonthly.asp>.

———. *Statistical Yearbook 2007*. <http://www.csostat.gov.mm/csocd.asp>.

Myanmar Ministry of Commerce. *Commerce Journal* 8, no. 48 (5 November 2008).

Myanmar News Agency. "State aims to build up industrial nation based on agricultural sector". *New Light of Myanmar*, 2 December 2008.

Myint, U. "The US Dollar, the IMF and the Global Financial Crisis". *The World Economic Journal* Anniversary presentation, 1 August 2009.

Steinberg, David. *Burma: the State of Myanmar*. Washington, D.C.: Georgetown University Press, 2001.

Thein Sein. Statement at the 64th UN General Assembly. 28 September 2009. Available at <myanmargeneva.org/statement&speech>.

Ye Lwin. "Financial crisis will have impact: Business community". *Myanmar Times* 23, no. 446, 14–30 November 2008.

8

RECAPITALIZING BURMA'S RURAL CREDIT SYSTEM

Sean Turnell

INTRODUCTION

Burma Is in Economic Crisis

For long-time observers of the country a statement such as the above would hardly come as a surprise. Indeed, it would be regarded as little more than commonplace, and just one of the given "facts" about Burma to be absorbed as background on the way to focusing upon other things.

But Burma's economy in 2009 and 2010 is not just the serial underperformer and outlier in a region that, despite its ups and downs, is otherwise a poster-child of purpose-driven economic development. Burma's economy in 2009 and 2010 is also not one that, notwithstanding decades of extraordinary mismanagement at the hands of its military leaders, is any longer able to rely upon its abundant natural resources and alluvial dowry to protect its people from widespread food insecurity. Burma's economy in 2009 is in extremis.

There are many causes of Burma's economic crisis, most of which have a common root in the incompetence and wilful indifference of the country's policymakers. Natural disasters and global crises exacerbate Burma's economic problems, yet they are but injuries to a body rotting from the inside. Failure to acknowledge this central fact would be to misdiagnose Burma's problems and, in a sympathetic search for remedy, risk exacerbating a situation already at the verge of the intractable.

Arguably looming above all of Burma's economic problems, however, is a chronic lack of financial capital. This deficiency is apparent at all levels and sectors of Burma's economy, but is at its most critical in agriculture and in rural areas generally — the source from which most of Burma's population attempt to derive their livelihoods. Burma's agriculture sector is now almost devoid of new and affordable credit, while the cash economy is collapsing under the weight of the chronic indebtedness of the cultivator, and the absence of wage employment. This situation is most apparent in those areas of Burma that were devastated by Cyclone Nargis in 2008, but it is likewise perceptible just about everywhere else in the country.

The purpose of this chapter is to review the recent evidence as to the credit and capital crisis in rural Burma, and to suggest ways forward. Such suggestions are not, in terms of the institutions and methods outlined, technically difficult. Nevertheless, they do involve a loosening of the stranglehold that Burma's current government attempts to exert over the economy. In this context any "liberalizing" proposals might be rejected by the same government (as have foundered such efforts in the past) but, if so, a chance provided by necessity, responsibility *and* opportunity (seldom has the international community been so primed for genuine initiatives out of Burma) will be missed.

The argument thus outlined proceeds in the chapter as follows. First, we attempt to paint the picture of Burma's credit and capital drought. This begins with an account of the post-Nargis situation, but we emphasize that while the damage wrought by the cyclone placed great stress on existing credit sources and infrastructure, the more lasting impact of the disaster in this context was to expose (rather than cause) a situation that was already dire. We then examine the existing institutions that are meant to provide agricultural and rural finance in Burma. The focus is on the Myanma Agricultural Development Bank (MADB), the institution that is the Burmese government's exclusive rural-credit instrument but which provides only a fraction of the needs of those engaged in rural livelihoods, as well as some microfinance institutions that are already in place. In the following section, we present the potential for hope — the new institutions that might be created, and the existing ones that might be reinvigorated. Arguing that it is in this arena that Burma's (gas-derived) cash reserves and foreign-aid windfalls can be best employed, we also emphasize methodological and technological innovation in bringing about real change.

Nargis: Destruction and Revelation

In May 2008, Cyclone Nargis struck lower Burma. Blighting much of the country's most-productive land in the Irrawaddy Delta, the cyclone killed an estimated 140,000 people, made homeless 800,000 more, and caused severe hardship for a third of the region's roughly 7.5 million inhabitants (Post-Nargis Recovery and Preparedness Plan [PONREPP], p. 3).[1] In its economic dimension, this hardship was manifested above all in a sudden and devastating shock to incomes, with surveys taken in the first few months after Nargis revealing that the poor (the vast majority) in affected areas "had suffered a drop in purchasing power to about half the pre-cyclone level" (PONREPP, p. 5). Much has been made of a post-Nargis recovery in paddy and food production in Burma (largely via the expansion of production in non-affected areas, and good climatic conditions in 2009), but the loss of income is not without relevance in the emerging consensus that Burma is presently facing chronic food insecurity — simply, because it matters little what happens to a country's aggregate food production if the population has no money to buy it.[2]

The human and physical destruction of Nargis understandably, and appropriately, captured the attention of much of the world. Less in focus were the institutional failures and shortcomings revealed in the cyclone's aftermath. Prominent amongst these has been the near-complete failure to provide the financial resources necessary for reconstruction, both of physical infrastructure, and that required for the rehabilitation of livelihoods. Amongst the early accounts, that of the Post-Nargis Joint Assessment taskforce (PONJA) set the trend of those that would follow in reporting (in June 2008) that some 78 per cent of households in cyclone-affected regions had "no access to credit".[3] Other reports told of the collapse of the traditional "informal" credit networks via which farmers paid advances to agricultural labourers in kind (mostly baskets of rice), but which were now no longer functioning because of the destruction of stored rice.[4] Another traditional savings mechanism, the accumulation of wealth in the form of livestock that could be sold in a crisis, was likewise rendered ineffective when so many animals were killed in the cyclone. Overall, according to PONREPP

(2009, p. 29), "80 per cent of those surveyed indicated that the *greatest* obstacle to rebuilding is a lack of money" (emphasis added).

BEYOND NARGIS: ONE YEAR ON

More than a year on from Cyclone Nargis, and Burma's rural credit system has essentially ceased to function. Even that credit traditionally available to cultivators from moneylenders, at (scarcely economically sustainable) interest rates of between 10 to 20 per cent *per month,* is unavailable in many parts of the country. According to testimonies of cultivators recorded by Dapice et al. (2009, p. 4), "cash had disappeared" from rural Burma, and "almost all farmers...[have] little if any paddy left over for home consumption right after harvest because they had to sell everything at harvest time". They do this to pay back (past) debt, and only after they have done so are many cultivators able to purchase their own food stocks — usually lower-quality rice than that grown by themselves. PONREPP (2008, p. 15) likewise noted the phenomenon: "[P]eople have not adequately regained their livelihoods and many face a debt trap ... interest rates are 5–25 per cent per month and now credit is very scarce."

Of course, Burma's rural financial system was dysfunctional well before Cyclone Nargis. A sector that provides over 70 per cent of employment in Burma and around 50 per cent of GDP, agriculture receives between 1 and 3 per cent of Burma's formal credit (FAO 2004, p. 215). Burma's rural-finance arrangements suffer from broad official neglect, a weak policy environment, an inappropriate regulatory structure, a lack of institutional capacities, and a dearth of formal expertise. Political interference in the regulatory structure of Burma's rural-finance system is particularly damaging, amongst the most egregious examples of which is the (truly bizarre) prohibition of commercial banks from lending for agricultural purposes. Other unhelpful government interventions include government-imposed interest-rate caps on all lenders (which, under Section 61 of the *Central Bank of Myanmar* [CBM] *Law* [1990], currently places a 17 per cent ceiling on the interest rates that banks can charge — against an inflation rate that is habitually above this), and the perennial issue of the inability of farmers to fully use their land as loan collateral.[5] PONJA acknowledged (2008, p. 138) the problems of politics in the provision of rural finance in Burma, noting also the pervasive corruption that channelled what little funds were available towards larger farmers with "connections".

The absence of affordable credit has also been a prominent cause of the decline in agricultural productivity in Burma, as fertiliser and other agricultural inputs have become unaffordable (FAO 2009, p. 26). As long ago as 2002 Aung Din Taylor (2002, p. 22) observed:

> [F]armers are using less and less fertiliser, families are abandoning farming and becoming landless, yields of key crops like paddy and sesame are declining and rice prices are rising ... more children are dropping out of school, large numbers of people appear to be criss-crossing the country in search of paid work, and farm families are going hungry.

Seven years later, surveys conducted by a team of economists and agricultural experts from Harvard University's Kennedy School (Dapice et al. 2009, p. 8), reveal a scenario that has only got more desperate:

> [I]t is our opinion that crop output will fall significantly unless much more credit becomes available and crop prices improve markedly. With the prospect of less intensive farming and fertilizer applications falling ... a significant reduction in paddy production is all but certain...
>
> [From this will come]... a slow motion humanitarian crisis that would become visible only if civil disorder rose as hungry parents stole food or money to feed themselves and their children.[6]

EXISTING INSTITUTIONS PROVIDING RURAL CREDIT

The Myanma Agricultural Development Bank (MADB)

The state-owned Myanma Agricultural Development Bank (MADB) is supposed to be the sole provider of rural credit in Burma, but its own modest objective of providing finance to meet just 30 per cent of a cultivator's production costs signifies internal recognition of its severe limitations. In practice the MADB falls well short of achieving even this modest target. Maximum loans to paddy cultivators (80 per cent of all MADB lending is to such farmers) is currently (2009) capped at K8,000 (US$7.20) per acre of paddy, against cultivation costs of the same crop of between K130,000 to K180,000 (US$118 to US$164) (Dapice et al. 2009, p. 13). The (minimum) 93 per cent financing "gap" is met via recourse to the moneylender — and, as we have seen, by simply going without.

A significant reason for the MADB's parsimony is that the bank itself is desperately short of funds — indeed, it has been effectively "decapitalizing" over recent years. As its primary source of funds, the

MADB claims to have two million depositors, but in truth it attracts little in the way of actual deposits (a mere K4.6 billion (US$3.7 million) in 2004) (FAO 2004, p. 25). Deposits in the MADB are inhibited by many of the same restrictions imposed on other banks in Burma, including those on the interest rates the Bank can pay. But in addition to this, and even more damaging, has been a policy in place since 2003 that greatly restricts the ability of depositors to withdraw their money (FAO 2004, p. 2).[7] In the wake of this, the only remaining matter of wonder is that the MADB attracts any deposits at all.

In 2004 (the latest year for which we have such data) the MADB's capital stood at just K1.2 billion (little more than US$1 million), an extraordinarily small financial platform upon which to pursue the functions of a countrywide bank with over 200 branches and engaged in a form of lending with strong covariant risks.[8] The MADB desperately needs an injection of capital, but the only recent policy in this direction is a most destructive order that compels the Bank to pay the government a dividend of 25 per cent of its annual profits. Alas, such profits that might be claimed by the MADB are almost certainly fictitious. Since 1991 the Bank has been forbidden from writing off bad and doubtful debts, and as a consequence it claims a repayment rate of 100 per cent (FAO 2004, p. 10). This fanciful figure may be compared to an annual provision against bad debts by Thailand's analogous Bank for Agriculture and Agricultural Cooperatives of around 15 per cent of its portfolio.[9] Restating the MADB's "earnings" to include any reasonable estimate of loan losses would eliminate any supposed profits, diminishing the Bank's capital even before the extraction of the government's dividend.

The Financial Sector is Broadly Dysfunctional

In Burma's present-day economic dystopia the MADB is not alone in its woes, and it sits amidst a financial system that is more broadly dysfunctional — especially, and critically, in channelling funds to genuinely productive private enterprise. With little access to foreign capital, and in the absence of functioning financial markets, formal finance for private enterprise in Burma is limited to that made available by the country's commercial banks. Here too, however, the circumstances are dire. Bank lending in Burma has recovered *somewhat* since a banking crisis tore through the sector in 2003, but it remains pitifully meagre.[10] In 2007, total funds lent by the banks were less than a quarter of those provided by the central bank to the state. Of course, as can be seen from the data in Table 8.1, a substantial component of commercial bank lending itself (nearly 50 per cent of the funds they provide to the private sector) also made its way to the government. Burma's banking sector, in short, scarcely performs the intermediation function that practice and history tells us is necessary for a country's economic development.

TABLE 8.1
State/Private Share of Burma's Financial Resources. Selected Indicators
(*kyat* millions)

Year	Central Bank Leading to Government	Commercial Bank Leading to Government	Commercial Bank Leading to Private Sector
1999	331,425	12,460	188,149
2000	447,581	36,159	266,466
2001	675,040	40,985	416,176
2002	892,581	43,248	608,401
2003	1,262,588	35,546	341,547
2004	1,686,341	89,217	428,391
2005	2,165,154	100,358	570,924
2006	2,762,626	186,998	652,892
2007	3,534,687	389,398	795,227
2008*	3,880,765	620,875	907,177

*As at end-December.
Source: International Monetary Fund, *International Financial Statistics* (Washington, D.C., June 2009).

Microfinance

Though they are little known to outsiders, Burma already fields substantial microfinance operations. Most of these are small schemes linked to various international and (some) domestic NGOs, and function as little more than charities.[11] Of more interest in the development of Burma's financial sector, however, are three large schemes (one each in the Irrawaddy Delta, in Burma's "Dry Zone", and in Shan State) operated by the US NGO "PACT" on behalf of the United Nations Development

Programme (UNDP). In addition to their substantial size (they are large even by global standards), these three schemes are relatively close to being financially self-sufficient, and offer a useful platform from which much could grow. Under Burma's current regime, however, the UNDP/PACT microfinance schemes are greatly inhibited in a number of ways, but especially by their lack of legal status — which, amongst other things, leave them vulnerable to state expropriation.[12]

The UNDP/PACT microfinance schemes currently operate in 22 townships and around 3,600 villages. Current clients number around 300,000 households, and the number of loans disbursed since the project started is in excess of 307,000, and to a total value of around US$10 million. The average loan size is US$32 and the average cost of making a loan is US$11. This high cost-to-loan ratio partially explains the high interest rates charged by the schemes. Meanwhile, the tiny size of the loans is indicative of Burma's grinding poverty.[13] Divided according to the three areas in which they are located, effective annual interest rates charged are 38.5 per cent in the Irrawaddy Delta, 43 per cent in the Dry Zone, and 45 per cent in Shan State (UNDP 2007b, p. 11).

Burma's UNDP/PACT microfinance schemes are Grameen Bank "replications". As such, loans (which are more or less exclusively made to women) are granted to borrowers in groups of five, and according to a 2:2:1 staggering (first two get a loan, next two group members follow after the first have successfully repaid) in order to capture the collateral-substituting properties of both peer pressure and progressive lending.[14] Other methodologies of the original Grameen Bank model are also employed, including restrictions on loan use (mostly in favour of income-generating activity), compulsory weekly group meetings of borrowers, weekly repayments, certain behavioural pledges, and devices designed to build social solidarity. Some of these methodologies have a degree of inflexibility about them which makes them largely unsuitable (for instance) for crop lending. At the Grameen Bank (in Bangladesh) itself, as well as at a selection of its replications elsewhere, many of the original methodologies have been abandoned in favour of a more flexible approach that is widely known as "Grameen II".[15]

The UNDP/PACT schemes continue to employ the older Grameen approach but, in an effort to better meet the needs of their clients, they offer a range of loan types beyond that of the standard loan (or "Main" loan in Grameen terminology). These include loans designed for microenterprises, for education, for health care, as well as seasonal agricultural loans. Such efforts have yielded only limited success thus far, however, and it is only in the Dry Zone scheme that seasonal agricultural loans have assumed any significance (20 per cent of loans there, but less than 1 per cent of the loan portfolios of the Delta and Shan State schemes). Similarly, micro-enterprise and education loans each comprise around 2 per cent of the Dry Zone scheme's loans, and less than 1 per cent of the others (UNDP 2006, p. 79). If and when the considerable legal and other obstacles on microfinance in Burma are alleviated (more below), the UNDP/PACT schemes should move further along the lines ventured above in introducing flexibility into their loan products. Above all, perhaps, existing loan-use restrictions should be abandoned. Money is highly "fungible", and it will be diverted regardless of whatever formalities might apply to its use, according to the priorities of borrowers. Recognizing this ineradicable fact will not undermine prudent lending, but it will promote honesty and openness between borrower and lender. The UNDP/PACT schemes should likewise consider making greater use of non-traditional collateral — that is, collateral pledged as security against a loan that may have very little market value (the conventional measure of its value), but which has great value to its owner, and who would thus be discomforted by its loss (basic tools are an example of such collateral). The use of non-traditional collateral, which has been successfully employed by a number of microfinance schemes around the world, is founded upon a true understanding of the real importance of collateral — which is not in its resale value upon foreclosure, but the discipline it provides against borrower malfeasance.[16] To the extent that it provides this, and helps signal borrower intent accordingly, potential benefits accrue to both lender (greater assurance of repayment) and borrower (loans so secured enjoy a lower risk premium, and thus a lower interest charge).

The UNDP/PACT microfinance schemes do not engage in savings mobilization beyond the "compulsory saving" of the original Grameen model, and so savings constitute only around 20 per cent of outstanding loans (UNDP 2006, p. 89). This lack of a savings emphasis is due to a number of factors, but not least because of a Memorandum of Understanding (MOU) made between UNDP/PACT and the Burmese government to not accept regular deposits — and so to escape Article 61 of the CBM Law regarding interest-rate ceilings. This is unfortunate, however, since savings facilities (the "forgotten half of rural finance" in the redolent phrase of Vogel 1984) are often more valued by microfinance clients than credit products. Allen (2007, p. 56) highlights in this context the aversion to risk of the poor (and especially poor farmers), and "the preference of the poor to work with their assets rather than assume liabilities". As with credit, savings allow for consumption smoothing, for small-scale investment, and to meet the various expenses associated with important social and cultural events (including births, deaths and marriages) — albeit without incurring debt. Likewise, the possession of savings allows for a potential solution to that problem (above) of cultivators in Burma needing to sell their production immediately at harvest (at less than optimal prices), because of their urgent need for cash. Like the poor everywhere, moreover, and contrary to the traditional scepticism, the poor in Burma do save — whatever and whenever they can. Such saving does not take place in financial institutions, but in stored commodities, foodstuffs, precious metals, precious stones, livestock, and so on. Of course, such "wealth" storage is accordingly vulnerable to theft, natural disasters (as Nargis amply demonstrated) and other depredations.

In the case of the UNDP/PACT microfinance operations, savings might also hold the key to their ultimate financial self-sustainability. At present none of the three regional schemes (Delta, Dry Zone, Shan State) are financially self-sufficient, with ratios of operating income to (inflation-adjusted) operating expenses in 2006 of 81 per cent, 88 per cent and 73 per cent respectively (UNDP 2006, p. 86). However, these numbers are unduly flattering, since they do not include the cost of technical assistance provided by PACT staff or those of UNDP itself. The end result, in short, is that the UNDP/PACT microfinance schemes remain dependent on their funders — and, accordingly, the whims of multilateral agencies and the aid community. The mobilization of savings offers an alternative to such dependence, as well as being a valuable financial service in its own right.

The MOUs signed by the UNDP/PACT schemes impose other restrictions on their operations — including the areas they can operate in, the products they can offer, the interest rates they can charge (which, as can be seen above, are far in excess of those legally sanctioned under the CBM Law), as well as the number of foreign staff they can employ (currently limited to two persons only). According to the FAO these specific restrictions, and Burma's political climate generally, creates a context in which microfinance operations are "legally uncertain ... lack adequate flexibility, and their growth is unnecessarily constrained" (FAO 2004, p. 216).

In the light of assessments such as these, the UNDP sought to remedy the legal ambiguity of its MFIs in numerous negotiations with the Burmese government. These came to nought until, unexpectedly, Burma's Ministry of Cooperatives suddenly announced in 2005 that it was "drafting legislation to frame the microfinance sector" (UNDP 2005, p. 21). In a fitting illustration of the care needed in Burma in dealing with officialdom, this announcement alarmed the UNDP and other interested parties. The legislation produced by the Ministry (which was not made public) fell well short of international norms and standards and, much worse, included machinery that could be used to transfer control of all MFIs to the government and/or local NGOs.[17] To all of this the UNDP had few ready answers. Its 2005 assessment mission plaintively called upon the "international community" to provide "as a matter of urgency" technical assistance to the Ministry of Cooperatives to come up with a better law — otherwise, it noted, it was "not clear what options are available" (UNDP 2005, p. 27). Little progress or movement followed, and in 2007 the latest of the UNDP "independent assessment missions" called for "dialogue" on "legal framework and institutional strategy" for microfinance in Burma (UNDP 2007b, p. 7). Finally, in 2008 the UNDP gave up, directing its Rangoon office to cease "pursuing the creation of a legal framework", adopting the "fig-leaf" that it had discovered that such a quest "was not within [the schemes] mandate".[18]

The UNDP/PACT microfinance schemes were greatly disrupted by Cyclone Nargis. The scheme centred in the Irrawaddy Delta lost five of its staff and many hundreds of its clients. In the wake of the cyclone, PACT returned some client savings, made grants, provided other in-kind assistance, and declared a moratorium on loans made in affected areas.[19]

NEW INSTITUTIONS AND WAYS FORWARD

As noted throughout these pages, Burma's agricultural sector is in desperate need of new financial capital. Moreover, given the long-term nature of the problem, it is necessary that any solution be similarly long term in focus. All of this means, in turn, that what is necessary in Burma is not on-again off-again cycles of donor-directed aid, but the creation of sustainable financial institutions that respond to the needs and preferences of their clients.

The sums required to create such institutions will be vast. Burma's Ministry of Agriculture and Irrigation put rural credit needs for post-Nargis reconstruction alone at between US$121.5 and US$243 million.[20] Significantly, David Dapice and the team from Harvard's Kennedy School estimated (in the wake of their 2009 surveys) that around US$1 billion would be necessary to recapitalize Burma's agricultural sector as a whole (Dapice et al. 2009, p. 14). Of course, such a number does not represent a permanent cost to the budget since, at reasonable interest rates, the loans generated will eventually be repaid. Where to source the funds to finance such a recapitalization? According to the Harvard team: "Capital could be provided out of Myanmar's foreign exchange reserves or borrowed on international markets against oil and gas revenues." (Dapice et al. 2009, p. 14)

At present, Burma earns gas revenues sufficient to meet a US$1 billion recapitalization target *every six months*.[21] The financial wherewithal to dramatically transform Burma's rural credit system, in short, is not in doubt. What *is* in doubt (perhaps intractably so, given the nature of Burma's political circumstances), is whether the current ruling regime has the *will* to make such funds available.[22]

The author of this paper is in firm agreement that the recapitalization of Burma's rural sector would represent the best possible use of the substantial foreign reserves Burma has built up (and will continue to accumulate) via its exports of natural gas. As argued elsewhere (Turnell 2008; Turnell, Bradford and Vicary 2009), an extra urgency here moreover is the fact that presently these foreign-exchange earnings are fuelling something of a "resources curse" in Burma — the windfalls allowing the state to spend on an ever-growing list of grandiose "national prestige" projects, and in other destructive ways.[23]

In practice, we argue that the recapitalization of Burma's rural financial system can be best achieved through a two-way use of the country's windfall gas revenues:

1. The dramatic expansion of microfinance in Burma from the base of the existing PACT/UNDP schemes, financed through a wholesale microfinance-funding vehicle which can also double as an apex institution to the schemes it finances.
2. The recapitalization of the MADB, and its eventual transformation into an institution that (at best) functions along the lines of Bank Rakyat Indonesia (BRI, especially its path-breaking "*unit desas*"

system), or (at least) of Thailand's Bank of Agriculture and Agricultural Cooperatives.

Expansion of Microfinance

PONREPP makes much of the possibilities of an expanded role for microfinance in Burma, though its vision in this context is relatively modest. PONREPP calls (2008, p. 74) for the expansion of the PACT/UNDP schemes by 120,000 new clients by the end of 2012, funded via an extra allocation of US$12.2 million across the same period. Such an amount is reasonably significant against existing funding arrangements, but it is a drop in the bucket against the obvious needs.

We advocate the creation of a wholesale funding vehicle/apex institution to facilitate the expansion of microfinance in Burma — both in channelling funds and in the creation (and subsequent supervision) of new individual schemes. In this context, lessons can be learnt from the Microfinance Investment Support Facility for Afghanistan Ltd (MISFA) as an example of what works in very challenging circumstances — as well as the microfinance-linked banking institutions of the sort explored below.[24]

Beyond a capital expansion, however, are other changes that need to be made to the existing UNDP/PACT schemes. Paramount is the clarification of their legal status, but following close behind is the need to make the schemes financially self-sustaining. As noted, presently the UNDP/PACT schemes are not financially self-sufficient. Burma's high inflation rates are one of the prime causes of this, and the country's macroeconomic volatility is not something that can be simply remedied by (even) a well-managed MFI. That said, the mobilization of savings through well-crafted saving and deposit products is largely within the powers of such an institution, and should be the focus in the future of the UNDP/PACT schemes.[25] Analysis of the performance of microfinance in Indonesia (and consistent everywhere else), is that the greater a microfinance institution's ratio of savings deposits to its lending, "the better its performance is likely to be in terms of default rates, growth and profitability" (Henley 2009, p. 184).

But microfinance, whilst being useful in poverty alleviation in Burma, will not provide a sufficient base upon which a genuinely transformative financial system can be built. On its own, microfinance does not provide the aggregation of capital necessary for broad-based economic development. Its methodology, though well-suited to supporting petty trading of infinite varieties, is not readily adaptable to the provision of larger, and generally longer-term, capital needed by industrial enterprise. Nor is it especially well-suited to the highly variable credit needs of cultivators. For these and other reasons, Burma needs to develop large-scale financial institutions, run on commercial lines, that history demonstrates are necessary to support economic development.

Recapitalize and Reform the MADB

Dapice et al. (2009, p. 12) call for the reinvigoration of the MADB. Not, one suspects, because of any great confidence they might entertain in the Bank's existing capacities or efficiency, but for its widespread branch network, a degree a familiarity with it from farmers, and because it was "likely that its staff are reasonably well-informed about local conditions".

We are less sanguine about the "reformability" of the MADB, but we recognize that microfinance will not be enough. We also acknowledge that, amidst the present circumstances in global finance, a broad agricultural lender offering both savings services as well as long-term credit at the scale required will probably necessitate at least a high degree of state ownership. Nevertheless, state *direction* of such a lender must be minimized. A silver lining perhaps of the global financial crisis is that there are now many models of state-owned but commercially focused financial institutions — that in some circumstances may serve as a model.

Above all, a reconstituted MADB must be financially self-sustainable. In order to do this, it must be allowed to set its own interest rates. Dapice et al. (2009, p. 13) suggest that: "[A]n interest rate of 5 per cent [per month] would be sufficient to ensure the program's viability. Farmers, who are used to paying 10–15 per cent per month, responded enthusiastically to the prospect of 5 per cent credit, which is typically only available to borrowers with gold collateral."

While Dapice et al.'s interest-rate suggestion appears high by "normal" global standards, Burma's own economic and financial history would support their broad assumption that such a rate would still allow profitable cultivation and rural enterprise.[26] Longer term, and with a genuinely reforming government pursuing prudent economic and monetary policies, interest rates in Burma should fall to levels that better approximate those of other developing countries in the region.

With interest-rate ceilings removed, the opportunity then might open to turn the MADB into a financially self-sustainable institution that is oriented to the product and service demands of its clientele, rather than the "directed-lending" model that has been in place more or less since the advent of military rule in 1962. In this, what might be envisaged is a return to an institution not unlike Burma's old State Agricultural Bank (SAB). The SAB, which was formed in 1953, was based on a network of village banks which were primarily funded centrally (savings mobilization in the village braches was, unfortunately, only moderately successful). Interestingly, the SAB employed lending methodologies (including a type of joint-liability or peer-group lending) that was not dissimilar to those employed by MFIs today. During its tenure in the days of Burmese democracy the SAB proved remarkably successful, with average loan repayment rates in excess of 95 per cent.[27]

Farmers are as much savers as borrowers, and savings are the best device for smoothing consumption (and investment) in the face of seasonal and other fluctuations in income. Given this, and the problems that microfinance in Burma has in aggregating savings (above), a reformed MADB must aim to be an especially safe and efficient savings vehicle. In this context there are many constructive models, but none would be better than Indonesia's (justly) famous Bank Rakyat Indonesia (BRI), and its *unit desa* (village bank units). This bank, established in 1969, was for the first twenty years or so of its existence simply a vehicle for the distribution of state-subsidized credit. As with such schemes everywhere, this collapsed amidst impossible debt arrears in 1987. Thereafter, however, the BRI was transformed — the *unit desa* into sustainability-focused providers of microfinance at commercial interest rates, and as the providers of savings facilities designed to fund all lending without subsidy. Total savings deposits in the BRI's *unit desa* were more than double the volume of loans by 2000, and the ratio of deposit to loan accounts was an extraordinary 10:1. The *unit desa* have also been profitable (and financially self-sufficient) for over twenty years, including (uniquely in Indonesia) through the Asian financial crisis of 1997–98 (Siebel 2005, p. 7). By the turn of the twentieth century, the *unit desa* of the BRI had become the largest fully financially self-sufficient "micro-banking" institution in the world (Henley and Goenka 2009, p. 5).[28]

Thailand's Bank of Agriculture and Agricultural Cooperatives (BAAC) is in many ways a less attractive model for a reformed MADB (especially following the pressures placed on the Bank after 2001, when the Thaksin government moved away from the pursuit of financial viability in its lending). Nevertheless, since a reform programme introduced in 1987, the

BAAC has been particularly successful as a savings depository. The Bank's ten million deposit-account holders fund over 80 per cent of its loan book, and the BAAC's extraordinary outreach is such that its 1,500 branches connect to 92 per cent of Thailand's rural households (Siebel 2007, p. 4).

Scale is important in banking — in taking advantage of new techniques and technologies, in providing diversification, in providing a range of financial services, in having liquidity depth, and in assembling expertise. Especially vital in the future on the technological front for a reformed MADB could be the exploitation of mobile telephony. The use of the mobile phone to provide banking services is emerging (especially, if unexpectedly, in Africa) as a genuinely revolutionary moment. Burma could especially draw upon the experiences of Safaricom in Kenya, G-cash in the Philippines, and those of many other emergent "telco-financial institutions" around the world.[29] Naturally, in the context of the MADB this would require a relaxation of Burma's draconian telecoms "laws" and restrictions, and a general liberalization of telecommunications. That such liberalization would in itself help spur economic development in Burma is just one of its fortunate externalities.[30]

A reformed MADB could itself become a wholesale finance provider to MFIs in order to broaden outreach combined with local knowledge. In this sense it could start to replicate the BRI's *unit desa* and, indeed, the village-bank approach of the old SAB.

Of course, some *immediate* reform steps will be required with respect to the MADB, and before the longer term "transformational" changes briefly noted above. The entire structure of MADB operations must be reviewed from top to bottom to get a true picture of the bank — beginning with its relationship to government. The MADB will require a genuine external audit to determine the quality or otherwise of its existing loan portfolio, of its loan classification and provisioning, of its true capital and liquidity positions, of all aspects of its internal culture (management quality, staff skills, incentives and morale, hiring practices, risk-management systems, lending policies), and internal governance generally (FAO 2004, p. 221).[31] Such steps are likely to be resisted by Burma's present government.

CONCLUSION

Recapitalizing Burma's rural-credit system would do much to alleviate the suffering and widespread food insecurity that is the present lot of much of the country's population. The funds to do so are available courtesy of Burma's growing role as a significant regional energy producer. These are currently being wasted by Burma's military government, but they could be used to construct the viable and economic development-enhancing financial institutions that internationally have achieved much. Burma's own history is similarly illustrative of the transformative power of a functioning rural-finance system. Reconstructing and recapitalizing Burma's rural finance system is urgently due.

Notes

1. The Post-Nargis Joint Assessment taskforce (PONJA) was established under the "Tripartite Core Group" comprising the representatives of Burma's government, ASEAN, and the UN and its agencies.
2. A similar point is noted in Dapice et al. (2009, p.8).
3. "Preliminary findings of post-Nargis joint assessment confirm need for continued relief assistance", 25 June 2008, press release, United Nations Office for the Coordination of Humanitarian Affairs. <http://www.reliefweb.int/rw/RWB.NSF/db900SID/AMMF-7FYBZL?OpenDocument> (accessed 31 July 2009).
4. Such in-kind credit (sabape loans in Burmese) has a long history in Burma. For more, see Turnell (2009).
5. For more on the many issues surrounding land-ownership in Burma, see Sein Htay and Hudson-Rodd (2008).
6. The results of the Harvard team's surveys are supported by those of the FAO (2009).
7. As at mid-2009 these restrictions remain in place.
8. Covariant risk in this context refers to the situation in which all borrowers face circumstances that may inhibit their ability to repay their loans. Agricultural lending is especially susceptible to covariant risk because seasonal factors tend to have an impact upon all borrowers simultaneously (FAO 2004, p. 5).
9. Bank for Agriculture and Agricultural Cooperatives, <http://www.baac.or.tha> (accessed 21 October 2009).
10. For a comprehensive analysis of Burma's 2003 financial crisis, see Turnell (2009), pp. 297–318.
11. For more on microfinance in Burma, its background, beginnings, and an account of the smaller as well as the larger schemes, see Turnell (2009), pp. 319–352.
12. For a full discussion of the implications of the lack of legal status of MFIs in Burma, see Turnell (2009), pp. 346–47.
13. The average size of a microfinance loan internationally is around US$150 (UNDP 2006, p. 80).

14. Around 95 per cent of loans made by the UNDP/PACT microfinance schemes are granted to women (UNDP 2006, p. 77).
15. For more on the methodology of Grameen II, and the emergent problems of the original Grameen approach that spurred its creation, see Collins et al. (2009), pp. 154–62.
16. For more on the use of non-traditional collateral, see Amend·riz de Aghion and Morduch (2005), pp.134–36.
17. A copy of the proposed Law was viewed by the author.
18. This directive is taken from an audit report of the UNDP/PACT schemes undertaken for the UNDP in 2008. The report, "Audit of the Project 'sustainable Microfinance to Improve the Livelihoods of the Poor' in Myanmar", can be found at <www.undp.org/execbrd/word/dp08-21_web per cent20annexes.doc> (accessed 31 October 2009). In truth, what the UNDP feared was that their advocacy was drawing the attention of Burmese government officials (hitherto ignorant of the MFIs), and who suddenly saw them as potential "cash cows". It should not go unrecorded that efforts to inhibit the UNDP/PACT MFIs by Burmese government officials, and/or to fleece them, have emerged on and off throughout their short history. The author is also aware of a number of occasions and situations in which the Burmese government has actively sought to sabotage the PACT/UNDP microfinance schemes — including encouraging rumours amongst their clients as to the schemes' financial soundness.
19. Altogether, nearly US$2 million in savings were returned to clients. Details of PACT's impressive response to Nargis can be found at <http://www.pactworld.org/cs/help_myanmar>, accessed 16 October 2009. PACT gave cash grants to nearly 30,000 households in Nargis-affected areas which, from July 2008, were primarily for the purposes of supporting livelihoods.
20. Brief on Preliminary Assessment of Damage on Agricultural Production Caused by Cyclone Nargis and Recovery Plan, prepared by the Ministry of Agriculture and Irrigation, 16 May 2008. The Burmese-language version of this report is at <http://www.mizzimaburmese.com/edop/songpa/1142-2008-05-20-11-51-47.html> (accessed 31 October 2009).
21. For an analysis of Burma's gas earnings, and the way they are currently wasted in the manner of a "resources curse", see Turnell, Bradford and Vicary (2009), pp. 645–46.
22. There must be a presumption that the present regime would not be so willing, given the lengths that they continue to go to in order to "hide" Burma's gas export earnings, and to keep them out of the country's public accounts. For more on this, and the way the subterfuge works via exchange-rate manipulation, see Turnell (2008).
23. These include the decision to create the new administrative capital of Naypyitaw, the entering into a contract with Russia to buy a nuclear reactor, the plan to

create a vast bio-fuel industry in Burma based on Jatropha, as well as some spectacular military pay increases — amidst, alas, a growing list.

24. MIFSA was created by the World Bank and its microfinance specialist affiliate — the Consultative Group to Assist the Poorest (CGAP) — in consultation with the Afghan government. MISFA is housed within Afghanistan's Ministry of Rural Rehabilitation and Development, and is funded by the World Bank's Afghanistan Reconstruction Trust Fund. MIFSA finances fifteen MFIs in Afghanistan which by July 2007 had nearly 400,000 clients, and had dispersed over 800,000 loans worth US$282 million. The MFIs operate throughout Afghanistan, including in conflict areas. Apart from raising and channelling funds for its MFIs, MIFSA serves as a source of advice and as a quasi-regulator. MIFSA is also the exclusive interlocutor with the many international donors that have provided funds specifically for microfinance. It has also helped keep politicians — from donor countries as well as those in Afghanistan — at arm's length from operational decisions. Five of MIFSA's subsidiary MFIs, representing over 85 per cent of clients, are already operationally self-sustaining. Details of MIFSA are drawn here from "CGAP, Building an Industry from Scratch: Donor Cooperation in Afghanistan", October 2007, available online at <http://cgap.org/portal/site/portfolio/Oct2007FAI/> (accessed 17 July 2009).
25. The author acknowledges that other challenges would be created by large-scale savings mobilization through MFIs — not least that such institutions should then be subject to appropriate prudential regulation. The likely emergence of a competent regulatory institution along these lines in present-day Burma must be considered as highly doubtful, and the record of the CBM in regulating the country's existing banks gives little room for comfort. Of course, a wholesale funding/apex institution could help somewhat in this context (its money will be at stake, after all), but such vehicles have a less-than-stellar record as quasi-regulators. As always, progress in this area may need to await more profound political and institutional change in Burma.
26. The interest rates charged to cultivators during Burma's emergence as the world's largest rice exporter were not too far away from those proposed by Dapice et al. For more on this, see Turnell (2009), pp. 40–48.
27. For more on the SAB, its model and methodologies, its performance in Burma's parliamentary-democracy years, as well as its destruction thereafter, see Turnell (2009), pp. 172–235.
28. In 2003, BRI accounted for an estimated 40 per cent of all loans granted by microfinance institutions around the world (Henley and Goenka 2009, p. 7).
29. For more on these developments, touched upon just briefly here, see Ivatury and Mas (2008) and McMurray (2009).
30. Through increasing the speed and volume of information flows, lowering cost

barriers to market entry, creating social networks and "social capital", and through the foreign investment such telecommunications infrastructure often attract. For more, see McMurray (2009).

31. Such reform programmes have been put in place in a number of countries, and for institutions similar to the MADB. For more on a recent experience in Mongolia, see Siebel (2007).

References

Allen, H. "Finance Begins with Savings, Not Loans". In *What's Wrong with Microfinance*, edited by T. Dichter and M. Harper. Warwickshire: Practical Action Publishing, 2007.

Amendáriz de Aghion, B. and J. Morduch. *The Economics of Microfinance*, Cambridge, MA: The MIT Press, 2005.

Aung Din Taylor, D. "Signs of Distress: Observations on Agriculture, Poverty, and the Environment in Myanmar". Conference on Burma: Reconciliation in Myanmar and the Crises of Change. Washington, D.C.: School of Advanced International Affairs, Johns Hopkins University, 22 November 2002.

Collins, D., J. Morduch, S. Rutherford, and O. Ruthven. *Portfolios of the Poor: How the World's Poor Live on $2 a Day*. Princeton: Princeton University Press, 2009.

Dapice, D., T. Vallely, and B. Wilkinson. "Assessment of the Myanmar Agricultural Economy". Paper prepared for International Development Enterprises, Harvard Kennedy School, January 2009.

Food and Agriculture Organization of the United Nations (FAO). *Myanmar: Agricultural Sector Review and Investment Strategy, Working Paper No. 9, Rural Finance*, Rome: Food and Agriculture Organization, 2004.

———. *FAO/WFP Crop and Food Security Assessment Mission to Myanmar*, Special Report. Rome: FAO, 22 January 2009.

Henley, D. "Microfinance in Indonesia, Evolution and Revolution, 1900–2000". In *Southeast Asia's Credit Revolution: From Moneylenders to Microfinance*, edited by D. Henley and A. Goenka. London: Routledge, 2009.

Henley, D. and Goenka, A. "Introduction: From Moneylenders to Microfinance". In *Southeast Asia's Credit Revolution: From Moneylenders to Microfinance*. London: Routledge, 2009.

Hudson-Rodd, N. and Sein Htay. *Arbitrary Confiscation of Farmers' Land by the State Peace and Development Council Military Regime in Burma*. Rockville, MD: The Burma Fund, 2008.

International Monetary Fund (IMF). *International Financial Statistics*. Washington, D.C.: IMF, July 2009.

Ivatury, G. and I. Mas. "The early experience with branchless banking". Consultative Group to Assist the Poor Focus Note 46, April, Washington, D.C.: Consultative Group to Assist the Poor, The World Bank, 2008.

McMurray, A. *Mobile Financial Services: Extending the Reach of Financial Services Through Mobile Payment Systems*, Brisbane: The Foundation for Development Cooperation, 2009.

Seibel, H.D. "The Microbanking Division of Bank Rakyat Indonesia: A Flagship of Rural Microfinance in Asia". In *Small Customers, Big Market: Commercial Banks in Microfinance*, edited by M. Harper and A. Sukhwinder . Rugby: ITDG Publications, 2005.

———. "Reforming Agricultural Development Banks". *Development Research Center Working Paper no. 2007-3*, University of Cologne, 2007.

Tripartite Core Group. *Post-Nargis Joint Assessment*. Yangon: Tripartite Core Group, 2008.

———. *Post-Nargis Recovery and Preparedness Plan*. Yangon: Tripartite Core Group, 2009.

Turnell, S.R. "Burma's Insatiable State". *Asian Survey* 48, no. 6 (2008): 958–76.

———. *Fiery Dragons: Banks, Moneylenders and Microfinance in Burma*. Copenhagen: Nordic Institute of Asian Studies Press, 2009.

Turnell, S.R., W. Bradford, and A.M. Vicary. "Burma's Economy in 2009: Disaster, Reconstruction…and Reform". *Asian Politics and Policy* 1, no. 4 (2009): 631–60.

United Nations Development Programme (UNDP). *Human Development Initiative, Myanmar: Report of Independent Assessment Mission*, New York: United Nations Development Programme, 2003.

———. *Human Development Initiative, Myanmar: Report of Independent Assessment Mission*, New York: United Nations Development Programme, 2005.

———. *Impact of the UNDP Human Development Initiative in Myanmar, 1994–2006*, Yangon: United Nations Development Programme, 2006.

———. *Integrated Household Living Conditions Survey in Myanmar*, Yangon: United Nations Development Programme, 2007a, in association with Government of the Union of Myanmar, Ministry of National Planning and Economic Development, and IDEA International Institute (Canada).

———. *Report of the Independent Assessment Mission of the Human Development Initiative, Myanmar*. United Nations Development Programme, Yangon, June 2007*b*. Available online at <http://74.125.153.132/search?q=cache:ZFY6O0lsP3EJ:www.undp.org/execbrd/word/IAM per cent25202007 per cent2520Report per cent2520final per cent252030-7-07.doc+Independent+assessment+mission+microfinance+burma+myanmar+2007+2008&cd=23&hl=en&ct=clnk&gl=au>. Accessed 10 August 2009.

———. *UNDP in Myanmar: Human Development Initiative Phase IV, Proposal for Extension (2008–2010)*, Yangon: United Nations Development Programme, 2007*c*.

Vogel, R.C. "Savings Mobilization: The Forgotten Half of Rural Finance". In *Undermining Rural Development with Cheap Credit*, edited by D.W. Adams, D.H. Graham and J.D. Von Pischke. Boulder, Colorado: Westview Press, 1984.

9

FARMERS, LAND AND MILITARY RULE IN BURMA

Nancy Hudson-Rodd and Sein Htay

> In August 2008, villagers were allegedly shot dead by soldiers while they worked in their paddy fields west of Papun Township. Incidents of forced labour are also reported, including in the construction and maintenance of eight roads and the portering of supplies to military posts. In Kayah State, the confiscation of land and work without remuneration in the agriculture sector was reported. In Thanbyuzayat Township, land was confiscated for the construction of rubber and castor-oil plantations and farmers were arbitrarily taxed. (UNGA 2009, pp. 57, 59, 60)

INTRODUCTION

Seventy-five per cent of Burma's 54 million people live in rural areas. The country's economic structure depends on agriculture and farm-related activities that provide livelihoods to more than 65 per cent of the population. While most rural households are engaged in farming as operators or labourers, and agriculture accounts for over half of the country's gross domestic product, only about one-fifth of rural households currently run viable farms of at least five acres (Dapice 2009, p. 11). Despite Burma's highly fertile agricultural land, some 32 per cent of the population are deprived of adequate food, nutrition and essential non-food items, with poverty levels particularly higher in rural areas (UN Human Development Initiative 2009).

Farmers with no clear rights of land ownership face severe survival pressures in Burma. An estimated one-half to two-thirds of rural households are landless farmers or farm labourers. Farmers' survival is further threatened when their land is confiscated. The State Peace and Development Council (SPDC) has implemented large-scale, arbitrary land confiscations in order to relocate civilian populations deemed supportive of armed opposition groups; to establish military bases in disputed areas by constructing or supporting new army battalions; to create infrastructure development projects such as the proposed Salween River dams; to facilitate natural-resource extractions such as the offshore Arakan Shwe Gas project; and to privilege interest groups such as military and foreign investors with commercial opportunities, in mining, logging and agriculture. The United Nations General Assembly has reported the broad negative cultural, social, environmental, and economic consequences of these confiscations (2006, p. 14).

The SPDC's forced displacement of ethnic populations in border areas has gained most international attention and continues to be well documented (All Arakan Students' and Youths' Congress 2009; Burma Environmental Working Group 2009; Human Rights Foundation of Monland 2009; Lahu National Development Organization 2009). Less is known about the arbitrary confiscation of farmers' land in central Burma. In this chapter we explore the plight of these farmers.

Rights to land, livelihood, food, property, and adequate housing are human rights established in several international conventions, resolutions, and declarations adopted by different bodies of the United Nations. According to article 17 of the Universal Declaration of Human Rights (1948), "everyone has the right to own property alone as well as in association with others" and "no one shall be arbitrarily deprived of his property". New international legal frameworks provide clear ways of restoring housing, land, and property to individuals affected. Articles on State Responsibility by the International Law Commission offer broad international legal rules and principles of definite preference for restitution as a remedy for violations of international law, specifically violations involving the illegal confiscation of housing, land, or property (Leckie and Simperingham 2009, pp. 12–13).

Being a farmer in Burma is a difficult, frustrating, and sometimes dangerous livelihood. As the major source of wealth and power, land has been the focus of successive ruling regimes of Burma. The present SPDC denies citizens rights of ownership and rights of cultivation. Depriving people of their economic and social livelihood is a serious denial of human rights.

REGIME LAWS AND PRACTICES

> The State is the ultimate owner of all lands (Section 30, Article 1, Constitution of the Union of Burma, 1947).
>
> The State is the sovereign owner of the land and the water (Section 18, Article 1, Constitution of the Burma Socialist Programme Party [BSPP] 1974).
>
> All land belongs to the State. Persons with permission to grow paddy have the duty to yield harvest to the full capacity of the field. Only after the paddy season is over and the set paddy season is over is it sold to the government (State Law and Order Restoration Council [SLORC], Order No. 32/88, 31 December 1988).
>
> The Union is the ultimate owner of all lands and all natural resources above and below the ground, above and beneath the water and in the atmosphere in the Union (Section 37a, Constitution of the Republic of the Union of Myanmar, 2008).

In Burma, the ownership of rural land is vested in the state. Legal control and classification of land was initiated by the British for a revenue collection and taxation system as were cadastral surveys and land classification according to ownership and use. With independence, a series of Land Nationalization Acts abolished all lease, rental or sharecropping arrangements, and established size limitations on agricultural holdings according to classification, use and family size. A basic limit of fifty acres was decreed for paddy and sugarcane, and smaller holdings for other land types. These limits remained through the socialist and military regimes, with no changes to land laws until the SPDC announced large land grants of over 5,000 acres for thirty-year leases to organizations and private entrepreneurs under the management of the Central Committee for Cultivable Land, Fallow Land and Waste Land. By 2001, over one million acres were distributed among 100 enterprises (Hudson-Rodd and Myo Nyunt 2001; Hudson-Rodd et al. 2003).

Despite these large land grants, more than 30 per cent of rural households are landless and another 37 per cent have small, marginal landholdings of five acres or less, the minimum required for subsistence farming. As farmers have only cultivation rights to the land they occupy, there is no legal ability to sell, lease or dispose of their land rights to others or consolidate holdings. Village-level committees can only provide cultivation rights when higher-level land committees approve them. Under normal situations, land cannot be used as collateral to access rural finance and there is no legal basis for transfer of land between farmers. But rural land transactions are widespread throughout Burma. Farmers informally mortgage land with moneylenders, or sell land to get immediate cash, or repay high-interest household loans (FAO and World Bank 2004, pp. 15, 29, 30). Widespread family indebtedness means a high percentage of households must sell their food stocks after harvest to meet debts. Forced farm sales due to debt contribute to increasing landlessness (Dapice 2009, p. 5).

In spite of complying with government regulations, having legal registration to land and having paid taxes for use of land, farmers are made landless. For example, in 2005 the armed forces in Natmauk, Magwe Division, claimed more than 5,000 acres of farmers' land. The army demanded 50,000 kyat and twenty baskets of physic nuts per acre to any farmer who wanted to use the land on a permit system. The physic nut was to be used for bio-fuel under a government scheme. Some fifty farmers lodged a complaint over their loss of land to the International Labour Organization (ILO) representative in October 2008. In response to this complaint, the army unit detained, interrogated and tortured four villagers, whom it held inside the army compound. The case finally went to court in January 2009. Zaw Htay, found guilty of giving out official secrets, was sentenced to ten years in jail because he had allegedly arranged for someone to take footage of the confiscated land and send the video abroad. U Phoe Phyu, the lawyer representing Zaw Htay, was also arrested (AHRC-UAC 2009). After strong ILO intervention, U Phoe Phyu's sentence was reduced to one year. He was released from prison on 5 March 2010. However, shortly after release, his licence to work as a lawyer was revoked (AHRC-UAC 2010).

NO RULE OF LAW

The military regime constantly iterates its intentions of building a modern and developed state, but with no functioning courts or independent judiciary where persons with legitimate grievances can bring their complaints, this is an absurdity. Individuals lack any public space in which to communicate or discuss grievances. In Burma communication is discouraged not only as a matter of principle. Measures are enacted so officials can silence with criminal sanctions those who irritate them by making complaints. As a bureaucratic agency, the courts perform an executive function, not a judicial one (AHRC-SPR 2009, pp. 14–15).

The United Nations has for years reported systemic and widespread human-rights abuses committed in Burma through a "culture of impunity and inoperability of the Burmese judiciary" (IHRC 2009, p. 3). Laws are applied selectively and arbitrarily. Courts adjudicate cases under decrees promulgated by the SPDC that effectively hold the force of law to be "what the generals from day to day decide it to be" (Gutter and Sen 2001, p. 14). There is no predictable outcome of any discourse or exchange between citizens and the criminal-justice system. There are no objective criteria upon which to determine consequences of a visit to a police station, a complaint to a ministry, or a case before a court.

According to the Asian Legal Resource Centre (ALRC), "This arbitrariness is the true indicator of the un-rule of law" (ALRC 2007, p. 15). The ALRC (2007, pp. 77–108) reported on many cases of persecution of Burmese farmers taken through the courts by petty local officials using "state apparatus" (laws, directives, and proclamations) for their own benefit of financial gain or personal revenge. For example, U Tin Kyi, a 65-year-old farmer, was jailed for "insulting government officials" when four men cleared local village land for a new castor-oil plantation; Farmer U Tin Nyein was jailed for complaining about destruction of his crops due to actions of government officials; Daw Khin Win was sentenced to one year in jail for complaining about various activities of local authorities; and U Thein Zan, Ko Zaw Htay and U Aung Than Htun were prosecuted for helping villagers to complain about the death of a man on a military forced-labour project. Farmers risk jail sentences if they complain that their crops are destroyed, land taken, or they are forced to labour.

Tomas Ojea Quintana, Special Rapporteur on the Situation of Human Rights in Myanmar, was disturbed that not only four farmers remained in prison after they made complaints of forced labour to ILO, but also imprisoned were a facilitator and lawyer who assisted the farmers (UNGA 2010, p. 117). The SPDC uses its courts to silence and punish farmers and all others who dare to speak out. Near the end of 2008, at least six lawyers were accused of criminal offences because of their attempts to defend clients whom the government intended to put in prison regardless of the trial process. The courts work effectively as regime agents to protect continued authoritarian rule. Nick Cheesman (2009/2010, p. 613) suggests this "role of law in Myanmar rather than the rule of law" is going to expand further when the 2008 Constitution is enacted. It gives the army-endorsed president powers of appointment and removal of superior judges, and calls for setting up new high courts at the state and regional levels, and expanded Supreme Court powers.

HUMAN-RIGHTS APPROACH TO DEVELOPMENT

Our research is informed by a human-rights approach to development. The Copenhagen Declaration on Social Development and Programme of Social Action sought to make human rights the framework for achieving the goals of the World Summit for Social Development (UN 1995). This strategy assumed that the norms and processes of implementing human rights would inform decisions on development policies. Norms and processes of human rights can empower social and economic groups hitherto excluded from or disadvantaged in entitlements and development. Specifically, human-rights norms that require and support democracy can provide the basis for political and social stability, and social and economic rights can eliminate the worst consequences of poverty (Ghai 2001).

According to Amartya Sen (1999), development consists of the removing of a variety of "un-freedoms" that leave people with restricted options to explore and create their lives. Economic and political freedoms act to reinforce each other. Rather than waiting for economic growth before ensuring human rights, there is a synergistic effect wherein one stimulates the other. Sen identifies the following five distinct types of freedoms: political freedoms; economic facilities; social opportunities; transparency guarantees; and protective security. He argues that each of these rights helps to promote the individual's overall capability. Each of these rights, important in its own way, when interconnected becomes stronger.

Democratic freedoms are not only the primary ends of development but they are the principal means of development. Political freedoms (free speech and elections) help to promote economic security. Social opportunities in the form of universal education and health services facilitate economic participation. Economic freedoms in the form of opportunities for participation in trade and production help to generate personal abundance as well as public resources for the common good. The realization of economic rights and social rights is closely linked to the condition of civil and political rights. Burma is one of the least democratic states in the world, ranked 163rd out of 167 countries surveyed by the Economist Intelligence Unit (2009, p. 11). The SPDC prevents people from pursuing their lives in peace, with no checks on its power. It takes all major policy decisions and appoints all government members, the majority with military backgrounds. Individuals are denied their political and civil liberties. Restrictions are imposed on individual and group freedoms, denying citizens their opportunities of participation in the social, economic, and political life of their country. Academics and farmers have no freedoms to contribute to research-based policy creation.

One aim of our research was to increase awareness of the plight of farmers through wide dissemination of the research back into Burma. The language of human rights has been used to develop a critical consciousness in the person and to encourage social action to overcome oppressive social structures. Awareness of universal rights is a powerful tool empowering individuals in their struggles against state rule, denying control to the military regime. Farmers' livelihoods in all townships, states/divisions, and ecological areas are severely threatened by the arbitrary confiscation of their land.

According to the government:

> The important role played by agriculture for national economic development needs no elaboration so that achieving a rapid, sustainable development of agriculture can be analogous to rapid sustainable development of our national economy. In this respect, comprehensive and reliable agricultural statistics, among other things, is [sic] regarded as crucial for policy and planning purposes (Government of Myanmar 2009, p. 1).

Despite this professed need for comprehensive data crucial for national development purposes, economic planning proceeds in Burma without public input, reliable data or official accountability. Facts are more a matter of negotiation than of observation. The regime claims a data gap exists in agriculture statistics because "farmers don't want to talk about real income and expenditure to avoid income tax" (Government of Myanmar 2009). Farmers know they will lose rights to cultivate land if they do not plant and produce a good harvest, so officially report what they think is expected (Dapice 2009, p. 2).

There is no government document specifically addressing agricultural policy. Rather, there are periodic pronouncements. In Burma, with no freedom of expression, with no free academic research or ability to disseminate research findings and heavy censorship of all writing, there can be no public debate informed by independent sources (Hudson-Rodd 2008). As one economist in Burma points out cogently: "As well known to all responsible members of Burmese mass media, both within the country and abroad, academics like us play no role and are completely out of the picture in the decision-making process regarding issues that are of major concern to the people of Myanmar" (Maung Myint 2007).

It is important to recognize the lack of knowledge and understanding of coherent economic and political mechanisms in Burma. Accurate research, information dissemination and analysis are urgently required. Little is known about agriculture, the lives of farmers and their families inside Burma due to a restrictive research climate and lack of any enjoyment of human rights. The following studies highlight farmers' lives affected by restrictive and punishing regime practices.

RESEARCH LITERATURE

A significant study explored the behaviour and welfare of rural households in Burma during transition from a planned economy to a market system. Research conducted in 2001 with 500 households in eight villages from different agro-ecological environments revealed paradoxes in Burma compared with experiences of other Asian countries. Farmers with increased-size paddy-based irrigated crops had lower farm incomes than those with smaller, mixed-crop, non-irrigated systems. Kurosaki et al. (2004, p. 31) found regime interference through agricultural policies restricted land use by farmers and marketing by traders, thereby lowering their incomes. The authors concluded that vast room for an expansion of agricultural output and rural income existed "without innovation in technology or further investment in irrigation. All that would be necessary to tap this potential is to give farmers more freedom in land use and liberalize paddy/rice marketing."

In the first field-work based study of rural politics and development in Burma, Ardeth Maung Thawnghmung (2004) analyzed multiple ways in which rice farmers responded to often arbitrary and irrational government directives concerning agricultural policies. Especially pertinent are the author's conclusions suggesting reasons for lack of collective farmer revolt against the military regime: "Burmese farmers have generally shunned overt protests to express their grievances and have utilized a wide variety of strategies to evade irrational state demands and simultaneously avoid its brutal suppression" (Maung Thawnghmung 2004, p. 202).

Another study documented dispossession from land, forced evictions from villages, and confiscation of labour and materials of ethnic minorities in seven districts of eastern Burma (Hudson-Rodd et al. 2004, pp. 3–16). Household interviews were clandestinely conducted over three consecutive years (2001 to 2003) in Karen State. Findings revealed individuals, families, households, and villages barely surviving under a regime that systematically denied people their right to subsistence. Land, crops, food and household possessions were confiscated, farms and homes were burned, while people were forced to labour building roads and bridges, and act as porters for military battalions. Systematic acts of violence, including rape and extrajudicial killings, revealed the extreme conditions which increased people's vulnerability.

David Arnott (2007) conducted a major survey of 560 refugees and migrants from Burma now living in India, Thailand, and Malaysia which revealed lack of secure land tenure among the following reasons for forced migration: land confiscation (39.1 per cent); food insecurity (69.8 per cent); forced labour (59.9 per cent); extortion/heavy and arbitrary taxation (60 per cent); and ruinous agricultural cropping and marketing policies (18.6 per cent). Respondents came from Irrawaddy, Magwe, Mandalay, West Pegu, Rangoon and Sagaing Divisions, and Kachin, Chin, Arakan, northern and eastern Shan States. Despite large numbers of people forced to flee, the majority remain inside Burma living under increasingly severe conditions.

In the next section we describe our research into the plight of farmers and their families in villages of fourteen townships in Rangoon, Pegu, and Irrawaddy Divisions and Arakan, Karenni and Shan States.

RESEARCH METHODOLOGIES

Between January and November 2007, a team of fourteen researchers clandestinely conducted interviews with 467 farm households in homes and fields to document the current situation of arbitrary confiscation of land, labour and livelihoods of farmers inside Burma. All respondents had been displaced from their farms. No farmers were refugees. Most now work as labourers in nearby villages, on their former farms, or in city factories.

The researchers collected a range of documentation, including interviews, photographs, hand-drawn maps, letters, and videos, based on availability, resulting in inconsistent data sets and uneven distribution of interviews. They analyzed official SPDC reports, correspondence, scholarly papers, unpublished and published research findings, reports, and news articles in Burmese and non-Burmese sources.

A human rights-based approach to development (UNHCHR 2006) guided formulation of interview questions seeking farmers' descriptions, including who confiscated what, when, for what stated reason and was there any compensation or contestation of the confiscation? Open-ended questions elicited responses concerning social, economic, health, and general household impacts of confiscation.

Research was informed by discussion among elected members of the National Coalition Government of the Union of Burma (NCGUB) in exile, Burmese and non-Burmese scholars, and inside researchers, as well as previous findings, reports, international studies, and statements of people forced into exile. Khun Mak Ko Ban (1990), elected member of parliament for Phekon and Kayah representative for the Democratic Organization for Kayan National Unity (DOKNU), and Kyaw Htet of the Democratic Development Committee of the NCGUB and of Yoma News Group organized research teams inside Burma. Research aims were explained to fourteen men — two in Karenni State and twelve in the other states and divisions — with experience in collecting information concerning forced labour and other human rights issues in Burma. Farm leaders and lawyers representing farmers were approached directly by our inside team. Results of clandestinely conducted interviews including videos, hand-drawn maps, photographs, official letters, interview notes, and other documentation were couriered across borders into Thailand. All original documents were translated into English. Diverse methodologies were used depending upon the security of the researchers and the respondents.

Many Burmese farmers are not formally educated, and for good reason are very frightened of speaking openly about confiscation of their land and crops. Questions concerning confiscation details were difficult to answer. The majority of farmers do not have detailed accounts of their household expenditures so could not give specific responses but offered values in a range of ways. Children wanted to inform researchers of severe family losses of livelihood and the threat to their future survival as a result of farm confiscations. Some farmers' children led researchers by bicycle and by foot, sometimes at night, to show what land had been taken.

Research was conducted inside Burma at a time of increased surveillance and restrictions on the movements and activities of international organizations. Civilians' personal freedom to move is always restricted (ICG 2006). Burmese citizens live within an insecure environment, with limited means of contesting regime actions, no real legal recourse, and scarce access to independent observers. Layers of surveillance exist from the military intelligence, police Special Branch, and community wardens watching all individual families in their districts. Open discussion is impossible. SPDC informers — village authorities, members of the Union Solidarity Development Association (USDA), and Swanahshin (paramilitary enforcers) — watch over all unauthorized activities in villages. Interviews were conducted when and where it was considered safe to talk.

At great risk of detention, people spoke about their plight. Others interviewed farmers, collected information, and couriered confiscation details across the border into Thailand. Because of security risks involved in data collection, there are inconsistent data sets for the townships. Information not anticipated, data of different kinds, was collected, and some questions were not answered. A large network of people working inside Burma and along the Thailand/Burma border made this research possible. In light of high levels of regime surveillance, we did not want to put any person in danger of detention. Research participants were aware of the dangers to their personal security.

RESEARCH FINDINGS

Table 9.1 indicates the geographic extent of regime confiscation of farmland. It also reflects where information was able to be collected, with great variety of sample sizes in each township. Out of our sample of 467 respondents, from fourteen townships in six Divisions and States, only six farmers (1.2 per cent) were given any compensation. Three were granted alternative plots of land and three were given small cash payments. The plots of land and the cash payments were far below the value of land and crops confiscated. Over 5,000 acres of land, worth more than 300 million kyat, were confiscated. Loss of income varied depending on the type of crop planted. Five acres of farmland were sufficient to support a family, but village authorities abused their powers, acting as land councils, taking farmers' land and forcing them to move. Implications of uncompensated confiscation were dramatic losses in income, reduced quality of life and loss of residency rights in the village. Persons who lost these rights were required to report regularly to the Village Peace and Development Council (VPDC) and contribute cash on demand to VPDC officials. Children were denied rights to attend village schools, so households resorted to home education but had reduced time to dedicate to this.

Households showed a variety of survival tactics. Families who moved to cities found work in factories, or as casual labourers, earning low wages. Some used their savings to work as traders or start new businesses, but were inexperienced in commercial ventures. Those with no savings and not able to work as farm labourers, reported a variety of activities such as herding cows/buffaloes seven miles from their village, gathering vegetables from paddy fields, and doing casual work. All reported great reductions in income and reduced diet and nutritional levels, being forced into becoming fishers and eating frogs. Unanimously people stated that their lives would improve when their household-registration status was re-issued, farmland was returned, schools were constructed, children were granted an education and health clinics were available. Several farmers suggested better transportation services and access to clean water through construction of tube wells would help.

In south-eastern Pegu Division, land was confiscated between May and June 2003: eight farmers had their land "re-distributed" to be owned by the VPDC Land Department and the USDA; twelve were told their land was leased to others to be rented and re-cultivated; and the land of one farmer was given to the Land Department and rented out for cultivation. Disparate individuals and organizations linked with the government confiscated the land. Aside from the VPDC and USDA these included the Township Land Record Department, Military Battalion 105, Township Police Battalion, Township General Administration Department, and the SPDC. Farmers in south-eastern Pegu contested their confiscation, represented by a lawyer, Aye Myint, who demanded restitution through letters in 2007 to the Divisional Commander and Chairman, Divisional Peace and Development Council.

In north-western Pegu Division, seventeen farmers were forcibly removed from their seventy-two acres of paddy land, which was confiscated by the VPDC and Village Land Council chairman and Oat Pho Township Land Record Department. No farmer was compensated. In Irrawaddy Division, four respondents (two female-headed households) had their farmland confiscated in February 2002, by Myo Han, chairman of the Pantanaw Township Peace and Development Council in order to develop an urban block of land, to form a satellite town. One woman was given a

TABLE 9.1
Confiscation of Land, Crops and Other Assets in Fourteen Townships of Six States/Divisions, Burma

				Confiscated items					
No.	Township	State/Division	Sample	Land Acres	Value Lakh/Kyat	Crops, other losses Lakh/Kyat	Total value Lakh/Kyat	Compensation Lakh/Kyat	Yearly loss of income Lakh/Kyat
1	Kawa	Pegu	20	795	795	612	1,407	none	1,573
2	Oat Pho	Pegu	17	72	n/a	n/a	n/a	none	n/a
3	Pantanaw	Irrawaddy	4	18.5	10.3	5.3	15.6	one plot (40–60 ft)	46.5
4	Nyaung Done	Irrawaddy	1	12	18	n/a	18	none	24
5	Maubin	Irrawaddy	1	20	20	n/a	20	6	7.5
6	Kyaung Kone	Irrawaddy	39	171	n/a	n/a	n/a	none	n/a
7	Hlaingthaya	Rangoon	1	26	78	n/a	68	10 (one plot)	65
8	Htantabin	Rangoon	1	18	59	12	61	10 (one plot)	24
9	Hmawbi	Rangoon	1	40	80	41	121	16	48
10	Hlaegu	Rangoon	3	14	28	22	50	none	34
11	Thandwe	Arakan	23	344.3	n/a	n/a	n/a	0.3	n/a
12	Shwe Nyaung	Shan	1	6.12	10	n/a	10	none	20
13	Phekon	Karenni	218	2,040	1,908.5	213.4	2,121.9	none	n/a
14	Moebyel	Karenni	137	1,507	253	228	480	none	n/a
	Total		467	5,083.92	3,259.8	1,133.7	4,372.5	42.3	1,842.0

Note: One lakh is equal to 100,000 kyat.
Source: Hudson-Rodd and Sein Htay 2008, p. 67.

small residential block of land as compensation. She was compensated a fraction of the value of her loss. This urban land was no substitute for the income from five acres formerly planted in rice, beans, sugarcane, and bananas. The other four farmers were not compensated for their losses. One female head of a seven-member household lost twenty acres of paddy fields in Maubin Township, Irrawaddy Division, confiscated by Thein Myint, chairman of the Htanee Village Tract PDC, in order "to dig ground" for the construction of a lake. One male head of a household of seven members had his twelve acres of paddy forcibly taken from him by Aung San Oo of the Bawathit Prison Labour Camp. No reason was given for the confiscation. The farmer was given no compensation for his loss.

Township authorities confiscated 171 acres of paddy land of thirty-nine farmers (including three female-headed households) in Chaungwa, Tetseik and Magyigon villages, Kyaung Kone Township, Irrawaddy Division. Not only was the land taken and no compensation given to the farmers, but the Township authorities also denied access to common land normally used for grazing animals. This harsh and punitive action denied the livelihood of the 201 members of these farms.

In Rangoon Division, the SPDC confiscated farmland of five out of six farmers surveyed (all male-headed households). In two cases, the local Police Battalion and Htantanbin Township administration officials were responsible. The confiscated land was sold to a private company (Olympic) to profit the No. 9 Police Battalion and the SPDC, and used to build a power plant, a water distribution factory, a canal, and a road. One farmer had his land confiscated directly by the Myanmar Pyi Thar Hyat Company to make a fishpond. Htin Linn was compensated 1.6 million kyat after complaining to Lieutenant General Khin Nyunt, then Secretary 1 of the SPDC. No other farmer was compensated.

In Arakan State, one farmer had twenty-six acres of rubber plantation confiscated by the Thandwe Township Police and the USDA on 11 October 1997. Farmers' land was given to the USDA and the State Police Commissioner. The Township Fishery Department took 318 acres of paddy land from twenty-two farmers on 15 February 2000. The land was given to the Everlight Company to construct a prawn/shrimp pond. No compensation was given to the farmers.

In Shan State, Zaw Zaw, Chairman, Quarter Peace and Development Council confiscated over six acres of a man's farmland on which paddy, maize, and beans were growing. No compensation was given to the farmer. His farmland was "rented" out by the PDC chairman for cultivation purposes.

In Karenni State, 355 farmers' land was confiscated in 1991, 1995, and 1996. No compensation was given to any farmer. Most farmers grew corn and beans, with some paddy land; others depended on fishing. The land was taken for a military base establishment and for the construction of Mobye Dam. All 218 farmers' land west of the dam was confiscated. Over 130 houses were confiscated in villages on two islands for dam construction. Confiscated residential and farming land in Phekon and Mobye towns was given to retired army personnel and their relatives were invited to move into the township. Both towns are now virtual military bases, with Engineering and Artillery Battalions, Medical Corps, Light Infantry Battalion Bases 336, 421, 422 and Regional Military Command No. 7 Base. The military footprint is dominant as people are pushed off their land with no access to farming or means to support their families.

CONCLUSION

Land is confiscated in Burma for a variety of reasons, including for development of infrastructure such as roads, the building of a water distribution factory, for private shrimp pond enterprises, and for the personal use of the USDA members, police, and infantry battalion personnel. Farmers and their families are finding it increasingly difficult to survive with no real livelihood options when their land is taken from them. A high level of corruption; the lack of any freedom of association, expression, movement, or the right to own property; the absence of an independent judiciary and rule of law; and a regime dedicated to stifling any questioning of their lawless actions all contribute to a state of despair. Our research sample was small, but revealed harsh conditions of farmers in fourteen townships of six states and divisions. All farmers stated that they wanted their land returned to them, to be able to grow crops and support their families.

A vast network of individuals, organizations, and authorities linked to the regime at local, regional and national levels are involved in the arbitrary confiscation of farmers' land and benefiting from this theft. Rent-seeking is well embedded and occurs in every transaction. There is systemic official corruption. The administrative system represents a crazy patchwork quilt of surveillance and corruption, from village to national levels. Denial of access to resources or economic, social, and political power keeps people in a state of poverty, an "extreme form of deprivation" (OHCHR 2002). Poverty is induced through a systematic and sustained violation of human rights. Individuals have no freedom to publicly discuss violations of their rights. In this process, systematic violation of farmers' rights perpetuates poverty by constantly reproducing generations of poor.

The military elites extract rents, strengthening their position of power. Corruption thrives as secrecy and suppression of worker rights (no freedom of association, forced labour) further undermine human rights. Rent-seeking thus prevents the emergence of civil society and good governance (Mehmet 2001). Rent-seeking exists at all levels of Burmese society and includes the extortion of money through official and unofficial tax levies; the confiscation of crops, labour and goods; the destruction of property; looting; and the creation of capital-intensive agri-businesses. A large underground economy operates mostly outside government rules and regulations, over which much uncertainty and confusion exists arising from the lack of transparency, accountability and consistency.

Burma was the most corrupt nation in the region during 2006, according to the World Bank's Control of Corruption Index (CCI) conducted for nine countries of South and West Asia, seventeen countries in the Pacific and eighteen countries of East Asia. The CCI measures the extent to which public power is exercised for private gain. This includes both petty and grand forms of corruption as well as the "capture" of the state by elites and private actors. Burma has the least effective government, corresponding to provision of the fewest public services and lowest credibility. Burma rated worst for democratic accountability, indicating the smallest responsiveness of the government to the people; scored the lowest on voice and accountability measures, meaning that citizens have the least freedom to participate in selecting their government, as well as the least freedom of expression, association, and media. Burma scored the lowest on regulatory quality. This index measured the inability of the government to formulate and implement sound policies and regulations that would permit and promote the private sector (UNDP 2008, pp. 184ff).

Households in Burma are finding it more difficult to feed, clothe, and educate their children in face of the lack of land to farm. With no land as security, the next generation is disadvantaged. Children are not receiving education and illness often goes untreated. The research findings highlight ways in which land is arbitrarily confiscated due to increasing regime presence. Several individuals and groups are benefiting through their links with the regime, being granted leases on large tracts of land ostensibly to create entrepreneurial agricultural developments. Often, land formerly farmed by small households remains vacant and unused. This discrepancy, inequality, and arbitrariness in administration of farmland creates social tensions. It also contributes to nutritional deficits, as the crops grown and the market system are less able to provide sufficient food for local farmers.

Individual farmers and village groups are contesting their rights to land, demanding compensation despite the risks of arrest and detention, while recognizing that there is no independent judiciary in Burma. Farmers have no trust in government officials, the Village Peace and Development Councils, the Township Peace and Development Councils, the Union Solidarity Development Association, military battalions, or the Departments of Land and Fisheries, which often abuse their authority for personal gain. With no clear laws or rights to a clear, independent legal process, claims to confiscation of land rest on official whims. Farmers have nothing more left to lose. Land is their life and represents the future of their families. It also means the future of food security in Burma. Without land as security, the next generation is disadvantaged.

Farmers and lawyers have not given up hope of redress, and struggle to hold the SPDC accountable for illegal confiscation. The work of lawyer U Aye Myint contributed to our research.[1] He set up a legal-aid group to handle cases of forced labour, arbitrary land confiscation and farmers who were left uncompensated, and abuses against workers. Twice imprisoned for cases he brought to courts and to the ILO, he suffered cruelly. On receiving the 2008 European Bar's Ludovic-Trarieux 13th International Human Rights Prize for work under repressive conditions, he vowed to continue "to fight any government or individual acting against the law".

Our research sought to expand the limited space for Burmese and international researchers to contribute to knowledge concerning farming and land rights. People who conduct research inside Burma are courageous and put their lives at risk. Ko Kyaw Soe, one of our inside researchers, a member of the Human Rights Defender Group in Taunggyi Township, Shan State, was arrested in early 2008. He died in Myingyan Prison in May 2010.

We recognize the complexities in creating a democratic process in Burma after decades of military rule. A democratic Burma will need to find ways to resolve many conflicting claims on land, property, and housing, including those displaced after their houses and property were destroyed or confiscated. Resolution of just land title and land use is essential to this process. Farmers need freedom to own and sell land, cultivate crops of their choice and market these goods. This means making clear, precise legislation for land ownership, land use, land transfer, and for the enforcement of legal claims for land in dispute. There needs to be certainty of law, the rule of law, guarantees of human rights and political participation. Only by lifting the "un-freedoms" in Burma can an environment conducive to development be created.

Notes

1. Nancy Hudson-Rodd's (2008) meeting with U Aye Myint never happened. Special Branch police, army and immigration officers detained her and her husband, denied them access to the Australian embassy, and took their passports and air tickets. They were deported eight hours later. Nancy was accused of meeting with Burmese people, of not acting like a tourist, of travelling too much, and of "doing something wrong".

References

All Arakan Students' and Youths' Congress. *Holding Our Ground: Land Confiscation in Arakan & Mon States and Pa-O Area of Southern Shan State*. AASYC: Mae Sot, March 2009.

Arnott, David. "Forced Migration/Internal Displacement in Burma with an Emphasis on Government-Controlled Areas". Draft, 2007.

Asian Human Rights Commission — Urgent Appeals Programme (AHRC-UAC-032-2010). "Burma: Another human rights lawyer's license unlawfully revoked". AHRC, Hong Kong, 26 March 2010.

——— (AHRC-UAC-009-2009). "Burma: Man jailed over footage of army-confiscated farmlands". AHRC, Hong Kong, 2 February 2009.

——— (AHRC-SPR-002-2009). "The State of Human Rights in Burma in 2009". AHRC, Hong Kong, March 2009.

Asian Legal Resource Centre (ALRC). "Ten Cases in Legal Dementia". *Article* 2, no. 5-6 (October–December 2007).

Burma Environmental Working Group (BEWG). *Accessible Alternatives: Ethnic*

Communities' Contribution to Social Development and Environmental. Chiang Mai: Wanida Press, September 2009.

Cheesman, Nick. "Thin Rule of Law or Un-Rule of Law in Myanmar?". *Pacific Affairs* 82, no. 4 (Winter, 2009/2010).

Collignon, Stefan. "Human Rights and the Economy in Burma". In *Burma: Political Economy under Military Rule*, edited by Robert Taylor. London: Hurst, 2001.

Dapice, David. *Assessment of the Myanmar Agricultural Economy*. Cambridge, MA: Asia Programs, Harvard Kennedy School, January 2009.

Economist Intelligence Unit (EIU). Myanmar (Burma) Country Report. London: EIU, April 2009.

Food and Agriculture Organization and World Bank. Myanmar Agricultural Sector Review Investment Strategy. Volume 1 — Sector Review, 2004, <www.ibiblio.org/obl/docs4/FAO-ASR-MainReport2004.pdf>. Accessed 9 December 2008.

Ghai, Yash. *Human Rights and Social Development: Toward Democratization and Social Justice*. Geneva: UNRISD, 2001.

Gutter, P. and B.K. Sen. *Burma's State Protection Law: An Analysis of the Broadest Law in the World*. Bangkok: Burma Lawyers' Council, December 2001.

Hudson-Rodd, Nancy. " 'Not a rice eating robot': Freedom to speak in Burma". In *Political Regimes and the Media in Asia*, edited by K. Sen and T. Lee. London & New York: Routledge, 2008.

Hudson-Rodd, Nancy and Myo Nyunt. "Control of Land and Life in Burma". Tenure Brief, Land Tenure Centre, University of Wisconsin-Madison, No. 3, 2001.

Hudson-Rodd, Nancy, Myo Nyunt, Saw Thamain Tun, and Sein Htay. "State Induced Violence and Poverty in Burma". Research Report submitted to ILO Geneva on behalf of Federation of Trade Unions-Burma (FTUB), June 2004.

———. *The Impact of Confiscation of Land, Labour, Capital Assets and Forced Relocation in Burma by the Military Regime*. Bangkok: NCUB/ FTUB, 2003.

Hudson-Rodd, Nancy and Sein Htay. *Arbitrary Confiscation of Farmers' Land by the State Peace and Development Council (SPDC) Military Regime in Burma*. Washington, D.C.: The Burma Fund, 2008.

Human Rights Foundation of Monland (HURFOM), "Laid Waste: Human Rights Along the Kanbauk to Myaing Kalang Gas Pipeline". May 2009 at <http://rehmonya.org/data/Laid-waste.pdf>. Accessed 20 May 2010.

International Crisis Group (ICG). "Myanmar: New Threats to Humanitarian Aid". Asia Briefing No. 58, Yangon/Brussels: ICG, 8 December 2006.

International Human Rights Clinic (IHRC). *Crimes in Burma: A Report*. Cambridge, MA: IHRC, Harvard University, 2009.

Kurosaki, Takashi, Ikuko Okamoto, Kyosuke Kurita, and Koichi Fujita. "Rich Periphery, Poor Centre: Myanmar's Rural Economy under Partial Transition to

Market Economy". No. 23, Discussion Paper Series, Hitotsubashi University Research Unit for Statistical Analysis in Social Sciences, Institute of Economic Research, Hitotsubashi University, Tokyo, Japan, March 2004, <http://hi-stat.ier.hit-u.ac.jp/research/discussion/2003/pdf/D03-23.pdf>. Accessed 11 September 2009.

Lahu National Development Organisation, "Monitoring Development on Burma's Mekong". Issue 3, April 2009.

Leckie, Scott and Ezekiel Simperingham. *Housing, Land and Property Rights in Burma: The Current Legal Framework*. Geneva: Displacement Solutions, HLP Institute, 2009.

Maung Myint. "Open letter to editors of BBC, RFA, VOA, DVB, *Mizzima News*, *Irrawaddy News*, *Burma Net News*, and *Aljazeera*". 5 September 2007.

Mehmet, Ozay. "Corruption, Worker Rights and Good Governance". Paper presented at the Canada-China Project, Beijing, sponsored by Human Rights Centre, University of Ottawa, November 2001.

Ministry of Information. Constitution of the Republic of the Union of Myanmar (2008), Yangon: Printing and Publishing Enterprise, Ministry of Information, 2008.

Maung Thawnghmung, Ardeth. *Behind the Teak Curtain: Authoritarianism, Agricultural Policies and Political Legitimacy in Rural Burma/Myanmar*. London, New York, Bahrain: Kegan Paul, 2004.

Myanmar Central Statistics Organization. Agriculture Statistics, 2009 <www.statistics.gov.my/apcas/images/stories/files/apcas/papers/Country Report_Myanmar.pdf>. Accessed 9 December 2008.

Office of the High Commissioner for Human Rights (OHCHR). "Draft Guidelines: A Human Rights Approach to Poverty Reduction Strategies". UN, Geneva: September 2002.

Sen, Amartya. *Development as Freedom: Human Capability and Global Need*. New York: Anchor Press, 1999.

United Nations. World Summit for Social Development. Copenhagen, Denmark, 19 April 1995, <www.un.org/documents/ga/conf166/aconf166-9.htm>. Accessed 13 September 2009.

United Nations Development Programme (UNDP). *Tackling Corruption, Transforming Lives: Accelerating Human Development in Asia and the Pacific*. UNDP, 2008.

United Nations General Assembly (UNGA). "Situation of Human Rights in Myanmar". Sixty-first Session, Agenda Item 67(c), A/61/369, 21 September, 2006.

———. "Human Rights Situations that Require the Council's Attention, Report of the Special Rapporteur on the Situation of Human Rights in Myanmar", Tomas Ojea Quintana, Human Rights Council, Tenth Session, Agenda Item 4, A/HRC/10/19, 11 March, 2009.

———. "Human Rights Situations That Require the Council's Attention, Progress Report of the Special Rapporteur on the Situation of Human Rights in Myanmar", Tomas Ojea Quintana, Thirteenth Session, Agenda Item 4, A/HRC/13/48, 10 March 2010.

United Nations High Commissioner for Human Rights (UNHCHR). "Frequently asked questions on a human rights-based approach to development cooperation", Annex 11, UN: New York and Geneva, 2006.

United Nations Human Development Initiative (UNHDI). Annex Independent Assessment Mission (IAM) Terms of Reference, Human Development Initiative: Phase IV, Rangoon, Myanmar, 2009.

10

THE MOVEMENT OF RURAL LABOUR
A Case Study Based on Rakhine State

Ikuko Okamoto[1]

INTRODUCTION

There is no significant rural–urban migration in Myanmar.[2] This is mainly because full-scale industrialization was not implemented during the twenty-five years of the socialist regime or even after the twenty years of economic transition. The country's economic structure has barely changed over the past forty-five years and the capacity of the urban sector (industry as well as service) to absorb labour remains inadequate.

Nevertheless, limited rural–urban migration does not signify that rural Myanmar is static, with no population movement. We consider the following two population flows as being prominent since the start of economic transition in the late 1980s.

One is overseas emigration, which is rapidly increasing. The number of Myanmar migrants working on fishing boats, in factories, and at construction sites in Thailand has increased dramatically since around the mid-1990s (Bradford and Vicary 2005). Many Myanmar labourers are also working at ports and in factories in Malaysia. Even though the majority are fully aware of the severe working conditions in the destination countries, there is no end to the people who wish to migrate and are willing to pay exorbitant fees to migration brokers.[3]

The other population flow is intra-rural migration. Previous research on domestic migration from an economic standpoint is limited, with the exception of a study by Takahashi (1997). Takahashi conducted a field survey in 1993–95 and found that 20 per cent of the village population had been replaced. His study found, first, that the major class of people migrating were non-farmers, especially agricultural labourers who did not own any farmland or other assets. As pointed out in many studies, there is a large pool of agricultural labourers in rural Myanmar (Takahashi 2000; Fujita 2009; Okamoto 2008*a*), and they constitute the floating population. Second, it found that there was not much change in their occupation after their move. For example, agricultural seasonal labourers tended to also engage in seasonal labour in their new place of employment. Furthermore, the destination area was mostly confined to within the same township in which they lived.[4] In other words, the migrants' reason for moving was not necessarily to gain a larger income under a completely different economic environment. In this sense, their move could not contribute much to increasing the total household income. What is more important here is stability of livelihood or the minimization of fluctuations in household income throughout the year.

Takahashi's field survey was conducted during the initial phase of Myanmar's economic transition. Even though industrialization has not progressed very far since then, the movement of goods, people and capital has been brisk. In line with the increase in overseas migration, it is highly likely that intra-rural migration is also increasing — in scale as well as in area covered. However, due to the absence of sufficient and reliable statistics for grasping and analysing the whole picture of domestic labour movement, it is necessary to accumulate evidence from case studies.

To shed light on the issues affecting the movement of rural labour, this study adopted an empirical approach based on the case of labourers (crewmen) migrating to fishery villages in Rakhine State. Rakhine is generally regarded as a remote state, bordering Bangladesh. However, on the side facing the Gulf of Bengal is a newly developed area for Myanmar's commercial fisheries, along with those of the Tanintharyi Division in the far south. In particular, Thandwe District in southern Rakhine has shown remarkable development as a base for export-oriented shrimp fishing (both small-scale trawling and gill net) since the latter half of the 1990s (Okamoto 2008*b*). However, as competition among shrimp fishing intensified, shrimp resources started decreasing and subsequently the fishermen's catch also declined in recent years. Along with the declining shrimp catch, many fishermen turned to anchovy (*nganitu*) purse-seine fishing. Unlike shrimp fishing, purse-seine fishing is labour intensive, requiring a crew of between twenty-five and thirty men for each set of boats. Since local labourers alone could not meet this demand, many labourers began migrating to the area seeking employment for the anchovy fishing season. To the best of our knowledge, such large-scale domestic labour migration has never been reported and thus deserves scrutinizing.

Given the limited capacity for labour absorption by the urban and industrial sectors, and the fact that overseas migration is not widely available due to the high transaction cost and risk,[5] this type of labour-intensive industry in a remote area would be highly significant for the improvement of livelihood for rural households. Thus, this paper aims to clarify the following three points based on individual interviews with the migrating crewmen. First, who are the migrating labourers? Second, what are their major reasons for migrating? Third, to what extent has migration improved the economic standard of their household? By analysing the responses to these questions, we attempt to highlight the issues related to Myanmar's labour market in the mid-2000s, and provide a basis for further research.

The following sections analyse the research questions, while keeping in mind the findings of earlier research described above. The first section presents an overview of the survey area and general conditions of the fishing industry as well as of purse-seine fishing carried out in the area. The second section clarifies the characteristics of the migrating labourers. This is followed by an analysis of their background and the reasons for migrating in the third section. The last section presents our conclusions.

PURSE-SEINE FISHING IN RAKHINE STATE

Overview

Thandwe Township is a major fishing base in southern Rakhine State. During the socialist period, the township was the landing base for the state-owned Fishery Enterprise, but when liberalization of the fishing industry began in the 1990s, both inshore and offshore fisheries saw remarkable growth. The main actors of inshore fisheries are the small-scale fishermen in the coastal area (Okamoto 2008*b*). The shrimp-fishing boom opened up the way for development and anchovy purse-seine fishing became popular in the early 2000s.

One town and 63 village tracts make up Thandwe Township, with a total population of about 140,000 people. Village J in the M village tract and Village S in the S village tract were selected as the study site (see Table 10.1 and Figure 10.1). The reasons for selecting these two villages were that the anchovy purse-seine fishing is quite active in these villages and these are the two biggest destinations for the migrating fishing labourers. The interviews were conducted in February 2008.[6]

Village J is closer to Thandwe Town and has better transport infrastructure compared to Village S, which takes about 30–40 minutes to reach by car (the road to the village is very rough) and an hour by boat. Though there is a big difference in geographical convenience between the two villages, they are equally dependent on the fishery. Even though Village J has other employment opportunities because of its close proximity to the town — the hotels near the beach resort and the processing plants for marine products — about 85 per cent of the total households engage in fishing-related activities as the main household occupation.[7] Village S is a genuine fishing village. Some households own farmland, but it is usually a small area and is basically for home consumption. Also, since Village S is far from town, non-fishery and non-farm employment opportunities are limited.

The interviews were conducted with fishing labourers (crewmen) who had migrated from other areas. However, the analysis was not restricted

TABLE 10.1
Number of Households, 2006

Village Tract	M Village Tract		S Village Tract				
Village	J	M	S	N	I	K	C
Number of Households	1975	440	564	327	70	98	84

Source: Village Peace and Development Council.

FIGURE 10.1
Rakhine State and Study Area

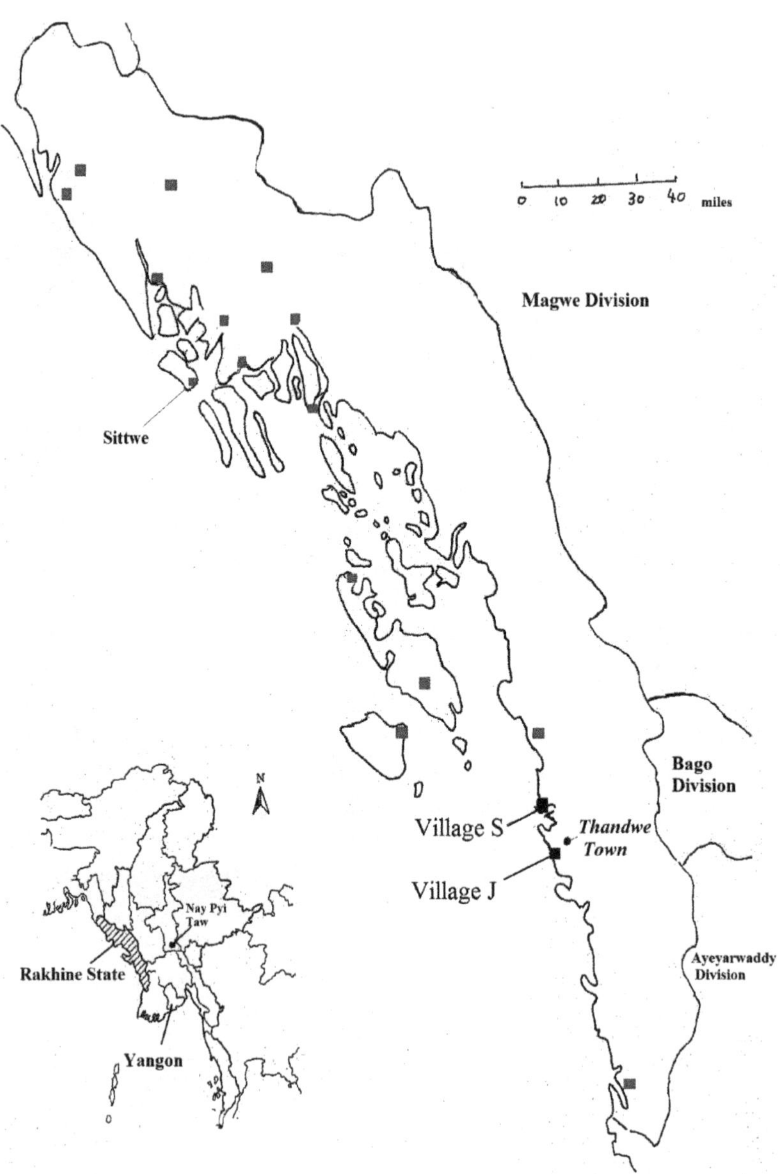

Source: Prepared by author.

to the individual crewmen since the decision to migrate is generally made by the entire "household". Thus, an attempt was made to grasp the details about the crewmen and their families. For example, income was estimated not only for each crewman, but also for the household by clarifying the income of each household member.

A total of 107 crewmen were interviewed: 60 in Village J and 47 in Village S. In both villages, a comprehensive list of crewmen from other areas was not available since these labourers are very mobile with varying duration of stay in these villages. Thus, it was not possible to select the interviewees randomly. We asked key villagers to select crewmen from different owners' boats, in order to minimize the bias. The main interview questions dealt with family structure, place of origin, motivation for migration, cost of migration, sector-wise income, consumption, and credit situation. The interviews were conducted by several local enumerators using our prepared questionnaires. After each interview, we checked the questionnaire and confirmed any points that were not clear with Burmese language.

Development of Anchovy Purse-seine Fishing

The season for anchovy purse-seine fishing is during the dry months from October to May. The fishing operation is conducted at night; the boats leave the shore at around five or six o'clock in the evening and return early the next morning. Two boats are required: one to light up the sea and the other to encircle the fish that gather around the lighted water. Considerable labour is required for pulling up the nets, with up to thirty crewmen generally being hired for each set of boats. The landed anchovies are sun dried on the nets spread out on the shore. The drying work is handled by women hired from the village together with the wives and daughters of the migrating crewmen. The boat owners do not go out to sea with the crewmen. When the boats return to shore, they weigh the landed fish and record the details, and at the same time, they distribute small fish (other than anchovies) to the crewmen for their daily meal.

Purse-seine fishing itself is not new to this area, having started around the early 1980s.[8] However, its initial target was small shrimp (sold as a dried product). Anchovies were caught by beach seine fishing at that time. The use of purse-seine (nets) to catch anchovies started around the late 1990s, when small-scale shrimp trawling started in the area,[9] which dramatically reduced the shrimp catch for purse-seine fishing. The target was changed to anchovies instead of shrimps at that time.

In the early years, the fishing ground for small shrimps and anchovies was within five nautical miles of the coast, so only small engines (five–six horsepower) were needed for the boats and fewer crewmen (twelve–fifteen) were required. These were mostly local villagers. Eventually, however, these boats started fishing in remote waters (ten–twenty nautical miles from the coast), most likely due to the decrease in catch near the coast. Accompanying the change in fishing ground was the need for larger boats and engines and a greater number of crewmen to handle the fishing operations.

The number of purse-seine fishing boats in Village J increased from fifty sets in the early 1990s to 100 sets in 1998 and 110 sets in 2008. In Village S, the number was fifteen in the mid-1990s, increasing to fifty in 2002 and sixty-eight in 2008.[10] The pace of development of purse-seine fishing was slower in Village S, but both villages have experienced a rapid increase in the number of operating boats.

Migration of Crewmen to the Study Area

How many crewmen in the study villages are from other areas? Suppose that each set of purse-seine boats has twenty-five crewmen. That would mean that 2,750 crewmen are needed in Village J and 1,775 in Village S. The actual number of crewmen from other areas fluctuates every year, and there is no system in place for keeping an accurate record. According to key villagers, the number of crewmen from other areas accounts for about 60–70 per cent of the total number working in each village. Thus, the number of crewmen from other areas is estimated to be 1,600–2,000 for Village J and 1,000–1,200 for Village S.

The duration of stay for crewmen in each village varies widely. In this study, crewmen are categorized as either "short-term" labourers who stay in the village for only a few months of the year specifically for anchovy purse-seine fishing, or "long-term" labourers who remain in the village throughout the year. Some of the short-term labourers go back and forth between their place of origin and the study village for several years, while others come to work in the study village only once. Given the fact that the survey year (2007/08) was the first year working in the study village for 45 per cent of the interviewed crewmen, we can assume that there is a high turnover of migrating labourers (see Figure 10. 2). Table 10.2 presents the pattern of movement for the crewmen based on the definition above. The share of short-term labourers is only slightly larger than the long-term labourers in Village J and Village S. Thus, there is a mix of short-term and long-term labourers in the area.

TABLE 10.2
Number of Samples

Village	J	S	Total
Number of Samples	60	47	107
Short Term	34	29	63
Long Term	26	18	44

Source: Author's survey.

FIGURE 10.2
Distribution of Crewmen for the First Year of their Arrival in the Two Villages

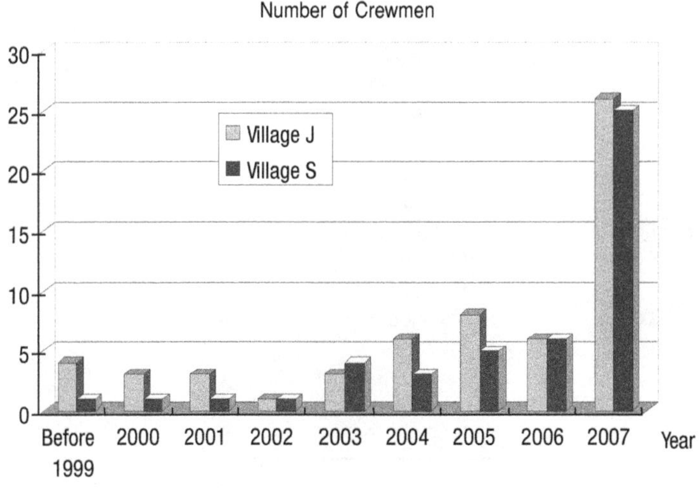

Source: Author's survey.

Where did these crewmen come from? And, how did they get here? The places of origin of the crewmen are shown in Table 10.3 and a location map is provided in Figure 10.1. The places of origin are widespread: northern, central and southern Rakhine State and even Ayeyarwaddy Division. The origin of migrating labourers was not concentrated in one location.

The majority of labourers decided to migrate to the study villages after hearing from friends or relatives that the area was booming with anchovy purse-seine fishing and would provide a high cash income. The first ones who came to the area tried to find an employer (boat owner) by contacting persons who used to work there.[11] In this sense, even though the places of origin were widespread, the labourers were part of a chain migration. The majority of labourers came to the villages to engage in purse-seine fishing only for a year as a trial. Some came alone and some came with other

TABLE 10.3
Distribution of Origin of Migrating Crewmen (number)

	Origin	Village J	Village S	Total
Northern Rakhine	Pon Na Kyin	13	11	24
	Kyauktaw	11	4	15
	Rathedaung	5	10	15
	Minbya	5	3	8
	Myauk U	3	4	7
	Buthidaung	1	4	5
	Sittwe	2	3	5
	Myebon	2	1	3
	Maungdaw	2	0	2
	Pauktaw	2	0	2
Central Rakhine	Kyaukphyu	3	0	3
	Man Aung	2	1	3
	Rambye	2	0	2
Southern Rakhine	Taungouk	4	0	4
	Thandwe	1	1	2
	Gwa	1	0	1
Ayeyarwaddy	Athouk	1	4	5
	Kyaiklat	0	1	1
Total		60	47	107

Source: Author's survey.

members of their household (such as brothers). In certain cases, the entire family came along (see Table 10.4).[12] Then, about 60 per cent of the crewmen returned to their original home after the season (Table 10.2). Among those who were not obligated to return to their home, some were fortunate enough to find local work — mainly shrimp fishing and repairing fishing nets — for the rainy season. For Village J, hotel construction was also on this list. Shrimp-fishing operations did not provide an opportunity for all crewmen since only three or four men were required for each shrimp boat. On the other hand, some crewmen who wanted to go home were forced to remain in the area because they did not have enough money for the return trip or to repay their debt to the boat owner (the reason is explained later). Hence, they engaged in any available casual labour to make ends meet.

We observed two prominent characteristics of the labourers from other areas. First, their average age was rather young (27.6 years old for Village J and 27.3 for Village S) and they were fairly new entrants into the labour market. Second, they had a relatively high level of education (see Figure 10.3). The dropout rate from middle school (in other words, they have completed primary education at least) was 45 per cent. In a previous survey conducted in various parts of Myanmar, the share of dropouts from middle school was 30 per cent on average, and 15 per cent in the case of non-farm-owners (agricultural labourers), which suggests that they stopped going to primary school at some earlier stage (Fujita 2009, pp. 295–300). The educational level of the migrant labourers in our study was thus comparatively high. For an occupation such as fishing crewman, which is generally categorized as simple but demanding and laborious work, the migrating labourers have an unexpectedly high level of education.

TABLE 10.4
Patterns of Migration (Number of Samples)

	Total	Short Term	Long Term
Single Migration	57	48	9
Migration of Part of the Household	8	6	2
Migration of All Household Members	42	9	33
Total	107	63	44

Source: Author's survey.

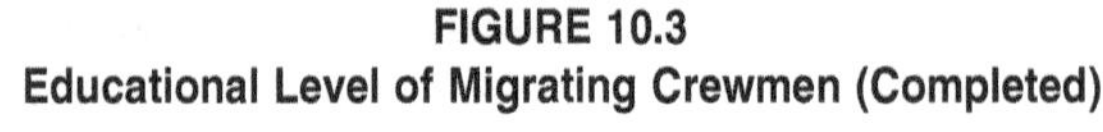

FIGURE 10.3
Educational Level of Migrating Crewmen (Completed)

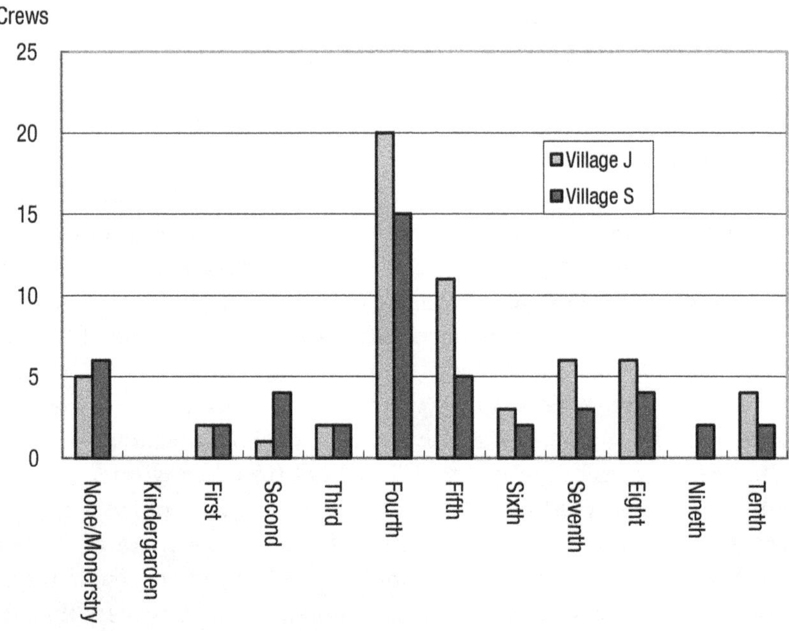

Note: In Myanmar's education system, primary school is from kindergarten to fourh grade, middle school is from fifth to seventh grade and high school is from eighth to tenth grade.
Source: Author's survey.

Looking at the places of origin and characteristics of the crewmen described so far, no large difference can be seen between Village J and Village S.[13] Thus, to avoid unnecessary complication, the following analysis will not differentiate between the two villages.

Background of Migrating Crewmen and Purpose for Migrating

The major occupation (the largest income source) of the households in local villages is shown in Table 10.5. It can be seen that the crewmen are from diverse classes that are not directly related to purse-seine fishing.

Labourers from farm-related households (self-employed farmers and agricultural labourers) account for the largest share. If the self-employed

TABLE 10.5
Main Household Occupation before Migration as Fishing Crewmen

Main Occupation of Household	%
Farming	31.8
Petty Trade	5.6
Public Servant	4.7
Carpenter/Plumber	2.8
Transportation	1.9
Agricultural Labour	35.5
Casual Labour	5.6
Fishing	8.4
Other	2.8
Unknown	0.9

Source: Author's survey.

farm households hold only a small area of land, their situation would not be very different from that of the agricultural-labour households. Table 10.6 shows that about 75 per cent of the households hold over five acres, indicating that these households are not necessarily small/marginal farmers. Medium and large farmers are also included. Therefore, farm-related households sending labourers to the study area are quite diverse, ranging from agricultural-labour households to large farm households.

TABLE 10.6
Acreage Held by Farming Households

	Number of Household
Under 5 acres	12
5 acres–10 acres	13
10 acres–15 acres	3
Over 15 acres	6
Total	34

Note: The acreage held by parent households was taken for 3 households.
Source: Author's survey.

There are also labourers from non-farm households such as petty trading, carpenters and public servants. Non-farm sectors such as petty trading generally provide a relatively high income in rural Myanmar, and these households often constitute the upper layer in the village economy (Takahashi 2000; Okamoto 2008*a*).

On the other hand, there are fishing households as well, but they are confined to very minor/marginal fishing. The infrastructure in northern Rakhine State is generally poor, and commercial fishing is not well developed there.[14] The fact that only two households own mechanized boats clearly shows that the type of fishing done in the north is quite different from the purse-seine fishing conducted in the study area.

Takahashi (1997) found that the occupation of migrant labourers remained constant before and after their move, and that agricultural-labour households were the main class of migrating people. On the other hand, the migrant labourers in this study were not only from the very poor class, but also from the rich class, which might be reflected in the high level of education pointed out earlier.

It is important to note that these migrating labourers are generally people who face fewer constraints against moving. Among the crewmen interviewed, only forty-eight of the 107 were the head of a household (that is, the main income earner). The remaining fifty-nine were all sons. Thus, many migrating labourers are the second- or third-generation workforce in the respective households. For example, in the case of farm households (thirty-four households), which may be the most constrained in terms of the necessity to manage their farmland, more than 70 per cent (twenty-five households) sent the sons rather than the head of the household to the study area. In the case of the households where the household head came to the study area (nine households), farming was not an issue when making the decision to move since they were independent of their farmer fathers (four households), or they had only a small area of land, which could be left idle and monitored by the remaining family members during the dry season (five households). Hence, the majority of crewmen came from households with few constraints on moving.

This trend can be confirmed by examining the kind of work that these crewmen previously did at their origins during the purse-seine season (see Table 10.7). The majority (80 per cent) were engaged in labour (agricultural or otherwise), assisting with their father's farming or fishing operations, attending school, or doing nothing at all.

TABLE 10.7
Activities Engaged in by Crewmen at their Home Village in the Dry Season

Agricultural Labour	25
Other Non-Agricultural	24
Assistance to Parent's Farm	15
Assistance to Fishing	7
Traditional Performing Arts	2
Student	6
Nothing	7
Fishing	9
Driver	7
Petty Trading	5
Total	107

Source: Author's survey.

Generally, migration was adopted as a strategy for diversification of income sources. Table 10.8 shows what the interviewees hoped to do with the income earned as crewmen. Note that this table only shows the crewmen's expectations, and not their actual usage. Nevertheless, since expectations are important in making the decision to migrate, it is useful to confirm the intended purpose of migration.

From this it is clear that there are two types of migrating labourers. The first are those who intend to earn a much higher income than they could have earned at home in order to expand their future economic opportunities through expanding their main occupation or entering a better-paying occupation. These labourers have positioned anchovy purse-seine fishing as a step towards upgrading their living standard. For example, of the thirty-one crewmen who intended to purchase farmland, nineteen were from agricultural-labour households, and seven from self-employed farm households. By engaging in anchovy fishing, they stood a chance of one day owning land or expanding their current acreage. Obtaining the capital to start a small business (such as operating a grocery store or brokering agricultural/fishery products, which can provide a relatively high and stable income in rural Myanmar) also figured prominently in the crewmen's hopes.

TABLE 10.8
Planned Usage for Crewmen's Earnings

	Planned Usage	Total	Main Occupation of Household before Migration				
			Self-employed Agriculture	Agricultural Wage Labour	Fishing	Non-farming	Unknown
Capital Accumulation Type 71	Purchase of Farmland	31	7	19	1	4	0
	Purchase of Livestock	5	2	1	0	2	0
	Initial Funds for Fishing	8	3	3	0	2	0
	Initial Funds for Petty Trading	21	6	6	1	8	0
	Purchase of Trishaw	1	0	1	0	0	0
	Initial Funds for Carpentry	1	0	0	0	1	0
	Initial Funds for Saw Mill	1	0	0	1	0	0
	Savings	3	0	0	0	3	0
Subsistance Type 33	Working Capital for Agriculture	10	10	0	0	0	0
	Working Capital for Fishery	12	3	1	3	5	0
	Consumption	8	1	4	2	0	1
	Repair and Construction of House	2	0	2	0	0	0
	Education & Medication	1	0	1	0	0	0
Other 3	To be a Buddhist novice	1	1	0	0	0	0
	Wish to Engage in Other Job	1	0	0	1	0	0
	Unknown	1	1	0	0	0	0
	Grand Total	107	34	38	9	25	1

Note: The crewman wanted to engage in some work other than the shrimp farming, which his father does.
Source: Author's Survey.

The second type was those who intended to minimize the effects of income fluctuations throughout the year. Some planned on using their fishing income for consumption, house construction and maintenance, education and medication. Those who planned on using the money to supplement the working capital for farming or fishing were also included here. Myanmar has a typically underdeveloped financial market that cannot be depended upon to raise working capital for farming and fishing, especially if it is for home consumption. Therefore, people need to raise their own capital through the labour market (that is, through migration). In some cases, even though the original intention was to expand their economic activities, crewmen ended up sending the money to their families for home consumption (see Table 10.9).

Hart (1994, p. 48) analysed the correlation between the income diversification strategy of the household and the land holding size, and pointed out that large farmers "diversify to accumulate", while small farmers "diversify to survive". The same two purposes can also be found for the migration of labourers to anchovy purse-seine fishing. The fact that labourers who differ in their purpose are pouring into the same employment opportunity signifies the absence of local opportunities for achieving either of the two goals.

IMPACT OF EARNINGS ON HOUSEHOLD INCOME

In the survey year (2007/08), the common practice was for the owner and the crew to take an equal share (50 per cent each) of the value of the daily catch. The share for the crew was divided equally among all the crewmen. A third of the fuel cost (diesel oil) was borne by the boat owner, but the rest (including engine oil and lamps used for lighting the water) was borne by the crewmen. Up until a few years ago, the crew had to bear the entire fuel cost.[15] However, the increase in fuel costs in recent years meant that very little cash was left for the crewmen and they soon lost their motivation to work. Therefore, the owners decided to bear part of the fuel cost.[16]

However, since the owner generally did not go out to sea with the crew, the two leading crewmen also received 10 per cent and 5 per cent, respectively, of the owner's share for monitoring and controlling the operation. Given the uncertainty surrounding the duration of stay of the migrants, the crew leaders were usually villagers. This does not mean that migrating crewmen are precluded from becoming leaders. At the

TABLE 10.9
Purpose of Remittances

Purpose of Remittance	Number of Samples	The Original Purpose of Migration								
		Purchase of Farmland	Working Capital for Agriculture	Purchase of Livestock	Working Capital for Fishery	Initial Funds for Trading	Initial Funds for Carpentry	Consumption	Repair of House	Unknown
Consumption	21	6	2	2	3	5	1	1	1	0
Repair of House	1	0	0	0	0	1	0	0	0	0
Medication	1	0	0	0	0	0	0	1	0	0
Saving	1	0	0	0	0	1	0	0	0	0
Unknown	1	0	0	0	0	0	0	0	0	1

Source: Author's survey.

time of our interviews, however, there were no leaders among the interviewed crewmen.

It was very difficult to estimate the exact income for each individual crewman because some may have received advances in the form of cash or rice from the owner and, in any event, their monthly income fluctuated widely depending on the size of the catch.

As a second-best approach, we considered the standard daily wage (2,000 kyat[17] per day) as the average reward for crewmen. Owners occasionally hire crewmen on a daily basis, to substitute for anyone unable to work on a particular day. The daily wages paid to these outside crewmen could well be determined based on the average catch and price. A daily wage of 2,000 kyat compares favourably with the 500 to 1,000 kyat they could expect to earn for agricultural work in their home villages. Our income estimates were based on this wage, assuming that crewmen worked twenty-four days per month for six months. Our estimates also allowed for an additional 400 kyat per day for fish provided by the owners for personal consumption. On this basis, the yearly income for crewmen would be about 350,000 kyat.

Table 10.10 shows the estimated household income, excluding the crewman earnings. As about half the households earned less than 500,000 kyat, the income of the migrant crewmen was significant for low-income households.

TABLE 10.10
Distribution of Household Income Excluding Crewmen's Earnings

Household Income excluding Crew Income	Total (Sample)	Contribution of Anchovy Crewman Earnings to Total Household Income (%)	Contribution of Total Crewman Earnings to Total Household Income (%)
Under 100,000	14	56.6	94.3
100,000–500,000	41	51.4	57.4
500,000–1,000,000	29	34.4	36.6
1,000,000–5,000,000	19	17.6	23.3
5,000,000–	4	5.2	9.4
Total Number of Samples	107		

Source: Author's survey.

To explain the full impact of the crewmen's earnings on their household income, it would be necessary to obtain more comprehensive data on the actual usage of the money than was allowed by our survey. (For more than half the crewmen, this was the first year they had been engaged in anchovy fishing and many did not know how much they would earn, while others did not know how the money would be spent until after they had returned home.)

Therefore, as a second-best approach again, we consider the significance of 350,000 kyat from various aspects. First of all, is this level of income sufficiently "high" compared to the crewmen's expectations?[18] What was clear from Table 10.11, which shows the income earned at home during the season, all but seven of the seventy-three respondents would have earned less than the 350,000 kyat they stood to earn as migrant crewmen if they had stayed at home during the dry season. In fact, more than eighty per cent of them would have earned less than 200,000 kyat. Therefore, purse-seine fishing provides migrant labourers with sufficiently good income, and this is particularly so if the crewmen are redundant labourers at home.

We calculated that the average cost for moving from home to the study area was about 20,000 kyat per person. Some labourers sold their assets or took out loans to be able to do so, but the majority (seventy-six per cent) used their savings or borrowed from their parents. Their living costs while they were away from home were negligible, the majority of crewmen living in small, shabby huts prepared by the owners or the village. While working on the fishing boats, they did not pay rent for the huts.[19]

TABLE 10.11
Earned Income of Crewmen before Migration in the Dry Season

No Job	24
Under 200,000	28
200,000-350,000	14
350,000	7
Total	73

Source: Author's survey.

So, what can be purchased with 350,000 kyat? We take rice as an example since it accounts for the largest share of household expenditures in Myanmar. According to the results of an official household-expenditure survey, monthly per-capita rice consumption for rural Rakhine State is 8.6 *pyi*[20] (CSO 1999, p. 185). The average retail price for rice was 700 kyat per *pyi* at the time of the survey, and the average number of family members was 4.8 per household. Based on this information, the yearly rice expenditure per household is calculated to be about 350,000 kyat. This means that a crewman's earnings were almost equal to the average annual expenditure on rice.[21]

The 350,000 kyat could, depending on the area and quality of the land, also buy approximately one acre of farmland in the home villages of the migrating crews.[22]

While relatively well-off farm households can use a crewman's earnings to purchase an additional acre of land every year, for poor households the story is somewhat different. While some migrating labourers from low-income households hoped to save money for new economic activities as well (Table 10.8), achieving such a goal seems very difficult.

The discussion thus far has been based on the assumption that the average earnings for a crewman were 2,000 kyat per day. However, the actual rewards fluctuate widely according to the size of the catch. The income fluctuations in fishing are far larger than those in farming.[23] In the case of anchovy purse-seine fishing, earnings fluctuate according to the catch from each boat, the number of crewmen and the seasonal and annual fluctuation in fish resources.

In the survey year, most of the fishing boats suffered from an unusually low catch of anchovies.[24] Consequently, many boats were forced to go to more remote waters. The low catch also resulted in payment being made to the crewmen three months into the season, even though it was supposed to be every month. (In the cases where payments were delayed, crewmen survived by receiving cash or rice as advance payment.) Some crewmen were so frustrated over the situation that they left in the middle of the season without repaying their debt (that is, advance payments) to the boat owner.[25]

There was a contrasting case as well, however. A boat from Village S had a lucky day's catch that was equivalent to ten million kyat from one trip[26] — an amount comparable to one-third of the average seasonal income for one set of anchovy purse-seine boats, according to our estimates

(Okamoto 2008*b*, Annex table). Therefore, the crewmen on that particular fishing boat received the equivalent to two months' earnings. This may be an extreme case, but it serves to demonstrate how income fluctuations can be quite large.

Of those who responded to the survey question on daily earnings, more than twenty earned only 1,000 kyat per day, which is no more than they would have earned at home.

A number of crewmen appeared to earn less than they had expected. This was clearly demonstrated by those who left in the middle of the season, and those who had a rather negative attitude about returning to work the following season (sixteen crewmen said that they would not be returning the following year, and seven responded that they would make their decision depending on the outcome of the present season).[27] Some crewmen did not have enough money for the trip back to their home village or to repay their advance wages to the owner, and thus were forced to continue working.

It is not possible for crewmen to foresee the annual fluctuation in catch or determine which boats will have the biggest catch. In this sense, anchovy purse-seine fishing is regarded as a very unstable employment opportunity.

CONCLUSION

This paper has attempted to point out the characteristics of (and economic outcome for) migrating labourers in two fishing villages in Rakhine State in order to highlight the issues affecting the current intra-rural movement in Myanmar. In a survey conducted in the mid-1990s, the floating class in rural areas, namely agricultural labourers, moved within the same township for the purpose of minimizing fluctuations in annual income. This study showed a more dynamic labour movement, even in the peripheral area of Myanmar. The characteristics of this labour movement are summarized as follows.

Labourers are migrating from remote areas, especially from northern Rakhine State. They are from diverse economic classes, which are not necessarily associated with the fishing industry. Not only the floating class that has fewer constraints against moving, such as agricultural and casual labourers, but also those from households with medium and large farms are migrating to the area to work as crewmen. In the case of those coming from relatively affluent households, surplus male labourers tend to migrate alone.

The diversity of economic class of migrating labourers is also reflected in the existence of two different motivations for migration. One is capital accumulation. There were labourers who expected a higher income than what would have been earned at home and who intended to further expand their income-earning opportunities. The other class mainly intended to smooth their annual household income. These were the labourers who had a difficult time finding employment during the dry season. Two types of crewmen coexisted here; namely, those who diversified their income sources for the purpose of accumulation and those who diversified their income in order to survive.

The average income level of the crewmen was generally higher than they could have earned at home during that specific time of the year. However, the earned income was only enough to meet the cost of rice for a year. In this sense, for low-income households that were highly dependent on a crewman's earnings, migration did not necessarily match their capital-accumulation expectations. Furthermore, the income fluctuated widely, influenced by uncontrollable factors such as the weather or the conditions of the fishing ground.

Three points can be drawn from the above findings. First, unlike the period just after the start of Myanmar's economic transition, the major objective for migration was not only annual income smoothing, but also to gain a much higher income than could be achieved at the present rate of increase, even within the (remote) rural areas of Myanmar.

In this process, the economic disparity within the areas of origin of these labourers is likely to expand. In other words, the disparity between those who successfully accumulate capital to expand their economic opportunities (classes that are relatively affluent and have redundant labourers within their households) and those who have yet to focus on maintaining a subsistence level or those who did not migrate from their village, is expected to increase (the gap between the latter two would not be large, as both are mainly focused on survival). As in the case of overseas migration (Takahashi 2007), the disparity would increase in terms of asset accumulation as well as living standard between those who succeed and those who do not succeed in intra-rural migration.

The second point is the emergence of regional economic disparity in Myanmar. The case of Rakhine State is a clear example. There is a large flow of people from the north to the south of the state. This can be simply interpreted as indicating that there are fewer economic opportunities in the north than in the south, which was quick to respond to the emerging opportunities for fishery development. Commercial fishing is limited to a small scale in the north. Behind this is the lagging development of basic infrastructure, resulting in less external economic stimulus reaching the area. If some of the people who have accumulated sufficient capital return home and contribute to activating the local economy, the regional economic disparity would surely be reduced. However, the reality is that the number of migrating labourers has increased year by year over the last decade. Thus, the regional economic disparity could widen further, depending on how successfully each area grasps the opening of the market economy, no matter how small it is in comparison to the experience of neighbouring countries.

Lastly, the study findings suggest that even after twenty years of economic transition, the Myanmar labour market has not developed sufficiently to meet either the purpose of income smoothing or capital accumulation for these rural households. Once again, anchovy purse-seine fishing is a very unstable and simple employment opportunity, but each year it attracts almost 2,000 labourers from diverse economic and social backgrounds. This fact clearly shows that there are no alternative employment opportunities for these migrating labourers. Attractive, stable and wide-ranging employment opportunities are not available either to those targeting capital accumulation or those only hoping to survive. This is the main reason for the concentration of migrant workers with different objectives in such an unstable employment opportunity.

What this suggests is the urgent need to create labour-intensive industries. Otherwise, more of the rural (and probably urban as well) population will seek high-cost, high-risk opportunities overseas if they think they can afford it. Not having the capacity to properly utilize its domestic labour force is certainly undesirable for Myanmar, which requires industrialization for mid- and long-term economic development, as the histories of other neighbouring Asian countries suggest.

Notes

1. I would like to thank U Khin Maung Soe, Department of Fisheries, Ministry of Livestock and Fisheries, Myanmar, for the continuous assistance and valuable inputs to the research. This chapter is a revised version of "Issues Affecting the Movement of Rural Labour in Myanmar: Rakhine Case Study," *IDE Discussion Paper* No. 206, July 2009.

2. Nang Mya Kay Khaing and Koichi Fujita (2009) found that those engaged in the informal sector in Yangon, the former capital, were not necessarily from villages but, rather, from towns in the rural area.
3. For example, the cost of migration from Chin State to Malaysia was equal to about one or two times the annual agricultural income, according to Takahashi (2007, p. 419). According to interviews conducted by the author in the dry zone in May 2010, the cost required for migrating to Malaysia is estimated in 13 million kyat per labourer.
4. The administration units of Myanmar are State and Division, District, Township and Village Tract.
5. In some cases, migrant workers were arrested and sent back to Myanmar without any money (Takahashi 2007).
6. Village tracts normally consist of several villages. M village tract consists of two villages, while the S village tract consists of five.
7. Interview with the former chairmen of Village S.
8. The start of this type of fishing was earlier in Village J than in Village S.
9. Small-scale trawling is illegal, but is given tacit approval in the field.
10. The exact change in number of boats is not available. The Department of Fisheries records the number of gear licenses, but these numbers often differ from the figures obtained at the village level.
11. The exception was crewmen from Ayeyarwaddy. One boat owner moved to Village S in order to start anchovy fishing. He recruited crewmen from his native area as he preferred to employ Burmese, rather than the Rakhine.
12. Included here are several crewmen who were single when they moved to the area, but later got married in the surveyed villages.
13. The average size of household is almost the same for the two villages (4.9 persons/household for Village J; 4.8 for Village S).
14. There are shrimp aquaculture ponds (extensive type) in the area, but the high start-up cost has been a barrier to new entrants.
15. As noted earlier, the owners of anchovy fishing boats do not go out to sea with the crewmen. Therefore, there is always a possibility of inappropriate fuel use (that is, consuming more than is necessary). Therefore, the owners preferred that the crewmen bear the fuel cost in order to reduce the monitoring cost.
16. Interview with boat owners in Village J (November 2007).
17. The season for anchovy purse-seine fishing is from October to May (eight months). However, the catch is usually low at both the start and the end of the season. Also, those who come from other areas tend to arrive late and leave early (before the Burmese New Year). Therefore, their working period is taken as six months in the calculation here.
18. The total number of respondents came to be seventy-three, excluding those who were unable to respond clearly and those who had arrived and settled in

the area more than three years earlier. The reason for excluding the latter is that it does not make sense to compare the income between the two different places and time, given the country's high inflation rate. However, exception here is the crewmen who received wages in kind. They were added to the analysis even if they had arrived more than three years earlier, as their income could be estimated using average paddy prices in the village.

19. Some of the crewmen who had worked in the area for a number of years and had their family with them lived in more solid houses.
20. One *pyi* equals 2.19 kg.
21. The expenditure for edible oil accounts for the second-largest share after rice. Crewmen eat fish supplied by the owners every morning, and they eat meat once a month at most.
22. Legally, the state owns the farmland and farmers only hold the tillage rights. Buying and selling is prohibited, but there are frequent informal transactions for tillage rights.
23. Refer to Okamoto (2008*b*) for the large fluctuation of income from prawn fishing in the study area.
24. The reason for the low catch is not clear. It may have been due to changes in the sea current or the increase in catch in recent years.
25. The owner would receive damages equivalent to the advanced wages. One boat owner said that ten crewmen had run away at the time of the survey.
26. Interview with the previous chairman of Village S.
27. Reasons given by crewmen included: "No matter where it is, casual labour is casual labour"; "Farming is better"; and "I can make ends meet working at home".

References

Bradford, W. and A.Vicary. "Preliminary Survey Results about Burmese Migrant Workers in Thailand: State/Division of Origin, Years of Entry, Minimum Wage, and Work Permit". *Burma Economic Watch* 1 (2005): 3–25.

Central Statistical Organization (CSO). *Report of 1997 Household Income and Expenditure Survey*. Yangon, Myanmar, 1999.

Fujita, Koichi. "Agricultural Labourers in Myanmar during the Economic Transition: Views from the Study of Selected Villages". In *The Economic Transition in Myanmar after 1988: Market Economy versus State Control*, edited by M. Fujita, F. Mieno and I. Okamoto. Singapore: National University of Singapore Press in association with Kyoto University Press, 2009.

Hart, G. "The Dynamics of Diversification in an Asian Rice Region". In *Development or deterioration? Work in Rural Asia*, edited by B. Koppel, J. Hawkins and W. James. Boulder: Lynne Reinner, 1994.

Nang Mya Kay Khaing and K. Fujita. "Urban Informal Sector Labourers in Yangon". In *The Economic Transition in Myanmar after 1988: Market Economy versus State Control*, edited by M. Fujita, F. Mieno and I. Okamoto. Singapore: National University of Singapore Press in association with Kyoto University Press, 2009.

Okamoto, Ikuko. *Economic Disparity in Rural Myanmar: Transformation under Market Liberalization*. Singapore: National University of Singapore Press 2008*a*.

———. "The Shrimp Export Boom and Small-Scale Fishermen in Myanmar" *IDE Discussion Paper* No.135. March 2008b.

Takahashi, Akio. "Intra-Rural Household Movement and Occupation in Myanmar". *Asian Economy* 38, no. 11 (1997): 2–24 (in Japanese).

———. *Myanmar's Village Economy in Transition: Peasant' and Non-Peasant' Lives under the Market-Oriented Economy*. Tokyo: University Tokyo Press, 2000 (in Japanese).

———. "Swiddens, Rice Terraces, and Malay Connections: Resource Use and Socio-economic Strata in the Chin Hills, Myanmar". *Southeast Asian Studies* 45, no. 3 (2007): 404–27 (in Japanese).

IV

The Role of International Cooperation and Governance

11

CYCLONE NARGIS AND ASEAN
A Window for More Meaningful Development Cooperation in Myanmar

William Sabandar

INTRODUCTION

Cyclone Nargis struck Myanmar in May 2008, severely affecting the lives of 2.4 million of the 7.5 million people who live in the Ayeyarwaddy Delta. Approximately 140,000 people were killed or unaccounted for following the cyclone; 800,000 homes were destroyed or damaged, vital infrastructure was severely damaged, and water sources were contaminated. The cyclone not only destroyed physical assets in villages and inundated paddy land with sea water, but also washed away household assets, including food stocks from the recent harvest in April/ May, livestock, seeds and tools, leaving hundreds of thousands of people in a situation of food insecurity. Cyclone Nargis is the eighth-deadliest cyclone ever recorded and by far the worst natural disaster in the history of Myanmar. Damage and loss from the cyclone was estimated at US$4.1 billion (Tripartite Core Group 2008).

The total economic losses caused by the cyclone were detrimental to Myanmar's already underdeveloped economy. According to the 2007/ 2008 Human Development Report, GDP per capita (Purchasing Power Parity in US dollars) for Myanmar is US$1,027, the lowest in the region, as compared to US$29,663 for Singapore, US$8,677 for Thailand, or US$3,843 for Indonesia. At the same time, Official Development Assistance (ODA) to Myanmar in recent years has been about US$3 per capita per year. This is one of the lowest in the world. As shown in Table 11.1, the comparative figure for Laos is US$63 per capita, for Cambodia US$38, Sudan US$55 and Zimbabwe US$21.

ASEAN was asked to step in and facilitate the communication between the international humanitarian community and the Myanmar Government. Acknowledging the unprecedented scale of the disaster, ASEAN rose to the challenge and collaborated with the government to allow international relief workers to operate in the country. At the Special Meeting of the ASEAN Foreign Ministers in Singapore on 19 May 2008, the ministers recognized with appreciation the outpouring of goodwill and strong determination of the international community to help the victims of Cyclone Nargis. Following the recommendation of the ASEAN-Emergency Rapid Assessment Team (ERAT) that was mobilized a week after Cyclone Nargis, ASEAN Foreign Ministers agreed to establish an ASEAN-led coordinating mechanism and set up the ASEAN Humanitarian Task Force (AHTF) for the Victims of Cyclone Nargis to facilitate effective distribution and utilization of assistance from the international community, including incoming international assistance to support the Government of Myanmar's

TABLE 11.1
GDP and ODA Comparisons, 2007/2008

	GDP per capita (PPP)	ODA per capita
Cambodia	US$2,727	US$38
Laos	US$2,039	US$63
Myanmar	US$1,027	US$3
Sudan	US$2,083	US$55
Zimbabwe	US$2,038	US$21

Source: <www.oecd.org/dac/stats/idsonline>, Development Assistance Committee, OECD, Paris.

ongoing relief, recovery and reconstruction efforts. The Task Force, chaired by the Secretary-General of ASEAN, Dr Surin Pitsuwan, provides policy decisions and sets the priorities and targets with regard to the implementation of this ASEAN-led initiative. In order to assist the AHTF in providing relevant technical expertise and inputs, an Advisory Group to the AHTF was established, consisting of representatives from Myanmar's neighbours (China, India, and Bangladesh), the United Nations, the Red Cross and Red Crescent Movement, the World Bank, the Asian Development Bank, non-governmental organizations, and international donors represented by the United Kingdom, Norway, and Australia. (Besides being a member of the Advisory Group, the Australian Government's support to the AHTF through technical expertise, operations and recovery efforts after Nargis has been vital for our success in Myanmar.)

For the purpose of day-to-day operations, the Tripartite Core Group (TCG) was set up following the decision of the First AHTF Meeting and with support from the ASEAN-UN International Pledging Conference held on 25 May 2008 in Yangon. The TCG, chaired by the Government of Myanmar, consists of three representatives each from the Government of Myanmar, ASEAN and the international humanitarian community led by the UN. The TCG mechanism has created an opportunity for international governments, civil-society organizations and international NGOs to take part in the massive humanitarian assistance to help the survivors of Cyclone Nargis. The dialogue and good cooperation between its members contributed to facilitate efficient, transparent and accountable provision of relief and recovery efforts, promoting governance in the longer-term development process. The TCG has built trust and confidence between the Government of Myanmar and the international community.

A UNIQUE ASEAN-LED COORDINATING MECHANISM

ASEAN has had a unique role to play in the aftermath of Cyclone Nargis. This role is mainly to bridge the gap in trust and confidence between the international community and the Government of Myanmar. Such a role strengthens, and is complementary to, the existing cooperation between the international community, through the United Nations system, and the national government. ASEAN's facilitating role has helped in accelerating the flow of international assistance to the victims and survivors of Cyclone Nargis. In a review of this role, Creac'h and Fan (2008) noted: "In response to the devastation caused by Cyclone Nargis, ASEAN as an organization took a bold step by proactively assuming a leadership role, both in convincing the Myanmar government to cooperate with the international community and in managing the response itself. In doing so, it has helped to open an unprecedented level of humanitarian space."

Working through the TCG mechanism, ASEAN has been able to:

1. facilitate unimpeded access for humanitarian workers. The TCG has granted nearly 4,000 visas for humanitarian workers since the relief phase.
2. conduct comprehensive assessment of need, loss and damage through the Post-Nargis Joint Assessment (PONJA) in the period immediately after the cyclone until late June 2008.
3. inform humanitarian assistance strategies and programme change to benefit affected communities through its Periodic Reviews and Social Impacts Monitoring.
4. develop a Post-Nargis Recovery and Preparedness Plan (PONREPP) which provides a framework for medium- and long-term recovery to promote productive, healthy and protected lives.
5. coordinate the transition from relief to the recovery phase and mobilize resources to address the critical needs for the recovery effort. Furthermore, ASEAN has also strengthened humanitarian coordination at the township level through ASEAN-UN hub co-location and collaboration to ensure focused assistance to the affected population.

PONJA was a landmark document on two counts. First was the full access given to the assessment team by the Myanmar Government to go to the areas the team chose, therefore making the assessment credible. Often, access is taken for granted, but in the case of PONJA, it was prerequisite and ASEAN played a significant role in securing this access. Second, the willingness of all concerned (that is, the Government itself, the NGOs, the UN, ASEAN, the World Bank, the ADB, the Red Cross and the whole humanitarian community) to cooperate with one another and to "own" the report, therefore making it a joint effort. PONJA reaffirms that the needs are at the community level. Therefore, to provide reassurance that assistance is delivered and to monitor the humanitarian needs and the socio-economic impacts of the assistance on the ground, ASEAN, together with the UN, the World Bank and the humanitarian community, pioneered the Periodic Reviews and the Social Impacts Monitoring process, to be done six months and then one year after the cyclone.

Cyclone Nargis occurred on the eve of the ASEAN Charter's inauguration, a critical juncture in the region's progressive integration. The ASEAN response was an opportunity to begin working towards the goals of the Charter, such as bringing ASEAN closer to the people, enhancing the well-being and livelihood of the people, alleviating poverty and narrowing the development gap within ASEAN through close cooperation with civil society, national and international agencies. Nargis has also challenged us to draw upon our resources at every step, for the first time, launching ASEAN's Youth Volunteer programme in the Delta. ASEAN's partnership with the civil society in the implementation of these projects not only enhances people's well-being and livelihoods, building more resilient communities, but also empowers the communities. Through the participatory approach, communities have become more engaged and conversant in planning to address their pressing needs, strengthening accountability and transparency to increase proper coordination, trust and confidence among communities, local authorities and other humanitarian agencies.

One of the successful examples of the ASEAN Volunteers Project is the project named "Rebuilding small farm livelihoods" in Tha Leik Gyi Village Tract, Pyapon Township, which was implemented by a Myanmar NGO with the support of ASEAN Volunteers. Committed to a community-led approach, the project ensured community participation and feedback about the project's activities by undertaking periodic needs assessments and surveys to monitor progress. The ASEAN Volunteers were also involved in facilitating consultation meetings among the villagers and local village authorities to debate among themselves and identify their priority needs, which fostered community empowerment and volunteerism. The formation of informal committees in each village promoted a sense of responsibility, ensured the participation of women and vulnerable groups, and created a venue for interaction and cooperation among the ASEAN volunteers, villagers, local village authorities, and the village tract heads.

CHALLENGES REMAIN

Although there have been many achievements to date (that is, the end of 2009), much remains to be done in helping to rebuild the lives of those affected by Cyclone Nargis. Significant efforts have been made to ensure that aid reaches survivors of the cyclone. One year after Nargis, ASEAN is still conducting community monitoring to gauge relief-and-recovery efforts. The published findings of the Periodic Review have indicated that, despite progress being made in all sectors, immediate efforts are still required to address the critical needs in such sectors as livelihoods, shelter/disaster-risk reduction, education, water sanitation and hygiene, and health. For example, 90 per cent of the households surveyed do not consider their shelter safe from another cyclone; 76 per cent still use unimproved water resources, particularly during the dry season; 41 per cent of those relying on agriculture lack capital and credit; and 90 per cent have their babies delivered at home rather than at health-care facilities (Tripartite Core Group 2009).

As of June 2009, Myanmar had received 67 per cent of the US$477 million promised in the revised flash appeal, and there has been great difficulty in securing the US$691 million earmarked as the total budget for the three-year recovery and preparedness plan. By way of comparison, following the Indian Ocean tsunami, an event of a similar scale to Cyclone Nargis in its impact on lives and the size of the affected populations, Aceh received US$5,140 million in international assistance during the first three years.

No doubt politics might influence the level of humanitarian assistance. However, experience from the field, such as the ASEAN community-driven and other humanitarian assistance programmes, have shown that ASEAN volunteers and civil-society organizations help local communities to strengthen their local institutions and formulate their strategies for reducing disaster risk and poverty. Such assistance helps local communities become more vocal and more participatory in building up their communities, thus fostering development, governance and democracy.

It is also noteworthy that humanitarian aid does work satisfactorily in Myanmar. The governance of the relief-and-recovery process under the ASEAN-led coordination has been good and strong. During a conference to discuss the way forward for the implementation of the recovery and preparedness plan in Yangon in May 2009, Mark Canning, then UK Ambassador to Myanmar, noted that the humanitarian assistance fund had been correctly spent and that no cases of inappropriate use had been reported.

With an effective coordination mechanism already in place, ASEAN, in collaboration with other members of the TCG, is currently sustaining a coordinated effort to address the existing gaps in all sectors as recovery enters the medium- to long-term stage based on the guiding framework articulated in the PONREPP.

The TCG has successfully facilitated international assistance for cyclone-affected areas in the relief and early-recovery phase. However, as the recovery phase has unfolded, the original mandate of the TCG has not been adjusted satisfactorily in line with the shifting development context. If not addressed urgently, this will impede the work of the international community, its national partners and communities.

THE WAY FORWARD: TRANSITION AND SUSTAINABILITY

The extension of the TCG mandate to July 2010 provides an opportunity for ASEAN to engage in dialogue on development policy in Myanmar at the regional level. Following the framework of the ASEAN Charter that works towards realizing an ASEAN community by 2015, ASEAN is working closely with the government of Myanmar to create a coordinated strategy for Myanmar's development. Myanmar will benefit from capacity-building support provided by regional neighbours, donor agencies and international organizations. Commitment from donors and the international development partners is essential to the sustainability of the recovery effort, which depends on their on-going integration into the country's long-term development strategy. ASEAN will support regional-development cooperation initiatives by ensuring that its post-Nargis efforts are closely coordinated with those of the wider international-development community.

At the 42nd ASEAN Ministerial Meeting in Phuket on 20 July 2009, ASEAN Foreign Ministers approved six recommendations from the Chair of the ASEAN Humanitarian Task Force. These recommendations lay out three main priorities: (i) addressing outstanding critical needs through the TCG; (ii) working with the Government of Myanmar to develop a transition strategy to ensure the sustainability of recovery efforts; and (iii) documenting and institutionalizing best practice to strengthen ASEAN's capacity to respond to future disasters. These are the strategic objectives that will define ASEAN's approach and work in Myanmar until July 2010.

The ASEAN Ministers affirmed that the TCG must continue to play a leading role in coordinating the international assistance for post-Nargis operations to July 2010, specifically in coordinating resources, facilitating operations, and monitoring and evaluating the progress and achievements of the relief and recovery work. In this effort, ASEAN is seeking support and funding commitments to the PONREPP Action Plan from ASEAN Member States and the international community in order to meet critical, outstanding humanitarian needs and provide essential recovery for those worst affected.

While the mandate of the TCG mechanism ends in July 2010 and the recovery process for many survivors of Cyclone Nargis will take many years, it is critical that ASEAN's contributions and activities from now until July 2010 are conducted in a way that ensures sustainability of recovery. Reflecting this concern, one of the calls by ASEAN Foreign Ministers was for both the AHTF and TCG to be given sufficient authority to work closely and openly with relevant line ministries to coordinate programmes that have a longer-term development outcome. This will involve handing over coordination structures and systems to the relevant authorities, as well as providing any capacity-building assistance to the respective authorities in such areas as disaster-risk reduction and information management. ASEAN has started this engagement already with the Ministry of National Planning and Economic Development and the Ministry of Agriculture and Irrigation, and will be pursuing this cooperation with the Ministry of Social Welfare, the Ministry of Health, and the Ministry of Education.

ASEAN is also documenting and institutionalizing the good practices from the post-Nargis operations to strengthen the implementation of the ASEAN Agreement on Disaster Management and Emergency Response (AADMER). AADMER is the newly established ASEAN mechanism that aims to achieve substantial reductions in loss of life and in the social, economic and environmental assets of the ASEAN Member States (ASEAN Secretariat 2009). In this way, the post-Nargis response in Myanmar will directly contribute to the capacity of the region to respond effectively to natural disasters. While AADMER is expected to come into force by the end of 2009, ASEAN needs to have a stronger role in responding to natural disasters within the region. ASEAN's experience in post-Nargis relief and recovery in Myanmar should be utilized to strengthen our response to disasters in the region.

In supporting Myanmar to become an equal member of ASEAN, ASEAN has a responsibility to continue to support Myanmar within the regional framework of the ASEAN Charter and progress towards realizing an ASEAN Community by 2015. Myanmar has been a member of ASEAN for only twelve years and there is much that ASEAN can do to help Myanmar (as well as other new members Cambodia, Laos and Vietnam) become more on par with other member-states in all sectors of development, from trade to education, from finance to agriculture. For example, ASEAN can provide specialized technical capacity-building for Myanmar officials to ensure meaningful participation in ASEAN meetings and negotiations, and facilitate regional policy dialogues among ASEAN members to share experiences, policy options and institutional frameworks in specific sectors. We will be developing our strategy for ASEAN's long-term support for Myanmar, even as we continue to coordinate the delivery of much-needed assistance to meet the critical outstanding needs of the victims of Cyclone Nargis.

ASEAN has opened a new chapter with the entry into force of the ASEAN Charter in December 2008. The Charter reaffirmed the commitment of all ASEAN States to internationally recognized principles, as contained in legal instruments. Among the Charter's 14 principles were adherence to the rule of law, good governance, the principles of democracy and constitutional government, upholding the Charter and upholding international law. The ASEAN Charter also conferred a legal personality on the organization.

The ASEAN Charter will transform the member-states into a truly rules-based, people-centred and closely integrated community by 2015. This community will be based on the three pillars of unity at the political and security level, and also the economic and the social-cultural levels. A dispute-settlement mechanism for the region will be implemented, as will an ASEAN Intergovernmental Commission on Human Rights. The terms of reference adopted by the meeting of regional foreign ministers in Phuket, Thailand, in July 2009, will be officially established at the next ASEAN Summit in Thailand in October 2009, and will be a first step in an evolving process to advance human rights in the region.

POST-NARGIS DEVELOPMENT: OPPORTUNITY FOR ALL

The ASEAN-led mechanism in the aftermath of Cyclone Nargis in Myanmar has paved the way for a new beginning for international engagement with Myanmar. First, it opens the window for more-effective international assistance in helping the country recover from the cyclone and in addressing other longstanding problems associated with underdevelopment. Second, it creates trust and confidence in a development mechanism that can promote accountability and transparency in Myanmar. But, more importantly, it demonstrates how international assistance works in the country and how the Government of Myanmar can work with the international community in fostering development and change in the country.

Cyclone Nargis has provided the world with an opportunity to engage in the humanitarian effort to help the people of Myanmar to rebuild their lives, and to demonstrate that it is possible to deliver effective and accountable programmes. The many projects and initiatives that have been introduced by the international community during the post-Nargis operation have brought confidence that development that promotes good governance can take place in Myanmar. The international community has seen at first hand how international assistance works effectively to support the recovery of the people and the region in the cyclone-affected area of Myanmar.

Cyclone Nargis provides an opportunity for ASEAN to engage constructively with Myanmar in addressing development issues, enhancing good governance via humanitarian and development processes to benefit the people. ASEAN engagement in post-Nargis relief and recovery indicate that ASEAN is not simply a meeting-based organization; it is also a body that works to address the real needs of its people. The ASEAN Humanitarian Task Force that coordinates the humanitarian effort and mobilizes ASEAN volunteers to promote community-driven programmes has represented a real engagement of ASEAN in the process to foster the achievement of an ASEAN community by 2015.

The Post-Nargis operation provides an opportunity for the Government of Myanmar to work cooperatively and effectively with the international community. The way in which local authorities cooperate and facilitate the work of humanitarian agencies on the ground creates hopes for effective governance in the country's future development. Cyclone Nargis also provides an opportunity for the people of Myanmar to benefit from the international assistance, to strengthen their local institutions and to bring development and change in the region.

The Post-Nargis operation illustrates that strong collaboration and partnership between ASEAN, the international community, the

Government of Myanmar and the people can foster development, creating an opportunity for effective governance to take place in Myanmar.

The humanitarian space that has been created after Cyclone Nargis should be effectively utilized to continue helping the people of Myanmar who need and deserve assistance to rebuild their lives but, more importantly, to continue the cooperation with Myanmar that will put the country back on the international development map.

References

ASEAN Secretariat. "ASEAN Agreement on Disaster Management and Emergency Response", Jakarta: 2009. <http://www.aseansec.org/PR-AADMER-EIF-End-2009.pdf>.

Tripartite Core Group. Post-Nargis Joint Asessment (PONJA), Yangon: July 2008.

———. Post-Nargis Recovery and Preparedness Plan (PONREPP), Yangon: December 2008.

———. Periodic Review II, Yangon: July 2009.

Creac'h, Yves-Kim and Lilianne Fan. "ASEAN's role in the Cyclone Nargis response: Implications, lessons and opportunities". *Humanitarian Exchange Magazine* (2008). Available at <http://www.odihpn.org/report.asp?id=2965>.

12

THE RELIEF AND RECONSTRUCTION PROGRAMME FOLLOWING CYCLONE NARGIS
A Review of SPDC Policy

Alison Vicary

INTRODUCTION

This chapter assesses the impact of the policy regime of Burma's ruling State Peace and Development Council (SPDC) on the relief and reconstruction programme that followed Cyclone Nargis, which struck lower Burma on 2–3 May 2008. The policy of the SPDC is only one determinant, albeit a critical one, of the success (or otherwise) of the aid effort. The chapter argues that its policy incompetence, neglect and brutality — hallmarks of the military regime more or less throughout its nearly 50-year rule — were once again evident in its response to the cyclone.

Of course, any analysis of the SPDC's role in the relief and reconstruction programme is limited by the availability and independence of public information, most of which derives from reports published by aid organizations. Given that one of the goals of aid organizations is to maximize the amount of donations received from the public and different governments, they have an incentive to censor information that might conflict with this goal. These same sources also frequently exaggerate the effectiveness of their projects (for the same motivation), while denying that problems arise from delivering aid under authoritarian systems of government of the sort in place in Burma.

The public information about the situation after Cyclone Nargis indicates that the aid programme was successful in averting famine in the face of widespread lost agricultural capacity in the delta. Yet, we also know that by the end of 2009 the situation for around one (of 2.4) million people severely affected by Cyclone Nargis had not returned to pre-cyclone conditions (TCG 2009b). We know that many households were still unable to command enough resources to feed themselves or rebuild their assets, except by incurring increasing and unsustainable levels of debt (Soe Lwin 2009; TCG 2009*b*; WFP 2009). We know that the regime allocated minimal resources to the relief and reconstruction programme, with most of the projects being undertaken by NGOs and UN agencies (ACTED 2009; Merlin 2008). Moreover, available evidence also indicates that even the low levels of stock and quality of infrastructure and public goods that existed prior to Cyclone Nargis have not been replaced (IRIN 2009; JRCS 2009; TCG 2009*b*).

There is, however, only enough information to undertake a partial analysis of the impact of the SPDC's policies on the relief and reconstruction programme. A thorough assessment is hampered by the limitations in public information. Thus, the following assessment is undertaken within these limitations, and is coupled with a critique of the information provided by official sources. The assessment and critique is divided into three sections. The first section provides an overview of the governance structure established to oversee the relief and reconstruction programme after Cyclone Nargis. The main purpose here is to outline the relationship between these structures and official sources that provided most of the information about the relief and reconstruction programme. The second section examines the SPDC's regulation of the relief and reconstruction programme, arguing that this regulation had an overall negative impact on the situation of the victims of Cyclone Nargis. The third section discusses the SPDC's limited financial contribution, ongoing neglect and the impact of its continuing inept policy on the relief and reconstruction programme.

GOVERNANCE OF THE POST-NARGIS RELIEF AND RECONSTRUCTION PROGRAMMES

The basic principles of delivering aid are designed to solve incentive problems that can emerge in humanitarian-aid programmes. In the absence of constraints, differences and competition amongst donors can lead to a "race to the bottom". The international aid industry, in response to problems of transparency and accountability, has developed methods to improve governance, including via the Good Humanitarian Donorship Initiative, the Inter-Agency Code of Conduct and the Humanitarian Accountability Project International. These intended constraints on self-interest include methods for evaluating the effectiveness of projects; requirements for the participation by recipients in the design, management and monitoring of projects; and the distribution of aid in an impartial and transparent system.

Other initiatives to improve the outcomes of aid programmes specifically relate to the provision of information — an issue of particular relevance to the aid programme following Cyclone Nargis. The importance of information for private-sector investment decisions shows that better disclosure assists investors to allocate capital efficiently (Bushman et al. 2004; Bushman and Smith 2003). There is also evidence that transparency and the general information environment affect not only the private sector but also the performance of non-profit organizations, which include NGOs and United Nations agencies. Stronger disclosure and enforcement have been associated with lower levels of compensation for the senior management of non-profit organizations, with consequently a greater proportion of those organizations' resources being allocated to projects. There is also evidence that rules mandating the provision of information are associated with improved quality of financial reporting.[1] Unfortunately, even in Western democracies mechanisms to improve the information environment governing aid remain poorly developed. There have, however, been improvements in recent times in the provision of information in the aid industry more broadly.

One improvement in information provision is the Consolidated Appeals Process (CAP) led by the United Nations Office for the Coordination of Humanitarian Affairs (OCHA), which is designed to solve the coordination problems that can arise among multilateral institutions and donor governments in the delivery of aid funds. This is coupled with the Financial Tracking System (FTS), which attempts to record the allocation of aid funds for a particular appeal and is designed to coordinate fundraising and the allocation of these funds to particular areas of need.[2] However, not all donors participate in these systems and not all contributions are recorded. The system is entirely voluntary, so not all countries provide funding information, and it does not cover non-financial donations. The FTS only provides information that allows for the most basic allocation of funds to be tracked. It is not, and is not intended to be, a mechanism to provide for financial oversight. In Burma, a coordinated and voluntary approach of this sort is also complicated by the politically contested nature of the regime and the giving of direct aid by countries such as Japan and China.

The difficulties and idiosyncrasies experienced by governments and aid organizations in negotiating with the SPDC led to the establishment of the Tripartite Core Group (TCG) on the 25 May 2008, about three weeks after Cyclone Nargis. Membership of the TCG consisted of a Rangoon-based diplomat from each member of the Association of Southeast Asian Nations (ASEAN), officials from the ASEAN Secretariat and an expert on disaster management from each ASEAN country, three SPDC-appointed officials and three UN representatives (the UN Humanitarian Coordinator, the Resident Coordinator and the head of a UN agency, assigned on a rotating basis). The TCG was the official senior level in the hierarchy overseeing the relief and reconstruction programme. An important (announced) function of the TCG was also to facilitate dialogue with the SPDC to mitigate its (unannounced) intransigence and incompetent policies. Given the limited success of past ASEAN diplomacy, the TCG could not be expected to convince the SPDC to introduce rational and considered policy after Cyclone Nargis. However, it does appear that the TCG did have some successes in facilitating minor changes in the policy of the regime.

Five important reports have been published under the auspices of the TCG, which were essentially designed as fundraising devices for NGOs and the different United Nations agencies.[3] In July 2008 the TCG produced the Post-Nargis Joint Assessment (PONJA) report assessing the damage wrought by the cyclone, as well as two subsequent reviews of the situation of those severely affected. Significantly, on 9 February 2009, the TCG released the Post-Nargis Recovery and Preparedness Plan (PONREPP), a three-year plan for the reconstruction and development of Burma. PONREPP estimated reconstruction costs at around US$691 million over the three-year period, though the Action Plan published later stated that an additional funding of US$103.5 million was required from international donors.[4]

In accordance with standard governance procedures following a natural disaster, the United Nations established a Logistics Cluster (originally in Bangkok) for the purpose of coordinating the delivery of humanitarian goods, initially to Rangoon and then to each of the six different hubs established in the areas devastated by the cyclone. Each hub consisted of those organizations implementing projects and distributing goods and services in a specific geographical area. These included international and local NGOs, and UN and government agencies. The projects and goods and services distributed were meant to cover each of ten programme areas, which are part of the United Nations standard humanitarian procedure: agriculture, early recovery, education, shelter, emergency telecoms, food, health, nutrition, protection of women and children, and water, sanitation and hygiene. Through this structure the "detailed operational planning and coordination at the technical level are addressed" (CAP 2008, p. 7).

Each field hub was responsible for "managing" the operations of the NGOs and United Nations Agencies in their respective areas. The governance structure within the hubs and the mechanisms used to manage the hubs were not specified, except that (typically) one aid organization was named as the programme coordinator within each hub. Relief goods were transported by aid organizations under the coordination of the Logistics Cluster, but were distributed from Burmese government stations. According to the OCHA, two monitors were placed at each relief station to oversee distributions of food alongside the (unspecified) local relief committee and the World Food Programme (WFP), and some of the medical supplies provided by the aid programme were distributed through first-aid posts run by the Myanmar Red Cross Society and Ministry of Health.[5] The Logistics Cluster was also responsible for initiating negotiations with the SPDC, such as concerning the issuing of visas, import taxes on relief goods, and the use of communications equipment. The Logistics Cluster ceased operations in August 2009 when the officially designated relief programme was completed.

There is some information available about the activities of the agencies within each of the hubs, as each provided reports on their activities on the second and fourth Friday of the month. The first report appeared in mid-October 2008, five months after Cyclone Nargis. The information included lists of distributed goods and services, but provided very little information about actual activities. The reports also recorded the many visits and opening of training programmes by diplomats and members of the SPDC and its ministries, but allowed little more than a diary of the movement of these officials within Burma. The actual programmes associated with the visits and openings were given little attention.

The most notable "absence" is information that indicates the success or otherwise of the projects implemented by NGOs and UN agencies, though this is not a problem solely associated with the response to Cyclone Nargis (ICCA 2006, p. 9; Woodward and Marshall 2004, p. 194). Most of the information provided is advertising for funds and pictorials providing little in the way of information about project performance and the impact on recipients. Any evaluations undertaken of NGO projects since Cyclone Nargis are difficult to find, and typically not available to the public.[6] There is very limited information about NGO projects in the wake of Nargis that allows for the outcomes of different NGO and UN projects to be compared. When opportunities do exist to assess the impact of an aid programme (and make this information public) they are not always taken. One example is the survey that forms the basis of the Periodic Review II undertaken under the auspices of the TCG, where questions were asked about the types of relief items received, but no questions were asked about the impact these items had on the situation of recipient households (TCG 2009*b*, p. 161). Another report written around the same time and published by the TCG reported finding no link between the recovery rates of villages and the amount of aid received (TCG 2009*c*, p. 9).

Many NGOs and UN agencies operate in jurisdictions where there is little, if any, requirement for the public provision of information, reducing the likelihood of disclosure. The extent to which the media and other organs of civil society can uncover and disseminate information to the public about NGO and UN activities determines how many gross derelictions in governance become scandalous (Fisman and Hubbard 2003, pp. 222–23). Scandals require freedom of expression, and the non-persecution and protection of activists and whistle-blowers. In societies where civil liberties are circumscribed there are limited mechanisms that act on NGO management to prevent them from satisfying their private interests, apart from those that institutional donors impose.

In Burma, where civil liberties are severely circumscribed, there is little public information with which to discipline stakeholders to any aid programme. Moreover, anyone in a position to receive goods and services from an NGO or UN agency is likely to be acquainted with corruption and poor governance, such that its occurrence in a local or foreign NGO occasions only cynical comment. If the foreign (mostly Western) press visits, the intricacies of project performance are (understandably) of limited interest, particularly since NGOs are often a source of information for journalists on the run between crises. Those adversely affected by the poor performance of aid projects rarely complain to the foreign press, not having contacts with it, and often constrained by language barriers. Nor is it always in their interest to do so. Publicly aired complaints may lead to the discontinuation of a project, rather than the instigation of improvements.

REGULATION OF AID AND CYCLONE NARGIS

States in Western liberal democracies regulate the non-profit sector, encompassing the legitimate allocation of revenue, notification of assets sales, standards for registration, and fundraising practices (Glaeser and Shleifer 2001; Hansmann 1987). Nevertheless, the impact of regulation and monitoring of non-profit organizations, even those operating in developed and democratic countries, has not been extensively addressed, except for a few recent studies that examine the repercussions of a narrow scope of regulation on a narrow range of behaviour (Core et al. 2004; Fisman and Hubbard 2003, 2005; Yetman and Yetman 2004). The results of these studies suggest that the regulation governing non-profit organizations in the developed and democratic countries improves their performance (Core et al. 2004; Fisman and Hubbard 2005; Yetman and Yetman 2004).

However, regulation in itself does not necessarily improve the performance of non-profit organizations. In many countries where NGOs and UN agencies operate, states are little interested in regulating and monitoring to determine whether funds or assets have been expropriated, misused or diverted to managerial compensation. States can also have nefarious objectives for requiring charities and other non-profit organizations to register.[7] In Burma (and many other countries) political considerations force local NGOs to operate clandestinely, or quietly, to stay beyond the control of the state. Many states either have no interest or no capacity to get involved in regulating, "monitoring" and "enforcing" regulations governing non-profit organizations. Any examination of the impact of regulation on the performance of NGOs requires state regulatory systems to be explored in a similar manner to the recent attention given to the impact of differing legal frameworks on the performance of corporations (La Porta et al. 1998).[8]

In addition to the "political controls" imposed on non-profit organizations, including NGOs and United Nations agencies, there are other restrictions in Burma. These include foreign-exchange controls exercised over all but a privileged few, which limit the access of competitor NGOs to funds from overseas. Sometimes accessing overseas funds can result in arrest and imprisonment, as in some cases after Cyclone Nargis (Wai Moe 2009). State controls over foreign exchange can have more nefarious consequences, with aid supporting a country's balance of payments, and the diverting of foreign exchange from food and materials required for reconstruction to other uses (Haggard and Noland 2007).

Inconsistent application and sudden changes of regulations, as well as unpredictable policy and behaviour towards foreign and local NGOs and United Nations agencies were commonplace in Burma prior to Cyclone Nargis.[9] These problems were coupled with sudden changes in regulation. After the cyclone, the continuation of this unpredictable regulatory system was the most notable contribution of the SPDC to the relief and reconstruction programme. After its well-publicized initial delay in refusing to accept foreign expertise, relief goods and services to assist those affected by Cyclone Nargis, the SPDC accepted delivered aid, whilst continuing to impose and transform the conditions upon its delivery. According to the OCHA on 13 May 2008:

> The Myanmar Minister of National Planning and Economic Development has now stated that aid from any nation will be accepted and that delivery of relief goods can be handled by local organizations and people working in international agencies provided this is carried out in cooperation with government. The movement of international relief workers to disaster-hit areas is still restricted.[10]

On 23 May Senior General Than Shwe agreed to relax restrictions on the issuing of visas to foreigners, which was one of the initial impediments to the emergency response.[11] Five days later all requests for visas from UN agencies were approved. The official relaxation did not resolve all the problems, with UN staff reporting delays sometimes of up to ten days in processing visas, though for NGO personnel the processing times were much longer.[12] On 10 June 2008, the government issued new regulations for the issuing of visas, which involved seeking authorization from the relevant ministry and the TCG, leading to a cessation in issuance.[13] The policy was overturned after intervention by the TCG, with visa applications and requests for travel within the country then handled by the Ministry of Social Welfare, Relief and Resettlement.[14] The "turnstile" regulatory system reappeared in April 2009 when restrictions on the issuing of visas for foreign-aid workers were re-imposed (Yeni 2009). Government permission was also required for foreign-aid workers to visit affected areas where their organizations were implementing projects.[15] Oversight of aid projects is necessary to ensure that materials and funds are being used to achieve their stated purposes, and unannounced monitoring is essential in this regard. Permission had to be obtained from the government for travel to project sites, though sometimes authorization was withdrawn and at other times aid agency employees were informed at checkpoints that they could not proceed to their destination.[16] The OCHA reported that: "The Dedaye Area Commander held a meeting with INGOs/NGOs on January 13, 2009 where he advised that for security reasons, all foreigners coming to Dedaye are requested to inform the Township Peace and Development Council (TPDC), Dedaye Area Commander, Immigration, Police Special Branch and Military Security Affairs."[17]

Local aid workers also faced restrictions, which included the provision of ongoing reports on their activities and their freedom of movement (EAT and JHU CPHHR 2009; Yeni 2009). Some local employees of aid organizations were even arrested and jailed for accepting funds from overseas (Phanida 2009; Saw Yan Naing 2009). These types of restrictions and intimidation made it extremely difficult for the foreign-aid organizations to monitor and evaluate the projects and programmes that they were funding.

Regulatory incompetence regarding the importation of relief goods also impeded the humanitarian response. This began with the regime taking more than five days to clarify customs regulations, which meant that the relief goods provided by the WFP and WHO did not begin to be cleared until 10 May. The goods of other organizations continued to be impounded at Rangoon Airport.[18] Regulations, when clarified, included the need to obtain twenty-four-hour approval for all relief goods from the Ministry of Foreign Affairs prior to their landing at Rangoon port or airport.[19] The Logistics Cluster could only obtain permission for clearance of goods sent for those aid organizations that were officially registered in Burma. Moreover, clearance of items had to be obtained for each individual organization with cargo on a plane, rather than for each individual plane. Each plane carrying relief cargo had to also obtain written permission from the government to be able to land.

Another regulation impeding operations was the import tax imposed on relief goods, unless an aid agency obtained an exemption. The Logistics Cluster reported that there were extended negotiations to obtain tax exemptions for relief goods.[20] Moreover, exemptions from import taxes had to be obtained from different government departments. There is no public information on the extent of tax exemptions or its corollary, the amount of import taxes that were paid to the SPDC. The regulations governing the importation of goods were also subject to turnstile policies when changes to import procedures for humanitarian goods were announced on 16 May, though aid organizations were quickly informed that the announced changes would not be implemented. However, the complex procedures associated with the importation of goods meant that some goods were inevitably impounded.[21] There is no information on the quantity and value of impounded goods. There were also irregularities in the items that NGOs were able to import, with some reporting that they were able to import boats, whilst others reported they could not.[22]

A further government intervention that wasted resources and hampered the humanitarian programme was the requirement that the WFP obtain permission to purchase food to distribute to cyclone victims. This was coupled with delays in the processing procedure. Food purchases were necessary, not only for those affected by the cyclone but also to prevent shortages arising from the destruction of agriculture in the delta. The WFP estimated that 55,000 metric tonnes of additional rice were required, of which it was only possible to purchase 50 per cent without upsetting agricultural markets inside Burma.[23] The WFP also sought permission to import pulses, salt and vegetable oil.[24] The government took thirteen days initially to decide, on 21 May 2008, that the WFP could only purchase less than half the requested amount of rice (10,000 metric tonnes) inside Burma, and only from the state-owned Myanma Agricultural Produce Trading. Two days later, permission to purchase another 10,000 tonnes of rice inside Burma was granted.[25] However, by 23 June the government had placed an embargo on the purchase of local rice by the WFP and other aid organizations.[26] On the 9 June the government finally agreed to allow the WFP to import the additional rice.[27] Even with approvals there were still problems with long clearance periods, with the rice sitting in warehouses before being distributed.[28] The distribution of goods after landing was a more general problem for all aid organizations.[29] The government's overall policy incompetence meant that by mid-August the WFP food purchases had temporarily ceased, leading to a reduction in rations.[30]

Yet another regulatory intervention arose from an apparent conflict over the exchange rate.[31] On 2 June in response to price rises, shortages of basic commodities and unemployment, the WFP began to distribute cash in lieu of food to those severely affected by the cyclone in Rangoon, but by the 11 June the government had closed down the programme.[32] Cash payments continued in other areas. The policy shifted again with approval given on 26 June for the cash payments programme to recommence in Rangoon. However, four days later it appears that permission for all cash-transfer programmes was withdrawn.[33] No explanation was provided by the WFP in its public literature nor, not surprisingly, by the SDPC.

Various regulations impeded the delivery of goods. One was the requirement that all goods be landed at Rangoon airport rather than directly delivered to the different relief hubs. The regime also delayed its negotiations with the International Organization for Migration (IOM) for goods to be transported from Thailand via Myawaddy. UNICEF reported that to be able to transport goods by road from Thailand "it is necessary to have in place the paper work requested by MOFA through a counter part in Myanmar".[34] UNICEF sent only five truckloads of goods from Bangkok to Rangoon by road.[35] Because of the poor state of Burma's roads, UNHCR transported goods by road from Thailand only once.[36] Global Refuge International also only transported relief goods by road from Thailand once, stating that it was "a long/expensive process".[37] Other regulations that impeded the delivery of relief goods and services, particularly in remote areas of the delta, involved the protracted negotiations and consequential delays to bring in helicopters with which to transport personnel conducting surveys for aid organizations. It was not until nearly six weeks after the cyclone, on 13 June, that the ten helicopters available were in operation.[38]

A ban on the use and importation of radio communication equipment by aid organizations also inhibited the relief operations, hampering their capacity to communicate with each other.[39] This was coupled by the absence of any mobile telephone infrastructure in the delta, and very poor landline service. Internet access was also a problem, being available only in a limited number of offices in Rangoon and not in the cluster hubs in the delta area. However, the government sold mobile phones to the aid organizations, though the number purchased and their price was not reported.[40]

The overall policy incompetence of the SPDC prior to the cyclone exacerbated the difficulties in implementing a relief and reconstruction programme. The poor state of the country's infrastructure — including its roads, Rangoon airport and its limited number of warehouses, the absence of off-loading equipment, and degraded ports — all hampered the humanitarian response. The poor infrastructure at the airport delayed the amount of goods that could be landed and distributed.[41] The lack of jetties and their poor quality also impeded the delivery of goods by water. The poor state of the roads limited the size of trucks that could be used to transport goods, a problem which was coupled with an insufficient number of trucks, along with nationwide rationing of fuel, which created problems in accessing supplies.

GOVERNMENT CONTRIBUTIONS (LACK THEREOF), POLICY AND CYCLONE NARGIS

PONREPP and other fund-raising documents described a surprisingly positive role for the government ministries and regime-controlled structures in the relief and reconstruction programme. According to PONREPP, the government ministries and the Township Peace and Development Councils (TPDCs) were to have an integral role in the relief and reconstruction programme. This positive representation of the role of Burma's bureaucracy is difficult to accept for a number of reasons. One reason was that the SPDC announced a contribution of only US$5 million, an insignificant amount, to assist those affected by Cyclone Nargis.[42] There are no public accounts that indicate how government funds were spent, let alone any information about the impact of the funds. In addition, the SPDC established the Natural Disaster Preparedness Central Committee (NDPCC), which then established ten additional subordinate committees (CAP 2008, p. 7). The public announcements of the NDPCC suggest that its main function was to collect donations from Burma's public, with the regime's media reporting that the government had received 12,418 million kyats (approximately US$12 million) in cash and in-kind contributions from this source.[43] Again, there are no public accounts or enforceable regulations governing the receipt, distribution and monitoring of resources received from Burma's public. The absence of even the pretence of accountability creates numerous opportunities for theft, diversion of resources and corruption, such as in the granting of contracts (though the terms of the contracts are unknown) to regime-linked companies to repair and rebuild mostly public buildings. Even these contracts were plagued with ineptitude and the companies did not always receive payment.[44] The limited funds provided by the SPDC to their ministries and the TPDCs means they could contribute little to the relief and reconstruction programme.

Another reason for suspecting that Burma's bureaucracy would not make a positive contribution to relief and reconstruction was the military government's long-term failure to allocate funds to develop infrastructure and provide basic public services, notably electricity, telecommunications, garbage collection, safe sewage (faeces) disposal and access to safe drinking water. In spite of this long-term funding failure, the public information provided by aid organizations had the relief and reconstruction programme supporting the development of non-existent government programmes to deliver these basic services: "There is also an opportunity to link into ongoing and proposed nationwide programme addressing issues in common with the recovery plan — health, shelter, water, sanitation, education, livelihoods and food security" (PONREPP 2009, p. 64).

The provision of services (and dealing with the problems associated with their absence) forms a considerable component of the official literature published by the Tripartite Core Group as part of its fundraising attempts for "reconstruction" (TCG 2009*b*). Some reconstruction issues certainly arise with the provision of public services, but the most significant problem is the absence of positive government involvement in their provision prior to, and after, Cyclone Nargis.

The suppression and control of the market was also a central impediment to post-cyclone reconstruction. The limited availability of farming inputs — such as seeds, fertilizer, tillers, spare parts and diesel — slowed agricultural recovery and employment. Limited availability of agricultural inputs such as these is a consequence of repressed markets, coupled with severe constraints on the availability of capital (Dapice et al. 2009; TCG 2009*b*, p. 9).[45] Other policy failures include the serious problems in accessing credit in the agricultural sector and for all businesses. These were coupled with the failure of the government banks to provide any debt relief after the cyclone.[46] Meanwhile, the government also closed the rice trade between towns in the delta, causing the rice price to plummet (ACT International 2009, p. 5). These failures, together with the problems created by the cyclone, meant that at the beginning of 2009 it was impossible for most farmers in the delta to make a profit from paddy production.[47]

The capacity of households to replace and repair their homes after the cyclone was hampered by the availability of materials. Of those households whose homes had been destroyed or severely damaged by the cyclone and still not repaired by June 2009, 50 per cent reported that reconstruction had not occurred because of lack of availability of materials required for repairs (TCG 2009*b*, p. 7).[48] Part of the problem was that thatch and bamboo — important materials in the construction of homes — were severely damaged by the cyclone. However, alternative construction materials were also in short supply. Market failure contributed to the problems households had in replacing fishing gear and boats, with a lack of materials and boat-building expertise cited again as a constraint on replacement (TCG 2009*b*, p. 10). Failures in these and other markets have not been given the attention devoted to agricultural markets, but there are many reasons that would explain the failure of the private sector to supply inputs required for reconstruction. Market failures could be due to the poor quality of the roads in the delta (and Burma generally), which would increase the costs of transportation, and potentially raise prices above those that people could pay. Other problems that would increase the prices of inputs necessary for reconstruction include the numerous military checkpoints that operate on the roads and rivers of Burma, where "payments" are collected. Problems could also relate to control over access to foreign exchange and rights to import. All these controls and the numerous others that suppress the private sector in Burma would act to inhibit the market to supply the inputs necessary for reconstruction.

The problems and dysfunctional incentives inherent in Burma's bureaucracy and other government structures also inhibit their capacity to design and implement policy for relief and reconstruction, yet the TPDCs, which are active in the suppression, control and monitoring of the population, are accorded a positive role in the relief and reconstruction programme by aid organizations (PONREPP 2009). Another fundraising report from ACT International even surprisingly referred to them in the following terms:

> The project will target the duty bearers and try to motivate them to address the problems such as poverty and issues of livelihood. LWF [Lutheran World Federation] will maintain good working relations with government officials at township and village tract levels. The project will organize

> awareness programmes and trainings for the duty bearers. Local councils (Government bodies) in the area, being an important change agent at village level, the project will try to motivate them to incorporate disaster preparedness components in their activities. The council members will be made aware of their duties and responsibility towards the communities. The project will work in close cooperation with township level government officials and others responsible for area development. (ACT International 2009, p. 17)

This positive role envisaged for Burma's ministries, the TPDCs and their village-level counterparts (VDPCs) contrasts with the endemic institutional failure arising from military rule. That aid organizations claim to cooperate only with the lower levels in the Burmese bureaucracy does not mean that inherent policy and incentive problems disappear. The limited capacity of these structures, the excessively centralized decision-making, and the existing dysfunctional incentive structure mean that they are incapable of performing the functions of local government that the aid organizations ascribed to them. The TPDCs and VPDCs are not designed to deliver, and do not engage in the delivery of, services such as electricity, garbage collection, the provision of safe drinking water and sanitation.[49]

There is also evidence of shortcomings in the cooperation and participation of the ministries and governmental structures with the foreign-aid organizations in the relief and reconstruction programme. All the information provided by OCHA in its official reports about the activities of the government to assist those affected by the cyclone came from the state-controlled media. Most of this information in the media consisted of rudimentary propaganda, with military figures performing the distribution of nominated quantities of in-kind aid to victims of the cyclone. There was a notable absence of other sources of information. This may have been deliberate, though ineptitude might account for the limited provision of information. Another indicator of poor cooperation (and coordination) are the references in OCHA Situation Reports that indicate aid organizations had limited information about the response of the government to Cyclone Nargis, such as: "It is hoped that once this information has been provided, a clearer picture of those who have been reached, and outstanding needs, would emerge."[50]

Aid organizations tried to promote interaction with government authorities reporting that "[s]upport to the national authorities is being strengthened through the increased participation of government representatives in the Cluster. Formal invitations from the Clusters to relevant line ministries and authorities have been sent and favourably received".[51] However, nearly six months after the cyclone the OCHA Situation and Hub Reports continued to indicate the limited constructive cooperation between the authorities and aid organizations. One report had the Minister for Progress of Border Areas and National Races informing aid organizations that they should inform local authorities on their activities so they could coordinate with the government's ministries.[52] Others suggest limited cooperation and participation by the local authorities in relief and reconstruction. Ensuring compliance with governmental controls appeared more important than the provision of services, with the chair of the TPDC for Labutta at a hub meeting reminding "agencies to share with him the permit to operate in the township".[53]

The unpredictable and pernicious policy of the government was also evident in the distribution of goods to cyclone victims, evidenced by the failure of TPDCs to inform people about the conditions of their receipt. According to ACT International, the government has not communicated clearly the conditions under which farmers have received power tillers and rice seeds. Farmers fear, and assume, they will eventually be asked to pay for the costs of these inputs received from the government for that season (2009, p. 23).

Another agency reported similar problems with a TPDC provision of fishing equipment:

> Besides being forced to hire equipment or take out loans to buy gear, fishermen have complained of the burden of paying for boats distributed by the government. ...Other complaints include those about the equipment distributed. Some say the nets they received were inappropriate — those who fish in rivers were given nets for sea fishing, and vice-versa. Some boats distributed have also been found wanting. (IRIN 2009)

The main function of the government in the reconstruction of the education and health sectors appears to have amounted to little more than the granting of permission to foreign-aid organizations to bear the costs and responsibility. Thus the Ministry of Health had "given approval to one of the cluster partners for the construction of rural and sub-rural health facilities" and the government was "taking an increasing responsibility for the coordination of reconstruction of permanent schools" and had "shared draft procedures for application to rebuild schools".[54] Lack of government funding meant that the responsibility for rebuilding was placed on NGOs and the UN agencies:

> The Ministry of Social Welfare, Relief and Rehabilitation confirmed that 13 humanitarian agencies have committed for the reconstruction of 74 basic education schools, to date. This represents around 5 per cent of the 1,407 needed in the eight highest priority townships alone. The Ministry and the Education Cluster are concerned by this significant gap.[55]

In a display of poor policy, Burma's Prime Minister on a visit to an area severely affected by the cyclone near Pyapon reportedly donated six million kyat (around US$6,000) to a district medical official for the renovation and expansion of the district hospital from 100 to 200 beds: a project that was reported to have been achieved in only two weeks.[56] The announced expansion of this hospital occurred in an environment where staff, equipment and medicine were not always available to treat patients.

The issue of the government forcibly returning people who had moved from their villages after Cyclone Nargis arose at an ASEAN-UN conference on the cyclone where the Emergency Relief Coordinator stated that "forced returns of any kind are completely unacceptable".[57] There are also references in the OCHA Situation Reports and those from other aid organizations that suggest government policy included forcibly relocating people who had gathered at relief centres.

All the references to forced relocation in official aid sources are obtuse, with euphemistic references to population movements, such as the government being concerned to "facilitate the return of internally displaced families".[58] The problem with the government's policy of managing people who had moved from their homes and villages began with the inability or refusal of TPDCs to share (or possibly implement) "clear information about how temporary settlements are managed".[59] Five days later and only two weeks after the cyclone, OCHA reported that, "Local authorities in Labutta have told relief workers that they have started sending villagers back to their villages."[60] Apparently the pace at which people were being returned to their villages was unacceptable, with aid organizations "requesting local authorities for a phased return of the internally displaced persons".[61] The government's policy of relocating victims of Cyclone Nargis was occurring even as people were travelling from the more remote areas into larger population centres seeking food and other basic provisions.[62] The frequent movement of people (both spontaneous and government-organized) reportedly created problems in the delivery of food aid and increased the number of children separated from their families.[63] Not only were the TPDCs involved in "facilitating" the return of people, but they also expected foreign-aid organizations to provide relief goods to assist people's return.[64] There were also reports that people in some settlements for the internally displaced had to sign agreements with their local government authorities that they would return to their places of origin upon receipt of assistance provided by foreign-aid organizations.[65] There was no discussion of the reasons for population movements (whether they were government-orchestrated or voluntary) in official aid reports.[66] There was no discussion of the views of the families, and limited provision of information about the choices people faced when the government arranged their return.

The distribution of relief services by the government authorities may have caused problems for people who had moved from their original locations and were not living in government-recognized relief camps. Relief services distributed by the local authorities (though provided by foreign NGOs and UN agencies) appear to have been linked to a household's place of registration. This means that people not living in officially recognized relief camps and without local registration may not have received assistance from government-controlled distribution services.[67] It is not known if people in this situation could obtain assistance from other sources, or the extent of any problems, as official aid sources are quiet on the issue.

People remaining in official relief camps at the end of August 2008, about four months after the cyclone, were reportedly given the option of moving to resettlement sites where government-built housing was provided.[68] Initially these relocation sites were not accessible to international staff without prior approval from the respective TPDCs, though restrictions were eventually removed.[69] There is little public information about the suitability of the sites in terms of opportunities for employment and the state of infrastructure, though the new villages reportedly did not contain any serious health problems.[70] Later reports had people in at least some of these new villages seeking permission from their TPDCs to return to their original homes, as they were unable to earn adequate incomes (Nan Kham Kaew 2009).

CONCLUSION

The above is by no means a thorough analysis of the relief and reconstruction programme that followed Cyclone Nargis. Yet it does remind us that aid programmes are implemented within the constraints imposed by the recipient country's government. It should not be a surprise that the policy of the SPDC and the limited capacity of the country's bureaucracy and administrative apparatus to oversee and implement policy inhibited the relief and reconstruction programme. Rebuilding physical infrastructure requires not only financial capital (that is, funds provided by foreign, mostly Western, donors), which is anyhow in short supply. Even if this supply was not constrained, the replacement of physical infrastructure and the provision of basic services require administration skills and local expertise. These skills are typically in short supply in poor countries and occasional visits by foreign experts do not make up for shortfalls. The building of infrastructure and the provision of basic services also occur within a particular policy environment, which is often not conducive or compatible with the production of these goods, let alone their upkeep. Given the government's neglect of infrastructure and the provision of basic services prior to Cyclone Nargis, it was never likely that any improvements would follow it.

Aid programmes that follow natural disasters also attempt to rebuild private assets, such as homes and businesses. The rebuilding of private assets likewise occurs within a particular policy environment and again the policy of the SPDC inhibited the replacement of private assets and the accumulation of private capital necessary for the restoration of employment. The significant constraints on rebuilding private capital destroyed by Cyclone Nargis were all those regulations and controls imposed by Burma's government, which have impinged and inhibited the development and functioning of the country's private sector for more than fifty years.

The primary purpose of much of the information about the relief and reconstruction programme was to raise funds for aid organizations, leading them to camouflage the problems inherent in the programme. The primary function of many of the sources was not to provide independent information. Nor was their primary function to assess the success or otherwise of the aid programme. Aid organizations exaggerate the outcomes that can be obtained from any reconstruction programme following a natural disaster, as was the case after Cyclone Nargis. This is particularly evident in the rhetoric of "build back better" with its utopian hue, implying that countries (or parts thereof) whose physical infrastructure has been destroyed can be simply improved, as if history can be eliminated and the clock reset at year zero. Unfortunately, bad government and poorly equipped administration do not disappear after a humanitarian disaster. All their inherent limitations remain.

The incentive for aid organizations to censor and mislead needs to be removed.

Recent improvements in the information environment governing aid programmes are not enough. If we are to learn from mistakes and know how to allocate scarce funds, the information environment needs to be improved further. For this to happen the sources of information and the assessment of aid programmes need to be in the hands of bodies that are not linked to the funding needs of aid organizations.

Notes

1. Desai and Yetman (2005); Fisman and Hubbard (2005); Yetman and Yetman (2004). In general the financial accountability of non-profits, which includes aid organizations, needs to be improved (ICCA 2006; Leat 2004; Wilson et al. 1999; Woodward and Marshall 2004).
2. Details available online at <http://reliefweb.int/fts/>.
3. Namely: TCG 2008*a*; TCG 2008*b*; TCG 2008*c*; TCG 2009*a*; TCG 2009*b*. The TCG was due to release another report, *Post-Nargis Social Impact Monitoring*, in early 2010.
4. In spite of the claims in PONJA and PONREPP about the outcomes that could be achieved from aid, there is an increasingly sceptical economic literature about the incentives that arise from the aid relationship on economic development (Burnside and Dollar 1997; Easterly et al. 2003; Svensson 1999).
5. OCHA *Situation Report* No. 15, 19 May 2008, p. 2.
6. For example, the Active Learning Network for Accountability and Performance (ALNAP) writes about a database of project evaluations: "A revamped version of the [evaluative reports database] ERD has been launched; this brings improved login facilities, but ALNAP Full Members need to reapply for access to confidential reports" (2003, p. 5). Moreover, some institutional donors, including ECHO, require NGOs to enter into a confidentiality agreement that prohibits them from making public any reports or evaluations of projects funded until five years after the completion of the project (2004, Article 5).
7. For example, in May 2007 prior to Cyclone Nargis, twenty-four non-profit organizations were refused registration by the regime's Ministry of Home Affairs, including a charity providing free funeral services (Free Funeral Services Association), two health clinics, three professional and trade associations (the Myanmar Engineers Association, the Indian Traders' Association and the Chinese Traders' Association) and various Buddhist organizations. The Free

Funeral Services Association was not allowed to register as two senior members had close connections with well-known campaigners for democracy (many of whom are in prison) (Htet Aung 2007*a*). The organizations were asked to resubmit their applications for registration after complaints — believed to have been made by China — about the ban placed on the Chinese Traders Association (Htet Aung 2007*b*). In June of the same year the Ministry of Culture refused to re-register cultural organizations associated with specific ethnic groups in the country (Shah Paung and Lawi Weng 2007).

8. NGOs can obtain competitive advantages from the state that allows them to survive despite being less effective (or efficient) than their competitors (Chang and Tuckman 1990; Hansmann 1987; Mullner and Hadley 1984; West 1989). The Myanmar Red Cross Society (MRCS) and the Myanmar Maternal and Child Welfare Association (MMCWA), along with other regime-sponsored NGOs in Burma, have gained a competitive advantage, which amongst other privileges provides them with greater opportunities to receive foreign donations. Intimidation, violence and imprisonment are not uncommon methods of circumventing competitor NGOs, particularly those with any political agenda. Privileges granted by the military state to selected organizations have allowed some for-profits to operate in the guise of NGOs. For example, donors to the MMCWA are typically local businesswomen giving in exchange for business concessions, such as licences to export (import), for telephone access and sometimes for protection when involved in illegal business activities. In exchange for these favours, some "donations" are allocated to the provision of rudimentary and poorly implemented "community" health programmes. The privileged position of the state-sponsored "NGOs" was evidenced during the aid programme following Cyclone Nargis, where some UN agencies and international NGOs utilized these organizations to distribute goods and services.
9. For example, many of the projects under the auspices of Human Development Initiative of the United Nations Development Programme were suspended for around twelve months in 2002, when the regime refused initially to grant permission for the continuation of the programme (Shaw and Rahman 2003, p. 5). In February 2006 it announced further restrictions on the operations of foreign NGOs and United Nations agencies. Approval for all projects had to be obtained from the relevant ministry and the Ministry for National Planning and Economic Development, rather than the local military authorities. Foreign employees of all NGOs were to be accompanied by a representative of the regime in any travels within the country, increasing the difficulties donors and aid organizations had in monitoring projects (USGAO 2007, pp. 18–19).
10. OCHA *Situation Report* No. 9, 13 May 2008.
11. OCHA *Situation Report* No. 19, 23 May 2008, p. 1.

12. CAP 2008, p. 5; OCHA *Situation Report* No. 27, 4 June 2008, p. 2.
13. OCHA *Situation Report* No. 30, 11 June 2008, p. 2; OCHA *Situation Report* No. 33, 19 June 2008, p. 1.
14. OCHA *Situation Report* No. 35, 26 June 2008, p. 1.
15. OCHA *Situation Report* No. 10, 12 May 2008.
16. OCHA *Situation Report* No. 22, 27 May 2008, p. 1; OCHA *Situation Report* No. 30, 11 June 2008, p. 1.
17. OCHA *Yangon Hub Update* No. 6, 27 January 2009, p. 1.
18. OCHA *Situation Report* No. 8, 12 May 2008.
19. OCHA *Situation Report*, 10 May 2008; *Logistics Cluster Report*, Bangkok, 10 May 2008.
20. OCHA *Logistics Cluster Report*, 10 May 2008.
21. OCHA *Logistics Cluster Report*, 19 May 2008.
22. OCHA *Logistics Cluster Report*, 23 May 2008.
23. OCHA *Situation Report* No. 8, 12 May 2008, p. 2.
24. OCHA *Situation Report* No. 23, 28 May 2008, p. 2.
25. OCHA *Situation Report* No. 25, 30 May 2008, p. 1.
26. OCHA *Situation Report* No. 34, 23 June 2008, p. 5.
27. OCHA *Situation Report* No. 29, 9 June 2008, p. 2.
28. OCHA *Situation Report* No. 42, 24 July 2008, p. 1.
29. OCHA *Logistics Cluster Report*, 19 May 2008.
30. OCHA *Situation Report* No. 45, 14 August 2008, pp. 1, 4; No. 46, 21 August 2008, p. 4.
31. OCHA *Situation Report* No. 30, 11 June 2008, p. 4.
32. OCHA *Situation Report* No. 26, 2 June 2008, p. 1; No. 29, 9 June 2008, p. 2; No. 30, 11 June 2008, p. 4.
33. OCHA *Situation Report* No. 36, 30 June 2008, p. 3.
34. OCHA *Logistics Cluster* Report, 16 May 2008, p. 1.
35. OCHA *Logistics Cluster* Report, 2 June 2008.
36. OCHA *Situation Report* No. 9, 13 May 2008, p. 2.
37. OCHA *Logistics Cluster Report*, 16 May 2008, p. 2.
38. OCHA *Situation Report* No. 30, 11 June 2008, p. 1.
39. OCHA *Situation Report* No. 13, 17 May 2008, p. 1.
40. OCHA *Situation Report* No. 18, 22 May, 2008.
41. OCHA *Logistics Cluster Report*, 16 May 2008, p. 2.
42. OCHA *Situation Report* No. 3, 6 May 2008.
43. OCHA *Situation Report* No. 32, 16 June 2008, p. 5. Donations from the public were officially made to the Rehabilitation and Reconstruction sub-committee of the NDPCC and through the TPDCs and their district-level counterparts. OCHA *Situation Report* No. 32, 16 June 2008, p. 5.
44. OCHA *Yangon Hub Update* No. 5, 2009, p. 2.

45. Only 7 per cent of households surveyed reported receiving any agricultural inputs as part of the relief and reconstruction programme (TCG 2009*b*, p. 10).
46. OCHA *Yangon Hub Update* No. 5, 2009, p. 1; see also the paper by Sean Turnell in this volume.
47. OCHA *Yangon Hub Update* No. 5, 2009, p. 2.
48. Ninety-three per cent of households reported that repairs had not been undertaken due to lack of cash.
49. The incentive structures in bureaucracies controlled by authoritarian regimes such as Burma's are incapable of eliciting the appropriate effort and responses from public servants, regardless of the desires of individual members within the hierarchy. Burmese public servants are no different from individuals elsewhere, in that they respond to the incentive structures that exist in their workplaces. But the incentive structure within the Burmese bureaucracy means that even committed public servants cannot make the necessary decisions required to implement successful policies. Wages are too low to elicit enough effort to implement good policies, even if they exist. Public servants have to supplement their meagre incomes either through other employment or by diverting resources either from intended recipients or aid sources to supplement incomes. This is nothing peculiar to Burma, being standard practice in countries where public servants are paid inadequate salaries. In addition, hiring and promotion is not based on merit, but on signals that indicate that correct political allegiances, and family and business relationships. Individuals in search of payments for performing duties or allocating resources might purchase jobs in any of the more lucrative ministries. The systems of penalties that permeate Burma's bureaucracy mean that public servants make decisions to avoid large penalties that can result from deviating from accepted practices. This means that public servants follow orders to the extent required to satisfy their superiors and, most importantly, do not make decisions independent of obtaining permission from a superior. This increases the cost and time associated with programme implementation, and limits the initiative required for a bureaucracy to design and implement policy. Even with the best of intentions, aid organizations cannot overcome these institutional failures and dysfunctional incentive structures.
50. OCHA *Situation Report* No. 27, 4 June 2008, p. 1.
51. OCHA *Situation Report* No. 23, 28 May 2008, p. 1.
52. OCHA *Labutta Hub Update* No. 1, 27 October 2008, p. 1.
53. OCHA *Situation Report* No. 48, 12 September 2008, p. 9.
54. OCHA *Situation Report* No. 48, 12 September 2008, pp. 4, 5.
55. OCHA *Situation Report* No. 51, 24 October 2008, p. 3.
56. OCHA *Pyapon Hub Update* No. 2, 13 November 2008, p. 1.
57. OCHA *Situation Report* No. 21, 26 May 2008, p. 1.

58. OCHA *Situation Report* No. 40, 17 July 2008, p. 1.
59. OCHA *Situation Report* No. 9, 13 May 2008, p. 4.
60. OCHA *Situation Report* No. 14, 18 May 2008, p. 1.
61. OCHA *Situation Report* No. 41, 21 July 2008, p. 5.
62. OCHA *Situation Report* No. 14, 18 May 2008, p. 1.
63. OCHA *Situation Report* No. 13, 17 May 2008, p. 3; No. 33, 19 June 2008, p. 4.
64. OCHA *Situation Report* No. 40, 17 July 2008, p. 1. MSF provided US$50 to households at camps in Labutta to encourage them to return to their villages (OCHA *Situation Report* No. 47, 28 August 2008, p. 1).
65. OCHA *Situation Report* No. 49, 26 September 2008, p. 2; No. 50, 10 October 2008, p. 6.
66. OCHA *Situation Report* No. 27, 4 June 2008, p. 3; No. 31, 13 June 2008, p. 3.
67. OCHA *Situation Report* No. 50, 10 October 2008, p. 7.
68. OCHA *Situation Report* No. 47, 28 August 2008, p. 1.
69. OCHA *Situation Report* No. 49, 26 September 2008, pp. 1–2; No. 50, 10 October 2008, p. 6.
70. OCHA *Situation Report* No. 48, 12 September 2008, p. 1.

References

ACT International. Cyclone Nargis Rehabilitation ASMY82 Revision 3. Action by Churches Together, December 2009.

Agency for Technical Cooperation (ACTED). "Myanmar: Building Boats in the Delta". 2009, <www.reliefweb.int/rw/>.

Active Learning Network for Accountability and Performance in Action Humanitarian Action (ALNAP). *Participation by Crisis-Affected Populations in Humanitarian Action: A Handbook for Practitioners*. London: Overseas Development Institute, 2003.

Ministry of National Planning and Economic Development. "Guidelines for UN Agencies, International Organisations, NGO/INGOS on Cooperative Programs in Myanmar". Yangon: February 2006.

Burnside, Craig and David Dollar. "Aid, Policies and Growth". Policy Research Working Paper 1777, Washington, D.C.: World Bank, 1997.

Bushman, Robert and Abbie Smith. "Transparency, Financial Action by Accounting Information, and Corporate Governance". Federal Reserve Bank of New York Economic Policy Review 9, no. 1 (2003): 65–87.

Bushman, Robert J. Piotroski and Abbie Smith. "What Determines Corporate Transparency?". *Journal of Accounting Research* 42, no. 2 (2004): 207–52.

Chang, Cyril and Howard Tuckman. "Do Higher Property Tax Rates Increase the Market Share of Nonprofit Hospitals?". *National Tax Journal* 43, no. 2 (1990): 175–87.

Consolidated Appeals Process (CAP). Myanmar, Revised Appeal: Action Cyclone Nargis Response Plan. United Nations, 2008.

Core, John, Wayne Guay and Rodrigo Verdi. "Agency Problems of Excess Endowment Holdings in Not-For-Profit Firms". Wharton School, University of Pennsylvania, 24 September 2004. <www.newyorkfed.org/research/conference/2004>.

Dapice, David, Tom Vallely and Ben Wilkinson. "Assessments of the Myanmar Agricultural Economy". International Development Enterprise, Harvard Kennedy School, January 2009.

Desai, Mihir and Robert Yetman. "Constraining Managers Without Owners: Governance of the Not-for-Profit Enterprise". NBER Working Paper Series. No.11140, National Bureau of Economic Research, 2005.

Easterly, William, Robert Levine and David Roodmand. "New Data, New Doubts: Revisiting Aid, Policies and Growth". Working Paper 26. Washington, D.C.: Center for Global Development, 2003.

European Commission Humanitarian Aid (ECHO). "Framework Action by Partnership Agreement with Humanitarian Organizations". 21 December 2004. <http://ec.europa.eu/partners/index_en.htm>.

Emergency Assistance Team (Burma) and Johns Hopkins Bloomberg School of Public Health (EAT and JHU CPHHR). *After the Storm: Voices from the Delta*, March 2009.

Fisman, Raymond and Glen Hubbard. "Endowments, Governance and the Nonprofit Firm". In *The Governance of Not-for-Profit Organizations*. Chicago: University of Chicago Press, 2003.

———. "Precautionary Savings and the Governance of Nonprofit Action by Organizations". *Journal of Public Economics* 89 (2005): 2,231–43.

Glaeser, Edward and Andrei Shleifer. "Not-For-Profit Entrepreneurs." *Journal of Public Economics* 81, no. 1 (2001): 99–115.

Global Fund. "Termination of Grants to Myanmar: Fact Sheet". 18 August 2005. <www.theglobalfund.org>.

Global Link Management. "Evaluation Study on the Grassroots Grant Programme: Case Studies in Myanmar, Cambodia, Vietnam". Tokyo, October 2001.

Hansmann, Henry. "The Effect of Tax Exemption and Other Factors on the Market Share of Nonprofit versus For-profit Firms". *National Tax Journal* 40, no. 1 (1987): 71–82.

Haggard, Stephan and Marcus Noland. *Famine in North Korea: Markets, Aid and Reform*. New York: Columbia University Press, 2007.

Humanitarian Accountability Partnership–International (HAP). "The Humanitarian Accountability Report 2005". Humanitarian Accountability Partnership, 2005. <www.hap.2005>.

Htet Aung. "Burmese Junta Bans Civil Organizations". *Irrawaddy Online Edition*, 16 May 2007*a*. <www.irrawaddy.org>.

———. "Junta Reconsiders Ban on Social Organizations". *Irrawaddy Online Edition*, 24 May 2007*b*. <www.irrawaddy.org>.

Inter-Agency Standing Committee (IASC). *Annual Report 2008*. Geneva/New York: April 2009.

Institute of Chartered Accountants in Australia (ICAA). *Not-for-Profit Sector Reporting: A Research Project*. Institute of Chartered Accountants, Sydney: September 2006. <www.charteredaccountants.com.au>.

Integrated Regional Information Networks (IRIN). "Myanmar: Cyclone-affected Fishermen Still Need Help". 10 November 2009. <www.reliefweb.int/>.

Japanese Red Cross Society (JRCS). "Myanmar Cyclone: Reconstruction of Primary Schools". 6 November 2009. <www.reliefweb.int/>.

La Porta, Rafael, Florencio Lopez-de-Silanes, Andrei Shleifer and Action Robert Vishny. "Law and Finance". *Journal of Political Economy* 106, no. 6 (1998): 1,113–55.

Lawi Weng. "Myanmar: Homeless Cyclone Survivors Demonstrate". *Irrawaddy Online Edition*, 23 March 2009. <www.irrawaddy.org>.

Leat, Diana. "What Do Australian Foundations Do: Who Knows and Who Cares?" *Australian Journal of Public Administration* 63, no. 2 (2004): 96–105.

Mai Phuong Tang. "ASEAN Hub Officers: Frontrunners of Humanitarian Coordination in the Delta Affected Townships of Myanmar". 2009. <www.asean.org/CN-PR-ASEANHubOfficer.pdf>.

Macrae, Joanna and Adele Harmer. "Good Humanitarian Donorship: A Mouse or a Lion?". *Humanitarian Exchange* 24 (2003): 9–12.

Medical Emergency International (Merlin). "Myanmar (Burma): Greater Funding Needed to Meet Most Critical Needs". 3 November 2009. <www.reliefweb.int/>.

Mullner, R. and J. Hadley. "Interstate Variations in the Growth of Chain Owned Proprietary Hospitals, 1973–1982". *Inquiry* 21 (1984): 144–51.

Nan Kham Kaew. "Farming in Delta Remains Underfunded". *Democratic Voice of Burma*, 3 December 2009.

New Light of Myanmar. "State Placing Emphasis on Development of Agricultural, Fishery, Marine and Transport Sectors of Seaside Regions: Senior General Than Shwe Inspects Progress in Rehabilitation and Reconstruction Tasks in Storm-hit Regions of Ayeyawady Division", *New Light of Myanmar*, 4 November 2009.

Office for the Coordination of Humanitarian Affairs (OCHA). Cyclone Nargis Myanmar Situation Reports. Nos. 1–52, 2008–2009. <www.reliefweb.int>.

———. Logistics Cluster Report. Bangkok, 2008. <www.logcluster.org/mm08a/>.

———. Myanmar Cyclone Nargis Bogale Hub Update, Nos. 1–6, 2008–2009. <www.reliefweb.int>.

———. Myanmar Cyclone Nargis Labbuta Hub Update, Nos. 1–6, 2008–2009. <www.reliefweb.int>.

———. Myanmar Cyclone Nargis Mawlamyinegyun Hub Update, Nos. 1–3, 2008–2009. <www.reliefweb.int>.

———. Myanmar Cyclone Nargis Pathein Hub Update, Nos. 1–6, 2008–2009. <www.reliefweb.int>.

——— Myanmar Cyclone Nargis Pyapon Hub Update, Nos. 1–6, 2008–2009. <www.reliefweb.int.

———. Myanmar Cyclone Nargis Yangon Hub Update, Nos. 1–6, 2008–2009. <www.reliefweb.int>.

Phanida. "Junta Sentences Six Relief Volunteers". *Mizzima*, 12 April 2009.

Saw Yan Naing. "Stop Arresting Cyclone Aid Activists: AI". *Irrawaddy Online Edition*, 24 November 2009. <www.irrawaddy.org>.

Shah Paung and Lawi Weng. "Junta Clamps Down on Ethnic Culture Groups". *Irrawaddy Online Edition*, 8 June 2007. <www.irrawaddy.org>.

Shaw, Robert and M. Shafiquer Rahman. "Report of the Independent Assessment Mission 11–30 August". Human Development Initiative Myanmar. United Nations Development Programme, July 2003.

Soe Lwin. "Drowning in Debt". *Irrawaddy Online Edition*, 26 October 2009. <www.irrawaddy.org>.

Sphere Project. Humanitarian Charter and Minimum Standards in Action Disaster Response. Sphere Project, Geneva: 2004.

Svensson, Jakob. "Aid, Growth and Democracy". *Economics and Politics* 11, no. 3 (1999): 275–98.

The Irrawaddy. "FFSS Founder Defies Court Summons".

Irrawaddy Online Edition, 30 October 2009. <www.irrawaddy.org>.

Tripartite Core Group (TCG). Post-Nargis Joint Assessment (PONJA). Yangon: July, 2008a.

———. Post-Nargis Periodic Review 1. Yangon: December, 2008b.

———. Post-Nargis Recovery and Preparedness Plan (PONREPP). Yangon: December 2008*c*.

———. Post Nargis Periodic Review II. Yangon: July 2009*a*.

———. Post-Nargis Recovery and Preparedness Plan, Prioritized Action Plan Yangon: October 2009*b*.

———. Post-Nargis Social Impacts Monitoring. Yangon: December, 2009*c*.

United States Government Accountability Office (USGAO). *International Organizations: Assistance Programs Constrained in Burma*, Report to the Committee on Foreign Affairs, House of Representatives, Washington, D.C., 2007 (GAO-07-457).

Wai Moe. "Journalists, Volunteer Relief Workers Arrested in Rangoon". *Irrawaddy Online Edition*, 29 October 2009. <www.irrawaddy.org>.

West, Edwin. "Nonprofit Organizations: Revised Theory and New Evidence". *Public Choice* 63 (1989): 165–74.

Wilson, E.R., L.E. Hay and S.C. Keating. *Accounting for Government and Nonprofit Entities*. New York: Irwin McGraw-Hill, 1999.

Woodward, Susan and Shelley Marshall. "A Better Framework: Reforming Not-For-Profit Regulation". Centre for Corporate Law and Securities Regulation, Faculty of Law, University of Melbourne, 2004. <http://cclsr.law.unimelb.edu.au/activities/not-for-profit/>.

World Food Programme (WFP). *Rapid Food Security Assessment in the Townships of Bogale and Laputta*. Vulnerability Analysis and Mapping Unit, WFP, Rome: March 2009.

Yeni. "Is Burma Stumbling Towards Another Disaster?". *Irrawaddy Online Edition*, 23 March 2009. <www.irrawaddy.org>.

Yetman, Michelle and Robert Yetman. "The Effects of Governance on the Financial Reporting Quality of Nonprofit Organizations". Working Paper, University of California (at Davis), 2004.

13

POSITIVE ENGAGEMENT IN MYANMAR
Some Current Examples and Thoughts for the Future

David Allan

INTRODUCTION

Myanmar approaches 2010 with only a few areas of certainty — one being that external observers will differ in the many possible interpretations of the events and process in the lead-up to the election, and another that there will be many dissatisfied with the result, regardless of the process. The new constitution offers potential opportunities for change and improvement in Myanmar, but various aspects of the transition are still unclear, yet critical for stability. Given the conflicting views, the process of change should be gradual.

National development goals are diverse. The consideration of this diversity should be coupled with the understanding that the Myanmar government is not monolithic, as often portrayed, and that at times a surprising mix of approaches is shown in methodology. Myanmar is a country of enormous richness and variety, and home to many groups characterized by great resilience, courage and a passion for national development.

Myanmar has rarely received positive press, or commendation for work done well, despite a considerable amount of progress that has taken place. A flow on from this has been more negativity in foreign policy or attitudes than is appropriate for the context. Failure to recognize progress for what it is devalues the efforts of a host of people working hard to create change in many ways. Yet few news reports or studies are written on positive achievements, although it can be expected that an increasing number of diverse, positive case studies will emerge as more summaries of accounts of work done as part of the overall response to Cyclone Nargis accumulate. The December 2008 edition of *Humanitarian Exchange*, published by the Overseas Development Institute, included a number of these. In general, as reporting on Nargis-related activities has been far better publicized than other examples, this chapter will seek to draw on other lesser-known examples. It acknowledges the many criticisms made of complex issues in Myanmar and makes no attempt to refute them, or to add to the shortcomings detailed elsewhere. The main purpose is to present some more positive and lesser-known perspectives on progress in Myanmar as alternatives that can be built on as a means of offering different pathways to future national development.

However, for Myanmar, even defining what constitutes "progress" is problematic. Khin Zaw Win highlights the difficulties which remain today. He questioned the simple formula that "lack of democracy equals lack of progress", and argues that "a more productive endeavour would be to identify turning points" that could "make a difference for the country".[1]

SOME POSITIVE EXAMPLES

Of particular significance is the breadth of examples that represent areas of progress, which take place quietly and consistently but which are usually overshadowed by political factors. In spite of the context difficulties, these examples demonstrate that opportunity is far more common than most would expect, and also imply that many more people are working successfully in positive engagement activities than is generally realized. Examples have been chosen in an attempt to show breadth, to illustrate the importance of work being done and, in some cases, to highlight unusual characteristics that many might have thought impossible in Myanmar.

Those who promote engagement as a strategy find small pockets of support; however, opponents strenuously reject this proposition. A tenet for this chapter is that support for positive engagement is sometimes not forthcoming because little external publicity is given to evidence of success, or to the examples of small but significant steps that it has been possible to take. One aim is to try and draw lessons learnt from these examples for help in applying this approach to other sectors. Many who have spent some years in Myanmar will recall areas of work where lack of achievement or progress remains frustrating, as well as isolated areas of progress that seem worthy of celebration. The richness of Myanmar's history, geography, and cultural and ethnic diversity ensure a complexity sufficient to make external interpretation of factors difficult, so this is hardly surprising. Yet if one looks at enough of the pockets of success, patterns begin to emerge. While the diversity in the administration means that nothing can be taken for granted, lessons are available in many places. Often these may be considered in relatively mundane activities, and not of any particular great national significance. Yet changes accumulate, and success in some areas makes success easier in others, and build confidence in the engagement process.

Some recent areas of change chosen for brief discussion are:

1. The work to counter human trafficking
2. Work in drug control, reducing opium cultivation, and harm reduction
3. Progress towards a national disability strategy
4. Improvements in the education of agricultural officers and in food security
5. Reforms in forestry policy
6. Improvements regarding resettlement through dialogue
7. Progress in developing national HIV, malaria and TB strategies.

For changes such as these it is clear that there are many dedicated individuals working hard for progress. The examples listed are mostly pre-Nargis programmes and do not cover the many triumphs, small and large, that allowed a far better result in dealing with the aftermath of the cyclone than most observers would have expected.

Countering Human Trafficking

Efforts by the Myanmar Government, together with national and international non-governmental organizations (NGOs) and organizations to prevent human trafficking, have increased in recent years. Since 2002, United Nations agencies and NGOs working on human trafficking in Myanmar have met on a regular basis in what later became the "Human Trafficking Working Group" (HTWG). Initially formed to share information about ongoing interventions, the focus of the group has shifted in recent years towards formulating a cohesive, multi-sectoral response to trafficking. In May 2003, the Myanmar National Committee for Women's Affairs (MNCWA), in cooperation with UNICEF, UNIAP, and Save the Children (UK), organized the first national seminar on trafficking in persons.[2]

In March 2004, Myanmar signed and ratified the Convention Against Transnational Organized Crime and the supplementary Protocol Against Trafficking in Persons. The government established a Department Against Transnational Organized Crime within the Ministry of Home Affairs to coordinate efforts against transnational crime, including human trafficking, reviewed existing national legislation and began drafting a national anti-trafficking law, through consultations with concerned government ministries and a review workshop with NGOs. On 13 September 2005, the resulting law, the "Anti-Trafficking in Persons Law" was enacted.

In addition, in 2004 an anti-trafficking unit of the Myanmar Police Force was established, and trained in part through the Asia Regional Cooperation to Prevent People Trafficking (ARCPPT) project, a regional Australian Government (AusAID)-funded project that also encouraged cooperation on intelligence and investigations with regional police forces. Myanmar is also participating in the six-country "Coordinated Mekong Ministerial Initiative against Trafficking" (COMMIT) process, which aims to increase regional collaboration to fight trafficking. The six countries involved — Cambodia, China, Lao PDR, Myanmar, Thailand and Vietnam — signed a memorandum of understanding to fight trafficking and began work on a Sub-regional Plan of Action (SPA) through national COMMIT task forces.

With the legislation enacted, and a special unit to support it, the Myanmar Government has put into place a clear framework to fight human trafficking. On the ground, challenges remain to operationalize this framework, particularly in the remote areas where much of the trafficking takes place. Table 13.1 summarizes work being done by the HTWG and others to achieve this.[3]

Arrest data and interviews with victims have led to the identification of four trafficking "hot spots" along the country's borders: Muse in the north (bordering China), Tachileik and Myawaddy in the east (bordering Thailand), and Kawthoung in the south (also along the Thai border). Victims come from all over Myanmar and often initially move to one of these hot spots before crossing the border. Table 13.2 summarizes the police data showing the work of the established enforcement system.[4]

Save the Children has been a key agency involved in the anti-trafficking reform work in Myanmar over a long period, at both a community and policy level. The organization's Director of Programmes, Guy Cave, made the following observations:

> The Myanmar Government has actually taken anti-trafficking more seriously than many others in the region.…Myanmar's thinking and action on trafficking stands up well when compared with others in the region.

TABLE 13.1
Elements of the Anti Human-trafficking Plan

Component	Goal	Objective
1: Prevention	Decrease the number of adults and children trafficked.	Increase general awareness of human trafficking and safe migration for both adults and children. Reduce vulnerabilities to trafficking.
2: Protection, Care and Support	Increase the protection and support provided to trafficked persons, without discrimination.	Offer protection and support to address the needs of trafficking survivors, both adults and children.
3: Prosecution	Increase effective prosecutions of traffickers and those involved in trafficking outcomes.	Improve the criminal-justice response to human trafficking.
4: Enabling Environment	Strengthen the national commitment to address trafficking and help to translate that commitment into action.	Support development of an enabling policy and operational environment to combat trafficking.

Source: Adapted from "Human Trafficking in Myanmar: A Response Strategy", Human Trafficking Working Group, May 2006.

TABLE 13.2
Convicted Human Trafficking Cases Under Anti-Trafficking in Persons Law (1 January 2006 to 31 December 2008)

State/Division	Convicted human trafficking cases	Under 5 years' imprisonment			Over 5 years' imprisonment			Over 10 years' imprisonment			Over 15 years' imprisonment			Over 20 years' imprisonment			Over 25 years' imprisonment			Life Sentenced			Grand Total		
		Male	Female	Total	M	F	Total	M	F	Total	M	F	Total	M	F	Total	M	F	Total	M	F	Total	M	F	Total
Shan (North)	101	–	–	–	–	–	–	28	99	127	2	3	5	4	6	10	1	2	3	21	19	40	56	129	185
Mandalay	21	–	–	–	–	–	–	13	16	29	1	1	2	1	2	3	1	1	2	10	8	18	26	28	54
Kachin	15	–	–	–	–	2	2	1	17	18	1	4	5	–	–	–	–	–	–	–	–	–	2	23	25
Yangon	15	–	–	–	1	–	1	12	10	22	4	7	11	–	1	1	–	–	–	2	3	5	19	21	40
Shan (East)	4	1	–	1	–	–	–	10	3	13	1	–	1	–	–	–	–	–	–	–	–	–	12	3	15
Shan (South)	3	–	–	–	–	–	–	–	4	4	–	–	–	–	–	–	–	–	–	1	1	2	1	5	6
Magway	2	–	–	–	–	–	–	2	4	6	–	–	–	–	–	–	–	–	–	–	–	–	2	4	6
Sagaing	2	–	–	–	–	–	–	1	1	2	–	–	–	–	–	–	–	–	–	–	–	–	1	1	2
Kayin	2	–	–	–	–	–	–	–	1	1	–	1	1	–	–	–	–	–	–	–	–	–	–	2	2
Ayeyarwaddy	2	–	–	–	–	–	–	3	–	3	–	–	–	–	–	–	–	–	–	–	–	–	3	–	3
Bago	2	–	–	–	–	–	–	1	2	3	–	–	–	–	–	–	–	–	–	2	–	2	3	2	5
Rakhine	1	–	–	–	–	–	–	1	1	2	–	1	1	–	–	–	–	–	–	–	–	–	1	2	3
Total	170	1	–	1	1	2	3	72	158	230	9	17	26	5	9	14	2	3	5	36	31	67	126	220	346

Source: Ministry of Home Affairs, 2009. Anti-Trafficking Unit, Myanmar Police Force, received from UNIAP 26/2/09, Naypyitaw.

> The government, including the police, has been very willing to engage with NGOs on the issue...The cooperative work on trafficking has been a good entry point into broader work on other child-protection issues. (Personal interview, 27 May 2009.)

Controlling Drugs and Reducing Production

While the reduction rate in the supply of Southeast Asian opium is a debated issue (for example, over claims that over-inflated starting figures were used), supply reduction generally in the region has been the result of various factors, including supply-side controls in the Golden Triangle region, a change to amphetamine-type substances (ATS) within the market, and record cultivation in Afghanistan.[5]

The Myanmar government's drug-control objectives have been focused on eliminating supply. Under the leadership of the Central Committee for Drug Abuse Control (CCDAC), a 15-year plan to eliminate narcotics, using a coordinated approach, started its first phase in 1999. The Myanmar Government has been largely successful in achieving these supply-level objectives (UNODC 2006, p. 21).

Over the eight years from 1998 to 2006, there is credible reporting that Myanmar's opium poppy cultivation decreased rapidly from 130,300 ha in 1998 to 81,400 in 2002 and 21,500 ha in 2006.[6] This represents an enormous reduction within a radically compressed time-frame. The main areas under poppy cultivation are Southern Shan State (65 per cent) and Eastern Shan State (25 per cent).

An overall flavour of the work done is one of "good progress, but missed opportunity".[7] Progress is hampered by inadequate funding, as the allocated Overseas Development Assistance (ODA) and Myanmar government funding is insufficient for social development and services — the sectors through which drug-control objectives are typically "mainstreamed". This is a major obstacle for attempting such work. In his survey work on mainstreaming, Theuss (2007) highlighted the fact that some respondents wondered whether it was possible to "mainstream without a stream".

The reductions, regardless of the exact amounts, have been influenced by the government's policy on reduction. Given the lack of funding allocated for social programmes in general, one could argue that at that point in the country's history the supply-side control was one of the few practical and achievable options. However, the poppy bans caused significant community impacts with respect to poverty and an alternative method of controlling supply may have been a better option. The fact remains that a huge impact on supply-side figures was achieved.

Drug control in Myanmar remains controversial. Initiatives like the UN Office of Drugs and Crime's Kokang and Wa Initiaitive (KOWI) show efforts to bring improved policy coherence and coordination to multi-sectoral and integrated development programming in poppy-growing areas. Many will say that much more is needed. KOWI is evolving into an organization that could support mainstreaming in a strategic manner if sufficient resources are allocated and the conflict environment permits. In southern Shan State, the Ministry of Agriculture and Irrigation's (MoAI) focus on agricultural projects designed to reduce poverty attempts to avoid some of the hardship introduced by previous reduction programmes, and appears to be the result of improved policy coherence. From the demand side, embryonic work in mainstreaming is taking place through an expansion of harm-reduction programmes into "drugs and society" approaches (MoAI/FAO 2009).

For the future, many desire to see increased funding to both supply and demand sides, increased policy coherence, replication of potential mainstreaming initiatives in Southern and Eastern Shan and Kachin States, and more-humane approaches to supply-side reduction than poppy bans. Increased attention to "drugs and society" approaches should be supported.

To reiterate and conclude — dramatic reductions have been achieved on the supply side as part of programmed drug-control work. Given the funding invested in this complex area, some will say the progress has been outstanding. Others maintain that much opportunity has been missed simply due to insufficient support for mainstreaming or demand work.

Progress Towards a National Disability Strategy

The Nargis disaster presented an opportunity for more comprehensive work on plans of action for people in Myanmar with disabilities. Work amongst a variety of agencies, through the Ministry of Social Welfare, Relief and Resettlement, and with The Leprosy Mission International (TLMI) acting as focal agency, has facilitated development of an Emergency Plan of Action for Persons with Disability, the overall goal of which is that: "Persons with disability have increased mobility, access and opportunity to be able to participate in society as equal members, and contribute to the economic and social goals of the State as active and responsible citizens."[8]

The plan of action uses a twin-track approach of advocacy for the needs and rights of persons with disability, leading to changes in attitude, capacity and action of stakeholders. The aim is that these, in turn, will result in the development of necessary programmes and support frameworks to enable rehabilitation of persons with disability in their community.

The specific objectives of the three-year strategic plan of action are clear and comprehensive. Comprehensive survey work has accompanied this process, representing major progress and providing the information necessary for implementing the plan. Quite simply, in the Myanmar context this is a remarkable achievement. While the work done under this plan is limited to the emergency areas, a similar process is now under way on a national scale, building on all aspects of the development work to date. A draft National Plan has now been developed.

Agricultural Education Programmes and Food Security

While national objectives for Myanmar support the development of agriculture as the base of the economy, it is widely recognized that the mechanisms for doing so need to be greatly improved. MoAI and its operational arm Myanma Agricultural Services (MAS) have supported agencies seeking to work for development in the field. Among the various agencies is the Food Security Working Group (FSWG), which has a membership of some 40 community organizations, LNGOs and INGOs. In May 2007, FSWG and World Concern Myanmar ran a National Symposium on Farmer-Led Agricultural Extension Approaches, which opened up with presentations from farmers, agricultural-college staff, NGO workers and the various departments in MoAI and MAS. From the open discussions between the various levels of participants that ensued, some clear steps forward were identified.[9]

One of these pathways has been the delivery by NGOs in June 2009 of lectures in the Farmer Field School process (a group-based learning approach that has been used by a number of governments, NGOs and international agencies to promote integrated pest management), and Training of Trainers (TOT) courses to final-year agriculture students at the government-operated agricultural university at Yezin, as part of

MoAI's desire to upgrade the service provision to communities. Other significant steps have included the commencement of the multi-donor Livelihood Improvement and Food Security Trust Fund, (LIFT) fund on livelihoods in conjunction with MoAI, and the "Roundtable and Development Forum on Economic Policies for Growth and Poverty Reduction" conducted in December 2009 by UNESCAP in conjunction with MoAI and Ministry of Planning.

Reforms in Forestry Policy

Another particularly important opportunity for multi-stakeholder engagement came from a February 2009 workshop focused on experience and practice in community forestry.[10] In attendance were representatives from the forestry community, academics, NGOs, donor organizations and various departments of the Ministry of Forestry (MoF).

Presentations were made on local and international practice. There was particularly open discussion on issues associated with ways forward to improve operation of community-forestry projects. Pathways were mapped out to allow reform of the legislation which provides the current legality of tenure via perhaps one of the most progressive pieces of land-use legislation in Myanmar. In-principle commitments made by the MoF have been followed up and ratified by the Minister of Forestry, and are awaiting Cabinet's Foreign Affairs Policy Committee (FAPC) approval.

While this may seem small in the overall scheme of things, the initiative has enormous potential. The outcomes specifically paved the way for further dialogue and progress on such things as:

- land-use reform
- commitment to multi-stakeholder, multi-sectoral legislative review processes
- focusing on indigenous people's needs, rights and entitlements
- extending tenure beyond the current 30-year limit
- teak ownership by communities, rather than the current ownership by the government
- recognition of swidden agriculture as a viable land-use component in community forest
- recognition that multi-sectoral and multi-agency approaches are necessary to resolve land-use conflicts that are increasingly arising from agro-forestry and agribusiness land allocations made at the state level.

Many specific issues are covered in this list. Arguably more important has been progress by communities in learning to practise conflict resolution on these issues, where communities have retained access rights to land, allocated under sometimes confusing circumstances. Case studies of these successful resolutions of land-use conflict are infrequent and, although not yet documented, are very important for promulgating the use of different mechanisms of conflict resolution.

Improving Resettlement Issues through Dialogue

Following Cyclone Nargis, many people were relocated to temporary shelters. Over time many returned to their former areas to restart their lives. However, at two temporary shelter areas (Labutta "7½ and 15 mile") some 375 families did not wish to relocate to coastal areas for fear of other disasters. The Norwegian Refugee Council (NRC) offered to provide shelter assistance, as well as upgrading local schools to cater for the additional children. The Township Peace and Development Council (TPDC) planned to reallocate people amongst 37 villages, and sought support for this. The NRC's offer of assistance was conditional on the resettlement being voluntary and access being assured to confirm that no force or undue pressure had been applied. Access was arranged and, through interviews conducted by NRC and UNHCR staff, the organizations were satisfied that the resettlement was voluntary.

As relocations progressed, it was observed that some of the locations selected could not offer sufficient livelihood opportunities for the new families and discussions began on an alternative scheme based on twenty-one more-suitable locations, rather than the thirty-seven villages proposed. Township authorities quickly approved this and through negotiations with local village headmen, additional land was identified. To quote NRC's Director Joern Kristensen:

> NRC's cooperation with township authorities has been carried out through an open dialogue, UNHCR has monitored the resettlement and confirm that there have been no attempts by the authorities to use force or to not accept the conditions for engagement put forward by NRC at the beginning of the process. Following the completion of the resettlement each family will receive a document, signed by the respective village headmen and by NRC, stating their ownership to the house and right to the land it is built on. (Personal interview, 19 June 2009)

Follow-up in November 2009 showed that all 375 families had been relocated in the manner planned and that relationships with authorities remained positive.

This short case study is of interest because there are so many stories of relocation from ethnic areas in Myanmar that do not have such positive outcomes. Stories of success are therefore worth taking note of to see what factors can be replicated. Extension of this type of work is being considered in some troubled border areas.

Developing National Strategies for HIV, Malaria and TB

The last five years (2006–2010) has seen major change in the response to HIV, malaria and TB in Myanmar. Integral and critical to this improvement has been the development of national strategic plans for each of these diseases. These plans are considered best practice, and each has been tuned for a further ongoing period. Each faces difficulties of funding availability and a relatively low level of resourcing available to the Ministry of Health, upon whom all groups operating in the health sector rely to some extent.

A brief overview of the current situation and plans for each disease follows.

HIV/AIDS

In 2007, the prevalence of HIV in the adult population was estimated to be 0.7 per cent, with an estimated 242,000 people living with HIV. Of these, 75,000 were in need of antiretroviral therapy, with estimates of over 20,000 deaths from AIDS-related causes.[11] The three largest groups as a percentage of those affected are injecting drug users (37.5 per cent), men who have sex with men (28.8 per cent) and female sex workers (18.4 per cent).[12]

The Ministry of Health has issued a "National Strategic Plan on AIDS 2006–2010", which prioritizes service provision for the most at-risk populations. The government-led plan is supported by a technical coordination group. According to the ministry, the plan provides "a basis for greater multi-sectoral involvement (for example prisons, the police, the uniformed services, the transport sector and the judicial sector); a focus on the most at-risk populations, including sex workers and clients, drug users and men who have sex with men; a participatory coordination structure; and explicit references to human rights" (Ministry of Health 2006, 2009).

Some summarizing comments on the National Strategic Plan by the NGO/UN Joint Team on HIV/AIDS concluded that "increased resources and policy engagement can result in increased services for people in need and facilitate the evolution of HIV policies" and that "International donors should recognize the evidence of increased coverage possibilities by increasing commitments".

Difficulties noted include: constraining administrative procedures, controlled access, limited research and a highly politicized context (PSI et al. 2008).

Clearly, there is a great deal of scope for improvement, and the difficulties must not be underestimated. Factors that create communication difficulties, such as relocation of government officials to Naypyitaw and a general environment of mistrust of international organizations, make this more difficult. Still, increased dialogue is considered a key route forward towards resolution, and parties closest to the areas of work remain committed to this.

Reductions in ODA commitments mean that levels of available assistance meet a comparatively low level of needs. Preliminary data for 2008 show HIV/AIDS resources are the equivalent of around US$0.50 per capita, which is less than half the level recommended by the Commission on AIDS in Asia for priority interventions and programme-related costs in expanding and declining epidemics (UNAIDS 2007; Commission on AIDS 2008). With current levels of funding, service coverage will not increase sufficiently to address the pressing needs for care and prevention. More resources are therefore required, both from international sources and from the government.

The operation of the Fund for HIV/AIDS in Myanmar (FHAM), which operated from April 2003 through March 2007 with a total of US$27 million spent, and that of the Three Diseases Fund demonstrate that international resources can be used to finance HIV services for people in need in an accountable and transparent manner. (The Three Diseases Fund is a US$100 million fund established in 2006 by six donors — Australia, EC, United Kingdom, Netherlands, Norway and Sweden — to respond to the funding gap for HIV, tuberculosis and malaria as a result of the withdrawal of the Global Fund from Myanmar in 2005.)

The public-health infrastructure, upon which all partners depend to varying degrees, is chronically under-funded, both by both the government and donors unwilling to invest in health systems in Myanmar. Government expenditure on health is less than US$0.50 per person per year, which is the second-lowest in the world (SC-MM 2006).

Malaria

Around 75 per cent of Myanmar's population live in villages considered to have high malaria risk. Myanmar's strategic plan for malaria control is considered to be well aligned with international best practice for prevention and control taking into account the socio-cultural setting, epidemiological situation and the development of the health system. A combination of tools is being used, and villages are being stratified to ensure classification and targeting can be satisfactory.

According to the joint Myanmar application to the Global Fund, the national malaria-control programme strategies are:

(1) Scaling up the coverage and consistent use of long-lasting insecticidal mosquito nets (LLINs) and insecticide-treated nets (ITNs), and selective application of indoor residual spraying (IRS) and other preventative measures where appropriate
(2) Improving early access to quality assured diagnosis and effective treatment
(3) Empowering communities at risk and building multi-sector partnerships
(4) Strengthening programme management and technical support

Global Fund application documents list in great detail the weaknesses in the systems and problems that need to be overcome, while recognizing that much progress has been made. Among the difficulties listed are insufficient budget for the Ministry of Health and the Vector Borne Disease Control Programme, low coverage of nets or treated nets, low coverage of diagnostics, weak information systems, poor access to behaviour-change communications, remote-area access issues and access to quality-assured drugs. Despite this, malaria work has progressed particularly well, although with limited effectiveness and coverage at this stage.

Inadequate financial resources emerge as the key constraint for this work.

Tuberculosis

According to the joint Myanmar application to the Global Fund, "Myanmar is among the 22 TB high burden countries, among the 41 high TB/HIV burden countries and among the 27 high multidrug resistant/extensively drug-resistant TB burden countries." TB is the most important opportunistic infection in cases of HIV/AIDS (affecting 60–80 per cent), in Myanmar and Southeast Asia overall. Activities in the national plan include improving detection, treatment and patient services, and access to medication.[13]

Based on learning from the previous Global Fund withdrawal, FHAM operation and 3D Fund experience, new applications have been prepared that aim to meet all the Global Fund requirements, with which Myanmar was considered to be non-compliant in 2005.[14] Governance is planned by a Myanmar Country Coordinating Mechanism of twenty-nine members, with wide representation. This demonstrates that compliance with international consultative mechanisms is possible. Such a comprehensive coordination mechanism could go a long way towards helping resolve some of the current operational constraints.

Considering more general health issues, there are overall serious financial constraints. "Funding sources for health care services are private out-of-own-pocket (73.4 per cent), government (13.6 per cent), external aid (12.1 per cent), community contribution (0.54 per cent) and social security system (0.36 per cent) according to 2001–2002 estimation of the national health expenditure."[15] Clearly, a greater input into health areas can assist the situation for the general population. While only three diseases have been discussed, opportunities exist to work on many additional health problems, with nutrition and maternal health key areas.

Significant progress in disease control has been possible in each of these three key diseases. Without strong cooperative work, the progress would not have been possible, and international-standard strategic plans for each disease would not be available. While the existing or future work is not and will not be free from difficulties, an astounding amount has been achieved in the Myanmar context. Funding availability appears to be the biggest single constraint to continued progress in these areas.

Perhaps the clearest evidence of general acknowledgement of progress made comes from the international assessments of Myanmar's submission for Round 9 Global Fund support, which received the highest tier of assessment for HIV/AIDS and the second-highest for Malaria and TB.

WHAT DOES ALL THIS SHOW, AND WHERE TO FROM HERE?

A diverse range of case studies has been presented (including discussion of some of the difficulties and constraints faced) at varying levels of detail to demonstrate that success stories are neither isolated to a specific area, nor as rare as one might imagine. Some obvious questions remain: Do these examples have anything in common? What is there to learn from this and what insight can they offer for the future? In what other fields might these sorts of small successes emerge if cultivated?

These examples have some significant common characteristics:

- A serious and intentional focus on engagement, on finding common ground with those interest groups who have a long-term desire for change and improvement.
- Openness and interest in acknowledging and discussing issues and problems.
- Avoidance of the elements that serve only to politicize the issues.
- Facilitation by groups working inside the country, who can demonstrate country- and culture-sensitive ways of doing things, and the building of mutual trust.
- A focus on issues where the needs can be acknowledged by all involved, and resulting in a situation change that can clearly be defined as progress.
- Cooperative work between multi-sectoral stakeholders and government.
- Legislation formation, review, ratification, training and enforcement.

Thant Myint Oo describes external presentation of Myanmar as very one-dimensional, with a portrayal of issues as principally a democracy issue. He goes on to describe the complexity of the ethnic situation, the long-running civil war, the massive social changes under way, the struggles of one of the world's poorest countries and a country with rapidly evolving relationships with extremely influential neighbours. His conclusion is that the situation is clearly very complex. The portions rarely described deserve further press coverage (McDermid 2009).

First-hand experience of some of these areas of progress perhaps helps rationalize the differences between external impressions and diversity of experience. Since the Myanmar government is a very diverse group of individuals, and not monolithic, then diversity of experience is to be expected over time.

Digging deeper into the above examples, what are some of the enabling elements? It is suggested that these include: maintaining a non-political approach; establishing trust; having ministries with clear mandates and interest in the specific fields in which programmes are able to realise the opportunities and development expectations; obtaining support that is sufficient and proportional to the tasks needed; and identifying champions and interest groups that are in a position to work in a field and deliver results.

The "Do No Harm" Approach

Ewing-Chow presents particularly interesting discussion on the interaction of international sanctions and human rights. To quote his concluding point, "the main concern of international actors seeking to address international ills should be, in the famous dictum of Hippocrates, to [first] do no harm and if harm is caused then to swiftly redress that mistake" (Ewing-Chow 2007). The "Do no harm" approach offers much to assist progress in Myanmar. Recent studies on the available tools and methodology have concluded the most important aspects are helping users to consider "dividers and connectors". The above examples are all connectors.[16] The use of dividers needs great care as harm almost always results.

Extending the previous discussion where many appear to have equated indicators on progress with indicators of democracy, harm would come where work on development retards progress towards democracy. From this perspective, none of the intervention examples discussed in this chapter would represent any risk.

Taking a more holistic perspective, particular care is needed with the rights of indigenous peoples, the disadvantaged poor, and many issues associated with land tenure, property rights and multi-sectoral land-use planning approaches. Finding "dividers" is easy in this work, whereas finding "connectors" is harder and needs creativity. As it turns out, the greatest overall connector can be the shared aspirational goal of national development, which provides diverse opportunities for connection and, therefore, for engagement.

Using these connector elements, what should one work on in the current climate? If various possible tasks are assessed against such criteria, more successful projects can be found and the amount of harm can be reduced.

Peace-building and Engagement with Ethnic and Ceasefire Groups

This area is critical to successful progress in Myanmar, and while including only a short paragraph on this is inadequate, omitting it completely seems even worse. The ceasefires have allowed considerable progress in ethnic areas and the author has yet to encounter any community that wishes to return to armed conflict. However, despite progress, many groups feel that the processes have not been sufficiently inclusive or paid sufficient attention to their specific needs. Kramer in recent work on ceasefire agreements deals well with the issues and critical needs for the future, and the complexity of the task given that the ceasefire groups need help to be able to deal with the participatory community processes likely to be needed for a peaceful future (Kramer 2009).

For many of these communities in border areas, all of the issues discussed in this chapter come to the fore — their current livelihoods and economy are integrated with activities that are often based on unsustainable utilisation of natural resources, with inadequate health, education and agricultural opportunity, and poor market access. Transition work for these communities needs considerable scaling up and needs to be integrated.

Two of Myanmar's current objectives are stability of the state, community peace and tranquility, prevalence of law and order; and national reconsolidation. Clearly these objectives provide "connector" opportunity. A number of groups in Myanmar have specialized in furthering work in peace building and dialogue processes in various forms. This work deserves far more support and encouragement than it currently receives, and epitomizes positive engagement opportunities.

Impact of the Economy on Socio-economic Development

A theme emerging from these case studies is that sufficient government funding is not being provided to meet the country's needs. After consideration of the implications of such low spending on critical nation-building elements such as education, health and food security, the economy has to be an area of focus. However, to have a chance of success, non-political approaches must be taken. While it is not within the scope of this chapter to provide detailed coverage of this, some points need to be made.

On Burma's macroeconomic instability and inflation, Turnell writes:

> Burma is in possession of almost every conceivable macroeconomic malady...The country lacks the fundamental institutions of a market economy, policy-making is arbitrary and uninformed, inflation is rampant, the currency is distrusted and trading is chaotic and the Government finances its spending by printing money. To this list can be added all-pervasive corruption, a growing trade deficit, foreign debt arrears, the imposition of economic sanctions and negligible foreign investment. (Turnell 2009)

This is quite a list of ills.

For continuing progress in Myanmar, serious economic reform, covering many aspects of the financial, banking and legal systems is needed, and these aspects continually provide blockages to development. From the author's experience in operating integrated development and livelihood programmes, involvement in small-business support, and observing other programmes, key economic priorities for work would involve:

- Liberalizing agriculture and trade
- Developing the financial and banking sectors to ensure that the availability of much-needed capital and access to credit
- Improving land tenure, land-use planning, and property and enterprise ownership for rural and indigenous peoples
- Simplifying and improving the business climate (particularly for small business)
- Improving financial transparency and accountability to encourage investment that will help long-term development, and not do further harm or create new problems
- Unifying exchange rates
- Reducing inflation.

These items are very similar to those proposed by Turnell and the IMF (Turnell 2009; IMF 2009).

An example of the dilemmas in improvement work and analysis in Myanmar can come from widely diverging views on some indicators. For example, Turnell says the inflation rate is around 50 per cent, while the IMF projections are around 25 per cent and 20 per cent into the future.

How can small-scale rural credit programmes be set up and operate sustainably with such uncertainty surrounding key matters such as the cost of credit?[17]

At present, most discussions on reform seem to become immediately embroiled in the highly political issues of sanctions and reasons why there cannot be further cooperation or international support, or assistance from the World Bank, IMF and ADB. Overseas development assistance (ODA) is extremely limited, as is foreign direct investment. For much-needed operating funds and investment, Myanmar turns to any possible sources of income, and as a result understandably pursues natural-resource developments. Without the ability or resources to develop resources itself, it relies on external relationships, some of which are exploitative and may not follow all the guidelines (legal or voluntary) that may be considered and used in ideal situations. These developments bring on further criticism, both from within and outside, but the alternatives are limited given the state of development. Unfortunately, without many of the needed economic reforms and specific attention to learning from elsewhere, the risk of Myanmar pursuing revenue from developing its natural resources, with the attendant risk of this becoming a "resource curse", increases greatly.

Transparency in Natural-resource Revenues

At present, gas revenues represent around 45 per cent of all export earnings and around 5 per cent of GDP, although considerable uncertainty surrounds the estimates, some of which range closer to 10 per cent of GDP. As the Shwe offshore gas fields in Rakhine State are developed, the percentage of exports can be expected to rise to 10–20 per cent and export earnings from gas to around 65 per cent of total exports. Again, the lack of clear information, uncertainty of understanding of how much is "off balance sheet", foreign-exchange issues and overall lack of transparency about such important figures are highly problematic and prevent full understanding of Myanmar's economic performance.

Given that gas and other natural resources already represent such a high proportion of the Myanmar economy, it would be helpful for the organizations operating in this sector to improve transparency standards, and begin processes that would allow a gradual improvement of trust.

Natural-resource revenues have provided financial independence for core operations of the government. Yet little of this has flowed through into spending on health, education and provision of food security or livelihoods for the extremely poor population. For a number of years now, natural-resource revenues have dwarfed ODA figures in Myanmar. (For example, compare current gas earnings of roughly $50/capita to ODA of roughly $3/capita, and also compare these to health spending of $0.50/capita and education of $0.60/capita.)

In developing economies, discussions on "natural-resource curse" factors abound.[18] Myanmar is currently highly vulnerable to all of the negative impacts of this phenomenon, and a "gas curse" is a likely scenario unless immediate measures are taken to reduce this risk. Ideally, Myanmar should follow the example of a host of developing countries with natural-resource wealth (including Indonesia) and engage with an initiative such as the Extractive Industry Transparency Initiative (EITI) to demonstrate accountability and transparency for its largest external funds flow. Further, the income should flow into a natural-resource fund (NRF), and a substantial portion of this should be allocated for spending on developing the education, health and livelihoods sectors. In a single simple move like this, Myanmar could greatly reduce criticism on economic matters and change entirely its development trajectory. Note that for NRFs to be successful, good governance is needed; and this would need particular attention in a country like Myanmar.

While the gas-resource revenues seem enormous, they are low compared with those of many oil-producing countries. They are inherently non-renewable and therefore represent one-off opportunities for Myanmar in this particularly difficult stage of its development. This makes the efficient and accountable handling and utilization of revenues particularly critical.

Corporations like Total and Chevron, which operate or are major shareholders in gas operations in Myanmar, are international signatories to transparency initiatives like EITI.[19] It is hoped their experience in this regard will enable increased transparency on payments in Myanmar. A worthwhile goal for the industry in Myanmar will be for all operators (particularly Petronas and Daewoo, in addition to those above) to adopt such important transparency standards in developing and practising corporate social responsibility (CSR).

Corporate Social Responsibility

Smith refers to Myanmar as being a "CSR Black Hole".[20] This claim can be contested, but it is true that the CSR field is embryonic in Myanmar.

The author has witnessed high interest in business ethics in Myanmar. However, to ensure that any such interest has the opportunity to develop healthily, much more stimulus is needed in the economy. Additionally, much of the foreign investment/development business activity comes from China, where CSR/sustainability practice, although a somewhat new field, is developing rapidly.[21] The net result is that business practice in Myanmar is generally not highly experienced in these fields, making it harder for developments to meet international standards. A focus on this area is recommended.

Myanmar's economy is dependent on development and exploitation of natural-resource based wealth. It is unfortunate that the country has been isolated from many of the positive benefits that best practice in CSR can offer. Business activities are enormous in comparison to humanitarian activities, and therefore have considerably more economic influence. They also carry huge potential for engagement in the process of guiding reform.

National Sustainable Development Strategy

Myanmar has been working for a number of years on a National Sustainable Development Strategy (NSDS). While still in draft form, this document offers opportunities for the country's development. The unique features of this strategy result from it having been developed by multi-sectoral panels of national experts and ministry representatives. As this work progresses through further drafting and approval processes, it should be recognized as a Myanmar-led, multi-sectoral plan that is the result of a significant process of learning, in a time of transition.

It is hoped that the NSDS will endorse the establishment of a National Council for Sustainable Development and the opportunity to move forward with legislation and enforcement mechanisms to fill some of the current legal gaps (for example, in environmental law). Planning issues surrounding sustainable land-use are an important part of this work, and will need continued engagement on the part of the many affected groups to move coordinated plans forward, recognizing the rights of individuals under national and international law.

Other issues to consider as a result of the NSDS drafting include:

- The Myanmar government has initiated this work, and for it to continue logical development, assistance and cooperation will be needed in many areas.

- Much crosscutting work is needed in the education, health and agricultural sectors — and a great deal of independent effort is going into these.
- Foreign groups will need to be more accountable — as a minimum, to the standards required in their home countries — and greater acknowledgement of the negative external factors affecting many projects is necessary. (China now has quite established guidelines for the area of "ecological compensation", as its way of approaching some of the market-based aspects of payments for ecological services (PES) which are emerging at present. These should also be applied to its operations in Myanmar.)
- Environmental-impact assessments (EIAs) and social-impact assessments (SIAs) will need to be part of the approval process for any new project.

Some of these aspects represent quite a change for Myanmar, and it is not unreasonable to expect that it will take some time to introduce all the necessary policy and legislative frameworks, education, training, awareness and enforcement mechanisms.

Agricultural-sector Performance, Food Security and Livelihoods

The MoAI/FAO national medium-term priority framework (NMTPF) for livelihoods and agriculture is due for public release, but still awaiting approval.[22] This is likely to advocate for close cooperative work with the Ministry of Agriculture in areas such as:

- improvements in the availability of rural credit and capital
- improvements in security of land tenure for farmers
- increased assistance from agricultural extension workers
- further market liberalization, market studies and secondary processing
- improvements in rural infrastructure for access to markets and irrigation.

A 2009 agricultural assessment by the FAO/WFP made some pointed observations on policy, referring to the "use of distorted macroeconomic, trade and sectoral policies", which resulted in "huge losses to the tax payer and corruption, and may have negative long-term impacts on Myanmar's agriculture sector". It called for the implementation of "market-oriented agricultural trade" with "strong policies that allow domestic prices to reflect world prices; redirect government intervention programmes toward tackling market failures and providing sufficient public goods/ services; create appropriate institutions that complement the market; remove regional (state/division) protectionism on agricultural produce" (FAO/WFP 2009).

To initiate these changes will take some considerable time and a massive coordinated effort. Much work is needed to help the agricultural sector flourish as the mainstay of the economy as the Myanmar government desires. In the meantime, the suffering of the people has to be alleviated to help improve the situation, build more resilience and improve national stability. Humanitarian assistance work outside the Nargis disaster zone can in the scheme of the overall economy be considered small. For the very poor, life is particularly difficult. Just how difficult can be gauged from the fact that in 2008 the per-capita GDP was $290, with 70 per cent likely to be spent on food.[23]

NEW MULTI-DONOR FUNDING OPPORTUNITIES

The LIFT fund and others like it should be important mechanisms for new funding. While funds directed towards improving livelihoods were much discussed prior to Nargis, it seems a mixed blessing that much of the early support from the LIFT fund may be channelled into cyclone recovery work. The need is far broader than this.

If Myanmar's Global Fund applications are successful, this will allow a significant further engagement in HIV/AIDS, malaria and TB programmes that go beyond the work of the 3D Fund. The reality is that with ODA currently so low, the need and opportunity exists for many such funds to be giving additional assistance at present.

Increases in Overseas Development Assistance (ODA)

Myanmar's aid assistance is the lowest in the region. Last available comparable figures were for 2005. "Myanmar received $3 per person compared with $9 per capita in Bangladesh, $38 in Cambodia, $49 in Laos.

The lack of development assistance compounds chronic weaknesses in social service provision caused by the limited investment made by the Government in health, education and other socio- economic programmes."[24] Figure 13.1 shows the level of support in 2005.

There now seems to be a consensus inside Myanmar as well as outside, for the proposition that "[c]onsidering its development profile, Myanmar receives a very low level of financial support from the international community".[25] An OECD study reported ODA for 2007 at $4 per capita, which is probably indicative of current support levels outside of Nargis-relief support. Relief funds should be considered as being specific to one of the world's worst-ever disasters, and the funds for this remedial work should not be counted as part of increases necessary to ensure a move to more appropriate ODA levels.

Engagement Process in Cambodia

Because there is much more active engagement in other countries, there are more formalized processes elsewhere than in Myanmar. As a geographically close and relevant example, the Cambodia Development Cooperation Forum (CDCF) is one that allows particularly useful multi-party formal dialogue. The issues faced there have much in common with Myanmar. For example, the NGO statements in 2008 identify three priority areas: land, agriculture and natural resources management; human development; and good governance (for which implementation of appropriate policies and reform programmes has the potential to improve the lives of millions of poor and vulnerable Cambodians). Most of these policies and reform programmes are described or referred to in the National Strategic Development Plan (NSDP) 2006–2010.[26]

Cambodian NGOs prepared 25 position papers to provide constructive feedback and input to the CDCF and NSDP implementation. Elements discussed in these were:

> Good Governance; Environment for the Implementation of the ... Strategy; Enhancement of Agricultural Sector; Rehabilitation and Construction of Physical Infrastructure; Private Sector Development and Employment; Capacity Building and Human Resource Development; Costs, Resources, Programming, Monitoring and Evaluation of the NSDP.[27]

FIGURE 13.1
Overall ODA Comparisons, 2005 (US$)

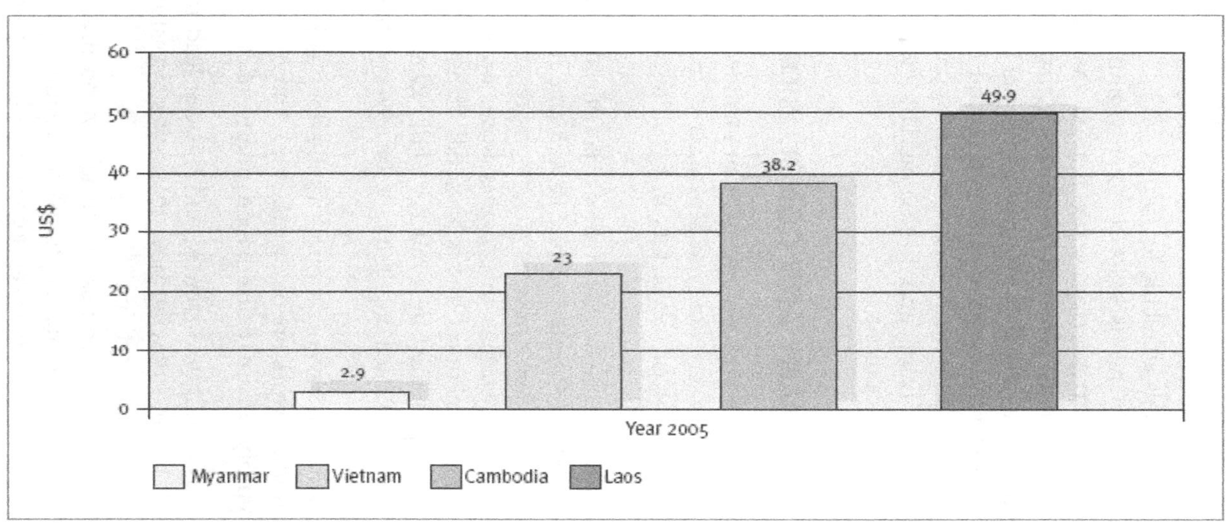

Source: Population Services International Myanmar, Save the Children and the UN Joint Team on AIDS in Myanmar, 2008. "HIV programming in Myanmar". *Humanitarian Exchange*, No. 41. London: Overseas Development Institute, December 2008, p. 29.

While some might consider opportunities for dialogue of this breadth far off in Myanmar, the author's view is that opportunities for expanding dialogue on sectoral work into these areas is very possible, and there are worthwhile opportunities available to prepare for.

Many similarities in needs exist regionally, and opportunities for information sharing currently are more limited than they should be, often due to the perhaps incorrect perceptions that Myanmar is not interested in those areas, and that progress would not be possible. Simple issues of isolation, communication difficulties, and budget constraints are more likely impediments. Much greater opportunities exist for regional sharing and learning, and these should be encouraged as part of ASEAN's overall development.

SUMMARY AND CONCLUSIONS

The diverse examples of positive engagement included here show that it is possible to work in many fields in Myanmar with excellent results if there are sufficient resources, connectors and a willingness to engage with multiple parties to do the work.

Hopefully, with the growing experience of beneficial results from ODA, the Myanmar government will continue to welcome further engagement opportunities, some evidence of which has been presented here. Ideally, it will be possible for Myanmar to progress to an open mechanism for development using something like a National Poverty Reduction Plan (NPRP). With input provided by a much broader group of stakeholders, the range of areas in which input might be given can be even more diverse.

At present, only a fraction of the opportunities for possible development and capacity-building work are being taken up, and more often than not opportunities simply are not realized, for a number of cumulative reasons:

- Myanmar is a complex country, and this can lead to international frustration in not knowing how to work successfully and to the "politicization of everything".
- It is often not considered possible to achieve positive results as past experiences reported and discussed internationally are frequently negative. These negative perceptions and understanding of operating difficulties create feedback processes which result in further isolation and exclusion than may be intended.
- ODA is too small in proportion to the work needed.

The priority areas for future international involvement, and the approaches needed, include:

- a clearer focus on economic reform
- mechanisms to ensure transparency in natural-resource revenue (for example, EITI)
- particular care with gas revenues, and more channelling of revenues into the social sector
- developing CSR practices in business
- stimulating agriculture and related economic reforms
- greater focus on developing small business
- significantly increasing ODA
- greater focus on peace-building and dialogue activities for unification
- broadening the overall areas of activity to ensure planning covers all areas.

Recent experience shows that while some things remain the same in Myanmar, other things have changed and many positive examples are listed. Myanmar is a country rich in natural resources, including its people. Current foreign policy often unwittingly helps maintain "grave hardship" as the reality for the many poor in Myanmar.[28] Similarly, further development of local policy can do much more to develop people, along with their living environment, and alleviate suffering effectively as a result.

The prime tenet of this chapter is that engagement should occur on a larger, broader and deeper scale than at present, and be satisfactorily resourced. Overall, this will surely result in stronger progress in the ongoing quest for Myanmar's national development.

Notes

1. Khin Zaw Win (2007).
2. See the Terms of Reference Adopted by the Human Trafficking Working Group (HTWG), on 5 May 2006, *Human Trafficking in Myanmar: A Response Strategy*, Yangon.
3. Van Myint (2007).
4. Ministry of Home Affairs (2009).
5. Kramer, Jelsma, and Blickman (2009).
6. Theuss (2007).
7. Interview with Senior UN Official based in Myanmar, Yangon, June 2009.
8. Ministry of Social Welfare Relief and Resettlement (2009).

9. Capacity Building for Food Security Project (2007).
10. Capacity Building for Food Security Project (2009).
11. HIV/AIDS TWG (2007).
12. Ministry of Health/World Health Organization (2008).
13. *Global Fund Round 9 Tuberculosis Proposal — Draft*, 14/5/09, Yangon.
14. M-CCM 2009.
15. Ministry of Health (2006).
16. Collaborative for Development Action (CDA). Do No Harm Project Occasional Paper, March 2008, "Three Key Lessons and their Implications for Training", CDA Collaborative Learning Project Website.
17. See also Turnell's chapter in this publication on rural credit.
18. Zaw Oo. "The Political Economy of Resource Curse in Burma: Implications for International Policies", in *SIIA Papers No. 4*, op. cit., p. 315.
19. The Extractive Industries Transparency Initiative (EITI) aims to strengthen governance by improving transparency and accountability in the extractives sector.
20. Presentation by M. F. Smith, "On Corporate Social Responsibility and Burma's Extractive Industries", at the International Quality and Productivity Center Conference on Local Content and Capability Development in the Extractive Industries, 15 April 2009, Jakarta.
21. SynTao (2007).
22. From the pending report released by the Ministry of Agriculture and Irrigation/ FAO. *National Medium-Term Priority Framework (2010–2014)*, Yangon: 2009.
23. Note the estimate is US$340/capita according to the 2008 IMF Article IV consultations. See also S. Turnell, *Burma's Economy 2008: Current Situation and Prospects for Reform*, Burma Economic Watch. Sydney: Economics Department, Macquarie University, May 2008.
24. From the FAO/WFP Crop and Food Security Assesment Mission to Myanmar, 22 January 2009, Yangon.
25. Population Services International Myanmar, Save the Children and the UN Joint team on AIDS in Myanmar (2008).
26. NGO Statement to the 2008 Cambodia Development Cooperation Forum (CDCF), NGO Forum, Phnom Penh, 2008.
27. NGO Forum 2008. *NGO Position Papers on Cambodia's Development in 2007–08*, Phnom Penh.
28. Pope John Paul II. Annual Address to the Diplomatic Corp (9 January 1995), <http://www.ewtn.com/library/PAPALDOC/JP2DIPCP.htm>.

References

Capacity Building for Food Security Project, 2007. Proceedings of the National Symposium of Farmer Led Agricultural Extension Approaches in Myanmar, 18–30 May 2007, Yangon.

Capacity Building for Food Security Project, 2009. Proceedings of the National Stakeholder Workshop for Community Forestry: Its experience and future in Myanmar, 11–12 February 2009, Yangon.

Commission on AIDS in Asia. *Redefining AIDS in Asia*, 2008.

Ewing-Chow, M. "First Do No Harm: Myanmar Trade Sanctions and Human Rights". *Northwestern Journal of International Human Rights* 5, no. 2 (2007).

Food and Agricultural Organization/World Food Programme. Crop and Food Security Assesment Mission to Myanmar, 22 January 2009, Yangon: 2009.

Gordon, J., and D. Desruelle, Staff Report for the 2008 Article IV Consultation, Myanmar. Washington, D.C.: International Monetary Fund, 2009.

Khin Zaw Win. "A Burmese perspective on prospects for progress". In *Myanmar: The State, Community and the Environment*, edited by M. Skidmore and T. Wilson. Canberra: Asia Pacific Press, The Australian National University, 2007.

Kramer, T. *Neither War nor Peace, The Future of the Ceasefire Agreements in Burma*. Amsterdam: Transnational Institute, 2009.

Kramer, T., M. Jelsma and T. Blickman. *Withdrawal Symptoms in the Golden Triangle: A Drugs Market in Disarray*. Amsterdam: Transnational Institute, 2009.

Myanmar Country Coordinating Mechanism [M-CCM] for HIV, TB and malaria Governance Manual, Global Fund Draft Application, Yangon, 2009.

McDermid, Charles. "Missing the Point on Myanmar, Interview with Thant Myint U". *Asia Times Online*, 4 July 2009.

Myanmar Ministry of Agriculture and Irrigation/FAO, (release pending) 2009. National Medium Term Priority Framework (2010–2014), Yangon.

Myanmar Ministry of Health. *Health in Myanmar 2006*, Yangon.

———. The National Strategic Plan for Malaria Control in Myanmar (2006–2010 and the updated version 2010–2015), Naypyitaw, 2006 and 2009.

Myanmar Ministry of Health/World Health Organization. "Report of the HIV Sentinel Sero-surveillance Survey 2008", Yangon, March 2009.

Myanmar HIV/AIDS TWG. "Report from the Technical Working Group on Estimation and Projection of HIV and AIDS in Myanmar", Yangon, 15–16 August 2007.

Myanmar Ministry of Home Affairs, Anti-Trafficking Unit, Myanmar Police Force, received from UNIAP 26/2/09, Naypyitaw, 2009.

Myanmar Ministry of Social Welfare Relief and Resettlement. Emergency Plan of Action for Persons with Disabilities, Yangon, 2009.

NGO Forum. NGO Statement to the 2008 Cambodia Development Cooperation Forum (CDCF), Phnom Penh, 2008.

Population Services International, Myanmar, Save the Children and the UN Joint team on AIDS in Myanmar. "HIV programming in Myanmar", Overseas Development Institute, Humanitarian Exchange No. 41, London, 27 December 2008.

Smith, M.F. "On Corporate Social Responsibility and Burma's Extractive Industries",

IQPC Conference on Local Content and Capability Development in the Extractive Industries, Jakarta, 15 April 2009.

SynTao. *Study of Sustainability Reporting in China, A Journey to Discover Values*. Beijing: SynTao, 2007.

Theuss, M. "Integrating Drug Reduction Strategies in Development — Practices and Visions for Alternative Development", Country Studies on Mainstreaming Drug Control, Myanmar. Workshop Proceedings, 31 October–2 November 2007, Bangkok.

Turnell, S. "Fiery Dragons — Banks, Moneylenders and Microfinance in Burma", NIAS — Nordic Institute of Asian Studies, Monograph Series, No. 114, Chapter 11, Copenhagen, 2009.

———. *Burma's Economy 2008: Current Situation and Prospects for Reform*. Burma Economic Watch/Economics Department Macquarie University, Sydney, May 2008.

Van Myint, N. "Inter-Agency Strategic Planning". Powerpoint Presentation, Human Trafficking Working Group Meeting Minutes 23/5/07, Yangon, 2007.

Zaw Oo. "The Political Economy of Resource Curse in Burma: Implications for International Policies". In SIIA Papers No. 4, *Between Isolation and Internationalization: The State of Burma*, edited by J. Lagerkvist. Reklam, 8–9 May 2008.

14

NORMATIVE EUROPE MEETS THE BURMESE GARRISON STATE
Processes, Policies, Blockages and Future Possibilities[1]

David Camroux and Renaud Egreteau

INTRODUCTION

Between 2007 and 2009, Burma experienced two major political crises that have drawn international focus and criticism upon the country and its military junta. In the aftermath of the September 2007 demonstrations and the passage of Cyclone Nargis in May 2008, European Union countries, both individually and as a whole through EU institutions (Council, Parliament and Commission), have had little leverage, let alone influence, over the gridlocked state of Burmese affairs (Selth 2008). A critical dilemma is caused by the tension between the EU's normative stance and its self-proclaimed willingness to assist, springing from its position as the world's largest provider of ODA. In practice, the easiest option has been followed since the 1990s; namely, that of isolating the regime on ethical grounds, rather than considering and elaborating another approach. Yet, strict implementation of the EU Common Position, first defined in October 1996 and reinforced several times since, which imposes restrictions on further aid and development assistance — albeit one that is little observed on the ground — has achieved little.

In spite of a few successes since the first sanctions decided by Brussels in the early 1990s, EU policies towards Burma have failed, both in encouraging a political breakthrough and in fostering economic growth, let alone socio-economic development. Even progress on the EU's bottom-line humanitarian agenda has been limited. Seen from Naypyitaw, Europeans are considered by the Burmese regime more as a potential threat than as a source of much-needed financial or humanitarian assistance, as Japan is. How can the EU's limited success be explained? We suggest that the present diplomatic and political configuration, both internally within the individual twenty-seven EU member states and the European Union as a whole, has neither facilitated in the past nor augurs well in the near future for any concrete policy change towards Burma. This is despite the fact that a change of approach to the Burmese conundrum undertaken by the Obama Administration may have a direct impact on other Western countries. Unfortunately, there are too many diplomatic obstacles, political constraints and internal EU divisions to revise the current EU Common Position significantly, including in a post-2010 elections context.

After offering a brief overview of the EU's global role and normative "inter-regionalist" ambitions in Southeast Asia, a second section of this chapter goes on to analyse the EU approach to the Burmese issue since 1988, highlighting the major geopolitical obstacles that hinder a more efficacious EU policy towards Burma. These obstacles range from political miscalculations, internal divisions and the influence of a persuasive European public opinion passionate about the iconic Aung San Suu Kyi, to indifference towards, and misinterpretations of, the current state of political affairs in Burma. In short, it will be argued that the EU approach to Burma reflects the same type of gridlock that can be observed within the country itself. Trapped within polarized and Manichaean political parameters, the present international stalemate in Burma will probably continue unless a complete change of mindset is decided upon by all the parties involved: the junta, the Burmese civil and ethnic opposition, and the international community, beginning with the EU.

Despite these constraints, we suggest a numbers of ways forward in revising EU policy. For example, while the inter-regionalist approach with

ASEAN has its drawbacks, it does provide one possible means for impacting on Burma's socio-economic situation. Moreover, through informed debate, European public opinion could be brought around to supporting much greater humanitarian assistance and a widening and deepening of development aid. Both approaches would help Europe further its involvement in Burma without requiring a drastic — and, in domestic political terms highly problematical — policy shift. As a prerequisite, the EU will need to redefine its normative approach to factor in the probability that any political transition in Burma will occur in the mid to long term. Thus Europeans would be able to focus on a crucial engagement with an emerging Burmese civil society and Burma's underdeveloped economy, and do so within a multilateral context that engages both political leaderships and civil society in other ASEAN countries. Such an approach would indeed respond both to the EU's assistance priorities and to the desperate needs of the Burmese people.

THE PECULIAR NATURE OF THE EU AS A GLOBAL ACTOR

The role of the European Union as a global actor on the international scene and some aspects of EU behaviour need to be mentioned briefly here. To paraphrase Clausewitz, "foreign policy is an extension of (domestic) politics by other means". As recent scholarship from the constructivist school of international relations suggests, a country's foreign policy is not only concerned with defending national interests and responding to domestic demands, it is also an expression of the intrinsic nature of the polity concerned. However, when the actor in question is not an individual nation-state but, rather, a highly institutionalized regional entity, then the situation is more complex. On one level, like ASEAN the European Union is an inter-governmental body, a kind of coalition or alliance. But inter-governmentalism, to use the common term, is only part of the story for the European Union, a regional entity that also acts like a nation-state as a supra-national body. The tension between inter-governmentalism and supra-nationalism lies at the heart of the capacity (or incapacity) of the European Union to perform as a global actor on the international scene (Bretherton and Vogler 2006). Other than this tension, three other parameters of EU behaviour provide a conceptual framework for the following empirical analysis. These are the notion of Europe as a normative power, its functioning within the parameters of a three-level game, and its promotion of a fourth, namely inter-regionalist level, within Southeast Asia.

Since its first incarnation as a *sui generis* actor as the European economic community, the European Union has been described as a "civilian power" (Hettne and S...derbaum 2005; Telò 2006; Orbie 2008), a "tranquil power" (Adam 2006) and/or "normative power" (Manners 2002) with a capacity to impose its normative preferences elsewhere in the world (Laïdi 2008). It is undoubtedly the notion of Europe as a normative power that is given the widest currency today. Yet such a characterization is loaded, denoting goals as much as descriptions, and the confusion between norm-setting, say in areas of environmental protection, and the ethically good is at the heart of European "actorness".

A second parameter worthy of our attention is that of the notion of three- and four-level games (Camroux 2010). In their studies of, respectively, agricultural policy and intra-European trade, Lee Ann Patterson (1997) and Hans Günther Deutsch (1999) build on Robert Putnam's (1988) seminal work on two-level games (the domestic and international) to propose the existence of a further sphere, namely the intra-regional, as a third-level game. In his study of trade liberalization in Europe, in particular in relation to the Common Agricultural Policy, Deutsch, like Patterson before him, points out that the governments of member-states are negotiating not only at two tables, namely, the domestic and multilateral, as Putnam has suggested, but at a third table at the same time; namely within the Council of the European Union and in interactions with the European Commission. On this "third table" sit also civil-society groups, NGOs and advocacy groups, which are increasingly pan-European in membership and approach. Take, for example, action over humanitarian intervention in Burma discussed below. Given that the NGOs most directly concerned with these questions are transnational, a national leader may at the same time be talking to a national audience (a local branch of Doctors Without Borders, for example), but also the overseas membership of the same organization.

A third and final salient parameter is that of inter-regionalism. To simplify, EU policy and practice concerning Burma is inscribed within relations between this regional entity and another, ASEAN. Europeans place great symbolic store on their first and oldest inter-regional relations. The promotion of intra-regional cooperation is, as Karen Smith cogently argues, "clearly an EU foreign policy objective that stems directly from its own internal identity" (2003, p. 95). The European Commission's approach to ASEAN is expressed in its Communication of July 2003, "A New Partnership with Southeast Asia". First amongst the six priorities elaborated in the communication is: "Supporting regional stability and the fight against terrorism... The European Union can contribute through using ASEAN and ASEM as frameworks for conducting policy dialogues, and through *providing its expertise in regional integration*" (European Commission 2003, p. 1, emphasis added).

Inter-regionalism, we argue elsewhere (Camroux 2010), is not so much a means employed by the EU as a global actor but, rather, an end in itself, or to use the classic distinction of Arnold Wolfers (1962, pp. 73–77) a milieu goal that is one designed to shape conditions of functioning beyond national boundaries.

THE EU APPROACH TO THE BURMESE CONUNDRUM SINCE 1988

For many observers in Europe, 1988 marked a turning point in EU–Burma relations. In response to the deterioration of the–human-rights situation and the crackdown on a revived Burmese democratic opposition, European countries swiftly opted for strong diplomatic condemnations of the new ruling military regime. The role of the democratic opposition had indeed been gradually — and passionately — symbolized in European media through the figure of Aung San Suu Kyi, daughter of Burma's national independence hero, Aung San. Since 1988 the EU, with the United States, has been the most vocal in condemnation of the Burmese authoritarian regime and in support of the democratic opposition.

Previously, several European countries had been at the forefront of the development assistance and aid programmes offered to the authoritarian Ne Win regime (1962–1988). While much of this assistance was easily siphoned off by the military elite and highly inefficient state-controlled companies, this situation was tolerated, with West Germany being Burma's second-largest donor after Japan. France was about to deliver diesel engines to Rangoon when the democratic turmoil broke out in early 1988. Burma's former strongman also had many linkages with Britain and Austria. For Britain, Ne Win had been influenced by his personal relationship with Lord Mountbatten and his favourite psychiatrist lived in Austria.

In the late 1980s, Western perceptions of Burma changed dramatically in the context of "People Power" in Asia (exemplified in the Philippines in

1986, South Korea in 1987, and Pakistan in 1988). Burma in early 1988 seemed to be yet another case of an Asian democratization process fostered by the ostensible success of Western liberal and democratic values. As with Cory Aquino in Manila or Benazir Bhutto in Karachi, the appearance of another charismatic female leader, Aung San Suu Kyi, fascinated the West. In response to her first appeals for international isolation of the SLORC in 1988–89, European countries collectively decided on tougher sanctions against the new Burmese junta after its refusal to recognize the results of the parliamentary elections it had organized on 27 May 1990.

Indeed, even more than the tragic events of 1988, with their more than 3,000 victims resulting from the *Tatmadaw*-orchestrated repression, the failure to respect the results of the May 1990 elections won by Aung San Suu Kyi's party, the National League for Democracy (NLD), drew far more massive condemnations from the international community and has been the benchmark for Europe's position on Burma ever since. As a direct consequence, the European Parliament in Strasbourg in December 1990 awarded the Sakharov Prize for Freedom of Thought to Aung San Suu Kyi, a prelude to her receiving the Nobel Peace Prize a year later. The systematic denunciation, collectively and individually by European countries, of the SLORC's refusal to recognize the results of the 1990 elections has been a key element in any European declaration since then (particularly at the UN General Assembly or the UN Council on Human Rights). Coupled with this has been a call for an immediate release of political prisoners — including Aung San Suu Kyi — and for a meaningful dialogue between the Burmese military government, the democratic opposition and Burma's other ethnic groups. For its part, and to show its support for the Burmese democratic forces, the European Council of Ministers imposed a complete arms embargo on the regime in 1990, and a year later all cooperation in defence and security matters between EU member-states and Burma ceased.

However, in 1995, the first release of Aung San Suu Kyi and U Tin Oo enabled the then fifteen-member EU — with France, the U.K. and Germany leading the debates on Burma — to propose a few political incentives to the Burmese regime, which had deftly consolidated its political and economic basis in the previous seven years. Besides the British, who were well connected to Aung San Suu Kyi's party (the NLD), the French government had in 1992 encouraged its largest oil company, Total, to negotiate a joint-venture with the SLORC to explore the Yadana Offshore Natural Gas fields. They were both perceived — rightly or wrongly — as non-regional states able to influence the investment-needy Burmese junta, while the Germans too benefited from older connections with the Burmese authorities dating from the time of Ne Win. Both Paris and Berlin sought then to build up a "constructive dialogue" among the three main partners — the European Commission, ASEAN and the SLORC — to promote the idea of a serious democratic transition in Burma.

But gradually, faced with the junta's refusal to negotiate and seeing the NLD becoming even more marginalized by the top Burmese leadership, strengthening the first EU sanctions was reaffirmed as the major European objective. This hard-line stance — mainly pushed by the Scandinavians and the British — was reinforced by the mysterious death in jail in 1996 of the Honorary Danish Consul who had been imprisoned in Rangoon for not having declared a fax machine. Thus the dramatic context of the mid-1990s militated towards a tougher EU position, pushing member-states to go beyond the mere diplomatic denunciation of the SLORC and to give the EU as a whole a legal arsenal in its dealings with Burma.

At the multilateral level, the growing friction between Brussels and ASEAN members became more pronounced over Burmese membership of the Association. Burma's participation in the Asia-Europe Meeting (ASEM) was a continuing irritant in EU–East Asian relations in the first ten years of the ASEM process, beginning with the first ASEM Summit in 1996 (Keva 2008). Burma's official admission to ASEAN in July 1997 initiated a long round of diplomatic EU–ASEAN frictions. For several years, the annual EU–ASEAN Foreign Ministers Meetings were cancelled because of Rangoon's presence. In September 2005, an EU–ASEAN meeting of trade ministers in Rotterdam was boycotted by ASEAN because the Burmese delegation had been subject to the visa ban imposed throughout the EU. When the junta agreed to pass over its turn at the ASEAN presidency in 2006, European diplomats publicly expressed their satisfaction (Egreteau and Jagan 2008). The desire to isolate the Burmese regime further increased since the imposition of a third house arrest on Aung San Suu Kyi in 2003 and became more obvious in the context of the month-long Burmese *Sangha* demonstrations in 2007.[2]

THE EU COMMON POSITION TOWARDS BURMA

The cornerstone of the European approach to the Burmese conundrum became the EU Common Position *1996/635/CFSP* which was adopted on 28 October 1996.[3] Its basis lies in the first 1990 embargo on arms, which prohibited the financing or providing of any European assistance to Burma in military or military-related activities. At the same time, EU members decided to expel all military personnel attached to Burmese diplomatic missions in Europe (Paris, Brussels, Bonn and London) and withdraw their own military attachés from the four European embassies (France, the U.K., Germany and Italy) based in the then Burmese capital of Rangoon. This remained a largely symbolic decision, which has not been emulated by the Americans or Asian regional powers, all of whom retained their military attachés in the Burmese garrison state, in order to be able to maintain closer interaction with the ruling *Tatmadaw* leadership.

Strict visa restrictions on the Burmese military elite and their families and a suspension of high-level bilateral relations were then imposed under this Common Position, which was reviewed six months afterwards, at the same time as the United States passed an even more restrictive law against Burma (1997). While not as strong as the original Clinton Administration proposals for a strict embargo of Burmese products (Seekins 2005), the EU Common Position has since been either renewed or reinforced on a regular basis, in the light of internal developments within Burma. The October 1996 Common Position measures were "extended and amended" in 2000 and 2001, then "repealed and replaced" in 2003, "renewed" and "reinforced" in 2004, "extended and amended" twice in 2005, to be "furthered" again in 2006 and 2007, and merely "extended" in April 2008 and in April 2009, or "renewed" in April 2010.[4]

In March 1997, in a supplementary step after the adoption of the Common Position, the EU withdrew Generalized System of Preferences (GSP) privileges from Burma for agricultural and industrial products, officially in response to forced-labour abuses by the Burmese authorities.[5] Previously the European Commission had allowed Burma to benefit from preferential tariffs for its exports to the EU countries, but, given the low level of bilateral EU–Burma trade, this had remained largely symbolic. As a consequence, Burma was also excluded from the "Everything-but-Arms" scheme for Least Developed Countries (LDC) in 2001. In reaction to every political step backwards taken by the Burmese military regime — the second arrest of Aung San Suu Kyi in September 2000, her third in May 2003 after the Depayin Incident, the repression of the Burmese monks demonstrations in September 2007, and lastly Aung San Suu Kyi's imprisonment and farcical trial in May–August 2009 — the EU chose to reinforce the restrictive measures initially adopted in 1996. But no real incentives were proffered for loosening or weakening those measures whenever what seemed a few steps forward in the democratization process were initiated by the Burmese generals. Indeed, a first EU delegation was able to visit Burma in July 1999 and met Khin Nyunt and Aung San Suu Kyi, followed by another in January 2001. Also, in May 2002, Aung San Suu Kyi was liberated after two years of talks with the UN Special Envoy, Dato Razali Ismail. But despite this progress, the EU has never toned down its approach, succumbing to the argument that pressure was effectively succeeding in swaying the junta.

Today, the EU Common Position is structured around three main constituent elements: military, economic and political. It first includes the ban on any defence cooperation with Burma and the exclusion of Burmese military personnel from the territory of EU members (as well as banning European military personnel in embassies in Rangoon). Secondly, in the economic domain it proposes largely implicit limitations on cooperation, including suspension of bilateral/multilateral investment/partnerships and any involvement in development or non-humanitarian programmes, restrictions on any imports/exports of Burmese-made products, as well as the freezing of the Burmese leaders' financial assets anywhere within the EU. Yet even the notable exception of the "strictly" humanitarian aid remains a cause of contention between European member-states and within their societies, for what is humanitarian aid, how is it to be defined, and to what extent is cooperation with foreign authorities (that is, the Burmese military) acceptable? Thirdly, the EU Common Position involves a wide range of political and diplomatic constraints, such as a visa ban for high-level Burmese officials (military officers, and people related to them — or thought to be — including their extended families), the systematic marginalization of Burmese representatives in international meetings and a series of public condemnations and critical official statements. Burma is, for example, also the only country — with Belarus — to have been sanctioned by the EU for its non-respect of core labour standards within the ILO.

In November 2007, immediately after the abortive Saffron Revolution, the EU reviewed its arsenal once more, strengthening a nominative list of 1,207 Burmese companies that were considered as "blacklisted"; that is, with whom there is a prohibition on any business contact. Furthermore, about 400 Burmese leaders or prominent people and their families were banned from travelling in Europe and their financial assets were to be frozen.[6] Consequently, with this three-fold arsenal — extended for one more year in April 2008 and then again in April 2009 — the EU has a broad legal base on which its approach to Burma is built. Though ostensibly aimed at encouraging the Burmese junta to engage in a "meaningful dialogue" with the democratic opposition, implicitly, the main objective is to suffocate it, so as to force it to open up and hand over power to Aung San Suu Kyi's leadership, and relinquish (even gradually) its authoritarian grip on Burmese society in order to comply with EU principles of human rights, liberty and democratic values.

As intimated in this chapter, the question of a political transformation and human rights within the country goes beyond the bilateral relations between individual EU member-states and Burma, to impact on the relations of the EU as a whole with its ostensibly privileged "interregional" partner, ASEAN. For example, while there are a number of other factors, such as the tremendous disparity among the ASEAN economies and their negotiating capacities, the failure of negotiations for an EU–ASEAN Free Trade Agreement (FTA) has been linked to the Burmese problem. European Trade Commissioner Karel de Gucht claimed that the political obstacle posed by fundamental disagreements with the ASEAN members on precluding Burma from the benefits of such an FTA was a major cause for the European Commission deciding to abandon the negotiations and turn towards negotiating FTAs with individual ASEAN members such as Singapore.[7]

EVALUATING THE EUROPEAN SANCTIONS POLICY

Achievements and Failures

In symbolic terms, the EU approach has fulfilled the Burmese democratic opposition's demands and comforted the Europeans in their ideological convictions. While responding to a liberal European orientation, the sanctions and diplomatic condemnations of Burma's authoritarian rulers have systematically held up a repressive regime to international opprobrium. Yet despite, or rather because of, its own isolationist tendencies, the regime remains — almost — unperturbed by the global ostracism of which it has been the object since 1988 (Egreteau and Jagan 2008). In both defining and implementing this international banishment, the exiled Burmese opposition is one of the most influential lobbies to which the EU (and the United States) has given almost-unconditional support since the early 1990s. The pariah status of the Burmese regime also is a response to the demands of European public opinion that is highly sympathetic to Aung San Suu Kyi. For Europeans she is a Burmese Mandela defending Gandhian values, unjustly trapped in her Rangoon home (Houtman 1999). European political leaderships are thus responding to the kinds of multiple-level influences referred to previously.

An alliance between elements of the Burmese diaspora and local, well-organized advocacy groups in the United Kingdom and in some Scandinavian countries maintains Burma as a subject of continued media interest in Europe. This situation contrasts with that pertaining to Vietnam, for instance. While a number of associations amongst the much larger Vietnamese diaspora in Europe, and in particular in France, are strongly anti-communist and critical of the Vietnamese regime, they do not agitate for it to be isolated. On the contrary, they tend to lobby for continued European economic assistance and engagement and are themselves actors in the economic development of the country, hoping to further some political leverage over Vietnam's future. For Burma the picture is different.

At the international level Burma is an issue over which Western solidarity is relatively easily obtained, although this finds different ways of expression. Unfortunately, however, we would argue that the ostensible means to bring about a political transition in Burma, namely sanctions, has become an end in itself. Yet this is in keeping with a tendency of the European Union to pursue normative goals as opposed to strategic goals (Tocci 2008). Outside the level of member-state governments, intra-European actors are also organized on a Europe-wide basis, with easy access to the ultimate expression of supra-nationalism, the European Parliament.[8] In January 2008 it expressed the view that it was not advisable to conclude a trade agreement with Burma/Myanmar under the current military regime, a position that was most recently approved in May 2010 (EESC 2010) by the tripartite European Economic and Social Council, which has an advisory, if influential, role in Brussels.

By putting additional pressure there on matters such as human-rights abuses, forced labour and other arbitrary policies, the European sanctions decided at the highest level have undoubtedly reduced the frequency of such problems in Burma, as noted by various NGO or UN agency reports (Altsean-Burma, ILO, UNDP).

Regular fieldwork and interviews with both Burmese and foreigners living in Burma leads us to assert that the military regime does indeed care about its international image, and has been repeatedly tempted to adopt softer political stances and practices when specifically sought by the international community. This has occurred despite a complete lack of understanding by the regime of the foreign-policy mechanisms and objectives and the military capacity of the EU compared, say, to the United States or ASEAN. Moreover, given the high profile role of British political leaders in EU–Burma relations, it is easy and convenient for the Burmese regime to label any European condemnation as "neo-colonialist".[9]

The benefits for European political leaders of maintaining strong ethical views on Burma far outweigh any economic costs: European economic stakes in Burma are minimal[10] and of no comparison with those in China or Thailand, for example. At the intra-European level, obtaining a consensus position on sanctions requires little compromise and virtually no political costs. An interesting comparison can, once again, be made here with the case of Vietnam, where the French have been able to impose a posture of "constructive engagement" on human-rights issues in relation to another authoritarian, if less-oppressive, regime. Admittedly, this has been facilitated by the Vietnamese government's ability — unlike that of its Burmese counterpart — to improve the well-being of its people (through *doi moi* measures), and its willingness to engage with the world (Vietnam's WTO agreement, for instance). It could even be argued that, by furthering isolation, European policy towards Burma is going in the direction that the regime wishes and helps it to maintain its inward-looking control over the country.

Moreover, a number of limitations in the European approach have gradually become obvious and, indeed, in some cases counterproductive. The essential problem has been to go beyond the "feel-good position" — namely giving moral support to the Burmese pro-democracy forces, "outsourcing" EU policy to them and pursuing an ethical approach commensurate with Western values — to adopting a "do-good position" (Aung-Thwin 2001–2002; Roberts 2006). Such an approach would mean seeking to bring about meaningful change in Burma by adopting a more pragmatic policy, and helping Burmese civil society flourish by itself within the context of peaceful development. While the strengthening of Burmese civil society may be palpable at the grass-roots level in Burma, it remains problematical after more than a decade of pressure and restrictions (Pedersen 2008).

The EU arms embargo is part of this "feel-good" component: few European countries are willing to sell weapons to the Burmese junta which has logically — and strategically — established key military partnerships with China, Pakistan, Russia, or even India. In continental Europe, only two non-EU members, the Ukraine and Yugoslavia/Serbia, have developed any significant military trade with the Burmese military in the past two decades. The embargo thus remains largely symbolic. Also, to indicate the counterproductive nature of some EU actions, we would argue that the absence of European military attachés in Burma since 1990 clearly does a disservice to the European diplomats in Rangoon, where many events, ceremonies and meetings are restricted exclusively to the military and provide a good vantage point to observe the current "who's who" of the Burmese military hierarchy.[11]

In this regard, as far as the EU visa restrictions are concerned, many limitations are also flagrant — even to the extent of seeing this particular restrictive measure being labelled as the "shopping visa ban" in European bureaucratic circles.[12] This ban does not target Burmese diplomats and officials invited to international gatherings or inter-governmental meetings, such as those organized in Brussels, Paris (UNESCO), Vienna or Geneva (various UN agencies). But the wealthy Burmese leadership has always gone to Singapore, Hong Kong, Bangkok or Dubai for their "shopping", medical and banking purposes. None of the top military leaders has funds and bank accounts in Europe, so less than €70,000 (US$100,000) has been frozen in Europe so far, which is clearly far from representing credible leverage against a junta that earns billions of dollars annually. Moreover, the names of the 400 blacklisted members of Burma's elite have been decided arbitrarily, often following the advice of the exiled Burmese opposition.[13]

Finally, one of the main flaws of the EU investment ban lies in its non-retroactivity, for a boycott cannot be retroactive in international law. All foreign companies whose joint ventures with the Burmese authorities had been set up before the adoption of the EU 1996 Common Position are not concerned by it, despite regular revisions. Amongst these companies the most important is the French oil company Total, which provides the Burmese government with an estimated US$500 million a year in taxes and royalties.[14] Yet given the strong aversion of European public opinion to the Burmese junta — and the unchallenged critical position of Aung San Suu Kyi against foreign investment and foreign tourism — many European companies have withdrawn from Burma since the mid-1990s. Amongst these are Heineken, Phillips, Accor and Premier Oil. Nevertheless, the main motivation for these decisions remains the negative publicity within Europe for companies working in a repressive Burma, rather than the legal pressures emanating from EU sanctions. Furthermore, few of the 1,207 banned Burmese firms and small trading companies have been involved in business relationships with Europe, except in the textile and timber industries. Restrictions on European trade with Burma, even in specific sectors such as timber or gems, have not proved to have had any great impact on the regime since the 2007 renewal of sanctions. The reality is that, while the Burmese economy may be particularly weak, it does not depend essentially on the West — as South Africa did in the early 1980s — but far more on Chinese, Thai, Singaporean and Indian trade and investment. Above all, Burma's economy remains highly informal, with underground transnational links and a still-volatile cross-border trade.[15]

Wrong Target, Wrong Assessment?

Despite the Burmese regime's shift of policy in the late 1980s, many analysts had then warned that economic sanctions and foreign political pressure against the Burmese military were doomed from the beginning (Steinberg 1991). Constrained by the miss-fit between symbolic political aims but mainly economic means, Western (and more specifically European) approaches towards the post-1988 Burmese situation were doomed to fail and miss their primary target. The Burmese Army, in power since the military coup staged in 1962, had in fact been at the forefront of Burma's political scene since the march toward independence in the early 1940s and managed to continually consolidate its ascendancy over the Burmese economy since the early 1950s. As the main institution dominating Burmese society, it has always propagated a nationalist ideology that has relied on an obsession with national security. As a result of a single-minded focus on defence against internal and external threats — coupled with the *Tatmadaw*'s rhetoric on the non-disintegration of the country, the safeguarding of the national unity and the moral duty of defending Myanmar identity — the regime has pushed economic and development priorities well into the background (Callahan 2001; Fink 2001; Taylor 2009).

Given this pattern, in which security goals prevail over economic ones, and the enrichment of the few, if Western sanctions first target the welfare of a military elite and not its security obsession, they simply miss the point. No matter how hard and extensive the economic pressure or the freezing of financial assets, the national security obsession will still be the priority for the Burmese Armed Forces. Thus they are quite likely to further their domination of the country's political landscape in the years to come if not challenged in a different way. To hope for a complete withdrawal of the Burmese Armed Forces from political life — either through external pressure and sanctions or a collapse due to internal divisions — is an illusion, at least in the mid-term. So is predicting the probability of the Burmese formal economy becoming bankrupt thanks to the asphyxia created by international sanctions. Both are based on a misguided assessment of the current Burmese state of affairs.

Moreover, it has always been a mistake to underestimate the xenophobic nationalism fuelled among the Burman elite, including among civilians and anti-junta circles, which are far from all being pro-NLD and pro-West. The imposition of boycotts and sanctions has only strengthened the negative perceptions the Burmese military has of the outside world, reinforcing their counterproductive effects, and hindering closer interactions in, *a priori*, non-political fields such as development and humanitarian activities. Put colloquially, from the Burmese junta's perspective, why should you allow in external powers that want you out? Why should you welcome humanitarian assistance and financial support from powerful states that have enacted laws to ban you and promote your own collapse? The fear of reliving the trauma of the colonial past re-imposed on Burma has reinforced the Burmese garrison state in its hatred against outsiders, whether Western, Indian, Chinese or Thai (Gravers 1999).

Finally, although these conclusions are strongly criticized by many Burma watchers, the new restrictive package decided by Europe and the United States after the third arrest of Aung San Suu Kyi in 2003 (the Depayin incident), followed by the repression of the "Saffron Revolution" in 2007, had a disastrous impact in Burma's rural and urban areas alike. Those affected are not only rich Burmese tycoons, traders or profiteers, but also ordinary workers in timber factories, rural labourers or small urban merchants (Kudo 2008; Pedersen 2008). As demonstrated in many reports and academic studies of international sanctions,[16] a better analysis of the direct costs of these policies, especially those defined by the EU, would help spark a review of the European Common Position (ICG 2004). However, endless intra-European bargaining has so far impeded any substantial reconsideration of policies and tactics.

The Internal EU Dimension

An overview of core European policymaking towards Burma would indicate that the approach each European country takes has been influenced by political actors, and not by the diplomatic or military sphere, nor even economic/business circles. This contrasts with the situation in neighbouring China, Thailand or India, which all have deep-rooted strategic concerns and profound economic interests in, and around, Burma. Despite strong support for the democratic opposition amongst some civil-society groups in Thailand or India, security and trade concerns dominate. Only in Southeast Asian countries geographically more distant, such as the Philippines and Indonesia, which both have more limited relations with Burma, do the pro-democracy civil-society groups have some impact over their political leaders. As a result, given the absence of economic and security concerns within Europe, and those who vector such concerns, Brussels and the member-states are much more receptive to public opinion and intellectual or philosophical debates within their vibrant civil societies. Through its inter-regionalist approach, the EU seeks to channel the support of such groups as part of its campaign against the Burmese junta.

In fact, European policymaking on Burma seems to have been the result of a delicate balance between the European countries willing to be outspoken in criticizing and to isolate Burma (the United Kingdom, Scandinavia and a few Eastern Europe countries[17]) and those who appear keener on adopting a softer diplomatic approach and opposing the mantra of ostracism (starting with France and Germany). Interestingly, a growing rift is now becoming apparent between the few European diplomats posted in Burma and those, far more numerous, based in Europe, whether in Brussels or in their central administrations. London's Foreign Office and the French Quai d'Orsay or Palais de l'Elysée appear indeed far more sensitive to the concerns of the domestic pro-democracy lobbies than British or French diplomats in Rangoon. The various declarations of British officials (Prime Minister Gordon Brown and Foreign Secretary David Miliband) during the Saffron Revolution in Rangoon (2007), as well as vitriolic statements by French President Nicolas Sarkozy and his Foreign Minister Bernard Kouchner in trying to impose the Responsibility to Protect (R2P) principles on Burma after the passage of Cyclone Nargis in May 2008, were coolly received by their respective embassy staffs in Burma. The latter — like NGO aid workers on the ground — had to find a way of dealing effectively with Burmese local officials during the post-Nargis humanitarian crisis.

In the end, the definition of the EU's global approach to Burma is a political compromise between leaderships in just a handful of European states, with France and the U.K. at the forefront as the two countries having the largest investments and greatest ideological stakes in Burma. The British have had a policy of strong criticism of the Burmese junta ever since 1988, while maintaining close contact with the pro-democratic opposition in Rangoon (both the NLD and the Generation 88, made up of former student leaders of the 1988 uprising). The French — also a UN Security Council veto power — have on the other hand been tempted to pursue a global agenda on Burma, having far fewer political connections there since it has never been part of the French colonial sphere of influence, but numerous active French NGOs (Aide Médicale Internationale, Groupe de Recherches et d'Echanges Technologiques, Médecins Sans Frontières, Partenaires, Enfants du Monde) and cultural activities (Alliance Française).

Furthermore, the growing difficulty of coordinating the EU policymaking process among twenty-seven countries having contending views on Burma is patent. Besides France and the U.K., Germany and Italy have at times proposed various diplomatic initiatives, often not welcomed by other EU members dealing with Burma from their embassies in Bangkok. The German presidency in 1999 brought an EU delegation (the troika) to Rangoon, despite the prohibition on high-level contacts between the EU and Burma. The ban concerns those above the level of Director General, but not "senior officials", particularly those responsible for dialogue with all of ASEAN. The German embassy in Rangoon regularly, and outspokenly, denounces the unilateral sanctions reinforced every year by the EU Common Position, inveighing against their lack of effectiveness.[18] The Italians too pushed for the EU Special Envoy, Piero Fassino, to play a key back-up role to the UN Special Envoy on Burma, Ibrahim Gambari, in 2007 and 2008, but this was far from being a success.[19] At the other end of the scale, European member-states like the Czech Republic, the Netherlands or Sweden — the latter two openly financing Burmese activist organizations and exiled news group in Europe, India and Thailand — have consistently expressed far stronger opposition to any diplomatic concessions to the Burmese generals unless the position of Aung San Suu Kyi and her party is improved. When one factors in the European countries with no interests whatsoever in Burma and those, such as Poland and Hungary, that are more willing to follow the tougher U.S. position, then the "multiple voices" dimension of the EU approach appears blatant.

The three-level game process in Europe involved in determining policy on Burma leads in the end to a kind of lowest-common-denominator approach; namely, consistent condemnation, involving sticks (in the form of sanctions) but very few carrots (development aid). This type of process also leads to a series of blockages that prevented revision of the Common Position, which remains immobilized in its present polarizing form, to the extent of seeing the EU having neither sticks nor carrots to offer to Burma.

TOWARDS A NEW EUROPEAN INVOLVEMENT IN BURMA: PROBLEMS AND PROSPECTS

Gradually, many European bureaucrats and Burma watchers have come to realize the limits, and counterproductive consequences, of EU ostracism against a xenophobic Burmese regime that is economically fuelled by its neighbours and which has only a few crucial diplomatic partnerships. Hence, a renewed focus on humanitarian aid has been proposed by various diplomatic and NGO circles, especially after the passage of Cyclone Nargis in 2008. Developing strong EU–Burmese cooperation in the humanitarian and development sectors, so as to more strategically consolidate Burmese civil society, has paradoxically always been a key objective of–Brussels. Yet achieving this objective has been hindered by the impossibility of building up any viable cooperation with the Burmese (read "military") authorities without earning harsh criticism from militant and pro-democracy organizations. Such groups denounce what they claim is an implicit endorsement of an oppressive regime. This "domestic" opposition within Europe has militated against even a better implementation of the positive elements in what is effectively proposed by the European position on Burma, notably regarding humanitarian assistance and development aid to Burma.

Before 2009, no major development schemes had been implemented by the Europeans in Burma, with the notable exception of the activities of a couple of dozen international NGOs in and around Rangoon and in Arakan State.[20] Besides individual initiatives by EU member-states (with the U.K. and France at the forefront), the European Commission Humanitarian Office (ECHO) opened an office in Rangoon only in October 2005. It has achieved an increase of EU humanitarian aid from a mere

€2 million in 2001 to €8.2 million in 2004. Nevertheless, this amount remains fairly low in proportion to the €570 million of humanitarian aid spent worldwide by the EU that year. However, understandably, European humanitarian assistance to Burma has been increased since the passage of Cyclone Nargis. A €40.5 million plan involving basic humanitarian assistance was decided upon in Brussels in December 2008;[21] another, of €35 million for food-security projects, in October 2009;[22] and lately a €17 million commitment to "vulnerable people" was announced in March 2010.[23] Still, the amount of development assistance Europe provides Burma lags far behind that granted to Laos, Bangladesh or even East Timor. ECHO funds only a dozen international NGOs operating in Burma including AMI, MSF and GRET, as well as the United Nations' High Commission on Refugees (UNHCR) activities through a Rohingya repatriation programme in Arakan state.

Yet, ironically, assistance in building a vibrant civil society has rhetorically always been the main motivation and primary argument underpinning the EU's approach towards Burma in particular, and ASEAN in general. Such an approach is consistent with the promotion of the European normative model of governance and springs from the nature of the EU itself. European diplomats have always defended the EU's role as preparing Burma for a political transition, by helping Burmese civil society to strengthen and flourish. So why is there this gap between declarations on the one hand, and effective actions and results at the grass-roots level? How can the incredibly low level of European humanitarian aid in Burma be explained? In the 1979/80 fiscal year, the isolationist Burma of Ne Win received US$473 million in grants and loans from external donors, including US$72.6 million from West Germany — that is, US$15 per capita at that time (Aung Kin 1980). Thirty years afterwards, a Burmese receives less than US$3 per year of humanitarian or development aid, while a Laotian could expect US$30 and an East Timorese more than US$140. The Manichaean view of the Burmese political situation has indeed also impacted on European humanitarian involvement.

In this regard, the Europeans are in a dilemma, for it is often perceived that giving aid to a country requires, one way or another, building close cooperation with the local authorities. However, in the Burmese case this means cooperation with the execrated military government, which is unacceptable according to the spirit of EU sanctions, though in contradiction with the mandate given by the EU Development Cooperation Instruments

(DCI). The fundamental issue lies here: is the West willing to compromise its ethical stance and enhance its development and humanitarian programmes despite this requiring visible collaboration with local Burmese authorities, the majority of whom are military personnel, as is done elsewhere in the world? Is the EU — collectively or individually — willing to increase its support for Burmese civil society, enhance its role in reforming and transforming the Burmese education system and build a wider assistance framework inside the country if this involves networking with local (military) officials and deeper interactions with a ruling entity that is not as monolithic as often assumed? In short, can European principles be compromised when dealing with a militarized garrison state? Here, an engagement with Burmese civil society is needed, beyond any direct face-to-face engagement with its top military leadership. The context after the 2010 election, with its planned civilianization of state politics, might offer an opportunity to the EU.

The current official EU position still stipulates that political progress and reforms in Burma should be observed first before assistance and cooperation are enhanced. But cooperating in education or health matters does not necessarily mean giving political endorsement to the authoritarian regime, especially when the latter has implemented a form of repressive rule that does not need this kind of cooperation to maintain itself. Europeans should be more creative, but also more modest, in their objectives in Burma. They have to begin by, alas, accepting their current lack of political influence in the short term in Burmese politics for the junta is, regrettably, now in a position to gradually implement its own transitional "roadmap" announced in 2003, according to its own agenda and at its own pace.

While opting for a toned-down form of political criticism, the European focus has to be reoriented into concrete humanitarian and development aid programmes, coupled with improved cultural relations designed to overcome the negative image of the Western world in Burma. It seems misguided to assume that a society that has been bruised by decades of colonial trauma, continuous civil wars and xenophobic propaganda will welcome the help of the Western community with open arms. It remains a misperception to picture Burma as being governed by only a cluster of xenophobic and ultranationalist Burmese generals, with the rest of the Burmese society widely and willingly open to the outside world. For many Burmese, the West is still perceived as a global threat, and the links with Aung San Suu Kyi and the essentially Burman opposition are too prominent, leaving the impression that Burma's other ethnic minorities or competing opposition voices are ignored and pushed into the background.

New bridges have to be built between European institutions/member-states and the Burmese administrative, political and cultural elites in order to foster a critical and beneficial role for Europeans in Burma. New mid-level linkages should be encouraged so as to balance the hierarchical nature of the Burmese decision-making process. Concomitant with this, new localized assistance programmes involving substantially increased aid should be implemented, as announced by ECHO in December 2008 and October 2009. Many such projects exist on the drawing-board, according to various interviews we have conducted. New projects sponsored by the EU to overcome Burma's under-development in various areas (not only in minority/ethnic zones, but also in Burman-dominated areas) have to be planned. Interestingly, a key issue lies in what is understood in Brussels (or Washington, Tokyo or Singapore) by "development assistance". While Japan labels the construction of airport facilities "development assistance", Western countries consider it as "infrastructure building", thus falling into the scope of sanctions. While an increase in aid might be perceived as a "reward", or an improper one-way incentive, for the current Burmese military rulers in the short term,[24] in the long run it might definitely bring visible results.

Burma is also desperately in need of a well-trained and open middle class. Today this class is entirely dominated by military people and the Chinese/Yunnanese or Indian communities. Facilitating the education of a Burmese elite inside the country (civil servants, lawyers) to prepare them for a transition, as has been tentatively done along Burma's borders (Thailand, Yunnan), would be another option for European policymakers to follow. Military oppression in Burma has meant lost generations of graduates capable of playing a role in a future political transition. In our view, Europeans (and the West in general) must, however reluctantly, accept that a political transition and renewed nation-building in Burma will be a lengthy and expensive process. The time to begin this process is now, through developing civilian governance capacities within Burma itself.

Compared to its other Western partners (the United States, Australia and New Zealand) the European Union has a weakness in its approach to Burma in always inscribing relations with Burma into the larger EU–ASEAN inter-regional context. Yet, on another level, this weakness could be made into a comparative advantage. After Cyclone Nargis, the EU chose to provide much of its humanitarian assistance through cooperative arrangements with ASEAN. Building on this approach in other areas, notably building capacity through joint EU–ASEAN educational projects within Burma, could offer a more effective way of preparing for a transition. The advantages are twofold: on the one hand, projects involving fellow Southeast Asians would have a better chance of acceptance by a "Western-phobic" military regime; on the other, the EU could tap into the civil-society resources in a number of the more democratic ASEAN countries.

CONCLUSIONS

At the time of writing, evidence of the reactive nature of the EU's approach to Burma was to the fore once again. Within European civil society there are signs of a movement away from an approach relies totally on sanctions. For example, in an opinion-piece in France's major right-of-centre daily, Françoise Sivignon, the head of one of the major humanitarian NGOs active in Burma, Médecins du Monde, argued that "a combination of diplomatic efforts and economic sanctions had produced no tangible movement towards a democratic process".[25] Instead, she argued, France (and the EU?) needed to significantly increase humanitarian assistance and that governments should concentrate their efforts on supporting the demands of NGOs for greater access to the Burmese population. This type of argument from those with experience in Burma appears to be having some impact at last, both in individual EU member-countries and in Brussels itself. European policy towards Burma is contingent on "domestic" considerations — that is, developments within EU member-countries. However, changes in European public opinion away from a "sanctions only" policy may finally be impacting on decision-makers. Indications from Brussels at the time of writing suggest this might result in a substantial increase in humanitarian assistance.

However, the primary cause of potential changes in EU policy is the shift in the position of the U.S. Administration, foreshadowed in Priscilla Clapp's chapter in this volume and symbolized by U.S. President Obama meeting with the Burmese Prime Minister at the ASEAN summit meeting in Singapore on 15 November 2009. The internal evaluation of U.S. policy towards Burma initiated by American Secretary of State Hillary Rodham Clinton upon her appointment has resulted in the announcement of more positive engagement, at least at the rhetorical level. While economic sanctions remain in place, there is also the promise of changes contingent on signs of political liberalization from the Burmese regime. EU member-states and the Commission, confronted with the change in the U.S. posture, have been obliged to undertake their own reassessment. Proponents of more positive engagement amongst (and within) member-countries and in the Commission would seem to have had their position strengthened with, notably, a reversal in the European Council of Ministers of the attitude of the Scandinavian members towards positive engagement. At the time of writing, only Britain was holding out for a continuation of existing policy.[26]

Much still remains to be done to bring about a change in European policy. For as long as it remains morally unthinkable to European political leaders, the return of European military attachés to Rangoon and the relaxation of the continuously strengthened EU sanctions are unlikely to occur, even in the event of a third release of Aung San Suu Kyi after 2010. As the iconic leader of the democratic opposition was not allowed by the junta to contest the state-controlled elections, the EU is not in position to offer the Burmese regime many political incentives. After those elections, the creation of some form of praetorian but civilian order will require a response from external actors, as will change in the military leadership following the inevitable departure of Senior General Than Shwe. Preparing for these eventualities should, in our view, be a priority task. Yet, despite our optimism, given the political risks and the intra-European stalemate caused by the three-level bargaining processes discussed above, as well as the uncertainties of the post-2010 Burmese political scene, overall EU Burma policies will not be altered in the near future unless a complete change of mindset takes place. The chapter by David Allan offers the case for such a change.

Notes

1. The concept of a "garrison state" was first developed by Harold Lasswell (1941) in the midst of World War II. This paper draws from two articles in a special issue of *East Asia: An International Quarterly*, Camroux (2010) and Egreteau (2010). Many thanks to Morten Pederson and Trevor Wilson for their helpful comments.
2. According to various interviews and discussions of the authors with European and Southeast Asian diplomats conducted in Paris, Brussels, Rangoon and Bangkok since 2002.
3. *Official Journal of the European Communities* No. L 287, 8 November 1996: p. 1.

4. *Official Journal of the European Communities* No. L66, 10 March 2008: p. 1; *Official Journal of the European Communities* No. L108, 29 April 2009: p. 1; and *Official Journal of the European Union* No. L105, 27 April 2010: p. 1.
5. *Official Journal of the European Communities* No. L 85, 27 March 1997: pp. 8–9. Only Belarus is in a similar position.
6. *Official Journal of the European Communities* No. L66, 10 March 2008: p. 81.
7. Declaration of Karel de Gucht in Brussels on 24th April 2010.
8. The Brussels-based Euro-Burma Office was initially financed by the European Commission and today mainly by Scandinavian governments. It remains a focus for pro-democracy advocacy and humanitarian development assistance in the EU.
9. As regularly read in the Burmese regime mouthpiece, the daily *New Light of Myanmar*.
10. In 2008, the EU 27–Burma bilateral trade reached only €289 million according to the EU Trade Commission. See <http://trade.ec.europa.eu/doclib/docs/2006/september/tradoc_113423.pdf>.
11. Extensive interviews with foreign diplomats based in Rangoon (2002–2008).
12. Interviews, Brussels, October and November 2008.
13. Although it remains difficult for those "sons or daughters of" to mix, socialize and build up friendship networks abroad. Apparently most of them tend to keep their inward-looking mentality, even when confronted by the outside world.
14. According to EarthRights International, Total provided US$4.83 billion to the Burmese government in the period 2000–2008: "Oil majors propping up Myanmar regime: rights group", *AFP*, 9 September 2009.
15. Interviews with Burmese businessmen, Ruili, Burma–Yunnan border, July 2009.
16. As noted, for instance, by Derek Tonkin, former British Ambassador now leading the charity group Network Myanmar: "Sanctions hurt Burma's people more than the generals", *Financial Times*, 10 November 2009.
17. Especially the Czech Republic following Vaclav Havel's all-weather support for Aung San Suu Kyi.
18. Interview, German Embassy, Rangoon, February 2008.
19. Larry Jagan, "EU envoy on Burma has nothing to offer the democratic process", *Mizzima News Commentary*, 30 January 2008.
20. Dealing with the statelessness and downtrodden position of the Muslim Rohingya community since 1992.
21. "EU provides extra EUR 40 million in aid to Myanmar", *AFP*, 19 December 2008.
22. "EU gives 35 million euros in aid to Myanmar, country still underfunded", *Reuters*, 21 October 2009.
23. "EU gives Myanmar 17 million euros in Humanitarian Aid", *Deutsche Presse-Agentur*, 2 March 2010.

24. As denounced by many Europeans diplomats and politicians; interviews Paris, Brussels, and Bangkok (2008–2009).
25. Francoise Sivignon, "Birmanie: des sanctions, rien que des sanctions?" *Le Figaro*, 24 August 2009.
26. Interview with DG Relex official, 20 November 2009.

References

Adam, Bernard. "Pour une Europe, puissance tranquille". In *Europe Puissance tranquille: Rôle et identité sur la scène mondiale*, edited by Bernard Adam, pp. 11–25. Brussels: Editions complexe, 2006.

Aung Kin. "Burma in 1979: Socialism with Foreign Aid and Strict Neutrality". *Southeast Asian Affairs*, pp. 93–117. Singapore: Institute of Southeast Asian Studies, 1980.

Aung-Thwin, Michael. "Parochial Universalism, Democracy, Jihad and the Orientalist Image of Burma: The New Evangelism". *Pacific Affairs* 74, no. 4 (Winter 2001–2002): 483–506.

Bretherton, Charlotte, and Vogler, John. *The European Union as a Global Actor*, 2nd ed. London: Routledge, 2006.

Callahan, Mary. "Burma: Soldiers as State Builders". In *Coercion and Governance: The Declining Role of the Military in Asia*, edited by Muthiah Alagappa, pp. 413–29. Stanford, CA: Stanford University Press, 2001.

Camroux, David. "Interregionalism or Merely a Fourth-Level Game? An Examination of the EU-ASEAN Relationship". *East Asia* 27, no. 1 (2010): 57–77.

Deutsch, Hans Günter. *The Politics of Freer Trade in Europe: Three-level Games in the Common Commercial Policy of the EU, 1985–1997*. Berlin: Lit Verlag, 1999.

Egreteau, Renaud. "Intra-European Bargaining and the 'Tower of Babel' EU Approach to the Burmese Conundrum". *East Asia* 27, no. 1 (2010): 15–33.

Egreteau, Renaud and Larry Jagan. "Back to the Old Habits: Isolationism or the Self-Preservation of the Burmese Military Regime". *IRASEC Occasional Paper* No. 7 (Bangkok, December 2008).

European Commission. *A New Partnership with South East Asia*. Communication from the Commission COM (2003) 399 final.

———. *Regional Programming for Asia: Strategy Document 2007–2013*, Brussels, May 2007.

European Economic and Social Committee, *Opinion on EU-ASEAN Relations, REX 276 EU-ASEAN Relations*, Brussels, 26 May 2010.

European Parliament. *Report on trade and economic relations with the Association of Southeast Asian Nations (ASEAN)*. Committee on International Trade, rapporteur: Glyn Ford. Ref. A6-0151/2008. Strasbourg, adopted on 27 February and tabled on 14 April 2008.

Fink, Christina. *Living Silence: Burma under Military Rule*. Second edition, London: Zed Books, 2009.

Gravers, Mikael. *Nationalism as Political Paranoia in Burma*. Copenhagen: NIAS Press, 1999.

Hettne, Björn and Fredrik Söderbaum. "Civilian Power or Soft Imperialism? The EU as a Global Actor and the Role of Interregionalism". *European Foreign Affairs Review* 10 (2005): 535–52.

Houtman, Gustaaf. *Mental Culture in Burmese Crisis Politics: Aung San Suu Kyi and the National League for Democracy*. Tokyo: ILCAA Monograph Series, 1999.

International Crisis Group. "Myanmar: Sanctions, Engagement or Another Way Forward?" *Asia Report* 78, 26 April 2004.

———. "Burma/Myanmar after Nargis: Time to Normalize Aid Relations". *Asia Report* 161 (20 October 2008).

Keva, Silja. "Human Rights and Burma/Myanmar in the ASEM Dialogue". In *Europe-Asia Interregional Relations: A Decade of ASEM*, edited by Bart Gaens, pp. 69–84. Aldershot UK: Ashgate, 2008.

Kudo Toshihiro. "The impact of the US Sanctions on the Myanmar Garment Industry". *Asian Survey* 48, no. 6 (2008): 997–1017.

Laïdi, Zaki, "European preferences and their reception". In *EU Foreign Policy in a Globalized World: Normative Power and Social Preferences*, edited by Zaki Laïdi, pp. 1–20. London: Routledge, 2008.

Lasswell, Harold. "The Garrison State". *American Journal of Sociology* 46, no. 4 (1941): 455–68.

Manners, Ian. "Normative power Europe: a contradiction in terms?". *Journal of Common Market Studies* 40, no. 2 (2002): 235–58.

Orbie, Jan. "A Civilian Power in the World? Instruments and Objectives in European Union External Policies". In *Europe's Global Role: External Policies of the European Union*, edited by Jan Orbie, pp. 1–33. Aldershot UK: Ashgate.

Patterson, Lee Ann. "Agricultural policy reform in the European Community: A three-level game analysis". *International Organization* 51, no. 1 (1997): 135–65.

Pedersen, Morten. *Promoting Human Rights in Burma: A Critique of Western Sanctions Policy*. Lanham MD: Rowman & Littlefield Publishers, 2008.

Putnam, Robert. "Diplomacy and domestic politics: The logic of two-level games". *International Organization* 42, no. 3 (1998): 427–60.

Roberts, Christopher. "Myanmar and the Argument for Engagement: A Clash of Contending Moralities". *East Asia: An International Quarterly* 23, no. 2 (2006): 34–62.

Seekins, Donald. "Burma and US Sanctions: Punishing an Authoritarian Regime". *Asian Survey* 45, no. 3 (2005): 437–52.

Selth, Andrew. "Burma's Saffron Revolution and the Limits of International Influence". *Australian Journal of International Affairs* 62, no. 3 (2008): 281–97.

Smith, Karen. *European Union Foreign Policy in a Changing World*. Cambridge: Polity, 2003.

Steinberg, David. "International Rivalries in Burma — The Rise of Economic Competition". *Asian Survey* 30, no. 6 (1990): 587–601.

———. "Democracy, Power, and the Economy in Myanmar: Donors Dilemmas", *Asian Survey* 31, no. 8 (1991): 729–42.

Taylor, Robert. *The State in Myanmar*. Singapore: National University of Singapore Press, 2009.

Telo, Mario. *Europe: A Civilian Power? European Union, Global Governance, World Order*. Basingstoke UK: Palgrave Macmillan, 2006.

Tocci, Nathalie. "Profiling Normative Foreign Policy: The European Union and its Global Partners". In *Who is a Normative Foreign Policy Actor? The European Union and its Global Partners*, edited by Nathalie Tocci, pp. 1–23. Brussels: Centre for European Policy Studies, 2008.

Wolfers, Arnold.–*Discord and Collaboration: Essays on International Politics*, Baltimore MD: Johns Hopkins Press, 1962.

15

THE USE OF NORMATIVE PROCESSES IN ACHIEVING BEHAVIOUR CHANGE IN MYANMAR

Trevor Wilson

INTRODUCTION

A common characteristic of most policies towards Myanmar/Burma is to seek to achieve some change for the better in the situation in the country despite the continued authoritarian rule of the military regime. This more modest change agenda was necessitated by the lack of any prospect of bringing the case of Burma to the UN Security Council. As at mid-2009 no external strategies (or, for that matter, internal strategies) have been especially successful in accomplishing much improvement, and certainly not in the sense of achieving "regime change". Few organizations conducting programmes there would even claim to have accomplished much success in pressing for systemic change, and so surprisingly few attempts have been made to rigorously assess or measure the extent of change attributable to these policies.

Nevertheless, there is some point in examining objectively what approaches have succeeded in accomplishing a modest degree of behaviour change by the military regime. Whether these changes have been caused by applying pressure, through sanctions or some other strategy, or, on the other hand, by using persuasion, or even some combination of the two, is not the ultimate test in this case. Yet, despite the claims to the contrary by the regime's critics, there is ample evidence of certain changes in its behaviour resulting from particular strategies. These changes may not have been sufficient to make Burma/Myanmar fully compliant with relevant international norms, but they can be documented, may have become "permanent", or may be a key step in a transitional process.

It would be instructive to look carefully and dispassionately at what changes have occurred in Myanmar/Burma and to try to establish why they happened. Where we are faced with a regime as averse to reform and "democratic" processes and as wedded to controlling events, an intelligent mix of strategies is likely to prove to be the best approach in seeking to bring about improvements. This is based on the obvious proposition that there clearly is no "magic bullet" solution and that, realistically, short of invading Myanmar/Burma, outside countries are extremely limited in what they can achieve there. It also accepts that considerable change has already occurred under the present military regime in Myanmar/Burma, despite the relatively small amount of external assistance going to the country, despite the regime's insistence that it will not be dictated to, and despite the extremely restricted and incomplete types of engagement that have been tried out there.

In reality, relatively few organizations are conducting activities on the ground inside Burma that are aimed deliberately at encouraging change or reform by working in conjunction with like-minded people or organizations inside the country. Some NGOs may seek such changes, but they lack the full authority of law-enforcing instruments. Some international agencies may seek such changes routinely as part of their programmes, and may not always seek publicity for their work, but are likely to be constrained in one way or another as to what they can do in the "difficult operating environment" of Myanmar/Burma. With different sanctions being aggressively applied, it is perhaps only to be expected that aid donors will be loath to expose themselves to political and other risk by conducting controversial programmes in Burma/Myanmar.

Many of the changes that have occurred under the SLORC/SPDC have probably been inspired or triggered by ideas generated by or programmes run by international agencies and, in some cases, by foreign governments. It is worth scrutinizing some of the cases closely to identify what specifically promoted the behaviour change and what conditions or circumstances made this change possible or likely when other changes have not occurred. This scrutiny should also shed light on what prevents change or reform occurring.

The chapter looks at some specific case studies of change in investigating what has been achieved where permanent fundamental "rules-based" reforms were pursued. It concentrates on only a few examples of these, but some other important changes could be equally relevant. It does not attempt to consider the political goal of bringing political change to Myanmar/Burma, which has been the subject of extensive analysis. This study takes three different types of situation and methodologies to investigate how and why change did occur, sometimes unexpectedly, sometimes predictably. It tries to identify the elements involved in these processes that might have promoted change, allowed the regime to shift in the right direction even if in a limited way, or to bring itself into greater harmony with its neighbours in particular. The three case studies examined are: the ILO and the use of forced labour; the Financial Action Task Force and the practice of money laundering; and the SPDC's somewhat selective, but nevertheless not insignificant, efforts to become a fully compliant member of ASEAN. This chapter does not consider Myanmar/Burma's conformity with political goals set by ASEAN, which have been the subject of quite extensive study, such as Stephen McCarthy's comprehensive contribution to *Asian Survey*'s 2008 special issue on Burma,[1] but rather the attempts to find practical improvement to regional collaboration, which have been covered in£very little independent analysis and commentary.

Other examples worthy of examination, where significant behaviour change also occurred, are: people trafficking; and narcotics trafficking, and topics mentioned by David Allan in his chapter. There are, equally, some cases where the regime is notable for *not* changing its behaviour, despite enormous pressures for it to do so. These include: human-rights abuses; child soldiers; political prisoners; and abuses of the judicial system. It may be that normative change in these latter areas is intrinsically more difficult to achieve, that ready-made reform programmes may not be suited to the conditions in Burma/Myanmar, or that the authorities in Burma/Myanmar simply refuse to countenance relevant international programmes.

FORCED LABOUR AND THE ILO

Burma ratified ILO core conventions, including No. 29 on forced labour, in 1955, but did not take specific action to implement the conventions. Since trade unions were not permitted under the SPDC, it was no surprise that in 1995 the International Confederation of Free Trade Unions (ICFTU) used a standard ILO mechanism, the Commission of Inquiry, to force the SPDC to take action to uphold its ILO obligations, particularly in relation to forced labour. Yozo Yokota, the first Special Rapporteur on Human Rights in Myanmar, in 1995 had questioned the SPDC's use of the Town and Village Act of 1930 to provide the legal justification for forced labour.[2] Across the world, acting in sympathy with Burmese trade unions represented by the Federation of Trade Unions Burma organization (FTUB), trade unions mobilized action against the military regime. This was a confrontational approach, with the overt threat of sanctions by trade unions (for example, dockworkers, whose strike action could be targeted against Myanmar shipping). But the SPDC's refusal to cooperate with the Commission or allow it access was neither surprising nor unprecedented, as countries such as Poland and Greece had declined to cooperate with Commissions of Enquiry in 1983 and 1970, respectively.

So what induced the SPDC in May 1999 to issue Order No. 1/1999 banning forced labour and to enter into dialogue with the ILO over its implementation? Pressure on the SPDC over forced labour built up in the international community after the ILO established the Commission of Inquiry in 1996. The Commission's report was delivered in November 1998, but even before then the European Parliament had, in February 1998, passed a resolution calling for economic sanctions against the SPDC, both for its human-rights abuses and for its practice of forced labour. During 1998 and 1999 there was a constant barrage of press reports and press statements suggesting that sanctions were about to be imposed by the ILO. This widespread media speculation would have contributed to the SPDC's alarm over the prospects of sanctions. Much of the media commentary was exaggerated, with references to "unprecedented" sanctions being "imminent".[3] This action was openly aimed at seeking the imposition of sanctions, even though the ILO's powers to do so were constrained.

From 1999 the ILO had begun imposing limited sanctions on Burma in accordance with its own processes and procedures, starting with ceasing technical cooperation with Burma, and suspending Burma from attending regular ILO meetings. Although the exact scope and impact of any such sanctions was still open to question, it would have been the first time any UN agency had imposed specific sanctions on Burma. However, ILO members were not convinced that action was being taken to implement this order, and Article 33 of the ILO Constitution was invoked to enforce compliance by Myanmar authorities.[4] Moreover, in July 1999 the EU dispatched its first "troika" mission to Yangon for discussions with the SPDC. As the senior ILO official, Francis Maupain, noted, the March 2000 decision by the ILO Governing Body to place the application of Article 33 on the agenda of the ILO's International Labour Conference (the politically driven peak body of the ILO) "immediately triggered a significant change in the attitude of the authorities".[5]

A number of features distinguish the ILO approach to Myanmar from those of other organizations charged with upholding international norms. To underline that it was the Burmese Government that had decided to sign and therefore uphold the conventions, Maupain repeatedly emphasized that Burma's commitment to the conventions was "voluntary", that is it was not the international community that was imposing its views on an unwilling government, and that it was not unusual for signatories to the conventions to need technical assistance to be able to fulfil their obligations under ILO conventions. In addition, ILO procedures emphasized discussion and dialogue before sanction-like measures were implemented. Formal ILO statements critical of Burma's abuse of standards tended to be accompanied by calls for dialogue and engagement. Typical is this 2000 summary by the ILO, which reported in a press release that: "While recognizing that the Minister's letter 'contains aspects which seem to reflect a welcome intention on the part of the Myanmar authorities to take measures to give effect to the Recommendations of the Commission of Inquiry',[6] the Conference considered that the factual situation (had) nevertheless remained unchanged to date."

Maupain makes a number of interesting points in his account:

- Myanmar's option of withdrawing from the ILO was recognized, and its choice to remain a signatory was critical.

- The ILO always insisted it was prepared to discuss issues with the SPDC, either through technical cooperation missions or high-level teams in Geneva, or through a special ombudsman. One result was that there was a great amount of direct contact and consultation on the ground in Burma.
- The ILO explained that threats of non-cooperation by Myanmar would not be in anyone's interest, that submitting to "independent" assessment and recommendations instead would delay further measures against Myanmar until its good faith could be assessed.
- The ILO made it clear that it intended to examine commitments and actions by the regime closely and would not accept generalized statements of intent unless it was demonstrated that these were being implemented in a reasonable, albeit long-term, way.

Despite its apparent isolation, and outward refusal to give way to pressure, the SPDC was generally careful in assessing its options and deciding its responses. Its public statements tended to be sharp and fairly hostile towards the ILO, and these statements were primarily tactical steps in the SPDC's overall defensive strategy. Around this time, the SPDC took the unusual step of appointing a committee of advisers composed of former ambassadors to Geneva and New York to advise it on dealing with the pressure from the ILO and the international community. These advisers, committed multilateralists, were generally recommending that Burma conform with ILO requirements, accept its obligations under the relevant conventions, and not withdraw from the ILO. They claimed to be offering honest advice to the military leadership, but were also realistic about the likelihood that their views would be accepted.[7]

From 2000 the ILO had been able to persuade the SPDC to accept "technical cooperation missions" from the ILO, which always held out the promise of technical assistance to Myanmar in meeting ILO requirements. These missions, often led by the experienced ILO official Francis Maupain, have continued on a more or less regular basis, but have not been able to elicit full cooperation with the ILO from the SPDC. In order to get the attention of the top military leadership, the ILO on two occasions felt obliged to despatch high-level teams to Myanmar in 2002 and 2005. Both of these missions were led by the former Governor-General (and Chief Justice) of Australia, Sir Ninian Stephen, who had also been mediator in the Northern Ireland Peace Talks in 2000. These visits succeeded in keeping the SPDC engaged at the highest level even when cooperation at lower levels was proving hard to achieve. While they often led to small breakthroughs, these missions did not succeed in securing the full implementation of Convention 29 by the Myanmar authorities, as is noted in the latest ILO report from the Committee of Applications.[8]

Intermittently, despite long periods of obstructionism and non-cooperation, the SPDC at times took significant steps towards working with the ILO in the direction of reducing forced labour. For example:

- In 2002 it agreed to an ILO Representative Office being established in Yangon; in 2003 it agreed to a work programme to demonstrate how labouring projects would be implemented without using forced labour (this project was never implemented, although never abandoned either).
- In early 2005, some local officials were prosecuted by the authorities for using forced labour,[9] but those who helped bring prosecutions were jailed or arrested.
- In 2007 the SPDC agreed to the establishment of a complaints mechanism allowing its citizens to lodge complaints over forced labour and enabling the ILO to investigate these complaints.

The establishment of a permanent ILO presence in Myanmar marked a quantitative strengthening in its attempts to drive a reform agenda in Myanmar. It significantly enhanced the effectiveness of the ILO and its ability to identify and respond to emerging developments, reinforced its ability to interact with stakeholders, including the SPDC, and was a powerful symbol of the ILO's determination to find creative and meaningful solutions to the difficult issues coming under its mandate. Once it had established a few modest in-country programmes, the ILO joined other UN agencies working on the ground to effect change in cooperation with the authorities, rather than operating at a distance.

The ILO complaints mechanism was unusual for Myanmar in that it allowed an outside organization to make findings in domestic matters, going against the consistently argued tenet of Myanmar policy of insistence on its sovereignty and non-interference in its affairs. The important issue here is that this allowed the development of skills and capacities by complainants and bureaucrats that otherwise would not have been encouraged by the authorities. It meant introducing standards of objective fact-finding that would have been unfamiliar to local bureaucrats. The operation of the complaints mechanism has been fraught with problems as the SPDC continued to arrest, harass and discourage anyone seeking to complain about forced labour, but it was extended in March 2009. In reality, forced labour continued to be widespread. However, although successful legal action was take in only 23 cases out of a total of 157 complaints (as of May 2009), increased scrutiny both from the ILO, and the increased international presence inside the country generally, meant that forced labour was no longer unchallenged.[10]

Until 2005, the SPDC was careful to keep open its options and lines of communication to the ILO. But in 2005, after the retired army officer and known hardliner U Thaung was appointed Labour Minister, the SPDC took exception to the tough line being pushed in the ILO by all representatives of Western countries, and began a propaganda campaign against the ILO, allowing (if not instigating) threats against the Yangon-based ILO Liaison Officer, Richard Horsey, and openly threatening to withdraw from the ILO. Eventually, the SPDC backed down on these uncalled-for and improper actions and threats, and after a time resumed its previous "cooperation" with the ILO. However, the ILO did not give up when others might have, in spite of strong pressure from the international trade-union movement, especially British trade unions.

What change in regime behaviour can be attributed, directly or indirectly, to the pressure being brought to bear through the ILO? Initially, after 2000, the ILO reported that there had been some slight reduction in the incidence of forced labour, although it was still being practised extensively. This was corroborated by anecdotal and other evidence of forced labour continuing. Moreover, despite the general reluctance of the SPDC to eliminate the use of forced labour by the army, the ILO in 2005 confirmed that the authorities had launched some prosecutions of persons charged with such offences.[11] More recent ILO reports have reported no noticeable further decline in forced labour and, at a special session of the Committee on the Application of Standards early in June 2009, described the SPDC's responses as "totally inadequate" and called on Myanmar to "move with urgency to implement all the actions requested" by the ILO.[12] However, some modest progress against underage recruitment into the army has been reported, indicating that the army can no longer act with absolute impunity, even though it remains the main offender in regard to all forms of forced labour.

Shifts in SPDC responses at different times can be partly explained by changes in the SPDC leadership over the years, including changing personalities of different Labour Ministers, even though the regime is usually highly disciplined. The quietly spoken Brigadier General Tin Ngwe presided over the initial rapprochement with the ILO until 2001. Tin Ngwe's replacement by the urbane former Ambassador to Washington and ex-military intelligence officer Tin Winn clearly presaged a period of greater cooperation with the ILO. Tin Winn was obviously following a policy line endorsed by Khin Nyunt, and he was dismissed at the same time as Khin Nyunt was purged in October 2004. However, he was replaced by retired army colonel U Thaung, described by one observer as a "hard-liner close to Than Shwe".[13] U Thaung was the minister when the SPDC publicly contemplated withdrawal from the ILO and orchestrated the campaign of threats against the ILO's Richard Horsey. Fortunately, these aggressive tactics did not last long and none of these threats was carried out. On his appointment as Deputy Minister for Labour in 2006, Brigadier General Aung Kyi took over the main role of liaising with the ILO and adopted a more conciliatory approach than U Thaung. The following year, Aung Kyi was promoted to Minister of Labour (as well as "Minister for Relations" with Aung San Suu Kyi).

SPDC representatives claim their position against forced labour is actually strengthening. They cite the provision in the 2008 Constitution which explicitly bans forced labour, while still allowing it as part of jail sentences, although any such qualification may still leave Myanmar in breach of its ILO obligations.[14] At the signing of the extension of the complaints mechanism on 26 February 2009, Labour Minister Aung Kyi maintained that extending the complaints mechanism reflected the SPDC's "high-level commitment". And at the ILO Governing Body meeting in June 2009 he amplified this by describing the SPDC's "political will" to eliminate forced labour.[15] A large gap still appears to exist between this SPDC rhetoric and reality, but perhaps it is starting to be narrowed. But achieving change in the behaviour of the army seems to be another matter; in May 2010, the ILO reported that it had detected no change in military behaviour on forced labour.[16]

THE FINANCIAL ACTION TASK FORCE AND MONEY LAUNDERING

The Financial Action Task Force (FATF) has been the lead agency in promoting conformity among economies in their anti-money-laundering efforts and in implementing national legislation as an effective means of achieving compliance with norms laid down in the relevant international conventions. The FATF was set up in 1989 to help enforce the various international treaties that were being negotiated to deal with all forms of trans-national crime that required some kind of financial action in response and derives its authority from these international treaties and arrangements. The FATF targets money laundering, illegal financial transfers (including in support of terrorism), and the proceeds of crime. The Myanmar Government acknowledged at quite an early point that the FATF's role was important for them because of the authority it carried (and almost certainly the capacity it had to impose measures against countries whether or not they were members).

The FATF operated on a basis of universality and objective criteria, which on the face of it did not presuppose either Western democratic values or capitalist market-oriented economic systems. It adopted a technical, rather than a political, approach, insisting on transparency and impartiality. It engaged in persistent, even protracted, consultations with authorities in breach of money-laundering principles, and worked hard at bringing non-complying countries "into the fold". But this team approach was combined with a tough attitude towards non-compliance, in which non-cooperating countries were named, and certain escalating sanctions could be imposed against them within the international financial system until they conformed. This "name and shame" strategy was particularly effective in inducing a change in behaviour in targeted countries.[17]

Although the FATF was an instrument of the developed countries that made up the OECD, it sought to apply a universal system of monitoring and policy adjustment based on objective rules that had global acceptance. All countries were treated in the same way, being judged firstly by their regional peers, not in Washington or London. Myanmar was only named as a non-cooperating county in 2001, and only then were financial transactions with Myanmar subjected to closer scrutiny than normal. (At that time, Indonesia and Nigeria were also among the countries deemed to be "non-cooperative".) But the FATF was able to express its satisfaction with a number of specific actions taken by the Myanmar authorities to comply with FATF standards.

The standard method adopted by the FATF and its sister organization the Asia-Pacific Group (APG) was to set up a financial investigations unit in the relevant central agency, provide detailed guidelines and training on its operations, and to then call for a detailed implementation plan to be submitted for endorsement by the FATF. These steps were followed in the case of Myanmar, with the APG (under Australian guidance) actively leading the process. Once these plans satisfied FATF/APG experts and standards, Myanmar was removed from the list of non-cooperating countries and welcomed as a member of the FATF. As it did not have official representation on the ground in Yangon, the FATF/APG's work was in the hands of its designated law-enforcement representatives (at this time, the Australian Federal Police had two representatives and local support staff in the Australian Embassy in Yangon.)

In June 2002, Myanmar enacted The Control of Money Laundering Law (CMLL SPDC Law No. 6/2002). In December 2003 it issued implementing rules for the CMLL (Notification 1/2003) and in January 2004 it issued three orders with reporting requirements for financial institutions and property-record offices. In April 2004, Myanmar adopted the Mutual Assistance in Criminal Matters Law (SPDC Law No. 4/2004) and in October that year it adopted the Mutual Assistance in Criminal Matters Rules.[18]

Australia was proactive in the APG, encouraging the Myanmar authorities to bring their legislative arrangements into conformity with FATF standards. In 2002, when the Australian Embassy was chairing the Mini-Dublin Group in Yangon, the Director of International Cooperation in the Myanmar Police Force briefed international representatives for the first time ever on the SPDC's proposed anti-money-laundering legislation, which was promulgated later that year. As the Australian Federal Police themselves explained: "The APG continued to work closely with members to implement the recommendations, identify areas for improvement and provide technical assistance and capacity building for anti-money-laundering and counterterrorist financing efforts throughout the region." In early 2004 the AFP represented Australia on an FATF technical mission to Myanmar through its liaison post in Yangon and on behalf of the APG.[19]

One measure of the Myanmar authorities' seriousness in dealing with money laundering is whether or not they have brought successful prosecutions against money launderers. In 2005 the SPDC took decisive action against certain breaches of money-laundering laws. In March 2005, the Central Bank of Myanmar revoked the operating licences of Myanmar Mayflower Bank and Asia Wealth Bank for money laundering. In August 2005, the Government of Myanmar also revoked the licence of Myanmar Universal Bank (MUB), and the chairman of the MUB was sentenced to a long prison sentence, in what is still the only significant prosecution under Myanmar's money-laundering laws. However, according to a 2008 APG report, "there has been only one conviction for money laundering itself since 2004 despite twenty-three money laundering investigations and fifty-four people having been convicted for predicate crimes under the 'Control of Money Laundering Law' ".[20]

Another singular method employed by the FATF that seems highly successful is its system of "mutual evaluations", which occur even after a country has been removed from the list of non-cooperative countries. This process enables countries struggling to maintain their status with the FATF to work to overcome problems they face, with technical assistance being provided for this purpose. It is a method for overcoming the distance to be covered before compliance can be assured. As part of the FATF's ongoing monitoring process, Burma became a member of the APG in 2006 and underwent a mutual evaluation by the APG on behalf of the FATF in July 2008. This evaluation assessed "Burma's regime as noncompliant or only partially compliant in all but four of the FATF 49 recommendations, a clear indication that Burma remains highly vulnerable to money laundering and terrorism finance threats".[21] This acknowledges fairly dramatically that compliance is not always achieved fully or immediately and that it is difficult to ensure that it is sustainable.

The most important measure was the ground-breaking 2002 anti-money-laundering law itself, drawn up under the former relatively "progressive" Minister for Home Affairs, Tin Hlaing. The SPDC was under no illusions about how seriously the United States took money laundering and recognized that sanctions imposed through the international banking system were quite likely and could be most harmful to its interests. At this time, SPDC leaders were prepared to go as far as necessary to avoid the ultimate penalty in expectation that internationally imposed sanctions could be rescinded. This law criminalized money laundering, required the establishment of monitoring bodies, and mandated reporting of suspicious transactions, all of which were regarded by the United States as essential. The law and the subsequent enactment of the related measures listed above were indeed sufficient to prompt the FATF to lift its sanctions against Myanmar. These are, so far, possibly the only sanctions against it that have been formally terminated. But the Bush Administration was not prepared to engage in a battle with the Congress to revoke the anti-money-laundering sanctions imposed under US law.

FATF measures against Myanmar were lifted in 2004 after it introduced mutual assistance legislation.[22] The FATF saw this mechanism, which involved a mix of sanctions and incentives, as highly successful.[23] In October 2006, the FATF removed Myanmar entirely from its list of non-cooperative countries but, to ensure continued effective implementation of reforms, it continues to monitor developments there through the APG.[24] The United States did not follow the FATF in lifting sanctions. In its 2009 annual report on international narcotics and crime, the US State Department draws attention to the limited progress made by the SPDC.[25] Obtaining congressional agreement to lift US sanctions is not easy at the best of times, especially as US bureaucratic assessments of compliance tended to present far less tolerant judgments about countries such as Myanmar.

Another source of technical assistance for Myanmar on transnational law enforcement was the UN Office of Drugs and Crime (UNODC), which maintained a reasonable-sized office in Yangon and which conducted substantial anti-narcotics capacity-building programmes on the ground in Myanmar. The FATF works closely with the UN Office of Drugs and Crime. UNODC's presence in the country over many years also enabled it to report accurately on the extent of Myanmar's compliance or non-compliance with international laws, and to develop a medium-term strategy with the Myanmar authorities to work towards elimination of systemic breaches of transnational law.[26] But unlike the FATF, UNODC did not have any sanctions at its disposal to encourage better behaviour.

Although Myanmar's poor compliance is one reason why the US Government has not lifted its money-laundering sanctions against Myanmar, both the FTAF and the APG were prepared to acknowledge the limited progress being made. While openly admitting the problems in Myanmar's performance in its report in 2006, the FATF stated that "Myanmar has made progress in implementing its AML regime and continues to take active measures to implement their legal reforms".[27] Reporting two years later, the APF says: "Despite the gaps highlighted in the preceding analysis, Myanmar has made steady progress in recent years in improving compliance with STR reporting".[28] Clearly the Myanmar authorities have a long way to go to improve their record. They need to allocate considerably more resources to the anti-money-laundering effort, and would have to accord much higher political priority to reducing this kind of criminal activity if real behavioural change were to become truly embedded.

But a significant start has been made and a few notable results achieved, which is more than was anticipated in the 1980s when these problems were already the subject of considerable international criticism. So far, in the course of taking action against money laundering, the SPDC has authorized the establishment of procedures to detect money laundering, provided a modest amount of training to relevant officials, and has actually issued Suspicious Transaction Reports, even if the number of reports remains small. Although money laundering no doubt continues, as it does in many borderline countries, its scale and seriousness in Myanmar seem to have receded.

While the FATF differed from the ILO in not maintaining an official presence on the ground in Myanmar, it made effective use of alternative capabilities at its disposal. Chief among these was the network of law-enforcement agencies represented in UN agencies (such as the UNDCP later UNODC) and various embassies. This network worked closely with the main law-enforcement agency outside the military, the Myanmar Police Force, with which a certain amount of camaraderie developed. Made up of law-enforcement officers from other countries dedicated to dealing with a variety in transnational crimes, the network actively sought ways to introduce new laws and procedures so that Myanmar was not left behind and could participate reasonably credibly in regional and, sometimes, international cooperation programmes against drugs, trafficking and the like. Australia was one of the countries which were prepared to invite the head of the MPF to participate in relevant anti-criminal meetings and programmes, including in the Asia-Pacific Group.

SEEKING CONFORMANCE WITH INTERNATIONAL NORMS THROUGH ASEAN

Myanmar's purposes in joining ASEAN, after years of refusing to join, included the economic, social and cultural benefits it could achieve thereby, finding an effective and reassuring way out of its previous policies of isolation, and the mutual support and collective solidarity it would enjoy when facing up to the outside world. SPDC Foreign Minister Nyan Win publicly expressed Myanmar's broad philosophy towards ASEAN in his formal statement when Myanmar (controversially) signed on to the ASEAN Charter in 2008. "Myanmar's ratification of the charter," he said, "demonstrates our strong commitment to embrace the common values and aspirations of the peoples of ASEAN."[29] Even discounting the rhetorical element in such a statement, its commitment is very clear. But one of the SPDC's main interests was the economic benefits it saw accruing from ASEAN membership.[30]

ASEAN's long-stated underlying operating principles revolve around "expanding collective efforts", "enhancing mutual assistance", "closer cohesion and economic integration", and developing "harmonized" systems and procedures to achieve world-class conformity.[31] They focus also on transparency and non-discrimination between members, coalescing into what became known as the "ASEAN Way", now the "national anthem" of ASEAN. This chapter considers examples of technical and similar conformity (which have received little attention from scholars) whereby ASEAN membership seems to have contributed towards some behaviour change by Myanmar's military regime. It does not consider Myanmar's problematic attitude towards political cooperation with ASEAN, which has received altogether a higher level of attention from scholars (see, for example, McCarthy 2008).

Economic Benefits

Compliance with the requirements of the ASEAN Free Trade Area (AFTA) have been a strong motivation for Myanmar's efforts, evident in the creation of a special National AFTA Unit within the Ministry of National Planning but with an unusual degree of independence. However, there are often suggestions that Myanmar has not benefited as much as might have been hoped.[32] While the SPDC has committed itself to achieving the various AFTA targets and is making progress towards those goals, often on a more lenient timetable,[33] it has not changed some of its economic polices, such as the high level of non-tariff barriers and its widespread use of state-owned enterprises. Despite its public espousal of "market-oriented" economic policies, the SPDC draws comfort from the retention of socialist policies by other ASEAN members such as Laos and (sometimes) Vietnam.

Other areas affecting economic interests more relevant for conformance and compliance are the many sectors where ASEAN endeavours to establish regimes for mutual recognition of products, standards, and the harmonization of procedures. These are areas given some priority within ASEAN but negotiations of arrangements have not always been achieved quickly.[34] The Myanmar authorities seized the opportunity of the e-ASEAN initiative to throw their weight behind efforts to translate ASEAN practices into electronically accessible formats at a time when this sector was developing rapidly in Myanmar. This enhanced regional conformance more quickly than would normally have occurred.[35]

Myanmar has joined some of these regimes, but not all. The reasons for it not participating would generally seem to be technical and related to its own capacity, effectiveness of internal regulation, and so on. Participation in these regimes is widely promulgated, including through the ASEAN Secretariat website. Myanmar's ability to participate in such arrangements is therefore a matter of public record. However, these schemes are voluntary, and there is no compulsion or pressure on members to join. But the downside of Myanmar not joining, in terms of being shown not to be an active or serious participant, undermining ASEAN campaigns, or simply standing aside from otherwise widely supported initiatives, are very apparent.

Cooperation on Public Health and Safety

Public health is one area where it was in the interests of all ASEAN members, and especially Myanmar's immediate neighbours, to achieve real progress towards a known set of standards. After the difficult experiences of SARS (in 2003–04) and avian influenza (from 2005), the authorities in all ASEAN countries recognized how quickly they would be called to account for any failings or successes in dealing with such transnational public emergencies. In 2006, ASEAN health ministers were moved to proclaim their "unity in health emergencies", but such declaratory statements tend not to identify problems in specific ASEAN countries, although these might be disclosed on websites displaying relevant technical information for the public.[36] By 2009, in responding to the "swine flu" outbreak, the ASEAN Secretary-General issued a statement which declared:

> ASEAN Member States *are better prepared now* following the experience from recent SARS and avian influenza outbreaks. *ASEAN has the existing mechanisms and networks for strengthening preparedness and response to a possible pandemic.* Key initiatives such as the establishment of the ASEAN Technical Working Group on Pandemic Preparedness and Response, ASEAN Communication and Integration Strategy, Minimum Standards for Joint Outbreak Investigation and Response, and the Non-Health Indicators for Pandemic Preparedness and Response will be contributory to addressing the current threats of an influenza pandemic.[37] [emphasis added]

Better remedial action and greater openness on shared public-health problems did not necessarily let Myanmar off the hook wherever suggestions remained that the authorities' performance was wanting. Thus on avian influenza, one 2005 media report described Myanmar as a "black hole",[38] although such a harsh assessment does not seem to have been justified. So far, strong criticisms of Myanmar's performance have not resulted in a major change of heart on the part of the regime towards ASEAN, or vice versa.

Conforming with Technical Standards

An example of Myanmar's improving compliance with international standards can be seen in its approach to the sanitary and phyto-sanitary measures set out in the FAO's "Plant Protection Profiles of Asia Pacific Countries" which identifies those areas where there is full, partial or no implementation of the necessary measures.[39] These are one way in which international performance can be assessed comparatively. Similarly, procedures under Myanmar's customs regime are now published on the website of the Ministry of Finance and Revenue, where the degree of compliance with ASEAN procedures is indicated. Compliance through ASEAN is increasingly being seen publicly in Myanmar as commercially advantageous as well. Early in 2009, a Fisheries Ministry official was quoted in the media as saying, in effect, that Myanmar could "piggy-back" on ASEAN fisheries standards to get access to the EU market.[40] In this way, acceptance of ASEAN's norms by Myanmar is a means of complying with international requirements.

The first ASEAN ministerial meeting that Myanmar hosted was the ASEAN Ministers of Labour meeting in May 1999.[41] The communiqué issued at the end of the meeting shows the positive and negative aspects of such direct involvement by Myanmar. While it resembles other ASEAN ministerial communiqués, it is silent on some issues that were problematic for Myanmar at the time, such as Myanmar's dispute with the ILO over forced labour, the lack of trade-union rights, and the use of child soldiers. These features of this meeting were consistent with the pattern of ASEAN efforts to advance its agenda of regional integration and conformity without focusing on known divisive problems, and illustrate the strengths and weaknesses of the mandatory and non-mandatory approaches it pursued, sometimes in parallel.

What Behaviour Change Has Really Occurred via ASEAN?

Little research has been carried out to assess the specific impacts of ASEAN membership on Myanmar, but the following comments are offered. Benefits Myanmar has received from its membership of ASEAN have not always resulted in a behaviour change on the part of the regime, and ASEAN membership is certainly no guarantee that behaviour change will occur. Moreover, sometimes behaviour change by Myanmar/Burma is more apparent than real, possibly amounting to little more than a token gesture on the part of the regime; or, alternatively, it is accompanied by less-than-adequate or complete implementation of ASEAN commitments. ASEAN monitoring or enforcement of its standards is not necessarily rigorous. Yet Myanmar technocrats who are already disposed to join useful plurilateral arrangements certainly use ASEAN membership as a vehicle for bringing about policy shifts and procedural change because they calculate that Myanmar's participation in these arrangements is more likely to be endorsed by the SPDC than if the measures were recommended for adoption in isolation. Before it was in ASEAN, it was difficult to get Myanmar's support for practical regional initiatives. Ministers who are members of the military also seem happier to go along with an ASEAN consensus response than if the measures were requested by any other outside source. To that extent, at least, Myanmar's engagement with the outside world has been advanced.

Moreover, some specific changes have been observed in Myanmar as a result of its ASEAN membership:

- Myanmar is included in regional consultations and its regular attendance at, and hosting of, ASEAN meetings certainly suggests that the cost and effort associated with this is worthwhile from the regime's point of view.
- In areas such as trade, customs and tourism, Myanmar is reasonably successful in meeting its ASEAN obligations. This makes it a much more open country than in the past, but it is not always able to meet timetables, or certain goals such as providing tourist visas on arrival, and it has probably been disappointed with the commercial gains made.
- In areas such as public health and quarantine, Myanmar is prepared to disclose details of emerging problems much more openly and

honestly than in the recent past, but this does not necessarily mean it will greatly increase its expenditure on health.

- In certain areas such as science and technology, e-commerce, or working conditions, ASEAN membership means Myanmar gives attention to difficult issues or long-term opportunities earlier than it might otherwise have done.
- Publishing ASEAN "scoresheets" on various activities means the SPDC cannot deny Myanmar's backwardness on many matters, and over time this may result in increased government spending in some areas than might have been the case otherwise.
- Generally, the Myanmar authorities are ready to commit themselves openly to goals and aspirations set by ASEAN, and are not evidently reluctant to take on suggestions or proposals from elsewhere for policy shifts.

There is a set of areas, however, where the Myanmar military regime has deliberately stood apart from ASEAN attempts to achieve closer regional collaboration. These relate almost entirely to measures which the regime deems to fall within the realm of its national defence and internal-security policies, which are areas of paramount concern and, indeed, fear on the part of the regime. For example, Myanmar has participated quite actively in the ASEAN Regional Forum, and provided briefings on its security situation at ARF meetings. But it has drawn the line and has so far declined to publish a defence white paper in accordance with the long-standing ARF policy of promoting transparency in defence and military matters, and remains one of a small number of ASEAN member-states that has not done so (the others are Malaysia and Laos). ARF membership may have influenced the Myanmar government to be slightly more open on defence matters, but the change is marginal at best.

Because of its obsession with "threats" to its internal security, Myanmar did not join ASEAN efforts in 2008 to conclude an ASEAN visa-free travel arrangement. This would have interfered with the regime's determination to decide who is allowed to visit Myanmar (a position at one time publicly adopted by John Howard as Australian Prime Minister). Nor was Myanmar always a ready participant in educational-exchange arrangements such as promotion of international students and academic exchanges at universities, which the authorities frequently closed on security grounds. So there are no regular foreign students at Myanmar universities; and while foreign academics can be invited as visitors to give seminars or lectures, they cannot be appointed to positions in Myanmar's national universities. (In other words, under Myanmar's military regime, the situation of universities is very different from that in most ASEAN counties and not really consistent with the cross-fertilization aspirations of the Southeast Asian Ministers of Education Organization (SEAMEO) in their University Mobility in Asia and the Pacific (UMAP) programme or ASEAN's University Network proposal.)

One can still reach some conclusions about the sort of outcomes and the extent of behavioural change that ASEAN is capable of achieving through these processes. Little of the processes goes on in the public arena; problems are not necessarily publicized; individual member-countries which do not conform or comply tend not to be named. Because of the "lowest common denominator" approach, high-quality outcomes are difficult to negotiate and enforce. Moreover, specific problems in individual member-countries are not openly targeted and so may not ever be properly addressed. There are few hard-edged incentives to encourage member-countries to lift their performance, and the tendency to have agreements containing "best endeavours" clauses perpetuates this mode of operation. The lack of any sanction that ASEAN can take against a defaulting member underlines one of the ongoing deficiencies of ASEAN as an organization.

CONCLUSIONS

Some clear, even obvious, conclusions from these studies are:

- An astute combination of sanctions and proactive encouragement probably stands the best chance of changing the regime's behaviour, but the effectiveness of sanctions measures depends on their authority and the extent of their acceptance.
- The case of the FATF's cooperation with Myanmar is arguably one of the more successful, reflecting a shrewd mixture of incentives and pressure. But is also reflects realism about the time frame and the extent of implementation that can occur, that time is needed before a drastic change of thinking can be fully absorbed, and the acknowledgement that a gradual accumulation of measures was the best that could be achieved.
- Important factors in the FATF's handling of its caseload were the

non-discriminatory approach taken (Indonesia could be under review at the same time as Myanmar), the insistence on transparency and openness, the focus on pre-determined technical, rather than political, issues, and the readiness of FATF representatives to engage in face-to-face discussions.

Constraints on how much change can be achieved will be influenced by a few key political factors, such as:

- The extent to which the activities impact directly on political controls judged by the military regime to be vital to its survival
- The extent to which the activities affect the direct interests of the Army, and to which alternative approaches impose unacceptable "costs" on the Army
- The distance that has to be travelled in achieving change or reform; the greater the distance, the more likely it is that any change will be small.

The international community — and the pro-democracy movement, in particular — needs to be much more realistic about what it can and cannot achieve in Myanmar/Burma. There is no point in seeking radical, far-reaching, change unless the means of achieving such change can be specified. This is not a recipe for minimalism, but a call for realism and better developed proactive agendas in aid programs. The international community needs better performance indicators by which it can judge what it might and might not achieve. The degree of difficulty (as in diving) needs to be considered.

Notes

1. Stephen McCarthy, "Burma and ASEAN: Estranged Bedfellows", *Asian Survey* 48, no. 6 (November/December 2008).
2. Venkateswaran (1996). For a regime that tried to follow the letter, if not the spirit, of the law, this would have been a worrying position.
3. The ILO's own press release of 14 June 2000, "International Labour Conference adopts Resolution targeting forced labour in Myanmar (Burma)", reflected the tone of the media pressure.
4. Article 33 provides that, if satisfactory compliance is not forthcoming, "the

governing body may recommend to the conference such action as it may deem wise and expedient to secure compliance therewith".

5. Maupain (2005).
6. "International Labour Conference adopts Resolution targeting forced labour in Myanmar", Press release ILO/00/27 14 June 2000.
7. Conversation with author in Yangon, 2002.
8. See Draft Report of Special Sitting of the Committee on the Application of Standards at <http://www.burmalibrary.org/docs07/ILC2009-SSMyanmar-concl.pdf>.
9. ILO Governing Body Discussion Paper "Developments concerning the question of the observance by the Government of Myanmar of the Forced Labour Convention, 1930 (No. 29)"
10. One prominent NLD figure and former political prisoner links the presence of more tourists after 1988 to a reduction in the practice of forced labour in areas tourists visited (private conversation 2002).
11. International Labour Organization Governing Body GB.292/7/2(Add.), 292nd Session March 2005.
12. International Labour Council, Committee on the Application of Standards, Special Sitting 98th Session, June 2009.
13. Win Min, "Internal dynamics of the Burmese military before, during and after the 2007 demonstrations", in *Dictatorship, Disorder and Decline in Myanmar*, edited by M. Skidmore and T. Wilson (Canberra: ANU E-Press, 2007).
14. S. 359 Ch 8 states: "The State prohibits any form of forced labour except hard labour as a punishment for crime duly convicted and duties assigned thereupon by the State in accord with the law in the interests of the people."
15. Press release No. 1, Myanmar Mission to the UN in Geneva. Available at <http://myanmargeneva.org>.
16. Media report by Agence France Presse, "ILO targets Myanmar's military over forced labour", 6 June 2010, quoting ILO Representative in Myanmar Steve Marshall.
17. FATF principles are laid down on the website <http://www.fatf-gafi.org/pages>. Its sanctions, or "counter measures" begin with: "Financial institutions should give special attention to business relationships and transactions with persons, including companies and financial institutions, from countries which do not or insufficiently apply the FATF Recommendations."
18. FATF, *Annual Report on Non-Cooperative Countries and Territories*, 2005.
19. AFP, Annual Report 2003–04.
20. Asia Pacific Group on Money Laundering, *Mutual Evaluation Report*, March 2008. Available at <http://www.apgml.org/documents/docs/17/Myanmar%202008.pdf>.
21. State Department, Bureau of International Narcotics and Law Enforcement

Affairs, 2009 International Narcotics Control Strategy Report (INCSR) Volume II: *Money Laundering and Financial Crimes*, 27 February 2009.

22. The 2005 FATF *Annual Report on Non-Cooperative Countries and Territories* stated that "the FATF welcomed Myanmar's enactment of mutual legal assistance legislation, implementing rules and regulations for its AML law and improvements to its suspicious transaction reporting regime. Consequently, the FATF withdrew counter-measures in October 2004."
23. In its report, the FATF offered the following assessment: "Overall, the NCCTs exercise has proved to be a very useful and very efficient tool to improve worldwide implementation of the FATF 40 Recommendations. Of the 23 jurisdictions designated as NCCTs in 2000 and 2001, only three remain. The de-listing of three countries in 2005 and progress by the remaining three NCCTs confirm that this initiative continues to trigger significant improvements in anti-money laundering systems throughout the world."
24. See n. 21 above.
25. Ibid.
26. See UNODC's Myanmar Strategic Programme Framework 2004–07 at <www.unodc.org/pdf/.../myanmar_strategic_programme_framework>.
27. FATF 2005, op. cit.
28. Asia Pacific Group *Mutual Evaluation Report* July 2008 available at <http://www.apgml.org/>.
29. Asia-Pacific News online, 21 July 2008.
30. Myanmar's purposes in joining ASEAN are described in Mya Than 2005, pp. 84–86.
31. ASEAN 2020 Vision Statement issued at Kuala Lumpur, 15 December 1997.
32. See "Trade expert warns of missed opportunities with ASEAN", *Myanmar Times* 20, no. 389 (22–28 October 2007), quoting the recently retired head of the National AFTA Unit, U Maung Maung Yi.
33. See Nandan (2006): "Progress has also been made in reducing the tariffs of Cambodia, Laos, Burma and Vietnam on intra-ASEAN trade" (p. 34).
34. Yoshimatsu 2006 says: "ASEAN members gradually intensified activities to promote the harmonization of technical standards and MRAs. However, actual processes of these activities were not smooth."
35. See, especially, Mya Than (2005), p. 102.
36. Joint Statement of the Second ASEAN Plus Three Health Ministers Meeting "Unity in Health Emergencies", Yangon, 22 June 2006, available at <www.aseansec.org>.
37. Statement by the Secretary-General of ASEAN on the Outbreak of Swine Influenza, ASEAN Secretariat, 27 April 2009, available at <www.aseansec.org>.
38. Ed Cropley, "Myanmar: The World's Bird Flu Black Hole", *Reuters*, 9 October 2005.

39. Food and Agricultural Organization at <http://wwhttp://www.fao.org/docrep/010/ag123e/AG123E00.HTMw.fao.org/docrep/010/ag123e/AG123E00.HTM>.
40. " 'The EU is not on our list of the top-10 buyers and there would be no effect even if we didn't adopt their standards. But ASEAN is now drawing up safety guidelines based on the EU standards, so compliance will help us sell in any international market,' said a Department of Fisheries (DOF) official." *Myanmar Times* 23, no. 454 (19–25 January 2009).
41. See <http://www.asean.org/6614.htm>.

References

ASEAN. Joint Statement of the Second ASEAN Plus Three Health Ministers Meeting "Unity in Health Emergencies". Yangon, 22 June 2006. Available at <www.aseansec.org>.

———. Statement by the Secretary-General of ASEAN on the Outbreak of Swine Influenza, ASEAN Secretariat, 27 April 2009. Available at <www.aseansec.org>.

Australian Federal Police. Annual Report, 2003–04. Canberra: Australian Government Publishing Service, 2004.

Elliott, Kimberly Ann. "The ILO and Enforcement of Core Labor Standards" in Institute for International Economics Policy Briefs, No. 00-6 July 2000.

Financial Action Task Force. Annual Report on Non-Cooperative Countries and Territories, Paris: 2005.

International Labour Council, Committee on the Application of Standards, Special Sitting 98th Session, Geneva: June 2009. Available at <http://www.burmalibrary.org/docs07/ILC2009-SSMyanmar-concl.pdf>.

International Labour Organization. Press release "International Labour Conference adopts Resolution targeting forced labour in Myanmar (Burma)", ILO/00/27. Geneva:14 June 2000.

———. Governing Body report GB.292/7/2(Add.), 292nd Session. Geneva, March 2005. Available at <http://www.oit.org/public/english/standards/relm/gb/docs/gb292/pdf/gb-7-2-ad.pdf>.

Kalathil, Shanthi. "Prodded by the Association of Southeast Asian Nations (ASEAN), Myanmar is starting to liberalize its draconian IcT laws", Dot.Com for Dictators, Washingtonpost.Newsweek Interactive, LLC. 2003.

Kenety, Brian. "EU toughens sanctions against Burma". *Asia Times*, 25 May 2000.

McCarthy, Stephen. "Burma and ASEAN: Estranged Bedfellows". *Asian Survey* 48, no. 6 (November/December 2008): 911–35.

Maupain, Francis. "Is the ILO Effective in Upholding Workers' Rights?: Reflections on the Myanmar Experience". In *Labour Rights as Human Rights* (Collected

Courses of the Academy of European Law) edited by Philip Alston. London: Oxford University Press, 2005.

Mya Than. *Myanmar in ASEAN*. Singapore: Institute of Southeast Asian Studies (ISEAS), 2005.

Nandan, Gita. *ASEAN: Building an Economic Community*. Canberra: East Asia Analytical Unit/AusAID, 2006.

Parker, Clive. "Forcing the issue on Myanmar labor" Asia Times online, 2007. Available at <http://www.atimes.com/atimes/Southeast_Asia/IC01Ae01.html>. Accessed 20 June 2009.

Sann Oo. "Fisheries prepares for EU standards". *Myanmar Times* 23, no. 454 (January 2009): 19–25.

The Irrawaddy. "Money Laundering in Burma: A chronology", 2004. Available at <http://www.irrawaddy.org/ theirrawaddy.com>.

United States State Department, Bureau of International Narcotics and Law Enforcement Affairs, 2009 International Narcotics Control Strategy Report (INCSR) Volume II: "Money Laundering and Financial Crimes", 27 February 2009.

Venkateswaran, K.S. "Burma — Beyond the Law", *Article 19*. London: 1996.

Win Kyaw Oo and San Oo. "Trade expert warns of missed opportunities with ASEAN", *Myanmar Times* 20, no. 389 (22–28 October 2007).

Yoshimatsu, Hidetaka. "Collective Action Problems and Regional Integration in ASEAN". *Contemporary Southeast Asia* 281 (2006): 115–40.

LIST OF ABBREVIATIONS

AADMER	ASEAN Agreement on Disaster Management and Emergency Response
ADB	Asian Development Bank
AFTA	ASEAN Free Trade Agreement
AHRC	Asian Human Rights Commission
AHTF	ASEAN Humanitarian Task Force
AIDS	acquired immuno-deficiency syndrome
ALNAP	Active Learning Network for Accountability and Performance
ALRC	Asian Legal Resource Centre
AMI	Aide Mèdicale Internationale
AML	anti-money laundering
ANU	Australian National University
APG	Asia-Pacific Group
ARCPPT	Asia Regional Cooperation to Prevent People Trafficking
ARF	ASEAN Regional Forum
ASEAN	Association of Southeast Asian Nations
ASEM	Asia-Europe Meeting
ATS	amphetamine-type substances
BAAC	Bank for Agriculture and Agricultural Cooperatives (Thailand)
BGF	border guard force(s)
BRI	Bank Rakyat Indonesia
BSPP	Burma Socialist Programme Party
CAP	Consolidated Appeals Process
CBM	Central Bank of Myanmar

CBO(s)	community-based organization(s)
CCDAC	Central Committee for Drug Abuse Control
CCI	Control of Corruption Index
CDCF	Cambodia Development Cooperation Forum
CGAP	Consultative Group to Assist the Poorest
CIA	Central Intelligence Agency (USA)
CMLL	Control of Money Laundering Law
COMMIT	Coordinated Mekong Ministerial Initiative against Trafficking
CPB	Communist Party of Burma
CSR	corporate social responsibility
DCI	Development Cooperation Instruments
DFID	Department for International Development (UK)
DKBA	Democratic Karen Buddhist Army
DOKNU	Democratic Organization for Kayan National Unity
DVD	digital video disk
EC	European Commission
ECHO	European Commission Humanitarian Office
EESC	European Economic and Social Council
EIA	environmental impact assessment
EITI	Extractive Industry Transparency Initiative
ERAT	ASEAN Emergency Rapid Assessment Team
ERD	evaluative reports database
ESCAP	Economic and Social Commission for Asia and the Pacific
EU	European Union
FAO	Food and Agriculture Organization
FAPC	Foreign Affairs Policy Committee
FATF	Financial Action Task Force
FC	[Yangon United] Football Club
FHAM	Fund for HIV/AIDS in Myanmar
FSWG	Food Security Working Group
FTA	free trade agreement
FTS	Financial Tracking System
FTUB	Federation of Trade Unions Burma
GDP	gross domestic product
GRET	Groupe de Recherches et d'Echanges Technologiques
GSP	Generalized System of Preferences
HIV	human immuno-deficient virus

HTWG	Human Trafficking Working Group
ICFTU	International Confederation of Free Trade Unions
IDP(s)	internally displaced person(s)
ILO	International Labour Organization
IMF	International Monetary Fund
INCSR	International Narcotics Control Strategy Report
INGO(s)	international non-government organization(s)
IOM	International Organization for Migration
IRS	indoor residual spraying
ITN(s)	insecticide-treated net(s)
KIO	Kachin Independence Organization
KNLA	Karen National Liberation Army
KNU	Karen National Union
KOWI	Kokang and Wa Initiative (UNODC)
KPF	Karen Peace Force
LDC	least developed country
LIFT	Livelihood Improvement and Food Security Trust Fund
LLIN(s)	long-lasting insecticidal mosquito net(s)
LNGO(s)	local non-government organization(s)
LWF	Lutheran World Federation
MADB	Myanma Agricultural Development Bank
MAS	Myanma Agricultural Services
MCRS	Myanmar Red Cross Society
MFI	microfinance institution
MISFA	Microfinance Investment Support Facility for Afghanistan Ltd
MMCWA	Myanmar Maternal and Child Welfare Association
MNL	Myanmar National League [soccer]
MoAI	Ministry of Agriculture and Irrigation
MoF	Ministry of Forestry
MOU	memorandum of understanding
MSF	Mèdecins Sans Frontières
MTA	Mong Tai Army
MUB	Myanmar Universal Bank
NCGUB	National Coalition Government of the Union of Burma
NDPCC	Natural Disaster Preparedness Central Committee
NGO(s)	non-government organization(s)
NLD	National League for Democracy

NMTPF	national medium-term priority framework
NPRP	National Poverty Reduction Plan
NRC	Norwegian Refugee Council
NRF	natural-resource fund
NSDP	National Strategic Development Plan (Cambodia)
NSDS	National Sustainable Development Strategy
OCHA	Office for the Coordination of Humanitarian Affairs (UN)
ODA	Official Development Assistance
OECD	Organization for Economic Co-operation and Development
PC	KNU/KNLA Peace Council
PDC	Peace and Development Council
PES	payment for ecological services
PONJA	Post-Nargis Joint Assessment
PONREPP	Post-Nargis Recovery and Preparedness Plan
PSDP	Ploung-Sqaw Democracy Party
R2P	Responsibility to Protect
SAB	State Agricultural Bank
SARS	severe acute respiratory syndrome
SEAMEO	Southeast Asian Ministers of Education Organization
SHAN	Shan Herald Agency for News
SIA	social impact assessment
SLORC	State Law and Order Restoration Council
SPA	Sub-regional Plan of Action
SPDC	State Peace and Development Council
STR	Special Transaction Reporting
TCG	Tripartite Core Group (SPDC, ASEAN, UN)
TLMI	The Leprosy Mission International
TOT	Training of Trainers
TPDC	Township Peace and Development Council
UMAP	Universal Mobility in Asia and the Pacific
UN	United Nations
UNDCP	United Nations International Drug Control Programme (later UNODC)
UNDP	United Nations Development Programme
UNESCAP	United Nations Economic and Social Commission for Asia and the Pacific (ESCAP)

UNESCO	United Nations Educational, Scientific and Cultural Organization
UNHCR	United Nations High Commissioner for Refugees (UN Refugee Agency)
UNIAP	United Nations Inter-Agency Project on Human Trafficking
UNICEF	United Nations Children's Fund
UNODC	United Nations Office on Drugs and Crime
USAID	United States Agency for International Development
USDA	Union Solidarity and Development Association
USDP	Union Solidarity and Development Party
UWSA	United Wa State Army
UWSP	United Wa State Party
VPDC	Village Peace and Development Council
WFP	World Food Programme
WHO	World Health Organization
WTO	World Trade Organization

INDEX

B

www.ingramcontent.com/pod-product-compliance
Lightning Source LLC
Chambersburg PA
CBHW020752300326
41914CB00050B/153

* 9 7 8 9 8 1 4 3 1 1 4 7 2 *